IN THEIR OWN WORDS

Voices of Jihad

COMPILATION AND COMMENTARY

DAVID AARON

This book results from the RAND Corporation's continuing program of self-initiated research. Support for such research is provided, in part, by donors and by the independent research and development provisions of RAND's contracts for the operation of its U.S. Department of Defense federally funded research and development centers. The project was conducted in conjunction with the RAND Center for Middle East Public Policy, part of International Programs at the RAND Corporation.

Library of Congress Cataloging-in-Publication Data

Aaron, David, 1938-
    In their own words : voices of Jihad : compilation and commentary / David Aaron.
        p. cm.
    Includes bibliographical references.
    ISBN 978-0-8330-4402-0 (pbk. : alk. paper)
    1. Jihad. 2. War—Religious aspects—Islam. 3. Islamic fundamentalism. I. Title.

BP182.A17 2008
363.325092'2—dc22

                                                                            2008002086

The RAND Corporation is a nonprofit research organization providing objective analysis and effective solutions that address the challenges facing the public and private sectors around the world. RAND's publications do not necessarily reflect the opinions of its research clients and sponsors.

RAND® is a registered trademark.

Published 2008 by the RAND Corporation
1776 Main Street, P.O. Box 2138, Santa Monica, CA 90407-2138
1200 South Hayes Street, Arlington, VA 22202-5050
4570 Fifth Avenue, Suite 600, Pittsburgh, PA 15213-2665
RAND URL: http://www.rand.org/
To order RAND documents or to obtain additional information, contact
Distribution Services: Telephone: (310) 451-7002;
Fax: (310) 451-6915; Email: order@rand.org

Preface

It must be stated at the outset that this book is not about Islam as it is practiced in its many varieties in Muslim communities throughout the world. It is not about Islamic fundamentalism or the various Islamist political movements. Rather, it is about a small group among the 1.2 billion Muslims on earth that carries out and promotes terrorism in the name of Islam. Respecting the difference is crucial if the terrorists are to be defeated. This can sometimes be difficult, because parts of the terrorists' messages resonate with the perceptions and experience of many Muslims. Nonetheless, the distinction is crucial, and the first step in making it is to listen to what the terrorists are actually saying. Their statements are often more appalling and more profoundly revealing than the accounts in many of the books that have been written about jihadi terrorism. This book offers unfiltered access to a broad range of the stories, rationales, ideas, and arguments of jihadi terrorists and those who support them. It presents a selected compendium of the actual words of jihadis expressing their views on virtually every subject relevant to their cause. A minimum of introductory and contextual material is provided, so that the reader may experience the full impact of what they are saying—to each other and to the world. It is hoped that this will provide greater insights into the motives, plans, and participants in jihadi terrorism, as well as the nature of the threat they pose. Further material is available at the RAND Voices of Jihad Database at http://www.rand.org/research_areas/terrorism/database/.

This book should be of interest to both students and researchers and to informed readers seeking a deeper understanding of jihadi terrorism. It may require more of the reader than other works on the subject, because it does not try to explain what is being said, nor does it speculate on why; rather, the jihadis speak for themselves.

This book results from the RAND Corporation's continuing program of self-initiated research. Support for such research is provided, in part, by donors and by the independent research and development provisions of RAND's contracts for the operation of its U.S. Department of Defense federally funded research and development centers.

This project was conducted in conjunction with the RAND Center for Middle East Public Policy. The RAND Center for Middle East Public Policy, part of International Programs at the RAND Corporation, aims to improve public policy by providing decisionmakers and the public with rigorous, objective research on critical policy issues affecting the Middle East.

For more information on the RAND Center for Middle East Public Policy, contact the Director, David Aaron. He can be reached by email at David_Aaron@rand.org; by phone at 310-393-0411, extension 7782; or by mail at RAND, 1776 Main Street, Santa Monica, California 90407-2138. More information about RAND is available at www.rand.org.

Contents

Acknowledgments

I would like to express my appreciation to the RAND Corporation and its CEO, James A. Thomson, for their support in making this book possible. I am also grateful to Rose Marie Vigil for her work in preparing drafts and particularly for locating and categorizing much of the original source material. Michael Egner provided valuable research assistance, and Katie Allen did an outstanding job in the exacting task of preparing the manuscript. Finally, I want to thank Bruce van Voorst, Frederick Wehrey, and John Esposito for their thoughtful reviews and very useful comments.

Note on Sources

This book consists largely of quotations from jihadi leaders and writers drawn from their books, manuals, fatwas, communiqués, interviews, web postings, and articles, as well as excerpts from the Qur'an, Hadith,[1] and earlier Islamic writers and scholars. The amount of primary material related to jihad is vast. In addition to the Qur'an and the Hadith quoted by jihadis, the Internet has exponentially increased the amount of available jihadi material. By one count, the number of terrorist-related web sites grew from 12 in 1997 to 4,500 by 2005 (Weimann, 2005). The subject of al-Qaeda in itself has generated hundreds of thousands of Internet postings.

Translated material is taken from a variety of sources, ranging from translations by the authors or publishers to the Open Source Center (OSC) (formerly the Foreign Broadcast Information Service (FBIS)) and the BBC, to private organizations such as the Middle East Media Research Institute (MEMRI) and SITE.[2] Several excerpts have been translated by RAND and are so noted.

Some of these sources are controversial and have been criticized for being biased. We have not attempted to present a balanced collection of Muslim views in this book. Because the book comprises original jihadi writings, the issue of balance is not germane, except as it pertains to conflicting jihadi views. These are fully reflected in this work. Moreover, the sheer volume and repetitiveness of jihadi statements help to ensure consistency and minimize misconstrual. Thus, while the translations may differ in quality and may even reflect particular agendas, they are more than adequate to capture the intent of the jihadi authors.

It should also be noted that, for brevity, we have included little jihadi poetry and few Qur'anic statements. This has the unfortunate effect of failing to convey the sense of fervor and even rapture contained in these excerpts or the extent to which jihadis seek to tap into the religious and emotional roots of Islamic culture.

Many Internet citations can be located only with difficulty or not at all. The web sites come and go, closed down by various authorities or abandoned by their

---

[1] Collections of reports on the sayings, decisions, and life of the Prophet.

[2] Previously a nonprofit service monitoring terrorist Web sites, SITE has become a for-pofit organization called SITE Intelligence Group.

creators, who may switch to password-protected sites. According to Jane's, authors frequently hijack existing URLs and move sites regularly to avoid attracting the attention of hackers or Internet service providers (Jane's Terrorism and Insurgency Centre, 2004). Aliases are common among authors of militant manuals and pamphlets who wish to hide their true identity from security forces (al-Zaydi, 2005).

The authors of jihadi statements may adopt multiple pseudonyms and *noms de guerre*. Complicating things still further, the names are translated from the Arabic, and many are spelled differently in different sources.

Not all the excerpts in this book are from prominent jihadis. Some have been selected because they are representative, others because they are contradictory, and still others because they provide a unique insight into the jihadi mentality.

Comments or insertions by the editor are enclosed within braces, while material in brackets and parentheses is from the selected text and may have been inserted by the source, the translator, or both.

CHAPTER ONE

Introduction

In the 20th century, the West confronted three totalitarian revolutionary movements: nazism, communism, and fascism. Now the world is under assault from a fourth such movement whose members operate under many labels—Islamic terrorists or extremists, Salafi militants, Islamo-Fascists, and jihadis, to name a few. In this book, I use the term jihadi, because the movement is focused on carrying out "holy war," which is one of the meanings of jihad.[1]

The four movements share an important characteristic: Their adherents go to great lengths to explain what they stand for and what they intend to do. Nazism followed the course laid out in Hitler's *Mein Kampf*; the Bolsheviks pursued the dreams of Marx and Engels and the plans of Lenin; fascism was fed by more than a decade of editorials by Benito Mussolini in his newspaper *Il Popolo d'Italia* (*"The People of Italy"*)[2] before he came to power. Interestingly, the societies targeted by these movements paid little heed to their murderous blueprints until late in the movements' development.

Before 9/11, the jihadis, who avowedly seek the destruction of Western democracy and the conversion of the world to their concept of Islam, were also given scant attention, although they had widely broadcast their intentions and had carried out numerous terrorist acts. Since the 9/11 attacks on New York and Washington, D.C., jihadis have redoubled their outreach efforts, increasingly exploiting the Internet to propagate their vision of the world, their interpretation of Islam, their version of the history of the Middle East, their grievances, their rationale for terror, their strategy, and even their tactics.

It can be argued that jihadism is more difficult for Americans to fathom than the earlier totalitarian movements, which originated in Europe, because jihad comes out of a culture largely unfamiliar to us and does not speak with a single voice. To bridge this gap in understanding, much has been written by analysts of the jihadi move-

---

[1] The literal definition of jihad is "struggle in the way of God." For a fuller description of various meanings of jihad, see pp. 5–7 and 79.

[2] *Il Popolo d'Italia* was founded by Mussolini and was published from November 15, 1914, through July 24, 1943. Its masthead bore the motto "A revolution is an idea that has found bayonets."

ment. This book takes a different approach, offering the actual words of the jihadis so that the reader can get closer to their thinking and mindset. It creates, in effect, a self-portrait of jihadism. Instead of describing what jihadis stand for, it presents their own descriptions. I have attempted to include as little editorial comment as possible, using it only to draw attention to the key points and put the material in context. This asks a bit more of the reader, but the unfiltered impact of the jihadi statements may lead to deeper and more powerful insights.

From Glory to Decline

Making sense of the rage and ruthlessness that characterize jihadism requires peering into the abyss of loss and humiliation felt by some Muslims over the collapse of Islamic civilization over the past 400 years.

After conquering and converting the largely pagan tribes of the Arabian Peninsula by the time of Muhammad's death in 632 CE,[3] the followers of Islam burst onto a world scene dominated by the empires of Persia and Byzantium. In slightly more than 100 years, the Muslims had vanquished the Persians, and the Islamic empire soon stretched from the Pyrenees Mountains in Spain to the foothills of the Himalayas. A magnificent civilization emerged at a time when Europe was frozen in the Dark Ages. Medicine, mathematics, and science flourished in the Muslim lands and provided the kindling for the Renaissance of Europe.

The Muslims repelled the onslaught of the Crusaders in the 12th century, and the absorption of the Turkish and Mongol invaders into Islam in the 10th and 13th centuries, respectively, was a testament to the religion's power and appeal. In 1453, the Ottoman Turks captured Constantinople and put an end to the last vestige of the Roman Empire. They then spread into southeastern Europe, occupying what are now Greece, Albania, Bulgaria, Romania, Hungary, Serbia, Macedonia, and parts of Ukraine. By the end of the 17th century, the crescent flag was planted outside the walls of Vienna. Had the Turkish armies succeeded in capturing the city, they might have rolled through much of Christendom. But they were driven back, and many historians mark that event as the beginning of the Muslim decline.

By the 19th century, industrializing Europe was picking apart pieces of the Ottoman Empire, which came to be known as the "sick man of Europe." World War I finished it off. The Versailles Peace Conference divided up the Ottoman caliphate, which had been on the losing side, and parceled it out to the European powers, which became colonialists in all but name.

The sense of loss and humiliation that resulted from the decline of the Ottomans and the ensuing colonialist period fueled a reform movement that had begun in the 19th century. It was aimed at overcoming the desuetude of Muslims, and in particu-

---

[3] Common Era, the term now frequently used instead of AD.

lar, of the Arab world. The movement marched in at least three ranks: the modernizers, who felt that Islam needed to be modified and adapted to the contemporary world by adding elements from the West; the secularists, from which Arab socialism, Arab nationalism, and Pan-Arabism derived; and the Salafis, a term currently used to describe fundamentalists who want to return to the pure Islam of the Prophet and the first four "rightly guided" caliphs[4] (the Salaf).[5] Today, Salafis seek to replace the civil institutions that were imported from or imposed by the West with Islamic or shari'a[6] law. Jihadism has its roots in this movement.

Since World War II, the region has been decolonized, but the birth of Israel and its repeated defeats of Arab armies, the failures and corruption of postcolonial secular Arab governments, and the repression of Islamic organizations all fed the growth of Salafi extremism. The invasion of Muslim Afghanistan by the "godless communists" of the former Soviet Union provoked the fundamentalists to unfurl the banner of jihad. At the time, they were supported by the United States, Pakistan, Saudi Arabia, and Egypt. After the Soviets were driven out, it became clear that the war had been a catalyst for turning a handful of small, scattered terror groups into an extensive, coherent, and skilled jihadi network that was not going to simply fade away. Al-Qaeda was, and remains, an important node in that network, even though it has metastasized into subgroups such as al-Qaeda in the Land of the Two Holy Places (Saudi Arabia) and al-Qaeda in the Land of the Two Rivers (Iraq), and it has spawned cells around the world that are inspired by its ideology.

Today, the targets of jihad are the secular regimes and monarchies that jihadis regard as apostate and the nations of the West that support them. Hence, 9/11. Additionally, the war in Iraq has become fertile ground for further jihadi recruitment, training, propaganda, and networking.

Who Are the Jihadis?

The term "war on terror" has produced significant confusion about how to define the enemy. Terrorism is, of course, a tactic, not an ideology. It has been used by the Irish

---

[4] The first caliph, Abu Bakr (632–634 CE); the second caliph, 'Umar (634–644 CE); the third caliph, Uthman (644–656 CE); and the fourth caliph, Ali (656–661 CE).

[5] Ironically, in the late 19th and early 20th centuries, Salafis were reformists who allied with secular modernists, in notable contrast to their current fundamental ideological manifestation. *The Oxford Encyclopedia of the Modern Islamic World* attributes this reformist mindset to the leadership of Egyptian Mufti Muhammad Abduh but states that after Abduh's death, his disciple Rashid Rida turned the movement toward conservatism and orthodoxy. This later, fundamentalist brand of Salafism is sometimes distinguished from its more moderate parent by the term "Neo-Salafism."

[6] The Arabic word shar'ia refers to the laws and way of life prescribed by Allah for his servants. The shari'a deals with ideology and faith, behavior and manners, and practical daily matters ("USC–MSA Compendium of Muslim Texts," undated).

Republican Army, the Zionist Stern Gang, the Mau Mau in Kenya, the Viet Cong, the Red Brigades in Italy, and other organizations. In the Middle East, a number of Arab organizations employ terror. In Palestine, there are several such groups: the Palestine Liberation Organization (PLO), a secular, socialist, national liberation movement that sponsors the Al Aqsa Martyrs Brigade; Hamas, a Sunni[7] fundamentalist Islamist organization committed to resistance to Israel; the Popular Front for the Liberation of Palestine (PFLP), a communist group. In Lebanon, Hezbollah ("Party of God") is a Shi'a[8] fundamentalist political party that was the first organization to use suicide bombing. And of course, there is al-Qaeda and its offshoots in Iraq and Saudi Arabia, as well as other similar groups elsewhere in the Middle East, Indonesia, the Philippines, Algeria, and Europe. This book focuses largely on al-Qaeda and its offshoots.

Jihadism is utopian. It seeks nothing less than the creation of a worldwide fundamentalist Islamic state. Its adherents believe that this can be achieved only through violence. It targets both governments in Muslim lands and those in the West that support them. Most jihadis claim to belong to the Sunni sect of Islam, and some regard all others as apostates whom they may kill. Like Wahhabis and other fundamentalists, they insist that the only true Islam is that which was practiced by Muhammad and his early followers, the Salaf, and therefore they sometimes call themselves Salafis. But jihadis go further, insisting that "holy war" is the central tenet and obligation of Islam. Increasingly, jihadis are regarded by established Muslim clerics (the *ulama*) as a separate and deviant sect. They reject the authority of even the most distinguished *ulama* if they disagree with them.

Some consider certain Shi'a groups, such as Hezbollah and the Moqtadar Sadr Mahdi Army (a militia fighting in Iraq,[9] which imitates Sunni jihadist terrorist tactics), to be jihadis as well. Although Hezbollah also follows certain jihadi doctrines (some quotes from Hezbollah members are included in this book), its agenda is focused on Lebanon, which distinguishes it from the broader jihadi movement. Moreover, the Shi'a, especially those like the Mahdi Army, have become mortal enemies of jihadis. Hamas is a Sunni organization, and much of its ideology is jihadist, but it has the more immediate objective of expelling Israel from Palestine. There are several Hamas excerpts in this book, especially relating to suicide bombing and martyrdom. Neither Hamas nor Hezbollah has the global ambitions and operations of the jihadis, although Iran appears to be using Hezbollah to expand its influence in the Middle East. All of these groups would call themselves mujahideen, the generic name for "holy warrior."

---

[7] The largest branch of Islam.

[8] A branch of Islam that broke away from the Sunni line in 632 CE over succession to the fourth caliph.

[9] The leader of al-Qaeda in Iraq, the late Abu Musab al-Zarqawi, declared war on the Shi'a, a sectarian war that rages today. He was opposed in this by Osama bin Laden's deputy, Ayman al-Zawahiri. See Chapter Eight for further elaboration of this conflict among jihadis.

Jihadis can also be categorized as Islamists, political movements that want to bring the practice of Islamic law into government. Here, too, the jihadis are at the extreme end of a spectrum. At the moderate end is the Islamist-oriented government of Turkey, a NATO ally and a nation where secularism is enshrined in the constitution. Further along the spectrum, the Muslim Brotherhood is the largest opposition group in the Egyptian Parliament. And finally, there are the Islamists in Sudan who countenance the genocide in Darfur (of non-Arab Muslims), the Taliban, and the jihadis.

The Islamic Factor

Jihadism should not be confused with Islam in general. However, it is necessary to be familiar with some of the features of the religion if one is to understand the background from which jihadism has emerged.

First, becoming a Muslim requires no ceremony, indoctrination, or blessing by a religious authority. One simply must commit oneself to the Five Pillars of Islam:

1. A declaration of faith in Allah alone and the belief that Muhammad is his Prophet
2. Praying five times a day
3. Paying alms (*zakat*)
4. Fasting during the holy month of Ramadan
5. Making the pilgrimage to Mecca (the Hajj)

To be a practicing Muslim, of course, entails much more. The sources of Muslim belief are based on the Qur'an, which is the revealed word of Allah, and for Sunnis, the Sunnah, the life of Muhammad, his statements, actions, and the things he approved, as set down in reports or stories called Hadith.

Second, Islam has no Pope or synods to decide what is correct doctrine. The proper interpretation of the Qur'an and the Sunnah results from consensus among prominent Islamic scholars (the *ulama*). However, there are no hard and fast rules about who is a prominent scholar or about how many of them form a consensus.

Not surprisingly, Islam has had its share of divisions into sects, the Sunni and Shi'a being the most prominent. Jihadis claim to be orthodox Sunni Muslims, but since they do not recognize the authority of the *ulama*, they shop for scholars who will support their ideology. Osama bin Laden has declared himself able to issue fatwas,[10] even though he lacks the religious qualifications. Though sometimes ambivalent, most mainstream Muslim scholars regard jihadis as "deviants." These scholars, and some

---

[10] Contrary to popular understanding, fatwas are not legally binding under Islamic law; they are "guidance."

fundamentalist leaders as well, criticize jihadi terrorists for exalting jihad above the Five Pillars of Islam.

Third, this somewhat unstructured system produces tolerance of divergence (*irja*—literally, "suspending judgment"—or, more colloquially, *tasamuler* (toleration) or *taqarub* (rapprochement)), as well as declarations by Muslims of excommunication (*takfir*) against one another. Jihadis have taken *takfir* to the point of declaring that all the governments in the Muslim world are *kuffar* (non-believers). This enables them to ignore traditional Islamic injunctions to not kill fellow Muslims and to obey authority. One seminal jihadi writer has claimed that the entire world is steeped in the pagan ignorance that existed before Islam. Jihadis thus feel justified in taking revolutionary action against their rulers and perpetrating violence against individuals they have declared to be heretics.

Fourth, the literal translation of jihad is "struggle in the way of Allah." The Qur'an, Hadith, and Sunnah all make reference to jihad as armed struggle. Yet the "struggle" that is jihad also has a meaning that involves introspection and preaching, aspects that predominate for most Muslims. Jihad in the sense of fighting is usually construed as the collective duty of the Muslim community as a whole (*fard kifayah*), rather than as an individual duty. That is, according to Islam, a Muslim ruler determines when and how to engage in jihad or to desist from it. It is not an individual religious duty, such as prayer or fasting, to be discharged by every Muslim (*fard 'ayn*). Only when infidels invade the lands of Islam does armed jihad become an individual religious duty.

Jihadis, however, incessantly hammer the alarm bell, claiming that Islam is under attack and therefore jihad is now a war of defense and as such has become not only a collective duty but an individual duty. That is, jihad is a total, all-encompassing duty to be carried out by all Muslims—men and women, young and old.

Fifth, Islamic law (shari'a) is referred to by jihadis as if it were a consistent and standardized compilation of laws, like the U.S. Federal Code. However, it is not. While shari'a is based on the Qur'an and the Sunnah, what it contains is not fixed. Shari'a is the product of centuries of commentaries by scholars and decisions by judges, reasoning by analogy and deduction. Ijtihad[11] interpretation of the Qur'an was common in the early days of Islam as it tried to come to grips with circumstances that differed from those on the Arabian Peninsula in the 7th century. In the 10th century, the door of ijtihad in Sunni Islam was closed by the consensus of scholars, and interpre-

---

[11] Ijtihad is the use of reasoning to interpret God's will in new situations, from the words of the Qur'an and Hadith of the Sunnah. This reasoning is usually done by analogy (equating an aspect of a new problem or situation with one for which a ruling already exists). Seyyed Hossein Nasr says that in the Sunni world, the gate of ijtihad was closed in the 10th century AD, and many authorities have been seeking to open it since the end of the 19th century. Jihadis both condemn and use ijtihad, for example, arguing that the use of nuclear bombs is permitted, because the Koran approves the use of catapults, which are also indiscriminate. According to Nasr, in the Shi'ite world, the gate of ijtihad has always been open, and it is considered essential that each generation practice it to refresh the body of the law (Nasr, 2002, pp. 79–80).

tation became a sin. Today, there are four separate schools of Sunni Islamic jurisprudence. Different versions of shari'a are practiced in Saudi Arabia and Central Africa, for example, and the shari'a of the Taliban is not the shari'a of the Saudis.

Sixth, Islam is strictly monotheistic, and Muslims consider Christianity to be in error because its followers believe Jesus is considered a part of God. Catholicism is denounced as polytheistic because of its devotion to the Trinity—the Father, the Son, and the Holy Spirit—not to mention the Virgin Mary and the saints. The Jews are regarded as infidels because they have not accepted Muhammad as God's final prophet. Yet both Christians and Jews are considered to be "people of the book," sharing a kinship with Islam, which recognizes the prophets of the Bible, including Jesus. Muhammad believed he was "reforming" Christianity and Judaism, not creating a new religion.

Finally, Islam was born in war and conflict, unlike Christianity, which, despite the crucifixion and occasional Roman repression, generally developed within the relatively peaceful political structure of a mighty empire. Muhammad was a political and military leader as much as a prophet, while Jesus was prepared to "render unto Caesar the things that are Caesar's and unto God the things that are God's" (Matthew 22:21).

In early Muslim society, there was no division of church and state, which is considered fundamental to contemporary government in the West. The early Muslim caliphates were headed by a caliph chosen by the community. He wielded authority, both temporal and religious, and ruled by a law, shari'a, that mixed together what the West would regard as civil and ecclesiastical rules. This is the system that today's jihadis are seeking to establish throughout the world.

This sketch of the historical and religious framework within which jihad has developed and operates provides some context for the excerpts that follow. It is far from a complete history or analysis, but the excerpts, which contain further context, should contribute to a fuller picture of jihadism.

Jihadism Is Not Islam

Middle East history goes far to explain the advent of jihadism. Some observers place responsibility for Muslim terrorism at the feet of Islamic fundamentalists. Certainly, jihadis constantly justify their actions and arguments by references to the verses on violence and war in the Qur'an and the Hadith. But there are also many such passages in the Bible, in both the Old and the New Testament, and Christian history is replete with wars waged in the name of God.[12] Jihadis use the term "Crusad-

---

[12] In Deuteronomy, book 20, verses 10 and beyond: "When you come near to a city to fight, call for peace; if it responds to your call for peace and opens its doors in front of you then all its people will be under your command and all will be your slaves. If it does not heed to your demands for peace then besiege it, and if your Lord God

ers" to mean Westerners, and none would forget the sack of Jerusalem in 1099. Is modern-day jihadi terrorism caused by or inherent in Islam? No more so than the Aryan Nations are the inevitable product of Christianity. While it is true that all jihadis consider themselves Muslim fundamentalists, few Muslims, or even fundamentalists, are jihadis. Fanaticism and violence are not unique to Islam, or even to religion.

As obvious as this point may be, it is important to stress it. This book focuses on what jihadis say and on their narrow view of Islam. As crucial as it is to understand their beliefs, they in no way represent the whole of Islam.

This book provides selected portions of jihadi writings organized to enable the reader to find quotations on particular topics. However, most of the excerpts deal with more than one topic, so the decision of where to place the quotes is inevitably subjective. For example, everything under 9/11 is about that tragic day, but not everything about 9/11 will be found in that section.

The purpose of this book is not to disseminate jihadi propaganda, but to follow the admonition to "know thine enemy" through its own words. As the following pages dramatically demonstrate, we do have an enemy, and we need to pay attention to how it thinks and what it plans to do to us.

---

pushes it to you then strike all its males with the edge of your sword. As for the women, children, and beasts and all that is in the city, they are all a booty for you." In the Gospel of Matthew, in the tenth book, verses 25 and onward: "Think not that I have come to spread peace in the land, but the sword. For, I have come to separate a man from his son, and the son from his father and the daughter-in-law from her mother-in-law. . . . and the animosity of the person with his household, whoever loves a son or a daughter more than I will not deserve me, and whosoever does not take his cross and follow me also does not deserve me. Whoever finds his life will lose it, and whoever loses his life for my sake will find me."

CHAPTER TWO

Life in Jihad

Jihad is a way of life, so any portrait of it must begin with a picture of the lives led by jihadis. Many of them are vagabonds searching for the next conflict, wandering from Afghanistan to Algeria, Bosnia to Baghdad, Chechnya to Cairo. Despite the lyric descriptions in the poems and songs of jihad, it is a life of hardship and personal sacrifice, not romantic adventure. The violence and brutality of this life produce in jihadis a lack of affect, an emotional deadness that does not seem to be relieved by their devotion to religion.

The reality and poverty of the lives of jihadis must be kept in mind as one reads this collection of excerpts. The voices of jihad are ultimately not only appalling, but sad.

The Story of Isam al-Qamari

The events in this story, which are related by al-Qaeda leader Ayman al-Zawahiri, take place in Cairo in the 1980s. As this account shows, random death is a jihadi's constant companion.

> "One of the most important jihad groups uncovered by the security agencies was that of Isam al-Qamari.[1]
>
> . . . .
>
> "Isam al-Qamari was a serious man who, since early in his youth, had taken the issue of Islam seriously. He decided to join the Military College to change the ruling regime in Egypt. That was his conviction as he finished his secondary school education. He once told me, God have mercy on him, that he asked his father once after joining the

---

[1] "Qamari was more of a charismatic leader than Zawahiri and was often deferred to on major decisions. In February 1981, Qamari's plots were found out by the government, which caused Sadat to order a major crackdown on diverse underground movements in Egypt. While most of the Egyptian Islamic Jihad leadership was arrested, Zawahiri remained a free man" (http://www.globalsecurity.org/military/world/para/zawahiri.htm).

Military College: Do you know why I joined the Military College? His father said no. Al-Qamari said: To carry out a military coup in Egypt. His father was shocked but he could do nothing. Isam had already been admitted to the Military College.

. . . .

"At the Military College, Isam al-Qamari met Muhammad Mustafa Ulaywah, brother of 'Ulwi Mustafa Ulaywah, one of the activists in the Al-Jihad Group[2] at the time. The two brothers made Al-Qamari join our jihad group.

. . . .

"When Anwar al-Sadat was assassinated {in 1981}, Isam asked me to connect him to the group that carried out the assassination[3]. . . .

"Isam thought about attempting to hit the funeral of Anwar al-Sadat, including the [former] Presidents of the United States and the leaders of Israel. He also thought about seizing some tanks and using them to hit a vital target or attack Al-Sadat's funeral. However, the resources available were short of his ambitions and it was too late.

. . . .

"An attack was conducted on the hideout of Isam al-Qamari, at the Cairo neighborhood of Al-Jammaliyah, where an interesting battle took place.

. . . .

"This battle took place in the Manshiyat Nasir area in the Al-Jammaliyah neighborhood. It is a poor area where poor homes are stacked next to each other, divided by narrow alleys and paths. Isam was hiding in a turner's workshop built by Muhammad Abd-al-Rahman al-Sharqawi {who went to jail in connection with Sadat's assassination}, along with Ibrahim Salamah Iskandarani and Nabil Na'im, to serve as one of our bases. . . . This workshop was in a modest house consisting of a roofless hallway, with two rooms on the right and two rooms on the left and an iron door at the beginning of the hallway.

"The workshop was located in a narrow alley with a dead end and surrounded by several houses, many of them one-storied.

"When the Interior Ministry learned that Isam was hiding in this workshop it surrounded the entire area with police and the Central Security Forces. It used the counterterror battalion in the Central

---

[2] The Al-Jihad Group (also known as Egyptian Islamic Jihad, Al-Islami Al-Jihad, and Islamic Jihad) is a Cairo-based terrorist organization which, under Zawahiri's leadership, joined with al-Qaeda to form the World Islamic Front in 1998. It later gave up terrorism, infuriating Zawahiri, who was in hiding with bin Laden.

[3] Egyptian Islamic Jihad.

Security Forces, the best unit available, to attack the workshop. The battalion surrounded the workshop for several hours and occupied the roofs of nearby buildings, where they mounted their machine guns.

"Before dawn, the police called our brothers through loudspeakers and told them that the workshop was under siege and that they ought to surrender. Immediately after that, the break-in unit, which is made up of the best Central Security officers wearing shields, began the attack by spraying the door with an endless hail of bullets and shouting to the brothers to surrender. . . .

"Isam and his companions were prepared for this eventuality. They had an electric wire fastened a few centimeters away from the iron door. They had two old short machine guns, two revolvers, and a number of hand grenades in their possession.

"When the break-in troops tried to storm their way into the gate they were jolted, and they immediately retreated in shock. Isam seized the opportunity and hurled a hand grenade over the door. It landed in the middle of the break-in team, killing or wounding the team members. The battalion officers and soldiers panicked when they heard the screams of the break-in team. There was complete silence in the air. Isam and his companions climbed to the roof of the workshop and started hailing the neighboring rooftops with bullets from their two machine guns, which soon stopped working. But Isam and his companions did not stop. They rained the force with 10 hand grenades, nine of which exploded. The resistance by the force stopped, and here Isam realized that it had been weakened. The brothers emerged from the workshop. They found a soldier in front of them pointing his weapon at them. However, he turned his back on them. Brother Nabil Na'im shot him in the head.

"Isam asked them to sit still and wait for him to throw a hand grenade then start running in the direction of the grenade. The brothers started running through the cordons of the siege. It was as if they were running amidst dead people and ghosts. They continued to run until they reached the neighboring hills of Al-Muqattam. From a distance, they sat down to watch the badly hurt troops as they gathered their wounded men and moved back to their vehicles. Ibrahim Salamah suggested that this was the best opportunity to attack the battalion with what was left with the brothers in terms of ammunition, but Isam decided it was enough.

"The brothers continued to walk on the hills of Al-Muqattam. Ibrahim Salamah had a hand grenade in his hand. He had removed the pin from it then returned it again. However, it seemed that the pin shifted out of place when he was running. The brothers stopped for a while near one of the caves.

"Ibrahim Salamah wanted to urinate. He turned around and faced the entrance of the cave. Isam and Nabil sat a few meters away from him with their backs to Ibrahim. The grenade dropped on the floor, causing the pin to shift a little. The brothers heard the capsule exploding. Ibrahim immediately threw himself on the bomb to protect his brothers. The silence of the night was broken by the explosion of the bomb, which ripped Ibrahim apart. He took the full power of the explosion.

"It was an act of destiny that was beyond any expectation. After escaping safely from over a 100-man force from the Central Security Forces, Ibrahim met his fate. Isam and Nabil were astonished by the gravity of the surprise.

. . . .

Subsequently, Isam al-Qamari was arrested and jailed.

"{While} Isam remained in prison . . . he continued to think of plans to escape. After several attempts, Isam, along with Khamis Musallam and Muhammad al-Aswani, managed to escape from the formidable Turah Prison on 17 July 1988. It was not an ordinary escape. It was preceded by long and complicated planning that was ultimately crowned with success. The escape involved a battle to cross the prison walls and go through the lines of guards watching the walls. It also involved crossing over to the other side of the Nile.

". . . the Interior Ministry was dumbfounded. It did not expect such a daring and noisy escape, which started with removing the bars of the cells, taking the warden guards prisoner, crossing the 4-meter high fence after throwing sound bombs, clashing with one of the guards and taking his weapon, and leaving the Turah Prison compound at midnight amidst the tight security.

"After the escape of Isam al-Qamari and his colleagues from prison, they crossed the Nile to the other side and walked in the fields until they reached the central Delta.

"Because they walked for such a long distance, Khamis Musallam's feet were injured and started to suppurate. He developed a fever and started to shiver. In an attempt to treat Khamis, the brothers resorted to Khalid Bakhit, a member of the Al-Jihad Group, who gave them his house in the Al-Sharrabiyah.

"As destiny would have it, a State Security Intelligence force came to the house of Khalid Bakhit early in the morning on 25 July 1988. It was part of the sweeping campaign of arrests that followed the escape of the three brothers.

"Another courageous battle took place. As soon as the force commander, a Colonel in the State Security Intelligence Department, knocked on the door, he came under a hail of sound bombs that the brothers had prepared. Isam al-Qamari attacked him with a kitchen knife. The officer escaped, leaving his pistol behind. The other soldiers and officers retreated in fear. Isam picked up the pistol of the force commander and the brothers started running down to the street.

"At the corner of the street, Isam al-Qamari engaged in a battle with the police force to cover his brothers' escape. He was hit in the stomach, and he fell. His companions returned to carry him, but he declined and gave them the pistol he had. He ordered them to continue to run away. He died on the spot." (al-Zawahiri, 2001)

The Story of Abu Hajer

". . . as you know, in those days, 13 years ago . . . everybody in those days heard what was going on in Afghanistan. The mosques were talking [about it] with support from the government, and so were the proselytizers and the television. Jihad was favorable in those days, and the government was subsidizing [airline] tickets for people. We had relatives, neighbors, loved ones, and friends who had gone to the land of jihad, so our ears were always listening for news about our brothers and the accomplishments of the jihad fighters in Afghanistan.

"The truth is that one's spirit was pining for one to be with the jihad fighters, but there were barriers. Some jurists used to say, and some still do, that jihad is not mandatory in Islam, and that a person may not go without the permission of his parents. Of course we tried to convince [our parents], but all of these attempts failed. Then one sheikh guided me to [the realization] that going to prepare [for the jihad] is mandatory and that, as such, it did not require permission from one's parents, so I left for the jihad. . . .

"[Abu Hajer then tells of the battles he fought in Afghanistan:] The fronts in which I have participated are: Afghanistan, then God was generous to me and I joined the brothers in Algeria where I worked with the equipment group, whose mission was to transport weapons and equipment from Europe to Morocco, and then into Algeria. Our job was to move these weapons and equipment. I stayed with this group for [a number of] months, until the majority of the members of the cell was captured and six members were killed. God was generous to me and I survived. . . . Then God was generous to me and I participated in Bosnia-Herzegovina. . . .

"Then I went from Bosnia to Yemen, and from Yemen I went to Somalia, then Oghadin, which is the Somali province occupied by the Crusader country of Ethiopia, which is working hard to Christianize the Muslim sons of Somalia.

"I saw the churches with my own eyes there. The Somalis are 100% Muslim, and there is a vicious campaign against them. I joined my brothers in the Islamic Union Group in Somalia, and we had a long story that ended in captivity for two years and seven months, after which I was turned over to the tyrants in Saudi Arabia who imprisoned me for a year. God was generous to me, so I was able to go to Afghanistan a month after my release. There I trained with the brothers and then in this latest war against the Americans.

"Today, praise God, we and the brothers are on the front that we had sought to purify and liberate it from the filth of the traitorous rulers and the Crusader Americans and their allies." (Abu-Hajer, 2003)[4]

How to Play Soccer

"1. Play soccer without the four lines, because they were created by the infidels and [are] the international rules of soccer, which require that they should be drawn when playing soccer.

"2. The terminology used by the international rules created by the infidels and polytheists such as [the English words] 'foul,' 'penalty,' 'corner,' 'goal,' and 'out'—all of these terms should be left behind and not uttered. Each person who uses them will be disciplined, berated, removed from the game. He will be told publicly: 'You have emulated the infidels, and this is forbidden to you.'

. . . .

"6. Playing with the ball, should [only] be done with the application of [these] rules and regulations, and with the intention of strengthening

---

[4] Abu Hajer (also known as Abdulaziz Issa Abdul-Mohsin al-Muqrin) was the former leader of al-Qaeda in Saudi Arabia. He was at one time number one on Saudi Arabia's 26-most-wanted list and was responsible for the beheading of Paul Johnson, an American employee of Lockheed-Martin, in Saudi Arabia. He was also editor of *Sword of Prophets*, an al-Qaeda training publication. Abu Hajer was killed in a shootout with Saudi security forces on June 18, 2004, while depositing Johnson's body in Riyadh.

the body for the purpose of waging jihad in the path of God and in preparation for such a time as the call for jihad is issued, not to waste time or for the enjoyment of the so-called 'victory.'

. . . .

"12. When you are done playing with the ball, do not talk about your game, saying 'I am a better player than the opponent,' or 'so-and-so is a better player,' and so forth. Your concern and speech should be about your bodies, their strength, and the muscles. Bear in mind that we only played with the intention of training to run and maneuver in preparation for jihad in God's path.

"13. Any of you who, when he kicks the ball between the wooden or iron posts, then runs so that his friends will run after him to embrace or adulate him as players do in America and France, spit in his face and discipline him and berate him. What do joy and embraces and kissing have to do with this sport?" (Abdallah al-Najdi, 2005)[5]

Nights in Iraq

"Let me tell you about some of the nights {in Iraq}. We could see them and they couldn't see us. One of those nights one of the brothers known as Abu Ahmad Afghani he was sitting and crying so they asked him why are you crying he said we used to pray to Allah (swt) that at the time of the Jihad against the Soviet Union and Russia they used to surround us from all directions but we could see them and we were waiting for the right time to start to kill them. I pray to Allah he gives me the same opportunity again. Where I am sitting in a place I can see them all moving around me and I am just waiting for the right time to kill from them. I wish I can have the same situation inshallah and Allah grant me to be in the land of Palestine where I will be in the same situation and have the same opportunity to fight there. After that he went out from his checkpoint and he started to reconnaissance and he came back and he said there are about 40 US patrol guards. The brothers said what do you think he said lets take them. So we all gathered together, all of us were happy and made Takbir[6] amongst ourselves as

[5] Abdallah al-Najdi was the alias of the head of the "Information Department" of al-Qaeda in the Arabian Peninsula; he published and often wrote in the online magazine *Sawt al-Jihad (The Voice of Jihad)*. Al-Najdi was arrested in June 2007.

[6] *Takbir* is the Arabic name for the expression, *Alluhu akbar!* (God is very great!) (*The Mishkat al-Anwar of Ibn 'Arabi*, book x, ch. ii). The ejaculation frequently occurs in the daily liturgy and in the funeral prayer.

if we were going to have a feast. By Allah we went out in an organized way and when the enemy came we was killing them the way you kill chicken and slaughtered them one after one. Each one of us came back with weapons we had taken off the enemy Alhumdulillah we killed 12, captured 8. Also amongst them were Sabees as well because we couldn't distinguish between man and woman from them; Wallahee what a Sabee[7] they are." (Abu Iyad, in Committee for the Defense of Legitimate Rights, 2003)[8]

Death in the Family

The attack referred to in this excerpt took place during the Afghan War, possibly in Tora Bora.

"And I {Zawahiri} say to you {Zarqawi} with sure feeling and I say: That the author of these lines has tasted the bitterness of American brutality, and that my favorite wife's chest was crushed by a concrete ceiling and she went on calling for aid to lift the stone block off her chest until she breathed her last, may God have mercy on her and accept her among the martyrs. As for my young daughter, she was afflicted by a cerebral hemorrhage, and she continued for a whole day suffering in pain until she expired. And to this day I do not know the location of the graves of my wife, my son, my daughter, and the rest of the three other families who were martyred in the incident and who were pulverized by the concrete ceiling, may God have mercy on them and the Muslim martyrs. Were they brought out of the rubble, or are they still buried beneath it to this day?" (al-Zawahiri, 2005b).

Death Notice

"We, in the Martyr Izz-al-Din al-Qassam Brigades,[9] announce the glad tidings of the ascension to heaven, God willing, of the martyr Al-

---

[7] A pun on Seabees and Sabians. Sabeans, also referred to as Sabian Mandaeans, follow a pre-Islamic faith and are a religious minority in Iraq and neighboring countries. In recent years, they have endured forced conversion and murder in Iraq (Crawford, 2007).

[8] Translation of the first press release given by Sheikh Abu Iyad, the Amir of the Mujahideen, in Baghdad.

[9] The armed wing of Hamas.

Qassam Brigades member Amjad Muhammad Rashid al-Hinnawi,[10] 32, commander of the Martyr Izz-al-Din al-Qassam Brigades in the northern West Bank, who was martyred by the occupation troops' gunfire at 0300 [0100 GMT] today, Monday, 12 Shawwal 1426 Hegira, corresponding to 14 November 2005, when they stormed the Al-Hamami Building in the low income residence area in Nabulus. The occupation troops evacuated the residents of the building and unleashed dogs inside it. Then, they shelled the house and opened fire on it. As a result, our martyr commander ascended to heaven after he was shot in the head. Afterward, the Zionist troops demolished the house wall over his body, which resulted in the crushing and disfigurement of his chaste body." (Izz-al-Din al-Qassam Brigades, 2005)

Al-Qaeda and the Battle of Kandahar

This military action took place toward the end of the war in Afghanistan. Kandahar was an al-Qaeda redoubt and still remains a hotbed of insurgent activity.

"On the following day, the signs of victory {in the battle for Qandahar} began when the Americans pushed Gal Agha's[11] forces to advance on the ground, saying that they had bombarded the area in the last days and there was no detection now of forces on the ground, so they needed to advance. The enemy advanced and reached the broken bridge and began to advance toward the trap points. One of the youngsters[12] was wondering about the hesitant vehicle on the bridge coming from the direction of the enemy. . . . When he surprised them, they fled and he fired at them and they exchanged fire while fleeing. This was, then, a first test to find out if the area was empty.

"Then hell broke out in the area. Airplanes came from every direction and in all kinds. C-130s attacked, jets attacked with missiles, helicopters attacked with missiles and guns. The area was transformed into a ball of fire for more than an hour. Gal Agha's forces began to advance again, assured that there were no breathing souls left in the area, other than their forces. As soon as they entered the killing field, bombs of the youngsters rained on them from every direction, and they were

---

[10] A well-known Palestinian explosives expert who was on the Israeli Forces' most-wanted list.

[11] Current governor of Nangarhar and former governor of Kandahar. He controlled the city before the Taliban took over in 1994.

[12] Arabs being trained by al-Qaeda in Afghanistan.

gunned down with machineguns. Calls of 'God is great' and victory were screamed aloud. The brothers killed many of them and captured two. . . .

"Quickly, the situation changed again and airplanes returned; . . . The Americans ended the bombardment close to sunset, while people were still fasting in their holes {this occurred during Ramadan}. No food was prepared. I contacted Abu al-Tayib . . . and asked him to buy food from the market and send it over to the brothers on the front, and told him that the following day we would turn the Religious Institute into a general kitchen for the front, serving three meals a day regularly. I contacted the youngsters on the front and told them that they had to eat their breakfast meal. Abu al-Tayib managed the kitchen very well and provided food throughout the following days, sometimes by cars, sometimes on foot, and sometimes by motorcycles. No meal was late to the holy warriors.

"Night descended and the bombardment was still on. The youngsters noticed the lights of an incoming car again, and here Amir al-Fateh (who named his tank the Elephant) asked Abi al-Hassan to watch the cars, so that when they reach the agreed-upon point, Amir, who prepared his tank for that, would attack them. Communication over the system was clear, aircrafts were hovering in the sky, and the cars were moving very slowly on the ground. Abu al-Hassan was slowly saying 'wait Amir . . . wait Amir' then he screamed 'now hit'. Amir released the forces of his Elephant and burned by God's blessing the first car. All the cars retreated, fleeing.

. . . .

"On the second day of the third week, we put the rocket launcher BM12 on a pickup truck. When Sheikh Abu al-BM heard about it, he hurried and asked me to be in charge of it. I could not turn him down.

. . .

"Fighting stopped in most of Afghanistan and the battle began in Qandahar at the outskirts of the airport and Aurzjan. We did not yet cover that sector, so I asked Sa'douf to contact the brothers in Khost and ask them to send a group to cover this breach. I went to Mullah Brader who was in charge of the fighting in the outskirts of Aurzjan and told him that we would support him with a hundred youngsters to strengthen the northern front.

"We had with us two trucks with a launcher from the Taliban. They were supporting the defense of the youngsters. On the following day, with repeated attacks from airplanes, and attempts of the Gal Agha forces to advance, and while the youngsters began to deflect the attack, the two trucks were hit and the Taliban operating them were martyred. They were the last Afghani group fighting with us. I asked them for weapons and ammunitions; they gave us the airport depots. . . . When we lost the two trucks, we immediately pushed the car {sic}, which had the launcher, and things returned to normal. Sheikh Abu al-BM was able through his experience to manage the portable launcher with rare military flexibility and skill. He turned points where Gal Agha groups gathered to hell. The only goal of the air force afterward was to search and find the portable launcher. When they gave up looking for it, they decided to attack the whole village. B-52s came and bombed the mountains and the flat lands, and flew over the village where the launcher was. They did not leave a home without bombing it, until they got to the place where the experienced sheikh was. He pushed his youngsters away from the launcher and the place collapsed. The whole village came under a cloud of dust, smoke and gunpowder, and communication with the sheikh was lost. I got worried about him, but half an hour later, heard his voice quietly over the communication system asking for some digging tools. . . . The launcher was hit after three days and nights of tough fighting. Among his crew, Abu Osama the Somali was martyred.

"The companies stationed around the airport were starting to wear out from the continuous fighting. They had been fighting all day and watching all night. I asked Abi al-Harith the Egyptian to rotate the groups so they might rest, provided that the companies stationed around the airport would take the positions of the companies who were in towns. . . . The battle intensified and lasted five days without respite, in which the Army of Allah won crushing victories and very few martyrs were killed, except for the third or fourth night, I do not recall, when the enemy advanced and was met by the hero Mowhad and the men of his company. . . . Mowhad said, 'Keep your position, Salah is coming from the right and I will attack from the center.' That is when Abu Hashim al-Sayyed, who came from a rear position when he heard of the advance, interfered rapidly in the transmission and said 'Oh Mowhad, do you need me?' Mowhad asked, 'Where are you, may Allah be pleased with you?' and Abu Hashim replied, 'I am on my way. Wait for me, may Allah reward you!' Then he left the car and ran on the road in company of Abu Hafs the Mauritanian, Hamza the Qatari, Abu Yussef the Mauritanian, Abu Amir . . . , Samir the Najdi and several youths who, in their excitement, took to the road, running without fear of the enemy, the airplanes, or the bombs. Abu Hashim al-Sayyed was ahead of everyone else. He was yelling in the radio, 'May Allah reward you, oh Mowhad. I am your brother, do not go without me!' Mowhad was prompting him, 'May Allah have mercy on your parents, where are you? You are late.' And Abu Hashim al-Sayyed replied, 'I am close.' Then, Abu Hashim was heard on the radio running and inciting the youths to jihad and he swore he could smell the scent of paradise. . . . I contacted Abi al-Harith the Egyptian and we changed to the private frequency. I told him to 'beware for Mowhad is upset and excited. Do not let the youths move [from their positions]. The company of Abu Hashim al-Sayyed should be enough for him. Do not let them move beyond the trap.' Then Sheikh Abu Harith the Egyptian said, 'I understand that, but it is getting hot here. I will try to calm the youths and make them keep their positions.' I went back to the 'general' frequency.

"Mowhad and his brothers were harvesting 'the souls of the enemy,' greatening Allah and walking between corpses. Then he started running ahead in pursuit of the enemy who was retreating. He took the youths with him. They left their positions and followed him running on the road, like the company of Abu Hashim. At this point, the airplanes intervened and started bombing the road, and as I mentioned, Abu Hashim said that he could smell the scent of paradise. Then the hero fell in martyrdom and other heroes fell around him. Thus fell the martyrs Sheikh Abu Yussef the Mauritanian, Hamza the Qatari, and I have personally felt the wonderful scent that was covering him and his face was wearing a beautiful smile, and what a smile that was – as well as Samir the Najdi who seemed very gracious and beautiful in death despite the blood covering his body.

". . . the two tanks . . . joined the battle, as well as the machinegun manned by Adham the Egyptian and Abu Amar the Palestinian. There were between them and the aircrafts impressive duels, and some extraordinarily courageous deeds. The aircrafts in the sky were firing everywhere, while they were shooting from their machinegun at the aircrafts. They could not reach the aircrafts, which were far in the sky, and the missiles dropping from the sky did not reach them. The duel lasted for quite a while. Amir al-Fatah used his tank to fire [at the airplanes] . . . . However, his tank was hit directly by a missile, and a second one exploded close by.

"The whole crew escaped safely except for Khalid who received a fragment in his head that deprived him from the use of his left side for four months. However, he recovered after that and only his left hand bears signs of the wound. Currently he is back to training in a secret base near the Pakistani-Afghani border in one of al-Qaeda's secret bases.

"As for Amir al-Fatah's Elephant, it was very respected by the Americans. They kept looking for it. Then they divided the area in squares and scanned them until they found the Elephant and destroyed it. However, Amir al-Fatah and his crew escaped to safety after a fierce battle where the Elephant humiliated the Apaches. However, the Elephant earned himself a 'medal of honor' in this battle.

"Thus, we lost our heavy back-up in tanks, as well as the missile launcher, and this is a serious matter. However, the enemy lost a large number of its fighters and their fighting spirit was crushed, and after that, they only shot [at us] from a distance. The Americans could not entice them to advance any more. We had won the ground battle[13] which lasted five days, without respite." (al-Adel, 2003)[14]

Terror in Konduz, Afghanistan

"A British Muslim woman called Umm-Hafsah carried out another operation during which she killed two Americans. She was with her husband and brother in the forces that were also besieged in Konduz.

". . . Her husband, an Arab, went with the forces that left the city safely. Umm-Hafsah and her brother were Jews who converted to Islam in Britain before they immigrated to Afghanistan and settled in it. But they still carried their original passports that were issued in their Jewish names.

"Umm-Hafsah hid explosives under her clothes and she and her brother surrendered to the Shiite Hezb-E Wahdat-E [Eslami] and Abdol Rashid Dostum factions. When they spoke in English with these forces' vanguards, the latter thought they were Americans because of their European looks and they were taken in a vehicle to Mazar-E Sharif where US units were deployed. They claimed there that they were working for Oxfam Relief Agency inside Konduz Province when the Taliban forces entered and took up positions in it after their withdrawal from Mazar-E Sharif. They were sent to the US Forces' command center in Kabul to check their claims.

---

[13] Kandahar finally fell on December 7, 2001, under a negotiated surrender agreement, but the Taliban and al-Qaeda fighters fled the city with their weapons.

[14] Saif al-Adel is an al-Qaeda commander and possible member of Egyptian Islamic Jihad. He was implicated in the 1998 African embassy bombings and is currently believed to reside in Iran.

"They left in a vehicle and were heavily guarded by a unit that included four Hezb-E Wahdat-E-Men. They sat in the back seat and the two Americans sat in the vehicle's cabin. At the right moment, she kicked her brother with her foot to make him move away from her and then blew herself up as her brother leapt from the vehicle that was driving at high speed." (al-Zawahiri, undated(a))

Testimonials: Why I Joined Jihad

"My name is Zakaullah and I belong to Tehsil Mansehra Warkan. I studied up to the ninth grade after which I became a labourer. I always liked jihad and had read in books that martyrs went to heaven without questioning by God. We were sinners and I thought this was the only way to redemption and therefore I joined madressah Syed Ahmed Shaheed, Balakot."

"My name is Abdul Rehman and I come from an area near District Faisalabad. I am totally illiterate. I used to carry baskets in the wholesale vegetable market in Faisalabad, finding work wherever I could. Once, in the market there was a hotel serving food during Ramadan and people were blatantly dishonouring the sanctity of the holy month when mujahids from Harkatul Ansar reached the scene and immediately had the hotel stop serving food. They gave a long sermon that touched my heart and I decided to commit myself to jihad. I went to madressah Khalid Bin Walid and since then have been to many fronts and am on my way to Kashmir now."

"My name is Mohammad Yar Afghani; I belong to Gardez, Afghanistan, and used to work in Jalalabad. From there I came to Peshawar and then accompanied a friend in search of work to Muzzaffarabad. As a child I had heard stories of jihad from my elders and was determined to participate in jihad when I grew up. One day I went to my friend Haq Nawaz Bhai and he told me that this world is finite and everyone must die, life after death is infinite therefore let us train for and join jihad. So I joined madressah Syed Ahmed Shaheed for training and am now going to Kashmir. If I am martyred, I have recorded a cassette of my poems please give that to my friend Haq Nawaz so that he remains in touch with the holy war."

"My name is Mu'awiya and I belong to District Bagh in Azad Kashmir. I am seventeen years old and have studied up to the fourth grade in a school, then I learnt the Holy Quran by heart from madressah Ta'aleemul Quran Hanafiya Chattar #2. I learnt fifteen chapters of the Quran at the mosque in my village then joined madressah Mahmood Ghaznavi for training. I joined jihad because of a sermon delivered by Ameer Muhtarim Hazrat Maulana Mohammad Masood Azhar at Bagh and am now going to Kashmir." (Mujahideen of Jaish-i-Mohammad, 2001)

Jihad Offers No Escape from Bureaucracy

"Noble brother Ezzat . . .

"Following are my comments on the summary accounting I received:

"With all due respect, this is not an accounting. It's a summary accounting. For example, you didn't write any dates, and many of the items are vague.

"The analysis of the summary shows the following:

"1. You received a total of $22,301. Of course, you didn't mention the period over which this sum was received. Our activities only benefited from a negligible portion of the money. This means that you received and distributed the money as you please . . .

"2. Salaries amounted to $10,085—45 percent of the money. I had told you in my fax . . . that we've been receiving only half salaries for five months. What is your reaction or response to this?

"3. Loans amounted to $2,190. Why did you give out loans? Didn't I give clear orders to Muhammad Saleh to . . . refer any loan requests to me? We have already had long discussions on this topic . . .

"4. Why have guesthouse expenses amounted to $1,573 when only Yunis is there, and he can be accommodated without the need for a guesthouse?

"5. Why did you buy a new fax for $470? Where are the two old faxes? Did you get permission before buying a new fax under such circumstances?

"6. Please explain the cell-phone invoice amounting to $756 (2,800 riyals) when you have mentioned communication expenses of $300.

"7. Why are you renovating the computer? Have I been informed of this?

"8. General expenses you mentioned amounted to $235. Can you explain what you mean?" (al-Zawahiri,[15] in Cullison, 2004)

Interview with the Wife of a Shaheed (Martyr), Umm Saburah

"Q. Ma Sha Allah, you are one of the most honoured women to be the wife of a Shaheed! I don't know what I would give to have that honour! Tell me, sister, how did you manage your (several) young children all through the years he was in jihad, and how are you managing now?

"Umm Saburah: I used to teach children and live with whatever I got out of that. Now, with the persecution of my government (they arrested and harassed her) I don't even know where I am going to go. People tell me all sorts of things. What can I do? I am just visiting family and friends moving from place to place at the moment. My dream would be to go to Chechnya and work with the refugee women there. I would want my children to be exposed to that life. I think the hardship will be good for them. There is too much luxury, too much ease over here.

"A.{sic} SubhanAllah sister, you encouraged your husband all along for jihad even though it was so difficult for you. I know of some sisters who just only think of themselves and their rights and stop their husbands from Jihad . . . and then there are others whose husbands simply don't want to go even though the sisters encourage them.

"Umm Saburah: Well, in my case, it was my husband who taught me and encouraged me. Sometimes I felt like that (referring to the women who discouraged their husbands), but I never tried to stop him or discourage him, as it is haraam {forbidden} to do so. Jihad is a fard from Allah. How could I stop him from that?!

"A.{sic} I have heard a lot about your husband . . . tell me more about him . . . how was he martyred? Of course, Allah only knows who is a martyr, but we like to think of him as such.

"Umm Saburah: Oh I know he was martyred (and her eyes filled with tears and she paused). He had all the signs of a Shaheed. They wouldn't send his body home after they killed him. They kept it for several days in cold storage. Finally, when they sent it home (a very short distance from the cold-storage facility), his body was so warm and he looked like he was still alive! He had all the signs of a Shaheed. He always wanted martyrdom. Once in a previous war he was badly

---

[15] Letter to Ezzat (real name unknown), February 11, 1999.

injured and doctors had said he would not be able to survive, but he did and became well. He was saddened by his recovery and often used to cry, thinking that perhaps he was not good enough to be accepted by Allah as a martyr. He was a very good husband and a very good man.

"Q. So what do you want your sons to be when they grow up?

"Umm Saburah: (Firmly) They will be Mujahideen insha'Allah. That was their father's wish and there is no choice about it.

"Q. How will you ensure that they do take that route?

"Umm Saburah: They do have other brothers (in Islam) who were my husband's friends and they have already instilled in them these values. They look up to their father and what he did with admiration and respect, and they look up to his friends now. My daughter feels angry at the whole situation though and I am working on trying to give as much love as I can to all my children. It's hard, but Alhamdulillah." (Umm Saburah, 2001)

Assassination in Cairo

"Members of the Egyptian Revolution Organization decided to assassinate a high-ranking Israeli living in Cairo.

. . . .

"2. Surveillance of the target was carried out for a period of time. The exits and entrances to the theater of operations were studied. The time was set to execute the operation at eight am 8/20/85, when the Israeli target would leave for work at the Israeli embassy in Cairo.

"3. A car was purchased for use in the operation. Someone's identification was purchased indirectly, the photo was removed, and that of one of the organization's members was put [in its place].

"4. The organization members participating in the operation (there were four of them) rode in a car belonging to one of them. They put their weapons in the car (they had hidden their weapons in tennis racket covers). Before arriving at the theater of operations, they left that car and got into the operations vehicle, which was close to the site of the operation.

"5. After riding in the car, it became apparent the car was not in good running order and had leaked a lot of oil, so they decided to delay the operation.

"6. While they were returning in the car in poor condition, they saw a man from the Israeli Mosad, and the operation leader decided to kill him. The Israeli Mosad man was riding in a car with two Israeli women with him.

"7. The assassins' car drove behind the Israeli target's car, which noticed the surveillance in the rear-view mirror, but the driver of the assassins' car was able to choke off the Mosad man's car and he wasn't able to escape. They blocked his way and forced him over by the curb.

"8. One of the four personnel got out of the car and emptied the magazine of his American rile in the direction of the Mosad man. The second one got out on the other side and emptied his bullets, and the third did likewise. After executing the operation, they fled to the other car and left the operations car on the street.

"9. After a period of time, the police force came and found the car with traces of blood.

"[It was not] known that the crime was committed by the organization until one of its members (the brother of the organization's leader) turned himself in to the American embassy and disclosed all the secrets of the operation which the Egyptian Revolution Organization undertook." (*Manchester Document*, undated)

Dreams

Osama bin Laden (UBL) and his cohorts place great store in dreams and visions. This is a discussion between him and an unidentified Sheikh after 9/11.

"UBL: . . . Abu-Al-Hasan Al-(Masri), who appeared on Al-Jazeera TV a couple of days ago and addressed the Americans saying: 'If you are true men, come down here and face us.' (. . . inaudible . . .) He told me a year ago: 'I saw in a dream, we were playing a soccer game against the Americans. When our team showed up in the field, they were all pilots!' He said: 'So I wondered if that was a soccer game or a pilot game? Our players were pilots.' He (Abu-Al-Hasan) didn't know anything about the operation until he heard it on the radio. He said the game went on and we defeated them. That was a good omen for us.

"Shaykh: May Allah be blessed.

"Unidentified man off camera: Abd Al Rahman Al-(Ghamri) said he saw a vision, before the operation, a plane crashed into a tall building. He knew nothing about it.

"Shaykh: May Allah be blessed!

. . . .

"Shaykh (referring to dreams and visions): The plane that he saw crashing into the building was seen before by more than one person. One of the good religious people has left everything and come here. He told me, 'I saw a vision, I was in a huge plane, long and wide. I was carrying it on my shoulders and I walked from the road to the desert for half a kilometer. I was dragging the plane.' I listened to him and I prayed to Allah to help him. Another person told me that last year he saw, but I didn't understand and I told him I don't understand. He said, 'I saw people who left for jihad . . . and they found themselves in New York . . . in Washington and New York.' I said, 'What is this?'

"He told me the plane hit the building. That was last year. We haven't thought much about it. But, when the incidents happened he came to me and said, 'Did you see . . . this is strange.' I have another man . . . my god . . . he said and swore by Allah that his wife had seen the incident a week earlier. She saw the plane crashing into a building . . . that was unbelievable, my god.

. . . .

"(Someone in the crowd asks UBL to tell the Shaykh about the dream of (Abu-Da'ud)).

"UBL: We were at a camp of one of the brother's guards in Qandahar. This brother belonged to the majority of the group. He came close and told me that he saw, in a dream, a tall building in America, and in the same dream he saw Mukhtar[16] teaching them how to play karate. At that point, I was worried that maybe the secret would be revealed if everyone starts seeing it in their dream. So I closed the subject. I told him if he sees another dream, not to tell anybody, because people will be upset with him." (bin Laden, 2001b).

Khobar Massacre, May 29, 2004: Interview with Fawwaz bin Muhammad al-Nashmi[17]

"*Voice of Jihad*: And how was the beginning [of the operation]?

"We left the house at exactly 5:45. When we approached the location, we changed our clothes and put on our packs and weapons. We asked God almighty for support and to facilitate our actions.

---

[16] Unknown individual.

[17] The self-declared leader of the "Jerusalem [al-Quds] Battalion," al-Nashmi (also known as Turki bin Fuheid al-Muteiry) was killed by Saudi security forces in June 2004.

"The company had two gates. We headed for the first. Our brother Nimr, may God accept him [as a martyr], got out with the rest of the brothers, and he ordered the guard to open the gate. There was a person behind the gate and the fence, and there were two security personnel outside, and one more inside. The one inside was the one who could open the gate. The brothers ordered the one inside to open the gate, but he refused. The brothers decided to force their way in, but he hid behind the counter [sic].

"We were in a hurry because we had to finish [our mission] at this company and then proceed to the second, so we went to the second gate and forced our way in, and we dealt with the guards protecting it.

"As soon as we entered, we saw the vehicle belonging to the British man (the director of investment at the company), and we killed him. The cell phone on the bloody car seat in the photograph that was so widely publicized was his.

"We left. We got into our vehicle [after tying] the infidel by one of his feet [to the car] and we left the company premises and saw the patrols. The first to arrive was a Jeep with one soldier, whom we killed. We engaged with the rest and managed to remove ourselves from their midst.

"Thank God that we had memorized more than one route to the second location because, when the patrols closed the road, there was no longer a way back on the same road, so we took another one (the coastal road, then the Khobar-Dammam Expressway) for 4 kilometers.

"The clothing of the infidel [tied behind the vehicle] had been ripped off, and he had become naked in the street. The street was full of people because this was during work hours, and everybody saw the corpse of the infidel dragged behind the vehicle, praise to God.

"When we reached one of the overpasses, we found a checkpoint mounted by the dogs of the tyrants and the guards of the Americans, so we engaged them. When we reached the middle of the overpass, the rope tore and the body of the infidel fell [off of the overpass into the intersection below], between the four traffic lights. Anybody who was stopped at any of the four traffic lights saw the infidel when he fell off the overpass.

"The brothers engaged the patrols as they loudly praised God. We wiped out that checkpoint with God's help. We continued on our way and headed toward the other company, the Petroleum Center, which was also in a business complex. We arrived at the gate and got out. Praise God, the brothers were in a state of great serenity and assurance. The brothers walked as if they were on a pleasant walk.

"We entered and found young Arabian men wearing Aramco company uniforms. They asked us, 'What is the matter? What happened?' We told them, 'Do not fear, we do not want you, we want the Americans.'

". . . All present in the reception area were very surprised. They all asked, 'What is the matter? Who are you?' We told them: 'We are jihad fighters and we want the Americans. We did not come to raise our weapons in the faces of Muslims. We came to purify the Arabian Peninsula from infidels and polytheists who kill our brethren in Afghanistan and Iraq, in accordance with the will of our Prophet, Muhammad, peace and blessings upon him. We want you to lead us to them.'

"We headed upstairs. The building contained a number of companies. There were a number of doors. Whenever we opened a door, we found a large hall containing many desks, and a main office with a glass front.

"We entered into one of the companies and found an American infidel who appeared to be the director. I entered into his office and called to him, and when he looked at me, I shot him in the head, which exploded. We entered another office and found another infidel. Our brother Hussein (we ask God to accept from him and from us) cut his throat—this was the South African infidel.

. . . .

"We left the company and found our heroic brother Nimr standing at the entrance to the company. He was drinking some water [and appeared] as though he was [as relaxed as if he were] on a pleasant walk, such was his bravery, may God have mercy on him. We exited and got into our vehicle, and found forces that had rushed to defend the Americans. Perhaps some of them were Marines. We engaged them for the third time. The strange cowardice was clear in their actions, for they stayed far away, while we were approaching them.

. . . .

"We proceeded to the third and most fortified location. Our plan was to remain in the vehicle until we came next to the American Humvee. When we came alongside it, the brothers stuck their heads out the windows and began to shout 'God is greater' and fire at them. I saw the skull of the soldier behind the machine gun explode before me, praise God, and I think the driver was killed also.

"We had planned to enter from the exit gateway and, as soon as we were in, I would blow up the vehicle in their midst, so that the brothers could continue to force their way in.

"As soon as we arrived, we passed passed by the Humvees and engaged them. At one of the gateways, God sent us a guard (we saw him in the street), whom we ordered to open the gates for us, so we didn't need to blow the vehicle up.

"Brother Nimr was strutting inside the compound, and we raced into the main road of the complex (the complex is huge; it covers an area of several kilometers and includes more than one compound).

"We went to one of the buildings where brother Nimr pushed the door forcibly until it opened, and we entered. We met a lot of people whom we asked about their religion and asked to see their identification papers. We used this process to call to God and make clear our objective. We talked to many of them.

"During this time, we found a Swedish infidel. Brother Nimr beheaded him and put his head at the entrance so that those entering and exiting would see it.

"We continued in our labor, looking for infidels and slaughtering those we found. As this was happening, we could hear the sounds of patrols and massed soldiers outside. The cowards did not dare force their way in. About 45 minutes or an hour had passed from the start of the operation.

"We began to comb the location in search of infidels. We found Pilipino Christians, so we cut their throats and dedicated them to our brothers, the jihad fighters of the Philippines. We found Hindu engineers and killed them, too, praise God. We purified the land of Muhammad from many Christians and polytheists on that day.

"After that, we headed to the hotel, where we found a restaurant, so we ate breakfast and rested. Then we went up to the first floor and found some Hindu dogs, so we slaughtered them. I told the brothers to put their corpses on the stairs, so that the soldiers of the tyrant would see them when they entered, and be filled with terror. It appears that I had overestimated those cowards somewhat, as they did not enter until after we had left.

"We then utilized the time by organizing a Qur'an class for the remaining Muslims. We taught them to recite the al-Fatiha chapter of the Qur'an in the proper manner. They were amazed at us, at how we could do this in the midst of these fiery happenings, so praise God who guided us to do this.

"We were informed by those Muslim Indians that their manager was an evil Hindu, and that he did not let them pray, and that he would be there after a short while. When he arrived, we verified his religion by checking his paperwork, and kept him with us for a while.

"Afterwards, I called Al-Jazeera TV channel and they conducted an interview with us that they did not broadcast. I told them that I was talking to them from inside the compound, and that we were only targeting infidels.

"Then I headed to one of the rooms and watched the news on television. About five hours had passed since the beginning of the operation, and the reports said that emergency forces were forcing their way into the complex at that time! So I distributed the brothers into various areas of the hotel in preparation to return the attack of the dogs of the state if they forced their way in.

"At 2:00 o'clock {sic} they forced their way in, and they had with them an officer. We could see them from where we were, so we threw bombs at them and the officer was killed, praise God, and his soldiers were wounded. They were screaming at the men behind them: 'We want to get out. Come on, let us out.' We were shouting: 'God is greater' and saying: 'God is our ally and you have no ally. To Hell [with you] and the worst destiny.'

"Nimr would shout to one of them: 'Come close, coward,' and the man would flee.

"They began to fire heavy weapons at the hotel and continued to do so until the time for mid-afternoon prayers. During this period, we slaughtered the evil Hindu who had been preventing his employees from praying. We put the Muslims on the higher floors so that they would not be hit by the bullets of the emergency forces and their stray projectiles. We stayed below to wait for those cowards.

"During this time, brother Hussein was on the stairs and saw the Italian infidel, so he pointed his weapon at him and commanded him to approach. The infidel approached and we saw his identification papers. We decided that he should call Al-Jazeera TV channel to talk to his countrymen and send them a message of warning against waging war on Islam and the Muslims, then we would slaughter him and dedicate him to the Italians who are participating in the war against our brethren in Iraq and the idiot president of Italy who wants to enter into a confrontation with the lions of Islam.

"We called Al-Jazeera and asked the anchor to speak to him, so he did. The anchor asked me whether the Italian spoke English. I asked the anchor whether he had any Italian translators. He said yes. I said: 'Then let him speak in his own language,' so he talked for a few minutes. Then I asked the anchor: 'Did you record?' He said yes, so the heroic Nimr cut [the Italian's] throat.

"*Voice of Jihad*: We ask God to accept this offering. What happened after that?

"Al-Nashmi: We were prepared and alert. One of the brothers suggested that we should force our way into those cowards because we had been waiting for them to try to force their way to us for so long, but they did not. We asked God for guidance and prayed, and after the sunset prayers, we asked God again. After the evening prayers we asked God for guidance yet again.

"The odd thing was that were feeling sleepy. Even stranger is the fact that we had been feeling sleepy since the start of the operation in the morning. We remembered the words of God '[Remember how it was] when He caused inner calm to enfold you, as an assurance from Him.'

. . . .

"After the evening prayers, we went to reconnoiter the situation. We moved after 9:00 o'clock {sic} p.m. We exited from the last position that the enemy would expect, and God made their eyes blind to us.

"We climbed one of the artificial waterfalls that overlooked the road, and the distance between us and the road was big—about 13 meters. Around these waterfalls there were tall trees. Five meters away from these trees were the concrete barriers around the compound.

"Brother Hussein jumped first, after throwing the ammunition bag before him. He bound the Kalashnikov to his back and tightened the belt, then he invoked God's name and leapt. When he reached the ground, he lay down, causing one of the brothers to believe that he was dead. It was God's mercy that the earth was moist from the spray of the waterfall, so brother Hussein was not harmed. We could hardly believe our eyes. We called out to him and he responded that he was well. We knew then that this was a blessing from God, because the distance was large: 13 meters. Praise God.

"Brother Nader leapt next, followed by me, and then brother Nimr jumped.

"*Voice of Jihad*: Allah Akbar . . . God is Greater . . . Praise God for this great blessing. You are now in the street?

"Yes. By now, we are in the street and the trees conceal us. All of the forces massed outside believe that we are inside the hotel. The hour was close to 10:30 p.m., and we were very tired and feeling sleepy, so we decided to rest before attacking them. Only meters separated us from them. God, in His mercy, drew their eyes to the hotel and provided us with the large trees to conceal us from them. They had not even the remotest expectation that we would jump this tall fence.

"The brothers slept for an hour while I stood watch. All of the brothers were certain that they would be killed, but we preferred to fight after resting. I then slept a sleep that I do not recall the like of in my life, in terms of relaxation, calmness, and clarity of conscience. Praise God.

"After that, we decided to attack them. We congregated and prayed insistently to God that he should grant us support and the succor of His soldiers. The plan was for all four of us to appear, and to stop the first military vehicle that appears before us. Then Nimr and Hussein would head to the vehicle and kill the dogs of America inside. I would head to the Hummer to engage it, distracting it from the brothers. Nader was to carry the remaining ammunition and place it in the vehicle because it would impede fast movement. Then, if we take the vehicle, we would drive it to the security cordon and engage with them.

"*Voice of Jihad*: How many soldiers were there, in your estimation?

"Al-Nashmi: In truth, there were a huge number of forces, armored vehicles, Hummers, and other vehicles. We wanted to take a vehicle because the security cordons were very long, measured in kilometers. To penetrate them, we would need a vehicle to carry us and our weapons.

"When we appeared from behind the trees, the soldiers were very surprised, and looked at us as if we were ghosts. The first of us to reach them was Nimr, who ran at a great speed as he fired at them and shouted 'God is greater.' We engaged them and we won with God's help, His generosity, His mercy, and His munificence.

"The remaining soldiers around the site kept firing, and I am not certain what they were firing at. Perhaps some of them were trying their weapons for the first time!

"We disabled two Jeeps and killed those aboard. I killed the driver of the third Jeep, and the vehicle rolled over several times. We were now in the middle of the road and we could not find a vehicle to ride, so we decided to enter into one of the nearby streets.

"Nimr took off with the speed of lightning and assumed a very difficult combat position and engaged the Hummer. I watched the tracer rounds that were fired from his weapon strike the turret gunner. We crossed the street with the bullets flying around us as we returned fire. It was a miracle from God and a weird blessing—we could see the bullets pass between our legs and all around us, but we were not hit. Praise to God alone.

"We entered the desired lane, and we managed to exit the cordon, and those idiots were still firing! We got into one of the vehicles and took off.

"I swear to God that I am surprised at what happened. For a distance of one and a half or two kilometers, we passed by tens of armored and other and patrols and personnel carriers. We engaged with all of them and passed them all, down the middle of the road in which they had amassed. The distance between us and every vehicle we passed was no more than one meter!

"They closed the road, but God facilitated our egress. We had accepted our deaths and had decided to launch ourselves into them in search of martyrdom. However, [the Prophet's companion] Abu-Bakr spoke the truth when he said: 'Seek death and you will be given life!'

"The tracer rounds had terrified all of those cowards. We were firing at them with Kalashnikovs and were throwing bombs at them that our brothers had made. We shouted and cheered, and God opened a great path for us.

"We broke through the first cordon, then the second, then the third. As we passed the third cordon, the hero, Nimr, had his body out the window to fire, and he was struck by a bullet in the middle of his chest. He continued to fire, however.

"We broke though the fourth and fifth cordons as Nimr's blood flowed freely while he continued to fight.

"As we passed the sixth cordon, Nimr fell inside the vehicle and raised his index finger.[18] We shook him and moved him, but he did not respond, so we had no doubt then that he had been killed. We ask God to elevate him. . . .

"When we passed the sixth cordon and reached the expressway, we could not believe that we had passed all those cordons. We became certain that there had been divine intervention.

"We drove for a distance of ten kilometers, checking our brother Nimr all the way, but he had apparently passed on. We prayed to God that He would accept him as a martyr. We found a National Guard pickup truck, so we took it. Our brother Nader sat in the bed of the truck with his weapon at the ready in order to engage if an engagement occurred. . . .

"We entered the city with God's help, and it was as if what we had been through was a dream, for all the blessings and support we received.

---

[18] A gesture symbolizing "There is no God but Allah and Muhammad is His Prophet."

Praise and thanks to God as befits the glory of His countenance and the greatness of his authority" (al-Nashmi, 2004)[19]

Poetry

"When I saw her eyes, the sweetness of her beauty lived in me
Her beauty is beyond description, God has poured beauty over beauty
I had many words to tell her, but they disappeared when my hands touched her hands
When I talked to her after I saw her I felt that the paradise is for me
I did not look at anyone but her when I could have looked at others
I did not write any poems for girls on this earth, I have nothing to do with them.
Without the perfume no man would have come close to her and praised her
If she came looking her best, I know that she is the devil under cover
Everyone was crying when they remembered women, while I am telling her poem
I ask God to give her to me, God never disappoints a faithful that comes to him praying" (al-Aslami, 2004)

"I witness that against the sharp blade
They always faced difficulties and stood together . . .
When the darkness comes upon us and we are bit by a
Sharp tooth, I say . . .
'Our homes are flooded with blood and the tyrant
Is freely wandering in our homes' . . .
And from the battlefield vanished
The brightness of swords and the horses . . .
And over weeping sounds now
We hear the beats of drums and rhythm . . .
They are storming his forts
And shouting: 'We will not stop our raids
Until you free our lands' . . ." (bin Laden, 2001b)

"Each day to the gardens go caravans of martyrs,
The Omniscient is pleased with them.

---

[19] Fawwaz bin Muhammad al-Nashmi was identified by al-Qaeda as the commander of the squad that attacked foreign workers in Khobar, Saudi Arabia, in May 2004. He was killed by Saudi security forces in June 2004.

What can I say to describe what they have done?
Rhetoric is powerless and the pens run dry" (al-Salim, 2003)[20]

---

[20] Muhammad bin Ahmad al-Salim is a Saudi jihadi who has contributed to the al-Qaeda magazine *Sawt al-Jihad*. He has called on Saudis to fight Americans in Saudi Arabia rather than go to Iraq.

CHAPTER THREE

Seeds of Jihad

The concept of jihad as "holy war" goes back to the beginnings of Islam and Muhammad's battles with the pagan[1] tribes that controlled Mecca and the Arabian Peninsula. Allah's revelations to Muhammad by the Angel Gabrael as set forth in the Qur'an addressed many of the practical, military, moral, ethical, and religious issues that emerged from those conflicts. Scholars and proponents of jihad quoted in this book cite these Qur'anic[2] statements (and Hadith) to justify and explain jihadi philosophy.

Islam developed in a time of war against not only pagans, but also Byzantines and Persians. Initially, when Muhammad was in Mecca, his revelations contained many admonitions to practice tolerance and peace. Later, when he was driven to Medina by persecution and then began to unify the tribes of Arabia, the revelations became more militant. Some of these later passages from the Qur'an and Hadith constitute the touchstones of jihadi ideology.

Many of the quotations are used without the context of the original revelation or story. Jihadis frequently reinterpret the texts and distort their original meaning. For example, the idolaters and polytheists who are the subjects of hostile references are freely translated as Jews, Christians, Americans, Westerners in general, and Muslims who disagree with the jihadis.

Equally important, jihadis also often provide only part of a quotation. For example, the Verse of the Sword (9:5), perhaps the most quoted Qur'an excerpt (cited on p. 38), is often truncated to "Kill the idolaters (polytheists) wherever you find them . . . lie in wait for them at every place of ambush," leaving out the tempering phrase "But if they turn [to God] . . . let them go their way."

The quotations presented in this chapter are in the form the jihadis most often use and therefore do not include the additional material that might change their meaning. However, sources are noted for those interested in exploring the full texts.

---

[1] Non-Muslim; typically also not Christian or Jewish.

[2] Qur'anic quotations, not within other citations, are from the translation of S'Abul a'la Maududi (1967a,b). A'La Maududi's interpretation and commentary were chosen on the basis of an online recommendation from the "USC–MSA Compendium of Muslim Texts," undated.

The Qur'an and Hadith references frequently quoted by jihadis[3] represent only a small fraction of these works and should not be taken as representing the Islamic religion. In this chapter, these references are followed by excerpts from the writings of principal figures in the jihadi pantheon; these excerpts provide snapshots of how jihadi thought developed into today's ideology of violence.

Allah

Muslims believe that the Qur'an contains the actual words of Allah as revealed to Muhammad between 610 CE and 632 CE. As such, the text is more akin to the Ten Commandments than it is to the Christian gospels. Since Muhammad was illiterate, he memorized the revelations and repeated them for others to memorize or write down. Several versions were collected, but the first standardized text was completed under Caliph Uthman between 650 CE and 656 CE (29 to 35 AH[4]). Most of the material on jihad is contained in what are called the "War Suwar"[5] (Chapters 8 and 9). These two chapters (out of 114 in the Qur'an) are devoted, for the most part, to rules of warfare, including constraints and rules on sharing booty.

These chapters were revealed to Muhammad at a time when he was engaging in his final battles to consolidate Islam in the Arabian Peninsula. There is a debate between jihadis and more-moderate Muslims as to whether the later bellicose revelations supersede earlier ones, which occurred when Muhammad's forces were weak and he was preaching peace and tolerance. Other relevant material is scattered among various chapters—in particular, Chapter 4 (An-Nisa), which is primarily about women and their rights and obligations.

> "Then, when the months made unlawful for fighting expire {Ramadan}, kill the mushriks [sic] [idolaters and enemies of Islam] wherever you find them, and seize them, and besiege them, and lie in wait for them at every place of ambush. . . ." (9:5)[6]

> "O Believers, fight with the disbelievers till there is no more mischief [fitna/discord] or persecution and the way of life prescribed by Allah is established in its entirety." (8:39)[7]

---

[3] Or misquoted and misinterpreted, according to many scholars.

[4] The dates in the Islamic calendar; AH stands for the Latin anno Hegirae (in the year of the Hijra).

[5] *Suwar* is the plural of *surah*, which means "chapter of the Qur'an." Each *surah* is divided into *ayat*, or verses.

[6] This is known as the Verse of the Sword and is the basis for jihadis declaring invalid the 114 verses contained in 54 chapters on peace and tolerance.

[7] Jihadis usually omit the rest of the passage: "If they desist, then God sees all that they do."

"O Prophet! Stir the Believers to the fight. If there be twenty men among you who show fortitude, they will overcome two hundred men, and if there be a hundred such men of you, they will overcome a thousand of the deniers of the Truth, for they are a people who lack understanding." (8:65)

"Why should you, then, not fight in the way of Allah for the sake of those helpless men, women and children who, being weak, have been oppressed, and are crying out, 'Our Lord, deliver us from this habitation whose inhabitants are unjust oppressors, and raise a protector for us by Thy grace and a helper from Thyself.'" (4:75)

"Those who follow the way of Faith fight in the way of Allah, and those who follow the way of disbelief fight in the way of taghut [idolatry]. So fight against the helpers of Satan with this conviction that Satan's crafty schemes are in fact very weak." (4:76)

"They ask you (O Muhammad) concerning warfare in the prohibited month. Say, 'Fighting is a heinous offence in this month [Ramadan], but in the sight of Allah it is far worse to hinder people from the Way of Allah . . . and persecution is far worse than bloodshed.' As for them [enemies], they will go on fighting with you till they succeed in turning you away from your Faith, if they can. . . ." (2:217)

"And remember when your Lord was inspiring the angels with this: 'I am with you: so keep the Believers steadfast. I am now going to fill the hearts of the disbelievers with awe: so smite their necks and beat every joint of their bodies.'" (8:12)

"But transgress not the limits. Truly, Allah likes not the transgressors." (2:190)

"Had Allah willed, He would Himself have dealt with them. But (He has adopted this way so that) He may test some of you by means of others. And those who are killed in the way of Allah, Allah will never let their deeds go waste." (47:4)

"So the fact is that you did not slay them but Allah slew them . . . ." (8:17)

"Do not regard as dead those who have been slain in the way of Allah: nay, they are really alive and are well provided for by their Lord." (3:169)

"They [martyrs] rejoice in what Allah with His bounty has given them, and they are happy to think that there is nothing to fear or to grieve also for those believers whom they have left behind and who have not yet joined them." (3:170)

"The pleasures of this worldly life are trifling and the life of the Hereafter is much better for a man who fears Allah, and you shall not be wronged in the least. As to death, it will overtake you wherever you may be, even though you be in fortified towers . . . ." (4:77–78)

"Though Allah has promised a good reward for all, he has a far richer reward for those who fight for Him than for those who stay at home: they have high ranks, forgiveness and mercy from Allah, for Allah is Forgiving and Merciful." (4:95–96)

"Indeed Allah has bought from the Believers their persons and their possessions in return for the Gardens; they fight in the Way of Allah, kill and are killed. This promise [of the Gardens] is the true pledge of Allah made in the Torah, the Gospel, and the Qur'an, and who is more true in fulfilling his promise than Allah? So rejoice in the bargain you have made with Him; and this is the greatest success." (9:111)

"You have been enjoined to go to war, and you dislike it; it may be that you dislike a thing and the same is good for you, and you love a thing and the same is bad for you: Allah knows but you do not." (2:216)

"O Believers, do not take the Jews nor the Christians as your friends; they are one another's friends only. If anyone of you takes them as friends, surely he shall be counted among them . . . ." (5:51)

"Fight with those from among the people of the Book [Christians and Jews] . . . until they pay Jizyah[8] with their own hands and are humbled." (9:29)

---

[8] *Jizyah* is a tax paid by non-Muslims living in a Muslim state ("USC–MSA Compendium of Muslim Texts," undated).

"Has it not always been so that every time they [the Jews] made a covenant, some of them set it aside? Nay, most of them never believe in it sincerely." (2:100)

"And recall the time when your Lord declared, 'I will set over the Israelites over and over again up to the Day of Resurrection, people who should inflict upon them the severest torment.'" (7:167)

"Now you are the best community which has been raised up for the guidance of mankind: you enjoin what is right and forbid what is wrong and believe in Allah. . . ." (3:110)

Muhammad

Muslims are guided not only by the Qur'an, but also by the Sunnah, Muhammad's sayings, deeds, and what he witnessed and approved, usually transmitted through narrations or reports called Hadith. Should the meaning of a Hadith conflict with the Qur'an, the Qu'ran takes precedence.

The authenticity of Hadith can be regarded as strong or weak, depending on the extent of validation by Islamic scholars of the chain of narrators from the time of the Prophet. There are more than 10,000 Hadith compiled in several different collections. The most widely accepted are the collections in Sahih al-Bukhari and Sahih Muslim.[9] The enormous number of Hadith and disputes over their authenticity have exacerbated the many conflicting interpretations of Islam.

". . . peace be upon our Prophet, Muhammad Bin-'Abdallah, who said, 'I have been sent with the sword between my hands to ensure that no one but God is worshipped, God who put my livelihood under the shadow of my lance and who inflicts humiliation and scorn on those who disobey my orders.'" (transmitted by As-Saghir)[10]

"A time will come when the nations (of the world) will surround you from every side, just as diners gather around the main dish. Somebody asked, 'Oh Messenger of Allah, will it be on account of our scarcity at that time?' He said, 'No, your numbers will be many but you will be scum, like the scum of flood water. Feebleness will be placed in your hearts, and fear will be removed from the hearts of your ene-

---

[9] Six sahihs are the main sources of Hadith: Sahih al-Bukhari, Sahih Muslim, Sunan Ibn Majah, Sunan Abu Dawud, Jami al-Tirmidhi, and Sunan al-Nisai.

[10] Sahih al-Jami, Number 2828.

mies, on account of your love for the World, and your abhorrence of death." (narrated by Imam Ahmad and Abu Dawud on the authority of Thawban)[11]

"Strive in the name of Allah in Allah's way! Fight those who disbelieve in Allah: campaign, but do not indulge in excesses, do not act treacherously, do not mutilate, and do not slay children." (transmitted by Muslim on the authority of Burayda)[12]

"War is deceit." (narrated by Abu Huraira)[13]

"And by the One in whose hand is my Soul, I wish I could be killed in the Way of Allah, then live again so that I may be killed again, then live again so that again I may be killed, then live again so that again I may be killed." (transmitted by Al Bukhari and Muslim on the authority of Abu Hurayrah)[14]

"The martyr feels nothing more from the pain of slaughter than any one of you feels from the sting of a gnat." (transmitted by An Nisaa'i at-Tirmidi and al-Darmi on the authority of Abu Hurayra)[15]

"Indeed the martyr has seven special favours from Allah: all his sins are forgiven at the first spurt of his blood, he sees his place in Paradise as his blood is shed [before his soul leaves the body], he tastes the sweetness of Iman, he is married to 72 of the Beautiful Maidens of Paradise, he is protected from the Punishment of the Grave, he is saved from the Great Terror [on The Day of Judgment], there is placed upon his head a crown of honour a jewel of which is better than the whole world and everything in it and he is granted permission to intercede for 70 members of his household [to bring them into Paradise and save them from the Hell Fire]." (narrated by Imam Ahmad at-Tirmidi)

"Whoever is killed while attempting to protect his belongings is a martyr; whoever is killed while attempting to protect himself is a martyr; whoever is killed while attempting to protect his religion is a

---

[11] Sahih al-Jami, Number 8035.

[12] Sahih Muslim, Book 19, Number 4294.

[13] Sahih Bukhari, Book 52, Number 268.

[14] Sahih Muslim, Book 20, Number 4626.

[15] Ahaadeeth on jihad, 1997. At Tirmidhi designates this as Hasan Gharib.

martyr; and whoever is killed while attempting to protect his family is a martyr" (narrated by Abu Dawood, Al-Tirmidhi, Al-Nisaa'I, and Ibn Majah, that Sa'd Ibn Yazeed said he heard the Prophet (PBUH) say)

"(The Apostle) – God's Peace be upon Him – says, 'Whoever truthfully asks for martyrdom will be put in the (heavenly) abodes of the martyrs even if he dies in his bed.' (This tradition is) reported by Muslim and Al-Bayhaqi on the authority of Abu Hurayrah." (Hadith quoted in Faraj, 1979, trans 1986, p. 205)

"He who provides for a mujahid in the Way of Allah the Almighty, it is as if he himself has made jihad; and he who has supported the family of a mujahid with an act of goodness, it is as if he himself has made jihad." (transmitted by Al Bukhari, Muslim, Abu Dawud, and at-Tirmidi on the authority of Zayd bin Khalid al Juhani)[16]

"Shall I tell you who is the best of men and who is the worst? Among the best of men is he who is active in Allah's way on the back of his horse or camel, or on foot, until death comes to him. And among the worst of men is he who reads the Book of Allah Almighty and remains unenlightened (he does not check himself, nor does he admonish and reprove himself)." (transmitted by An-Nisaa'I, on the authority of Abu Sa'eed al Khudari)

". . . and what is the Wahn,[17] O messenger of Allah? He (saw) said, 'Love of the world and the hate for fighting.'" (narrated by Ahmad with a good chain)[18]

"He who dies without having gone on campaign, and without having exhorted himself to do so, dies in a state of hypocrisy." (transmitted by Muslim and Abu Dawud, on the authority of Abu Hurayra)[19]

"The last hour would not come unless the Muslims will fight against the Jews and the Muslims would kill them until the Jews would hide themselves behind a stone or a tree and a stone or a tree would say:

---

[16] Sahih Muslim, Book 20, Number 4668.

[17] Wahn has several meanings. In this context, the relevant meanings are illusion, deadly disease, and enervation.

[18] Ahaadeeth on Jihad, quoted in al-Banna, undated(a). Also narrated by Abu Daud with the words "hate for death," it is a sahih Hadith.

[19] There are many reportings of the same meaning.

Muslim, or the servant of Allah, there is a Jew behind me; come and kill him. . . ." (reported by Abu Huraira)[20]

"Verily, this matter (i.e. this Religion) will reach what the night and the day has reached (i.e. the whole earth). Allah will not exclude an urban nor a nomad household without which this religion would have entered." (reported by Ahmad)[21]

"You are the best people for the people, you tie them in chains and shackles and drag them off to paradise." (narrated by Abu Huraira, in Ibn Taimiya, undated)

"The Prophet (peace be upon him) said: Three things are the roots of faith: to refrain from (killing) a person who utters, 'There is no god but Allah' and not to declare him unbeliever whatever sin he commits, and not to excommunicate him from Islam for his any action; and jihad will be performed continuously since the day Allah sent me as a prophet until the day the last member of my community will fight with the Dajjal (Antichrist). The tyranny of any tyrant and the justice of any just (ruler) will not invalidate it. One must have faith in Divine decree." (Book 14, Number 2526, narrated by Anas ibn Malik)[22]

Jihadi Writings

The thinking that underpins Islamic terrorists' ideology did not originate with Osama bin Laden. Both the idea of purifying Islam by a return to the orthodoxy of the Salaf and violent jihad have periodically come to the fore in Islamic society over the centuries. This section focuses on the writers who have had the greatest influence on contemporary jihadi ideology. Because Osama bin Laden's communications are more operational than philosophical, he is not included here, but his statements are represented extensively in subsequent chapters. Some new writers, too, are largely operational and are excerpted in later chapters. They include Abu Bakr Naji (*The Management of Savagery*), Abu Mus'ab al-Suri[23] (*The Call to Global Islamic Resis-*

---

[20] Sahih Muslim, Book 41, Number 6985.

[21] Hadith quoted in Abu al-Waleed al-Ansari, undated.

[22] This Hadith is one source of the common phrase "Prophet said . . . jihad continues until the Day of Judgment." It also runs counter to much of jihadi ideology.

[23] Abu Mus'ab al-Suri (the Syrian), also known as Mustafa Sitmariam Nasir, is a key al-Qaeda strategist and military trainer. He holds Spanish citizenship and may have been linked to the 2004 Madrid bombings. He is also the author of "The Call to Islamic Global Resistance," a 1,600-page text written in 2004, one of the most

tance), Abu Qatada al-Falistini (*The Markers of the Victorious Sect*), Abd-al-Aziz Bin Rashid al-Anzi ("The Religious Rule on Targeting Oil Interests"), Muhammad Khalil al-Hukaymah ("A New Strategic Method in the Resistance of the Occupier"), and Hamed bin Abdullah al-'Ali (several anti-Shi'ite tracts).

A point that applies not only here, but throughout the book, is the propensity of jihadi writers and speakers to indulge in exaggeration and hyperbole. It is not that they do not mean what they say, but rather that they are trying to communicate the emotional content of their messages rather than facts.

Sheikh Ahmad Ibn Taymiyyah (1263–1328)

Perhaps the jihadis' most widely quoted scholar from the past, Ibn Taymiyyah lived and preached during the time of the Mongol (Tatar) invasions of Islamic lands. He was a militant and strict fundamentalist. In his view, the Muslim world was suffering the calamity of the Mongol conquests because it had deviated from the precepts and example of the original four "rightly guided" caliphs.

Ibn Taymiyyah was greatly concerned that the Mongol rulers were not genuine Muslims, even though they converted to Islam, because they retained laws and practices from their pagan past. Because of his great concern over who was and who was not a real Muslim, he is credited with raising the prominence of *takfir*, whereby he declared both individuals and groups to be no longer Muslims—in effect, infidels. A self-appointed censor, he organized a militia to fight what he considered idolatrous sects and wrote a fatwa declaring that the adherents to the Ismaili sect[24] should be killed. Far more important in the contemporary context of sectarian warfare in Iraq, Taymiyyah declared the Shi'a leaders and extremists to be heretical but did not *takfir* (excommunicate) all Shi'a, nor did he call for their wholesale slaughter.[25]

Taymiyyah preached against "novelty" in interpreting the Qur'an and Sunnah. At the same time, he believed that he need not follow the tradition of the consensus of Islamic scholars in deciding what was the true interpretation of the Qur'an or what constituted orthodox Islamic practices. Rather, he could decide on his own. Interestingly, this view and his emphasis on *takfir* were themselves something of a novelty. Then, as now, Islam is quite tolerant of divergent interpretations and practices—

influential strategic documents in the jihadist community. Al-Suri was captured in Pakistan in November 2005 and is believed to be in U.S. custody.

[24] "The Ismailis break away from the main body of the Shi'as on the question of the line of imams in succession to Muhammad (precisely the issue on which the Shi'as and Sunnis have broken away from each other).

"By the 9th century the Ismailis are an identifiable sect, based in Syria and strongly opposed to the rule of the Abbasid caliphs in Baghdad. In the 10th century they establish their own dynasty in Egypt, the Fatamids, and rule over the entire coast of north Africa, which was technically part of the caliphate." (Historyworld, online at http://www.historyworld.net/wrldhis/PlainTextHistories.asp?historyid=ab17#1275)

[25] As cited by al-Maqdisi (2005c).

notwithstanding jihadis and fundamentalists who are at odds with the vast majority of Muslims in this respect.

Not only did Ibn Taymiyyah urge jihad against the Mongol heretics, he participated in the battle of Shaqhab in 702 AH (1302 CE), which for a time turned back the Mongol forces seeking to capture Damascus.

Ibn Taymiyyah also argued that offensive war was obligatory in order to fulfill the Qur'anic obligation to "enjoin the right and prohibit the wrong." He is considered one of Islam's great scholars, but his strict and sometimes unusual views were often unpopular with other Muslim scholars, as well as the Mameluke (Turkish) rulers in Cairo and Damascus. He was repeatedly jailed and died in prison.

> "'Jihad' linguistically means to exert one's utmost effort in word and action; in the Sharee'ah [shari'ah] it is the fighting of the unbelievers and involves all possible efforts that are necessary to dismantle the power of the enemies of Islam including beating them, plundering their wealth, destroying their places of worship and smashing their idols. This means that jihad is to strive to the utmost to ensure the strength of Islam by such means as fighting those who fight you and the dhimmies[26] (if they violate any of the terms of the treaty) and the apostates (who are the worst of unbelievers, for they disbelieved after they have affirmed their belief)." (Ibn Taymiyyah, in al-Banna, undated(a))

> "Know that jihad is the finest thing in this world and the next, and to neglect it is to lose this world and the next. . . . This means: either victory and triumph or martyrdom and paradise." (Ibn Taymiyyah, 699 AH, in al-Salim, 2003)

> "The most reliable Speech is the Book of God, and the best guidance is the guidance of Muhammad, may God's peace be upon him. The worst of all things are novelties, since every novelty is an innovation (bid'ah) and every innovation is a deviation, and all deviation is in Hell." (Ibn Taymiyyah, in Faraj, 1979, trans. 1986, p. 160)

> "Everyone who is with them {Mongols} in the state over which they rule has to be regarded as belonging to the most evil class of men. He is either an atheist (zindiq) and hypocrite who does not believe in the essence of the religion of Islam—this means that he (only) outwardly pretends to be Muslim—or he belongs to that worst class of

---

[26] *Dhimmies* (there are alternate spellings, e.g., *Zimmis*) are infidels (Christians and Jews) living in an Islamic state, accepting Muslim control, gaining their protection, paying the *jizyah* (alternate spelling, *jizyya*) tax and able to continue practicing their religion.

all people who are the people of the bida' (heretical innovations) . . . ."
(Ibn Taymiyyah, in Faraj, 1979, trans. 1986, p. 173)

"Any group of people that rebels against any single prescript of the clear
and reliably transmitted prescripts of Islam has to be fought, according to the leading scholars of Islam, even if the members of this group
pronounce the Islamic Confession of Faith {i.e., are Muslims}." (Ibn
Taymiyyah, in Faraj, 1979, trans. 1986, p. 170)

"The adulterers, homosexuals, those who abandon jihad, the innovators and the alcoholics, as well as those who associate with them, are
a source of harm to the religion of Islam. They will not co-operate in
matters of righteousness and piety. So whoever does not shun their
company is, in fact, abandoning what he has been commanded to do
and is committing a despicable deed." (Ibn Taymiyyah, in Azzam,
1987)

"Kufr {unbelief}, corruption, and disobedience {to Allah} are the cause
of evil and strife. . . . This is because man is by nature dhaloom (ever
given to criminality) and jahool (ever given to ignorance and foolish-
ness). . . .
   "Anyone who contemplates the strife and chaos which afflicts the
Muslims will see that this is indeed their reason. All of the confusion
which occurs between the rulers of the Ummah,[27] and its scholars, and
those who follow them among the common people has this as its root
cause." (Ibn Taimiya (Taymiyyah), undated)

". . . that someone who makes it possible to follow another religion
than the religion of Islam or to follow another law than the law of
Muhammad—God's Peace be upon him—(that such a person) is an
infidel (kafir)." (Ibn Taymiyyah, in Faraj, 1979, trans. 1986, p. 168)

"Since lawful warfare is essentially jihad and since its aim is that religion is entirely for Allah and the word of Allah is uppermost, therefore,
according to all Muslims, those who stand in the way of this aim must
be fought." (Ibn Taymiyyah, undated)

"As for the previous nations [before Islam], none of them enjoined all
people with all that is right, nor did they prohibit all that is wrong to all
people. Furthermore, they did not make jihad (struggle) in this cause.

----

[27] The *ummah* is an entire Muslim community.

Some of them did not take up armed struggle at all, and those who did, such as the Jews, their struggle was generally for the purpose of driving their enemy from their land, or as any oppressed people struggles against their oppressor, and not for sake of calling the people of the world to guidance and right, nor to enjoin on them right and to prohibit to them wrong." (Ibn Taimiya (Taymiyyah), undated)

"When the enemy has entered an Islamic land, there is no doubt that it is obligatory on those closest to the land to defend it, and then on those around them, . . . for the entire Islamic land is like a single country." (Ibn Taymiyyah, in Azzam, 1987)

"If with the Kuffar there are pious people from the best of mankind {Muslims} and it is not possible to fight these Kuffar except by killing them, then they are to be killed as well." (Ibn Taymiyyah, in Azzam, undated(c))

"Whoever doubts whether he has to fight them {mixed armies of infidels and Muslims} is most ignorant of the religion of Islam. Since fighting them is obligatory, they have to be fought, even if there is amongst them someone who has been forced to join their ranks. On this the Muslims are in agreement." (Ibn Taymiyyah, in Faraj, 1979, trans. 1986, p. 207)

"When they are killed, these Muslims are martyrs, and the prescribed jihad must not be neglected on account of those who are killed as martyrs. When the Muslims fight the unbelievers, a Muslim who is killed is a martyr, and someone who is killed while he is in reality a Muslim who cannot show this and who hence does not deserve to be killed on account of his religion, is (also) a martyr." (Ibn Taymiyyah, in Faraj, 1979, trans. 1986, p. 208)

"As for those who cannot offer resistance or cannot fight, such as women, children, monks, old people, the blind, handicapped and their likes, they shall not be killed, unless they actually fight with words [e.g., by propaganda] and acts [e.g., by spying or otherwise assisting in the warfare]. Some [jurists] are of the opinion that all of them may be killed, on the mere ground that they are unbelievers, but they make an exception for women and children since they constitute property for Muslims." (Ibn Taymiyyah, undated)

"The King and most wise men know that the majority of the Christians are non-adherents to the commands of the Messiah, his disciples or even the letters of Paul and other saints. A detailed look will show that what they have of Christianity is but wine-drinking, swine-eating, glorifying the cross and other innovated rites that were never commanded by Allaah. Some even render lawful what the Almighty had forbidden and these are things that cannot be disputed. They dispute over what we have of prophecies. . . ." (Ibn Taymeeyah (Taymiyyah), undated)

"It is of the authentic speech of the truthful and believed messenger of Allaah, Muhammad (saw), that the Messiah, 'Eesaa [Jesus], the son of Maryam {Mary}, will descend in our land by the white minaret in Damascus, his hands placed on the shoulders of two angels. He will break the cross, kill swine, impose the jizyah and not accept from any a belief save Islam. He will kill the anti-Christ, the one-eyed Dajjaal of evil whom the Jews will follow. The Messiah 'Eesaa, the son of Maryam, will then summon the Muslims for war with the Jews until the tree and the stone are made to speak to the Muslim, informing of a Jew's hideout, urging his killing. Allaah will then avenge the Messiah, the son of Maryam, the Messiah of Truth, against the Jews for the harm they inflicted upon him and their rejection of him when he was sent to them." (Ibn Taymeeyah (Taymiyyah), undated)

Muhammad Ibn 'Abd al-Wahhab (1703–1792)

Like Ibn Taymiyyah, Wahhab was the son of an Islamic teacher, but unlike Taymiyyah, who lived his life in the cosmopolitan capitals of Damascus and Cairo, Wahhab grew up in a small town on the Arabian Peninsula. Not a great deal is known about his early life except that he traveled a good deal and made his way to Basra, which is now in Iraq, where he became acquainted with the teachings of Ibn Taymiyyah. Seeing what he regarded as widespread idolatry around him, Wahhab sought to revive the fundamentalist Islam that had been advocated by Ibn Taymiyyah more than 400 years earlier. His ideology was organized around two key concepts: *tawhid* (the unitary nature of God) and *shirk* (the association of something other than God with God). He assumed the role of deciding which was which for the entire Muslim community.

Wahhab was not particularly popular. He destroyed revered tombs and was persecuted for his views and iconoclasm. His father warned against his teachings, and his brother wrote a book denouncing them. Ultimately he found refuge in Dar'iyya (a village) in Najd, northwest of Mecca. It was ruled by Muhammad ibn Saud, who formed a formal alliance with Wahhab under which he swore allegiance to ibn Saud and ibn Saud agreed to make Wahhab's version of Islam that of his domain. This alliance was sealed by marrying his son Abdul Aziz to Wahhab's daughter. Wahhab thus provided the ideology and religious basis for ibn Saud's quest to unify the tribes of Arabia.

Wahhab was captured by an army dispatched by the Ottoman caliph and was sent to Istanbul. A shari'a court convicted him of murder and rebellion and the Muftis (lawyers) declared him a non-believer and apostate. He was executed in 1792 and denied a Muslim burial.

After a century of further military struggle, Saud's direct descendent Abd al Aziz ibn Saud finally succeeded in unifying most of the peninsula in 1932, with the help of the British, and later named the country Saudi Arabia. The Wahhabi version of fundamentalist Islam became the state religion, which it continues to be today.

Adherents of the Wahhabi sect call themselves Salafis after the name of the first generation of "rightly guided" caliphs (salaf) and their converts. The Wahhabi movement gained great impetus from the resources generated by Saudi Arabian oil wealth. Wealthy Saudis and the government have funded Wahhabi mosques and schools (madrassas) throughout the Muslim world, many of which concentrate on teaching religion but little else.

The principal contribution Muhammad Ibn 'Abd Al-Wahhab made to jihadism is the creation of a puritanical vision of Islam which is the purported goal of jihadis today.

As pointed out in Chapter One, it is important to remember that Islamic fundamentalism is not the same as jihadism. Moreover, there are Islamic fundamentalists who would not consider themselves followers of ibn Wahhab.

". . . our way is the way of the Salaf . . ." (al-Wahhaab, undated)

"I do not entertain any opinion of people coming after the Qur'an which contains all that pertains to Islam, the fresh and the dry (cf. 6:59)." (al-Wahhab, undated)

". . . bid'ah (innovation), which is everything that was introduced into the religion after the three generations {salaf}, is in all of its forms blameworthy . . ." (al-Wahhaab, undated)

". . . we do not make takfeer of anyone except the one whom our da'wah {preaching} to the Truth has reached, and to whom the path has been clarified and the evidence established, and who then continues arrogantly and stubbornly, like the majority of those whom we are fighting today, who insist on attributing partners to Allaah, refusing to carry out the obligations of the religion, and openly committing the major sins and forbidden acts. And as for those other than the majority, we only fight them due to their aiding such people, their acceptance of them, their increasing of their numbers, and their participation with them in fighting us.

. . . .

". . . we do not make takfeer of anyone whose religion is correct, whose righteousness, knowledge, piety, and asceticism is well-known, whose life is praiseworthy, and who made his sincere effort for the Ummah by devoting himself to teaching the beneficial sciences and writing about them, even if he was mistaken in this matter or in other matters." (al-Wahhaab, undated)

"Those people who ask for intercession from Prophets and Angels and make du'a[28] through their waseela[29] to become closer to Allah, are committing sins. Due to this crime it is permitted to kill them and to take their possessions." (al-Wahhab, undated)

". . . [one who is] seeking by that [invoking the name of a saint or prophet] to avert an evil or bring a good from anything that Allaah ta'aalaa[30] alone is capable of doing, such as healing the sick, or granting victory over the enemy, or guarding from a misfortune, or the like: that he is a mushrik guilty of major shirk, whose blood may be shed and whose wealth is lawful, even if he believes that the ultimate controller of the universe is Allaah. . . ." (al-Wahhaab, undated)

"And we {do} not order the banning of any writings at all, except those that contain what the people have fallen into of shirk [attributing partners to Allah] . . . or which may result in defects in the 'aqeedah {creed they follow}, such as 'ilm al-mantiq (the science of logic), which a group of the 'ulamaa' have declared to be haraam {forbidden}. But we do not interrogate and search for the like of them." (al-Wahhaab, undated)

Hassan al-Banna (1906–1949)

An Egyptian, Hassan al-Banna founded the Muslim Brotherhood in 1928. The son of a part-time teacher and writer on Islamic jurisprudence, he was deeply religious and active in religious societies from a young age. While studying in Cairo, he became

---

[28] A term designating personal prayer, supplication, and communication with God, as distinct from *salah* (formal worship).

[29] *Waseelah* literally means to make a request or supplicate through a means {good deeds}" (http://www.central-mosque.com).

[30] Subhanahu Wa Ta'ala (SWT) is an expression that Muslims use whenever the name of Allah is pronounced or written. It means "Allah is pure of having partners and He is exalted from having a son" ("USC-MSA Compendium of Muslim Texts," undated).

concerned with the fact that other young people were being attracted by European ideas and culture. Writing not long after the fall of the Ottoman caliphate following World War I, al-Banna attributed the decline of Islamic civilization to the abandonment of fundamental Islamic beliefs.

He was attracted to the Islamic reform movement but saw the problem not as one of modernizing Islam, but rather of expunging Western secular ideas and recapturing the purity of early Islam, as Wahhab sought to do. And like Ibn Taymiyyah, he believed that war to spread Islamic proselytizing was justified.

Due in part to al-Banna's skill in recruiting and organization, the Muslim Brotherhood grew rapidly and by the 1940s had spread to other countries, including Syria and Jordan. Initially, it focused on religious and moral issues, but over time it became more engaged in political action. It also became increasingly radicalized, spawning several terrorist-oriented groups both outside and within the organization, including a "secret apparatus" which carried out assassinations. The organization was banned but was legalized again after the formation of Israel in 1948. Dissatisfied with Egyptian efforts against the "Zionist threat," the Brotherhood assassinated the prime minister of Egypt in late 1948, leading to the retributory killing of al-Banna in early 1949.[31]

The Muslim Brotherhood continues to be an influential Islamist force in several countries. In Egypt, after having forsworn violence, it began to emerge from the shadows. It scored significant political advances in the elections of 2005, becoming the largest opposition group in the Egyptian legislature.

"All pleasures brought by contemporary civilization will result in nothing other than pain. A pain that will overwhelm their enticement and remove their sweetness." (al-Banna, 1935)

"Reformist Feeling in the Islamic World

"Many political and social analysts as well as scholars, especially those interested in studying the development and evolution of nations, notice that the Islamic world (spearheaded by the Arab world) is pursuing an Islamic path in its fresh resurgence, and this new direction is gaining increasing momentum.

"Many writers, thinkers, scholars, and leaders who were advocating conformity with the values of western civilisation and adherence to its norms and the complete adoption of its principles began rethinking their ideas and started to change their tone and replace it with a new

---

[31] The Brotherhood was banned again in 1954 (because of an attempt to assassinate Egyptian President Gamal Abdal Nasser), and its members were dispersed into surrounding nations, including Jordan, Lebanon, and Syria. As it spread throughout the Middle East, the Brotherhood became increasingly associated with acts of violence, assassination, and terrorism.

more cautious and wary approach. The call for the return of Muslim society to the fundamentals and teachings of Islam became more powerful, paving the way for the re-islamisation of all aspects of life.

"The Causes

"It worries the Islamists that the governments and nations of the west have lived for centuries ignorant of Islam, knowing nothing about Islam except fanaticism and stagnation, and viewing the Muslim nations as nothing more than weak societies which can be easily led and conquered. When Islamic revival emerged, they began to analyse and explain this phenomenon according to many frameworks and theories totally alien to the true essence of this religion. Some researchers said that this Islamic resurgence was a result of the rising tide of extremist Islamic tendencies and intolerant Islamic organisations. Others argued that it was a reaction to the political and economic pressures felt by the Islamic nation. Still others saw the cause for the rise of this phenomena [sic] as a means by which those who seek power will achieve their desired goal. All these speculations are very far from the truth because this Islamic direction is due to three main developments:

"Materialism in the West

"The materialist pillars upon which modernity was established achieved an economic and technological advancement, but failed to satisfy human needs and fulfill the conditions of a stable social life. The western way of life which was founded on material knowledge, technical know-how, innovation, invention and the dominance of the world markets with its products, was not able to give the human soul a ray of light, a hint of (spiritual) inspiration or a strand of faith. It was not able to provide any means of peace and tranquility for anxious souls. This is why it was natural for a man living in these conditions to seek happiness in the purely material world and look for ways of alleviating his suffering in ways consistent with it. Indeed all that western life could offer him was material pleasure: an excess of wealth, sex and other corrupted vices, with which he temporarily indulges himself, only to find that he is not satisfied. With the decline of family values and the rise of individualism, the modern man, along with the 'modernised' one, felt his soul crying out for freedom from this material prison, searching for a release into the vastness of faith and spiritual light.

"The Perfection of Islam

"Secondly, and this is the positive aspect, the Islamic thinkers rediscovered the fundamental virtues of Islam and the comprehensiveness of its teachings; and they realised that Islam offers the most detailed, most complete, all-encompassing system compared to all other social philosophies that have ever emerged. . . .

"The Course of Modernity

. . . .

"{Third}, the democratic system led the world for a while, encouraging many intellectuals as well as the masses to think of it as the ideal system. Nobody can ignore the freedom it has secured for peoples and nations alike, and the justice it has introduced to the human mind in allowing it to think freely, and to the human being as a whole in allowing him the freedom to fulfill himself; and, apparently, giving power to the people. . . . However, it was not long before people realised that individuality and unlimited liberty can lead to chaos and many other shortcomings, which ultimately led to the fragmentation of the social structure and family systems, and the eventual re-emergence of totalitarianism." (al-Banna, 1948)

"Our lands have been besieged, and our hurruma'at (personal possessions, respect, honour, dignity and privacy) violated. Our enemies are overlooking our affairs, and the rites of our din [religion] are under their jurisdiction. Yet still the Muslims fail to fulfill the responsibility of Da'wah {preaching to spread Islam} that is on their shoulders. Hence in this situation it becomes the duty of each and every Muslim to make jihad. He should prepare himself mentally and physically such that when comes the decision of Allah, he will be ready.

. . . .

". . . preparation for war is the surest way to peace! Allah did not ordain jihad for the Muslims so that it may be used as a tool of oppression or tyranny or so that it may be used by some to further their personal gains. Rather jihad is used to safeguard the mission of spreading Islam. This would guarantee peace and the means of implementing the Supreme Message. This is a responsibility which the Muslims bear, this Message guiding mankind to truth and justice. For Islam, even as it ordains jihad, it extols peace.

. . . .

"The Islamic jihad is the noblest of endeavours and its method of realisation is the most sublime and exalted. For Allah has forbidden aggression. . . ." (al-Banna, undated(a))

"Wars are a social necessity: Civil life in Islam is aimed towards peace. Nevertheless, Islam deals with reality and as long as there are people that follow their own desires and self-interest, there will always be conflict and war. But if war is for the sake of stopping an aggressor, aiding truth and achieving justice, then it is a virtue since it encourages goodness and prosperity for the people. It is a source of evil, social vices and degradation for mankind when it is used as a tool for the wrong-doer, corruption, transgression and oppression of the weak." (al-Banna, 1948)

"Many Muslims today mistakenly believe that fighting the enemy is jihad asghar (a lesser jihad) and that fighting one's ego is jihad akbar (a greater jihad). The following narration {Hadith} [athar] is quoted as proof: 'We have returned from the lesser jihad to embark on the greater jihad.' They said: 'What is the greater jihad?' He {Muhammad} said: 'The jihad of the heart, or the jihad against one's ego.'

"This narration is used by some to lessen the importance of fighting, to discourage any preparation for combat, and to deter any offering of jihad in Allah's way. This narration is not a saheeh (sound) tradition."[32] (al-Banna, undated(a))

"The purposes of war in Islam: Though Islam acknowledges these realities, it prohibits war, the indulgence in it, the call to it and the encouragement of it, except for justifiable reasons, such as:

i – Resistance of transgression and self-defence as well as defence of family, possessions, nation and religion.

. . . .

ii – The protection of the freedoms of religion and the doctrine of the believers – those whom the disbelievers attempt to divert and mislead.

. . . .

iii – The protection of the Islamic call so that it reaches and becomes clear to everyone.

. . . .

---

[32] And thus, he argues, is not likely to be an authentic saying of Muhammad.

"Thus, it must remove from its path all sources of hindrance which may delay or prevent the propagation of its message; and the position of every individual and every nation must be clarified with regards to this call.

. . . .

". . . the good of all humanity is in the return of Muslims to their religion and that this will be the most important step towards peace on earth. Also, one must realise that the motive of that revival is not blind fanaticism but rather conviction in what the virtues of Islam have brought to mankind. These are the virtues that conform totally with the highest of what contemporary thought has managed to discover about righteous social principles and the pillars upon which they stand." (al-Banna, 1948)

"It is forbidden to slay women, children, and old people, to kill the wounded, or to disturb monks, hermits, and the peaceful who offer no resistance. Contrast this mercy with the murderous warfare of the 'civilised' people and their terrible atrocities! Compare their international law alongside this all-embracing, divinely ordained justice!" (al-Banna, undated(a))

"There is an amazing spiritual quality which we (Easterners), as well as others, perceive in our own souls; namely, that we believe in our ideology with a faith which, when we discuss it, leads people to believe that it will drive us to shatter mountains, to give up our persons and our wealth, bear misfortunes, and struggle against adversities until we triumph over it or it triumphs over us. . . ." (al-Banna, undated(b))

Mawlana Abul a'la Maududi[33] (1903–1979)

Born in India and descneded from a long line of prominent figures in the Sufi order of Islam, Maududi's early formal education was in a secondary school that mixed a traditional Islamic education with modern Western curricula. He attended a university but left when his father died, and at 15 he became a journalist to support his family. Over the next several years he became editor of a series of Islamic publications, including the leading Muslim newspaper in India, *al-Jam'iyat*.

During this period, Maududi continued his Islamic education independently but with some guidance from established scholars. He joined an anti-British group, Tahrik-e Hijrat, and called for the mass migration of Muslims out of India to Afghani-

---

[33] Often referred to as Maulana Maududi. There are many alternative spellings of his name (e.g., Syed Maudoodi, Sayyid Abul a'la Maududi).

stan. In 1930, his first major book, *Jihad in Islam* (*al-Jihad fi al-Islam*), on the Islamic law of war and peace, was published. He spent the rest of his life researching, writing, and speaking. He founded a political party in 1940 called Jamaat-e-Islami. Opposing nationalism, he was against the creation of Pakistan, arguing that the Islamic community should be transnational. Nevertheless, he moved to Pakistan in 1947 after it separated from India. His writings, which insisted that the new rulers create an Islamic state, caused him to spend long periods in jail.

Maududi wrote prolifically on a vast range of subjects, often trying to apply Islamic teachings to modern problems in politics, economics, and culture. He was a major force in the Islamic revival movement, and some consider him the most important figure in Islamist thought in the 20th century. His major work, *The Meaning of the Qur'an*, took him 30 years to complete. Its translations of the Qur'an are considered the best in both the Middle East and the West and are used in this book.

He died in 1979 of a kidney ailment in Buffalo, New York, where his son was a physician.

> "In reality Islam is a revolutionary ideology and programme which seeks to alter the social order of the whole world and rebuild it in conformity with its own tenets and ideals. 'Muslim' is the title of that International Revolutionary Party organized by Islam to carry into effect its revolutionary programme. And 'Jihad' refers to that revolutionary struggle and utmost exertion which the Islamic Party brings into play to achieve this objective.
>
> "Islam wishes to destroy all States and Governments anywhere on the face of the earth which are opposed to the ideology and programme of Islam regardless of the country or the Nation which rules it. The purpose of Islam is to set up a State on the basis of its own ideology and programme, regardless of which Nation assumes the role of the standard bearer of Islam or the rule of which nation is undermined in the process of the establishment of an ideological Islamic State.
>
> "Islam is not merely a religious creed or compound name for a few forms of worship, but a comprehensive system which envisages to annihilate all tyrannical and evil systems in the world and enforces its own programme of reform which it deems best for the well-being of mankind.
>
> . . . .
>
> "Islamic 'Jihad' does not seek to interfere with the faith, ideology, rituals of worship or social customs of the people. It allows them perfect freedom of religious belief and permits them to act according to their creed. However, Islamic 'Jihad' does not recognize their right to administer State affairs according to a system which, in the view of

Islam, is evil. Furthermore, Islamic 'Jihad' also refuses to admit their right to continue with such practices under an Islamic government which fatally affect the public interest from the viewpoint of Islam." (Sayyeed Abdul a'la Maududi, 1939)

"Instead of offering apologies on behalf of Islam for the measure that guarantees security of life, property and faith to those who choose to live under its protection [infidels], the Muslims should feel proud of such a humane law as that of jizyah. For it is obvious that the maximum freedom that can be allowed to those who do not adopt the Way of Allah but choose to tread the ways of error is that they should be tolerated to lead the life they like. That is why the Islamic State offers them protection, if they agree to live as its Zimmis by paying jizyah, but it cannot allow that they should remain supreme rulers in any place and establish wrong ways and impose them on others. As this state of things inevitably produces chaos and disorder, it is the duty of the true Muslims to exert their utmost to bring to an end their wicked rule and bring them under a righteous order." (S'Abul a'la Maududi, 1967a)

"But the fact is, and the majority of the earliest Muslim scholars have opined, that here the 'Way of Allah' stands for Jihad in the Way of Allah, that is, the struggle to eradicate the systems based on kufr and to establish the Islamic system in their stead.

. . . .

"But Jihad in the Way of Allah is a much more comprehensive term than mere fighting in the Way of Allah. Jihad applies to all those efforts that are made to degrade the word of kufr and to exalt the Word of Allah and to establish the Islamic System of life, whether by propagating the Message of Allah in the initial stage or by fighting in the final stage of the struggle." (S'Abul a'la Maududi, 1967b)

Sayyid Qutb (1906–1966)

Born in Egypt in the same year as al-Banna, Sayyid Qutb was at first a social reformer. He joined the Muslim Brotherhood later in life and became its most powerful advocate in the 1950s and 1960s. Indeed, his blending of Islamic fundamentalism with anti-Westernization and jihad against Middle Eastern governments has led him to be regarded as the foremost thinker of modern Islamism—to some, as the "father" of jihadism. But some younger-generation jihadis criticize him for not being sufficiently Salafist.

A novelist, critic, and educator, he came to the United States in 1948, where he studied modern educational techniques from 1948 to 1950. However, he seemed most struck and appalled by the open sexual mores and the materialism of Americans, as well as by the racism he may have experienced firsthand. When he returned to Egypt, he resigned from the Education Ministry to devote himself to the Muslim Brotherhood and to his writing. Nonetheless, these writings contained reflections of his earlier interest in Marxism.

Growing up in Egypt when it was a British protectorate, he was, like al-Banna, deeply concerned about the decline of Muslim civilization, which he, too, ultimately ascribed to the rising tide of Westernization and materialism. Qutb and his compatriots supported the July 1952 military coup against King Farouk but were deeply disappointed when President Nasser turned not to Islam to organize the Egyptian state, but to socialism.

Qutb saw a fundamentalist theocracy as the answer to Western materialism and the social inequities prevailing in Egypt. Muslims use the term *Jiahiliyyah* to denote the pagan period of ignorance before Muhammad. Qutb expanded the concept to cover all contemporary society, in particular, the non-Islamic governments in the Muslim world. This, he declared, required genuine Muslims to wage jihad against the authorities who were considered *kuffar* (non-believers). Qutb's writing was directed not only at Egyptians, but at the entire Muslim *ummah* (community), for he rejected the idea of national borders and nationalism.

Confrontation with the Nasser government further radicalized him, as did his experience of torture and imprisonment. After an attempt on Nasser's life in 1954, Qutb and many other members of the Muslim Brotherhood were arrested. He spent ten years in prison, where he composed his most important works, including *Milestones*, which has become the jihadi "bible," second only to the Qur'an and Sunnah. After a brief period of liberty, he was rearrested in 1965 and was promptly hanged.

> "The orientalists[34] have painted a picture of Islam as a violent movement which imposed its belief upon people by the sword. These vicious orientalists know very well that this is not true, but by this method they try to distort the true motives of Islamic Jihaad." (Qutb, 1964)

> ". . . Islam reckons itself to be a worldwide region {sic} and a universal religion; therefore, it could not confine itself to the limits of Arabia, but naturally desired to spread over the whole world in every direction. However, it found itself opposed by political forces in the Persian and Roman Empires, which were its neighbors; these stood in the way of Islam and would not allow its propagators to travel through their countries to inform their people of the nature of Islam, this new faith. Therefore, it followed that these political forces had to be destroyed, so

---

[34] Western scholars of the Middle East and Islam.

that there may be toleration for the true faith among men. Islam aimed only at obtaining a hearing for its message, so that anyone who might want to accept it would be free to do as he wished, while anyone who wanted to reject it could be the master of his own destiny; this was only possible when the political and material forces of the empires had been removed from the path.

"The Islamic conquests, then, were not wars of aggression, nor yet were they a system of colonization for economic gain, like the colonizing ventures of later centuries. They were simply a means of getting rid of the material and political opposition that stood between the nations and the new concept that Islam brought with it." (Qutb, 1949, pp. 198–199)

"So long as Muslim society adhered to Islam it manifested no weakness and no tendency to abdicate its control of life. It was when it fell away from Islam that these things took place. Emphasis on this fact will compensate for the idle aspersions that Westerners have cast on our faith, and which they have evidenced from history." (Qutb, 1949, p. 262)

"If we look at the sources and foundations of modern ways of living, it becomes clear that the whole world is steeped in Jahiliyyah [ignorance of the Divine guidance], and all the marvelous material comforts and high-level inventions do not diminish this ignorance. . . . It is now not in that simple and primitive form of the ancient Jahiliyyah, but takes the form of claiming that the right to create values, to legislate rules of collective behavior, and to choose any way of life rests with men, without regard to what God has prescribed." (Qutb, 1964)

"This movement uses the methods of preaching and persuasion for reforming ideas and beliefs; and it uses physical power and Jihaad for abolishing the organizations and authorities of the jahili system . . . ." (Qutb, 1964)

"If Islam is again to play the role of the leader of mankind, then it is necessary that the Muslim community be restored to its original form.

"It is necessary to revive that Muslim community which is buried under the debris of the man-made traditions of several generations, and which is crushed under the weight of those false laws and customs which are not even remotely related to the Islamic teachings, and which, in spite of all this, calls itself the 'world of Islam.'" (Qutb, 1964)

"Since the objective of the message of Islam is a decisive declaration of man's freedom, not merely on the philosophical plane but also in the actual conditions of life, it must employ Jihaad. . . ." (Qutb, 1964)

"Hence, certainly there must be Jihad . . . assuredly in every form. Unquestionably, it should begin in the realm of ideas, and then appear in and pervade the world of truth, reality and experience. . . . Undoubtedly, armed Evil must be taken on by armed Good. . . . Falsehood strengthened by numbers must be confronted by Truth garbed with preparation . . . otherwise it would be suicide, or jest not befitting Muslims." (Qutb, in Azzam, 1987)

"Those who say that Islamic Jihaad was merely for the defense of the 'homeland of Islam' diminish the greatness of the Islamic way of life and consider it less important than their 'homeland.' . . . The soil of the homeland has in itself no value or weight. From the Islamic point of view, the only value which the soil can achieve is because on that soil God's authority is established and God's guidance is followed; and thus it becomes a fortress for the belief, a place for its way of life to be entitled the 'homeland of Islam,' a center for the movement for the total freedom of man.

. . . .

"Of course, in that case the defense of the 'homeland of Islam' is the defense of the Islamic beliefs, the Islamic way of life, and the Islamic community. However, its defense is not the ultimate objective of the Islamic movement of Jihaad but is a means of establishing the Divine authority within it so that it becomes the headquarters for the movement of Islam, which is then to be carried throughout the earth to the whole of mankind, as the object of this religion is all humanity and its sphere of action is the whole earth." (Qutb, 1964)

". . . Islam is not merely 'belief.' As we have pointed out, Islam is a declaration of the freedom of man from servitude to other men. Thus it strives from the beginning to abolish all those systems and governments which are based on the rule of man over men and the servitude of one human being to another. When Islam releases people from this political pressure and presents to them its spiritual message, appealing to their reason, it gives them complete freedom to accept or not to accept its beliefs. However, this freedom does not mean that they can make their desires their gods, or that they can choose to remain in the servitude of other human beings, making some men lords over others.

Whatever system is to be established in the world ought to be on the authority of God, deriving its laws from Him alone. Then every individual is free, under the protection of this universal system, to adopt any belief he wishes to adopt." (Qutb, 1964)

"We have, then, not a single reason to make any separation between Islam and society, either from the point of view of the essential nature of Islam or from that of its historical course; such reasons as there are attach only to European Christianity. And yet the world has grown away from religion; to it the world has left only education of the conscience and the purification of the soul, while to the temporal and secular laws has been committed the ordering of society and the organizing of human life." (Qutb, 1949, p. 32)

"It is in the very nature of Islam to take initiative for freeing the human beings throughout the earth from servitude to anyone other than God; and so it cannot be restricted within any geographic or racial limits, leaving all mankind on the whole earth in evil, in chaos and in servitude to lords other than God." (Qutb, 1964)

"Islam has always represented the highest achievement in universal and comprehensive social justice; European civilization has never reached the same level, nor ever will. For it is a civilization founded on pure materialism, a civilization of murder and war, of conquest and of subjugation." (Qutb, 1949, p. 202)

"Brother, push ahead, for your path is soaked in blood. Do not turn your head right or left but look only up to heaven." (Qutb, undated, in al-Zawahiri, 2001)

Mohammed Abd al-Salam Faraj (1952–1982)

Strongly influenced by Sayyid Qutb and Ibn Taymiyyah, Muhammad abd al-Salam Faraj founded the group Jama'at al-Jihad, which organized the assassination of President Anwar Sadat in 1981 for his having made peace with Israel. Faraj's goal for the operation had been the overthrow of the government of Egypt and the establishment of an Islamic state, but poorly prepared for carrying out a coup, Jama'at Jihad was quickly crushed by Egyptian security forces.

Following the hanging of Qutb, the radical Islamists split into two groups, each believing that it was following his teachings. They both rejected the Muslim Brotherhood because it had taken the position that working with the government to fight Israel was more important than overthrowing it.

One faction believed that the Islamist groups, because of their weakness, had to physically retreat from society, much as Muhammad did in leaving Mecca for Medina.[35] Faraj rejected this idea because it would preclude waging jihad, which he proposed should be elevated to the "Sixth Pillar of Islam,"[36] a compulsory individual duty.

His principal work, *The Neglected Duty*, published in 1979, focuses on the arguments and divisions among the Salafis and how to deal with apostate rulers. In it, he addresses the issue of whether later entries in the Qur'an supersede earlier ones, whether the near or far enemy should take priority, and whether the correct route to an Islamic state is through political parties, infiltration of the institutions, preaching, or Islamic scholarship. Faraj also goes beyond the idea that the eclipse of the Muslim world was due to a failure to follow the fundamentalism of the Salafis. He attributes the decline to a neglect of jihad as an essential element in Islam.

Arrested after the assassination of Sadat, he was tried and executed in 1981.

> "Jihad (struggle) for God's cause, in spite of its extreme importance and its great significance for the future of this religion, has been neglected by the ulama (leading Muslim scholars) of this age. They have feigned ignorance of it, but they know that it is the only way to the return and the establishment of the glory of Islam anew. . . .
>
> "There is no doubt that the idols of this world can only be made to disappear through the power of the sword." (Faraj, 1979, pp. 160–161)

> "Neglecting jihad is the cause of the lowness, humiliation, division and fragmentation in which the Muslims live today. The word of the Lord – Exalted and Majestic He is – about them has come true: 'O ye who have believed, what is the matter with you? When one says to you, 'March out in the way of God,' ye are weighed down to the ground; are you so satisfied with this nearer life as to neglect the Hereafter? The enjoyment of this nearer life is in comparison with the Hereafter only a little thing. If ye do not march out He will inflict upon you a painful punishment, and will substitute for you another people; ye will not

---

[35] Muhammad first preached his message in Mecca, where he lived, but when he met opposition from the powerful Quraysh tribe that controlled Mecca (Muhammad's family belonged to the clan of Hashim, a branch of the Quraysh tribe), he and his followers migrated to Medina in 622 CE, where they resided for eight years, gathering strength. They reentered Mecca in 630 CE (8 AH).

[36] This would be an addition to the traditional Five Pillars of Islam: faith in Allah alone and belief that Muhammad is his prophet, paying alms, praying, fasting, and pilgrimage to Mecca. Oddly, he favorably quotes Ibn Taymiyyah: "The worst of all things are novelties, since every novelty is an innovation (*bid'ah*) and every innovation is a deviation, and all deviation is in Hell."

injure Him at all. God over everything has power.' This quotation is taken from Surah 9 (verses 38–39)." (Faraj, 1979, pp. 205–206)

". . . We should refute those who say that jihad in Islam is defensive, and that Islam was not spread by the sword.[37] This is a false view, which is (nevertheless) repeated by a great number of those who are prominent in the field of Islamic missionary activities. . . . To fight is, in Islam, to make supreme the Word of God in this world, whether it be by attacking or by defending. . . ." (Faraj, 1979, p. 193)

". . . The establishment of an Islamic State is an obligation for the Muslims. . . . If, moreover, (such a) state cannot be established without war, then this war is an obligation as well.

"Muslims are agreed on the obligatory character of the establishment of an Islamic Caliphate. To announce a Caliphate must be based on the existence of a (territorial) nucleus (from which it can grow). This (nucleus) is the Islamic State." (Faraj, 1979, p. 165)

"There are those who say, 'We must establish an Islamic political party (and add this party) to the list of extant political parties.' It is true that this is better than benevolent societies, because a party at least talks about politics. However, the purpose of the foundation (of such a party) is the destruction of the infidel State (and to replace it by an Islamic theocracy). To work through a political party will, however, have the opposite effect, since it means building the pagan State and collaborating with it. . . . (Moreover, such an Islamic political party) will participate in the membership of legislative councils that enact laws without consideration for God's Laws." (Faraj, 1979, p. 184)[38]

"There are those who say that the Muslims should do their best in order to obtain (socially) important positions. Only when all important centers are filled with Muslim doctors and Muslim engineers will the existing pagan order perish automatically and the Muslim Ruler (Al-Hakim al-Muslim) establish himself. . . . Someone who hears this argument for the first time will think it is a fantasy or a joke, but there are, as a matter of fact, people in the Muslim world who embrace such philosophies and arguments. . . ." (Faraj, 1979, p. 185)

---

[37] Note the conflict with Qutb's contrary assertion in *Milestones*. This is a continuing debate among jihadis.

[38] Note the difference with Hamas in Palestine and Hezbollah in Lebanon, both of which have formed political parties and stood for election.

"Some of them say that the right road to the establishment of an (Islamic) State is (nonviolent) propaganda (da'wah) only, and the creation of a broad base. . . ."

"But then, how can (nonviolent) propaganda be widely successful when all means of (mass) communication today are under the control of the pagan and wicked (State) and (under the control) of those who are at war with God's religion?" (Faraj, 1979, p. 186)

"Someone who says that (the quest for) knowledge (also) is (a form of) jihad has to understand that the duty (which is indicated by the Arabic word jihad) entails the obligation of fighting, for God – Praised and Exalted He is – says, 'Prescribed for you is fighting' (Qur'an 2.216)." (Faraj, 1979, pp. 188–189)[39]

"Scholarship is not the decisive weapon which will radically put an end to paganism. This can only be done with the weapon which the Lord – Exalted and Majestic He is – mentioned in His word: 'Fight them and God will punish them at your hands, will humiliate them and aid you against them. . . .' (Qur'an 9:14)" (Faraj, 1979, p. 190)

"How can someone who specialized in (Islamic) religious studies and who really knows all about small and great sins not have noticed the great importance of jihad, and the punishment for postponing or neglecting it?" (Faraj, 1979, p. 188)

"There are some who say that the true road to the establishment of an Islamic State is jihrah, emigration, to another locality and to establish the (new Islamic) State out there. Then they (want to) return again, as conquerors. . . .

. . . .

"All these strange ideas only result from having forsaken the only true and religiously allowed road towards establishing an Islamic State. So, what is this true road? God – Exalted He is – says: 'Fighting is prescribed for you, though it is distasteful to you. . . .' (Qur'an 2:216)" (Faraj, 1979, p. 187)

"With regard to the lands of Islam, the enemy lives right in the middle of them. The enemy even has got hold of the reins of power, for this

---

[39] Another translation by Maududi 2:216, presented under the heading "Allah" above, is "You have been enjoined to go to war, and you dislike it; it may be that you dislike a thing and the same is good for you, and you love a thing and the same is bad for you: Allah knows but you do not."

enemy is (none other than) these rulers who have (illegally) seized the Leadership of the Muslims. Therefore, waging jihad against them is an individual duty, in addition to the fact that Islamic jihad today requires a drop of sweat from every Muslim." (Faraj, 1979, p. 200)

". . . The basis of the existence of Imperialism in the Lands of Islam are {sic} (precisely) these Rulers. To begin by putting an end to imperialism is not a laudatory and not a useful act. It is only a waste of time. We must concentrate on our own Islamic situation: we have to establish the Rule of God's Religion in our own country first, and make the Word of God supreme. . . . There is no doubt that the first battlefield for jihad is the extermination of these infidel leaders and to replace them by a complete Islamic Order. From here we should start." (Faraj, 1979, p. 193)[40]

"The Qur'an scholar Muhammad ibn Ahmad ibn Muhammad ibn Juzayy al-Kalbi . . . says: 'The abrogation of the command to be at peace with the infidels, to forgive them, to be (passively) exposed to them and to endure their insults preceded here the command to fight them. This makes it superfluous to repeat the abrogation of the command to live in peace with the infidels at each Qur'anic passage (where this is relevant). (Such a command to live in peace with them) is found in 114 verses in 54 surahs.[41] This is all abrogated by His word: 'Slay the polytheists wherever ye find them' (Qur'an 9.5) and 'Fighting is prescribed for you' (Qur'an 2.216)." (Faraj, 1979, p. 195)

Abdulla Yussuf Azzam (1941–1989)

The invasion of Afghanistan by the Soviet Union in December 1979 was a turning point in the jihadi movement and in the life of Dr. Abdulla Yussuf Azzam. Prior to that event, he had been primarily a teacher at several Middle East universities and a sometime guerrilla fighter. While studying for his graduate degrees in Islamic jurisprudence at al Azar University in Cairo, Azzam met Sheikh Abdul Rahman, the so-called "Blind Sheikh" who masterminded the first World Trade Center attack, and also Ayman al-Zawahiri, al-Qaeda's chief ideologist. Like them, he was a follower of

---

[40] Faraj takes the position that fighting the near enemy is more important than fighting the far enemy. This is contrary to other jihadis, such as Osama bin Laden, who believe that the far enemy (i.e., the United States) is the most important target. See Chapter Seven, "Prescribed for You Is Fighting . . ." Faraj also quotes a hadith: "To fight an enemy who is near is more important than to fight an enemy who is far." (Faraj, 1979, trans. 1986)

[41] There are many passages in the Qur'an that call for peace with infidels, revealed when Muhammad was in Mecca and Medina. But as fighting intensified in the peninsula, the revelation came to "slay the polytheists." Jihadis insist that this command overrules the previous peaceful admonitions.

Sayyid Qutb. He taught the inevitability of a clash between Islam and the West and the individual's obligation to wage jihad against secular governments.

A Palestinian by birth, Azzam joined the Muslim Brotherhood after fleeing to Jordan when the Israelis took over the West Bank during the 1967 War. He participated in attacks on the Israelis under the umbrella of the PLO but ultimately rejected its secular, socialist, and nationalist agenda, envisioning instead a pan-Islamic movement that would obliterate the colonial boundaries of the Middle East imposed by the West.

When the PLO was expelled from Jordan in 1970, Azzam moved to Saudi Arabia. He taught at King Abdul Azziz University in Jeddah when Osama bin Laden was a student there, and given their subsequent relationship, it is speculated that this is where they first met. The Afghan war against the Soviet occupation opened new opportunities for Azzam to engage in jihad. He proclaimed a fatwa against the Soviet invasion, which was blessed by the Mufti[42] of Saudi Arabia. Azzam then moved to Pakistan, where he set up an organization in Peshawar that housed and trained foreign recruits for the war. Osama bin Laden gave him support that ultimately enabled him to establish his own guerrilla group operating inside Afghanistan.

Azzam was a charismatic and fiery speaker. During the 1980s, when the West supported the jihadi fighters in Afghanistan, he toured Europe and America seeking recruits and financial support, visiting and lecturing in 50 cities in the United States.

In 1989, after the Soviet Union had withdrawn from Afghanistan, Azzam was killed by an improvised explosive device (IED) in Peshawar. Many people were suspected of having been the assassin, including Osama bin-Laden, with whom Azzam had developed differences over whether al-Qaeda should focus on Palestine or go global.

During his lifetime, Azzam wrote many ideological tracts and developed several manuals on terrorism and guerrilla war. These continued to be disseminated by London-based Azzam Publications and a web site, but both were closed after 9/11. His contribution to jihadi ideology was the call to "global jihad" and his argument that jihad (in the sense of armed struggle) was an individual obligation on all Muslims, not a collective responsibility of the Muslim community.

> "Oh you Muslims! You have slept for a long time, long enough for the tyrants to take control over you. You accepted to live as slaves and submitted to tyrants. Now the time has come to revolt and destroy the shackle of slavery." (Azzam, undated(a))

---

[42] The highest religious authority.

"The sin upon this present generation, for not advancing towards Afghanistan, Palestine, the Philippines, Kashmir, Lebanon, Chad, Eritrea, etc., is greater than the sin inherited from the loss of the lands which have previously fallen into the possession of the Kuffar." (Azzam, undated(d))

". . . Yes, allowing Muslims to be slaughtered while the only thing that we do is to offer them lip service from a distance and rub our hands together without taking even one step towards elevating the suffering of Muslim (sic). Sure that is playing and ridiculing of the religion [Islam]." (Azzam, undated(a))

"The Jihad is in need of money, and men are in need of Jihad." (Azzam, 1987)

"Those who believe that Islam can flourish {and} be victorious without Jihaad, fighting, and blood indeed are illusioned and do not understand the nature of this religion. The prestige of preachers, the influence of Islam, the dignity of Muslims, cannot be attained without Jihaad." (Azzam, undated(a))

"The word Jihad, when mentioned on its own, only means combat with weapons . . . ." (Azzam, 1987)

"Jihad Against the Kuffar Is of Two Types

"*Offensive Jihad* (where the enemy is attacked in his own territory).

"Where the Kuffar are not gathering to fight the Muslims. The fighting becomes Fard Kifaya [a collective duty of the community] with the minimum requirement of appointing believers to guard borders, and the sending of an army at least once a year to terrorise the enemies of Allah. It is a duty of the Imam to assemble and send out an army unit into the land of war once or twice every year. Moreover, it is the responsibility of the Muslim population to assist him, and if he does not send an army he is in sin.

. . . .

"*Defensive Jihad*

"This is expelling the Kuffar from our land, and it is Fard Ayn, a compulsory duty upon all. It is the most important of all the compulsory duties . . . ." (Azzam, undated(d))

"A small group: they are the ones who carry convictions and ambitions. And an even smaller group from this small group are the ones who flee from the worldly life in order to spread and act upon these ambitions. And an even smaller group from this elite group are the ones who sacrifice their souls and their blood in order to bring victory to these ambitions and principles. So, they [jihadis] are the cream of the cream of the cream.[43]

. . . .

"Some thought that the Earth had become devastated and that this Ummah had been drained of the thirst for martyrdom. Therefore, Allah exploded the Jihad on the land of Afghanistan and groups of youths from the Islamic World marched forth to Afghanistan in search of Jihad and martyrdom.

"Indeed this small band of Arabs, whose number did not exceed a few hundred individuals, changed the tide of the battle, from an Islamic battle of one country to an Islamic world Jihad movement, in which all races participated and all colours, languages and cultures met; yet they were one, their direction was one, their ranks were one and the goal was one: that the Word of Allah is raised the highest and that this Deen is made victorious on the Earth." (Azzam, undated(b))

"Jihad must not be abandoned until Allah (SWT) alone is worshipped. Jihad continues until Allah's Word is raised high. Jihad until all the oppressed peoples are freed. Jihad to protect our dignity and restore our occupied lands. Jihad is the way of everlasting glory." (Azzam, 1987)

"O youths! O sons of Islam! What will cleanse our sins? What will purify our mistakes? And what will clean our dirt? It will not be washed except with the blood of martyrdom, and know that there is no path except this path." (Azzam, undated(b))

"So history does not write its lines except with blood. Glory does not build its lofty edifice except with skulls. Honour and respect cannot be established except on a foundation of cripples and corpses. Empires, noble persons, states and societies cannot be established except with [such] examples." (Azzam, undated(c))

---

[43] Azzam here adopts a Western concept of the "elite revolutionary vanguard," which was common to 20th century European totalitarian movements.

"Indeed nations are only brought to life by their beliefs and their concepts and they die only with their desires and their lusts." (Azzam, undated(b))

Ayman al-Zawahiri (1952–present)

Ayman al-Zawahiri has come to prominence as a principal spokesman for al-Qaeda since the 9/11 attacks, having released scores of videotapes and radio interviews. He is widely considered Osama bin Laden's top aide and al-Qaeda's principal ideologist.

Born into a prominent middle-class family in the suburbs of Cairo, Zawahiri showed an early penchant for Islamist politics by joining the Muslim Brotherhood at the age of 14—by some accounts, radicalized by the Arab defeat by Israel in the 1967 War. He was both a student and a follower of Qutb, as well as a trained and practicing physician. By age 28, he had moved on to the more militant and violent Egyptian Islamic Jihad, where he became a prominent leader.

As it had done for many other jihadis, the Soviet invasion of Afghanistan exerted an irresistible pull on Zawahiri, and soon after that event, he traveled to Peshawar, Pakistan, where he worked alongside Osama bin Laden as an acolyte of Abdulla Yusif Azzam. When the organization they were affiliated with broke up, Zawahiri joined bin Laden to form al-Qaeda.

Zawahiri returned to Egypt as an experienced terrorist in 1990. He led the Egyptian Islamic Jihad in a series of actions, including the murder of 66 foreign tourists in Luxor in 1997. He subsequently rejoined bin Laden in 1998 and merged the Egyptian Islamic Jihad with al-Qaeda. They issued a joint fatwa declaring a "world Islamic front against Jews and Crusaders," a manifesto for global jihad against the West.

Zawahiri's contribution to jihadi ideology is severalfold. The followers of Qutb had been debating about whether jihadis should migrate to a safe area to gather strength or, as Faraj argued, remain near their targets and penetrate the institutions of the enemy apostate governments. Similarly, there had been differences over whether to attack the "near enemy" (secular Muslim governments) or the "far enemy" (the West, in particular, the United States). Zawahiri, in effect, synthesized the conflicting arguments by stressing the importance of a secure base such as Afghanistan from which jihadi attacks could be launched at both the near and far enemies. He also sought to resolve that doctrinal dispute by insisting that the far enemy was the same as the near enemy, since the United States ruled the Middle East through local puppets in a system that he called "veiled colonialism." With the Iraq war, the distinction between "near" and "far" enemies collapsed, but other differences have emerged, particularly between Zawahiri and the late Abu Musab al-Zarqawi, the deceased "leader" of al-Qaeda in Iraq. Zawahiri criticized Zarqawi for deliberately attacking the Shi'a and for the beheadings broadcast on television.

The following few quotes capture the essence of Zawahiri's contributions to jihadi ideology, but many more quotations from him on a range of subjects are presented in other sections of this book.

". . . A new awareness is increasingly developing among the sons of Islam, who are eager to uphold it; namely, that there is no solution without jihad.

"The spread of this awareness has been augmented by the failure of all other methods that tried to evade assuming the burdens of jihad." (al-Zawahiri, 2001)

"He [Sayyid Qutb] affirmed that the issue of unification in Islam is important and that the battle between Islam and its enemies is primarily an ideological one over the issue of unification. It is also a battle over to whom authority and power should belong—to God's course and shari'ah, to man-made laws and material principles, or to those who claim to be intermediaries between the Creator and mankind.

"This affirmation greatly helped the Islamic movement to know and define its enemies. It also helped it to realize that the internal enemy was not less dangerous than the external enemy was and that the internal enemy was a tool used by the external enemy and a screen behind which it hid to launch its war on Islam." (al-Zawahiri, 2001)

"When the second Gulf War occurred, the US military arsenal with its fleets and strike forces moved to the region to oversee the management of its interests by itself. Hence, it transformed its role of hidden mover of events into the role of the Muslims' direct opponent." (al-Zawahiri, 2001)

"The Ummah [pan-Islamic nation] must snatch back its right to choose its ruler and call him to account and criticize him and depose him, and snatch back its right to enjoin good and end that which is abominable." (al-Zawahiri, 2005a)

"The persistence of the resistance will keep the volcano in a state of continual eruption and ready to blow up at the least provocation. The persistence of the resistance will transfer the popular wrath from one generation to another and keep the desire for revenge alive in the people's souls. In contrast, the spread of the concepts of conciliation, acquiescence, and acceptance of the facts will make our generation leave a legacy of despair and a willingness to surrender to the next generation." (al-Zawahiri, 2001)

"Our freedom is the freedom of monotheism, ethics, and virtue. Accordingly, the reform that we seek is based on three foundations.

"The first foundation is the rule of shari'ah [Islamic law]. Shari'ah is the course we should follow, since it is sent from God Almighty. No rational human being can adopt an unsteady or wavering position vis-à-vis shari'ah. It is an issue that should be taken seriously, since it does not accept disdain.

"The second foundation: This is the foundation on which reform should be based and is a branch of the first foundation, namely, the freedom of the Muslim lands and their liberation from every aggressor, thief, and plunderer. We should not imagine that we can carry out any reform so long as we are under the yoke of the US and Jewish occupation.

"It is not possible for us to carry out reforms so long as our rulers, merely to achieve their own personal gains, pursue a policy of normalization with Israel and allow it to ruin our economy. . . .

"The third foundation: This foundation is also a branch of the first foundation, namely, the liberation of the human being." (al-Zawahiri, 2001)

CHAPTER FOUR

Ideology

Ideology is characterized as a body of ideas upon which particular political, economic, or social systems and movements are based. Because jihadists (and other Islamists) view Islam as encompassing both temporal and spiritual realms, it can properly be called an ideology as well as a religion. Totalitarian ideologies are typically closed intellectual systems—that is, everything can be explained and justified by the body of thought.

The excerpts in this chapter make apparent the closed nature of jihadi ideology. They focus on the jihadi view of Islam as a revolutionary ideology that emphasizes jihad and martyrdom. The excerpts also present what might seem contradictory to many, a religious rationale for killing other Muslims and innocent people. The concluding section of the chapter comprises selections describing the goals of jihad that allegedly justify the ideology.

One of the unfamiliar characteristics of these writings is the way religious sayings and symbols are used to address issues that in the West would not take on such religious aspects. It is reminiscent of the way the communist movement in the 20th century discussed almost every political issue in terms of "class struggle," and in much of the Christian era, secular problems were debated in the language of church doctrine. Similarly, jihadis address contemporary problems in terms of their religious ideology.

The selections also reveal certain differences among jihadis—differences that are elaborated more fully in other chapters. For our purposes here, it is sufficient to note that while jihadi totalitarian ideology is a closed system, it has room for clashing conclusions about strategy, tactics, and other important issues.

Islam

The following excerpts reflect the way jihadis think about Islam and its role in their revolutionary efforts. These statements should be seen neither as a compendium of Islamic beliefs nor as a description of contemporary Islam—it would be a mistake to conclude that they express the beliefs of the Muslim community as a whole. In fact, jihadism is a fringe movement, albeit one whose grievances resonate with many in the Muslim community.

As noted in Chapter One, the Islamic religion consists of a wide variety of doctrines and practices manifested in many sects and subsects. The three largest sects are the Sunni, Shi'ite, and Sufi. The first split in Islam occurred between Sunni and Shi'a and was largely over succession to the position of caliph. The Sunnis wanted the caliph to be chosen by consensus, while the faction that became Shi'a insisted that the caliph be a relative of Muhammad. (In fact, the turmoil in early Islam was so intense that two of the four "rightly guided" successors of Muhammad were assassinated—one was possibly poisoned, and one was killed in an uprising.) In time, the rupture was reinforced by significant differences in religious practice, and it became all the more profound as the Persian Savafid dynasty adopted Shi'ism as the official religion for its empire and entered into a titanic struggle with the Sunni Ottoman Turks for dominance of the region.

Further complexity was introduced by the emergence of the Sufi, who may be either Sunni or Shi'a but who emphasize the spiritual dimension of Islam, in particular, man's individual relationship with Allah. In contrast, mainline Sunnis focus more on temporal issues, and jihadis, who are mostly Sunni, do so almost exclusively. Like Ibn Taymiyyah, jihadis view Sufis as heretics.

The jihadi view of Islam sets jihadis apart from the overwhelming majority of the world's 1.2 billion Muslims in many ways. As noted earlier, they believe in the "pure" Islam of the first four "rightly guided" caliphs and are known as Salafis, as are most fundamentalist sects, including as the puritan Wahhabis. Therefore, some of the excerpts in this chapter, though drawn from the jihadis, also reflect the views of nonviolent Salafis and fundamentalists.

Jihadis not only seek to restore the glory of the caliphate and the Muslim world by a return to fundamentalist Islam, they believe that this can be done only through violence—jihad—against apostate rulers in the Muslim world and their infidel supporters in the West. In addition to considering existing governments illegitimate, they also refuse to accept the religious authority of the *ulama* (the community of religious scholars). Finally, jihadis believe that their religion obliges them to spread their concept of Islam to the entire world by sweeping away all other governments, religious institutions, and cultures that might stand in the way.

These are the common beliefs of Sunni jihadis such as al-Qaeda and Hamas, although the latter have developed in the context of Palestinian nationalism and resistance to Israel. Hezbollah is an example of Shi'a jihadism, but it, too, is more appropriately defined by its Lebanese context and ties to Iran and its ambitions for regional hegemony. Neither seems largely motivated by the universalistic ambitions of al-Qaeda, but both make similar arguments on behalf of terrorism and suicide bombing.

Most Muslims, including Salafis, regard jihadi views as heretical. While it is true that all jihadis regard themselves as fundamentalists, it is important to reiterate that few fundamentalists are jihadis.

The following excerpts illustrate how jihadis see the nature, role, and purpose of Islam. They do not constitute an objective description of the Muslim religion, which would be far more extensive and quite different.

> "Islam alone can provide the power for Muslims to liberate oppressed peoples . . . capitalist, socialist, communist, or other manmade systems, either in whole or in part, constitute a denial of Isalm. . . . Islam teaches its followers that there is no segregation or separation between religion and worldy affairs. . . ." (Fathi Yakan, unknown, in Habeck, 2006)

> "Islam is a total way of life, both in this life and the hereafter." (al-Jaysh al-Islami fi Iraq, 2005)

> "Islam is an all-encompassing religion. It is a religion for people and for regimes. . . . Islam is the only alternative for the countries [of the world]. . . .
>
> "Therefore, the crime of the tyrants in infidel [i.e. non-Muslim] countries, who do not rule according to Allah's law, is an enormous sin . . . and we are obliged to fight them and initiate until they convert to Islam, or until Muslims rule the country and he who does not convert to Islam pays Jizya.
>
> "That is the religious ruling with regard to infidel countries and all the more so with regard to those who rule Muslim countries by way of the cursed law [i.e. a man-made law]." (al-Najdi, 2003b)

> ". . . Islam's way of life is unique, for in systems other that Islam, some people worship others in some form or another. Only in the Islamic way of life do all men become free from the servitude of some men to others and devote themselves to the worship of God alone, deriving guidance from Him alone, and bowing before Him alone." (Qutb, 1964)

> "The consequence of the Islamic doctrines, first that Islam is a universal religion, and second, that it must not employ physical or spiritual coercion, is this: Three possibilities are placed before the people of a conquered country, one of which everyone must choose—Islam, the poll tax {jizya} or war.
>
>   . . . .

". . . For to refuse both Islam and the payment of the poll tax indicates clear insistence on maintaining the material forces that intervene between Islam and the minds of men. Hence this insistence must be removed by physical force, which is ultimately the only way." (Qutb, 1949, pp. 199–200)

"As long as there is no intention to fight us and Islam continues to grow there can be peace. This is the doctrine of Islam. Islam can't be ruled by others. Allah's law can't be under human law. Allah's law must stand above human law. All laws must be under Islamic law. This is what the infidels fail to recognize, that's what America doesn't like to see." (Ba'asyir, 2005)[1]

"Islam grew up in an independent country owing allegiance to no empire and to no king, in a form of society never again achieved. It had to embody this society in itself, had to order, encourage, and promote it. It had to order and regulate this society, adopting from the beginning its principles and its spirit along with its methods of life and work. It had to join together the world and the faith by its exhortations and laws. So Islam chose to unite earth and heaven in a single system, present both in the heart of the individual and the actuality of society, recognizing no separation of practical exertion from religious impulse." (Qutb, 1949, pp. 26–27)

"Islam treats Muslims everywhere as one nation, and it does not recognize geographical borders or [differences of] race, color, or language. It sees Muslims as one nation in Dar Al-Islam, united in Islamic belief and Muslim brotherhood. Co-religionists must not rise up against each other for other peoples' causes, particularly when it is not proven that the crime[2] was carried out by one of those [Islamic] countries." (al-Qaradhawi, 2001b)[3]

---

[1] Abu Bakar Ba'asyir was a founder of the Indonesian extremist group Jemaah Islamiyah (JI). He was arrested in connection with the Bali and Jakarta Marriott bombings and was released in June 2006.

[2] The 9/11 attacks.

[3] A leader of the Muslim Brotherhood movement, as well as a prominent Egyptian thinker, writer, and TV host, Sheikh Yussef al-Qaradhawi espouses a conservative ideology that endorses suicide bombings against Israelis but condemns attacks in Muslim countries. He has said, "Islamic religious law dictates that we join the Taliban's Jihad, not the US coalition; it is forbidden to attack American citizens, but permitted to attack the American military." (al-Qaradhawi, 2001b).

". . . Some people may say that it is impossible for Islam to cope with certain matters and issues and that we have to depart from it, ease its rules and restrictions, and ignore its divine ordinance in order to be able to run our daily life affairs. This is a baseless allegation. Humanity has never known a system like Islam. It is a Koran and a sword, knowledge and worship, doctrine and law, ethics and politics, action and a penalty, and life and doomsday." (Ibrahim et al., 1984)[4]

"Islam, then, does not demand literal equality of wealth, because the distribution of wealth depends on men's endowments, which are not uniform. Hence absolute justice demands that men's rewards be similarly different and that some have more than others – so long as human justice is upheld by the provision of equal opportunity for all. Thus rank or upbringing, origin or class should not stand in the way of any individual, nor should anyone be fettered by the chains which shackle enterprise. Justice must be upheld also by the inclusion of all kinds of values in the reckoning, by the freeing of the human mind completely from the tyranny of the purely economic values, and by the relegation of these to their true and reasonable place. Economic values must not be given an inflatedly high standing, such as they enjoy in those human societies which lack a certainty of true values, or which give to them was slight an importance [sic]; in such conditions money alone becomes the supreme and fundamental value.

"In Islam money is not given this value; Islam refuses to admit that life can be reckoned in terms of a mouthful of bread, the appetites of the body, or a handful of money. Yet at the same time it demands a competence for every individual, and at times more than a competence, in order to remove the fear of destitution. On the other side, it forbids that unbridled luxury in possessions and desires which produces social divisions and classes. It prescribes the claims of the poor upon the wealth of the rich, according to their needs, and according to the best interests of society, so that social life may be balanced, just, and productive. Thus it is not unmindful of any one of the various aspects of life, material, intellectual, religious, and worldly; but it organizes them all, that they may be related together and thus furnish a coherent unity in which it will be difficult to neglect any one of their various

---

[4] Asim al-Majid Ibrahim Najih is a founder and former leader of the Egyptian al-Gama'a al-Islamiyya. After being imprisoned in connection with the 1981 assassination of Anwar Sadat, Ibrahim renounced violence in 1997 and was released in November 2005. Isam-al-Din Darablah was a leader of the Egyptian al Gama'a al-Islamiyya. He is now serving a life sentence for his role in the Sadat assassination and is among the group's leaders who have renounced violence and criticized al-Qaeda.

integral parts. So these departments of life become an organized unity, similar to the great oneness of the universe and to that of life and of all mankind." (Qutb, 1949, p. 49)

"If, then, we are to establish a sound Islamic theory of the universe, life, and mankind, it is essential that Western philosophies and their moral corollaries should not be studied at all in our secondary schools, and that they should be studied in the university only after at least two years in the department of philosophy. And by the very nature of the case they should not be studied in the Azhar colleges until the very end of the course. In every center of study such Western philosophies should be preceded by a course in pure Islamic thought, as distinct from the so-called 'Islamic philosophy,' in order to emphasize the true Islamic viewpoint." (Qutb, 1949, p. 291)

"On the issue of education, we want to teach the people our history, and we insist that the people must learn the Quran. Even if the Quran attacks the Jews in some of its verses, the people must read it. We cannot agree to the manipulation of the Quran and the religion." (al-Zahar, 2005a)[5]

"Know the truth and its roots. The book of God is our guide. Either Islam or atheism." (bin Laden, 2001a)

"Atheism causes the destruction of minds. People say that the universe is working automatically. They say that the universe is the creation of an accident. They say that the process of creation is automatically under way. This atheism is destroying the minds of our children in schools, colleges, and universities. Our curriculum and books of geology and other branches of science spread these ideologies of the atheists. Studying in these colleges, our children come out with these minds and spread it when they join practical life. They say that yes, the Koran is a sacred book and should be read, but it has nothing to do with the world, our circumstances, and new incidents. They say that it has nothing to do with these things. They say that the Koran has nothing to do with politics, the economy, and what is happening in the world. They say that it is only a sacred book.

"O cruel people! Christians can think of their amended and modified Bible in these terms, but our Koran is still alive in the same shape

---

[5] Mahmoud al-Zahar is a senior leader of Hamas and has been the spokesman of the organization since 1989. In 2006, he became Foreign Minister in the Hamas-led government.

as it was revealed from the skies. It is alive just as it was in the Prophet's days and will continue to remain unaltered as Allah says He promised to protect it. This book is screaming to tell you and to make you understand every issue. It explained every issue that erupted at any point in history. It provides solutions." (Saeed, 2005)[6]

"You encounter a long list of those who call themselves Islamic thinkers. These people put themselves above the divine message, and their arrogance deludes them into thinking that they can act as equals with the overpowering miracle of the Koran. Thus, they strongly demand a rereading of the Koran, or what is an even greater crime, they demand that one listen to those who offer a new allegorical interpretation of the religious text." (Azmi, 2005)[7]

Al-Wala' Wa al-Bara' and Takfir

While they share the fundamentalist opposition to "innovation" and "novelty" in Islam, jihadis greatly expand the concept and practice of "al-wala' wa al-bara'" (loyalty and disavowal) and takfir. The former requires jihadis to pledge their loyalty to their group and reject any relationship with others. It is based on the Qur'anic verse, "O you who believe! Do not take the Jews and the Christians for friends; they are friends of each other; and whoever amongst you takes them for a friend, then surely he is one of them; surely Allah does not guide the unjust people" (5:51). Takfir can involve excommunicating either an individual or entire groups (e.g., Shi'as). Its justification is based on the verse, "And whoever acts hostilely to the Apostle after that guidance has become manifest to him, and follows other than the way of the believers, we will turn him to that to which he has (himself) turned and make him enter hell; and it is an evil resort" (4:115). Extensive and, in particular, collective use of takfir by jihadis and other Salafis is controversial, because together with al-wala' wa al-bara', these concepts permit bloodshed against those who otherwise would be considered Muslims, whose blood could not be shed according to the Qur'an. Countering these concepts is the principle of irja, which is embraced by most Muslims. It means tolerance, or more specifically, the suspension of judgment. Under this concept, the issue of who is and who is not a Muslim is left to Allah. More generally, many Muslims would oppose takfir on the basis of taqarub or tasamuh (rapprochement or toleration).

---

[6] Hafiz Mohammad Saeed is a founder of Lashkar-e-Taiba, a Kashmiri militant group. He was arrested in 2006 in connection with violent protests of cartoons depicting the Prophet Mohammad, and his current status within the group is unclear.

[7] Rim Azmi is an Egyptian journalist best known for his 2005 condemnation of liberal Muslims.

"The expression, 'the children of Abraham,' which the tawhif[8] use nowadays to appease the Jews, and enter into peace conferences with them; an expression which is intended to annihilate the ties of faith (imam) and dissolve the very foundation of the religion and shake the basis of al-'Wala' Wal-Bara." (al-Maqdisi, 1985, p. 29)

"Muslims should consider with care the verses on loyalty, faith and jihad. They should sever any relations with the Jews and the Christians . . . whoever befriends Jews and Christians becomes like them, and becomes one of them in their religion and in their infidelity. God, Praise and Glory be to him, indicated in many verses that whoever befriends the infidels becomes one of them." (bin Laden, 1998c)

"Indeed, people are not Muslims, as they proclaim to be, as long as they live the life of Jahiliyyah. If someone wishes to deceive himself or to deceive others by believing that Islam can be brought in line with this Jahiliyyah, it is up to him. But whether this deception is for others, it cannot change anything of the actual reality. This is not Islam, and they are not Muslims." (Qutb, 1964)

"We believe that any sect of people organized around a principle that is not Ilsam is an apsostate, infidel sect, such as the nationalist, the communist, Ba'athist, secular, and democratic parties. . . ." (al-Falastini, 2005)[9]

"We also decree that any of the hypocrites in Iraq, or Arab rulers who have helped America in their murder of Muslims in Iraq, anyone who approved of their actions and followed them into this Crusader war by fighting with them or providing bases or administrative support, or any other kind of backing, should be aware that they are apostates who are outside the community of Islam; it is therefore permitted to take their money and their blood." (bin Laden, 2003a)

---

[8] This is most likely a misspelling. It is probably the broken plural form of *taghut* (*tawaghit*), meaning "false idol," an archaic term that jihadis have resurrected to denote an un-Islamic ruler, e.g., the al-Saud, Mubarak, etc.

[9] Abu Qatada al-Falastini (the Palestinian) is a Jordanian-Palestinian cleric who is imprisoned in London and faces deportation to Jordan. After arriving in London in 1993, he held leadership roles in several mosques, including the Baker Street mosque attended by Zacarias Moussaoui. His fatwas justified terrorist attacks, and tapes of his sermons were found in the Hamburg apartment of some of the 9/11 hijackers. His publications, including "The Markers of the Victorious Sect," espouse his *takfiri* view that many who claim to be Muslim are not in fact Muslim.

"We do not accuse Muslims or Muslim societies of unbelief. It is for their sake that we came out to defend them and want them to have security and peace, but not at the expense of disobeying Allah." (Abu-Hafs al-Masri Brigades (Al-Qa'ida), 2004)

Jihad

Jihad, the struggle in the way of Allah, has several aspects: struggle with oneself to live in the way of Allah; struggle to enlighten others as to the nature of Islam and the desirability of conversion; and armed struggle against the enemies of Islam. The first two interpretations govern the conduct of jihad for the vast majority of Muslims, but for the jihadi, armed struggle is the "forgotten obligation" of Islam and should predominate.

There are two kinds of armed struggle, or holy war, in Islam. Offensive jihad is war against infidels beyond the realm of Islam. Indeed, that part of the world is called the "abode of war" (dar al-Harb). This form of jihad is a collective obligation of the Islamic community and must be declared by an appropriate authority, e.g., a caliph. Not everyone is expected to participate in such a jihad.

Defensive jihad is waged when Muslim territory is attacked or occupied, or when Islam itself is threatened. This form of jihad is an individual duty, and it is incumbent on everyone to combat such enemies or occupiers. As spelled out in Chapter Five, jihadis insist that Islam and Muslims are under attack everywhere—hence the argument that waging jihad is every Muslim's personal obligation.

For those who cannot fight, there is financial jihad (boycotts); "jihad of the tongue" (propaganda); and even political jihad (engaging in elections), although the latter is highly controversial in violent jihadi circles.

"The walls of oppression and humiliation cannot be demolished except in a rain of bullets.

"The freeman does not surrender leadership to infidels and sinners.

"Without shedding blood no degradation and branding can be removed from the forehead." (bin Laden, 1996)

"We must understand the nature of the battle and conflict. Our enemies will not grant us our rights without Jihad." (al-Zawahiri, 2005e)

"Reform can only take place through Jihad for the sake of Allah, and any call for reform that is not through Jihad is doomed to death and failure." (al-Zawahiri, 2005e)

"Religious scholars also agree—as far as I know—that jihad is the greatest voluntary act. It is nobler than voluntary pilgrimage, fasting, or prayer." (Taymiyyah, quoted in al-Salim, 2003)

"Jihad in the path of God in spirit is the greatest and best means of drawing close to God. Everyone is aware of its excellence.

"The Koran and the tradition note the virtue of the mujahid {holy warrior} in spirit and the excellence of the martyr and martyrdom. They devote extensive space to this. The Koran contains more than 70 verses about jihad. In the tradition, scholars have dedicated entire sections of their collections of the prophet's sayings to jihad—the word, its rules, and its virtues. The word means fighting. Ibn Rushd says, 'The word jihad means to fight the infidels by the sword until they embrace Islam or pay the tax to which they are subject.'" (al-Salim, 2003)

"Among the aspects of distortion in this age is that some groups claim that one or ten or twenty or forty Muslims fighting is not really Jihad, as is the claim that fighting cannot be sanctioned without the presence of an imam to enable it. These are broad claims without foundation, and just a quick sketch of them is enough to rule them ignorant and ruinous." (al-Falastini, 2005)

"In a few hours or days, the Mujahid sees, with his own eyes, such hardships, trials, and tribulations, as others do not see in decades. It will be impossible for anyone who engages in this experience of Jihad to equate physical Jihad with other pacifistic means of Dawah. Therefore, anyone who disputes with the Mujahid in the issue of Jihad or who calls people to abandon fighting should join a camp, even if only as a servant. Or he should participate in a battle even if only as a cook. Then after that, we will see if, in his opinion, the pen is equal to the Kalashnikov." (Abu Khubayb and Abu Zubayr, undated)[10]

"The Da'wah {preaching of Islam} can spread only through the barrels of the cannons. One will of a martyr is much more efficient and effective than dozens of religious lessons and sermons. This is the first goal of the Jihad. Jihad is not only a military activity. It should be accom-

---

[10] Abu Khubayb was the pseudonym used by al-Qaeda in Iraq for Ali Hussein Ali al-Samari, one of the suicide bombers who carried out the 2005 Amman hotel bombings. Abu Zubayr was a prominent member of al-Qaeda in Iraq, attaining the title Emir of Mosul before being killed in August 2005.

panied by a proper Salafi Da'wah and incitement." (Abu Muhammad al-Hilali, 2005)[11]

"But the question is how the torments {of the infidel} that Allah wants carried out by our hands will be implemented. . . . The torments certainly will not be carried out by means of da'wa [preaching to Islam] . . . [but] by means of Jihad will Allah torment the [infidels] by killing, by means of Jihad will Allah torment them by financial loss, by means of Jihad will Allah torment them by loss of power." (Seif al-Din al-Ansari, 2002b)[12]

". . . We say to our Muslim brethren everywhere that our crime, by God, is no more than carrying on jihad against the Crusaders. . . . We shall proceed on the way of jihad. We have put our lives at risk and donned our shrouds. We have left family and children, desiring what is with God Almighty. We pray that God will strengthen us on this path until we meet Him." (al-Ayiri, undated, in Center for Islamic Studies and Research, 2003)[13]

"This is a message to you from Shaykh Ibn-al-Juzi,[14] may Allah have mercy on his soul: 'O people, the war has broken out, the call for jihad has been made, and the doors of heaven have opened. If you are not among the war knights, then open the way for the women to fight it, go and take the censer and kohl,[15] o women in turbans and beards!!'" (Abu-Hafs al-Masri Brigades (Al-Qa'ida), 2004)

"It is very clear, brothers and sisters, that the path of jihad and the desire for martyrdom is imbedded in the holy prophet and his beloved companions. By preparing ourselves for this kind of work, we are guaranteeing ourselves for paradise and gaining the pleasure of Allah. And by turning our back on this work, we are guaranteeing ourselves humiliation and the anger of Allah. Jihad is an obligation on every single one of us, men and women." (Kahn, 2005)

---

[11] Abu Muhammad al-Hilali is the name given to an al-Qaeda supporter, strategic thinker, and apparent student of Abu Musab al-Suri who has written on jihadi strategy for activities in Egypt.

[12] Seif al-Din al-Ansari is a pro–al-Qaeda writer. The name is likely a pseudonym, and little other biographical information about him is available.

[13] Yusuf Bin-Salih al-Ayiri was a prominent member of al-Qaeda who ran training camps and wrote a number of strategic and training documents for the organization. He was killed in 2003 by Saudi security forces.

[14] Historian, d.597 AH.

[15] A censer is a small dish used for burning incense. Kohl is a traditional Middle Eastern cosmetic.

"Jihad today is the only option for the Islamic community, for the enemy has come to occupy the countries of Muslims one after the other. As God said in the Koran, 'Nor will they cease fighting you until they turn you back from your faith if they can' [2:217]." (al-Salim, 2003)

"Until Islam as a Way of Life dominates the whole of the world and until Allah's Law is enforced everywhere in the world, it is binding and incumbent upon the Muslims to fight on against the disbelievers.

. . . .

". . . all the Muslims who have capacity enough but do not take part in Jihad are, in fact, living a sinful life." (bin Muhammad, undated)

"We must not neglect this great duty on the pretext that this is the duty of the mujahidin. If this is the duty of the mujahidin, the duty of the non-mujahidin is to become mujahidin." (Center for Islamic Studies and Research, 2003)

"The Muslims today love this world, hate death, and abandon Jihad, and therefore Allah has subjugated them to the infidel nations that humiliate them. This is the divine punishment meted out to anyone who abandons Jihad." (Mansour, 2004)

"Luxury has a deleterious effect on God's servants in the short term and the long term. It hardens the heart, breeds arrogance, encourages an attachment to this world and a hatred of death. The consequences go beyond the neglect of jihad and the truth, for the effect is to obscure jihad and the truth." (al-Salim, 2003)

"And may Allah lengthen our days to allow us to infuriate the enemies of Allah, kill them, and strike them by the sword until they either join the religion of Allah or we kill every last one of them. Our model is [the Prophet] Mohammad, who said to the infidels of Qureish, 'I have brought the slaughter upon you.'" (Abu Hajer, 2003)

"Intense hatred of the infidels is in and of itself support for the muja-hidin." (al-Salim, 2003)

"Some supporters stand alongside the mujahidin in the trenches with their souls, their money, and everything they have. They have linked their fate to the mujahidin and to jihad. They no longer have any earthly possessions or positions to lose or to fear for. They are an indispensable part of the jihad community. They obey its commands and prohibitions. They let the interests of jihad be their guide." (al-Amili, 2002)[16]

"If you are seeking the Jihad, you must know that it is not a promenade or a vacation trip. It involves losing money, relatives, and abandoning friends, companions, and home. This requires patience [for] hardships, and adherence to the principles." (Anonymous, undated(a))

"Let each of us spend the night with the sword and wrath as his bed-mate. Let the field of fierce battle be for him a spring pasture. Let the heat of battle's furnace be for him a refreshing rain. Let him answer the summoner of death obediently and willingly. Let him betake himself to fame, though he be thrown down and left slain." (Center for Islamic Studies and Research, 2003)

"Men of Jihad, this is your festive season {Ramadan} since Jihad, in a state of fasting, has a particularly delectable taste for the believers, especially [when together] with the dignity of the month of Ramadan. How wonderful it is to delight in the breaking of the fast and to taste the killing of infidels, to delight in the sound of the wailing of tyrants and lowly degenerates, and [in the sound of] the voices of the condemnations on the part of evil people and their collaborators broadcast on the TV stations . . . ." (al-Aamer, 2004)

"Jihad fighters everywhere! This month of Jihad {Ramadan} has come with all its blessings and with the double reward [granted to Jihad fighters] in its course. Come closer to Allah through the blood of infidels, do not relent in spilling [their blood], and through [this blood] wipe out humiliation and disgrace from among your Muslim nation! Make this month like the month of the Battle of Badr, the conquest of Mecca, [the conquest] of Shaqhab, and other Islamic victories." (Sa'ud Bin Hamoud al-Utaybi, 2004)[17]

---

[16] Abu Sa'd al-Amili is a pro–al-Qaeda writer, possibly from Saudi Arabia. The name may be a pseudonym, and little other biographical information is known.

[17] Sa'ud Bin Hamoud al-Utaybi was a leader of al-Qaeda in the Arabian Peninsula and is believed to have been killed by Saudi security forces in April 2005.

Terrorism

"This is a public statement: Terrorism is part of Islam, and whoever denies it is an Infidel." (al-Aziz, undated)[18]

"There is no Jihad without Terrorism." (Alusi, 2004)[19]

"Jihad literally means 'to struggle.' In the military sense it is meant in the context 'to struggle against oppression.' Jihad is therefore an act to liberate people from the oppression of tyrants. Jihad is not illegal acts of terror against innocent people. When tabloid journalism mistakenly informs the masses that Jihad is 'to commit illegal acts of terror,' they are revealing the lack of their research and the extent of their unprofessional approach to the subject." (Azzam Publications, undated)

"Islam has ordered us to terrorize our enemies and whoever denies that is an infidel himself. Terrorizing our infidel enemies is a legal obligation. Whoever says that Islam is not related to terrorism has committed an infidel act—terror comes from Islam." (Algerian Salafist Group for Prayer and Combat, 2005)

"America has made many accusations against us and many other Muslims around the world. Its charge that we are carrying out acts of terrorism is an unwarranted description.

. . . .

"They did this {the 9/11 hijackers} . . . as a matter of self-defense, in defense of our brothers and sons in Palestine, and to liberate our sacred religious sites/things. If inciting people to do that is terrorism, and if killing those who kill our sons is terrorism, then let history be witness that we are terrorists.

. . . .

". . . the truth {is} that we are not terrorists as they understand it but {acting in self-defense} because we are being attacked in Palestine, Iraq, Lebanon, Sudan, Somalia, Kashmir, the Philippines and everywhere else.

. . . .

---

[18] Abd al-Qader bin Abd al-Aziz was a founder and leader of Egyptian Islamic Jihad who lost his leadership role after disagreeing with al-Zawahiri on the use of violence. He was extradited in 2004 to Egypt.

[19] Muhammad Alusi is an Iraqi Shi'ite cleric who has promoted the idea that terrorism is an integral part of jihad.

"Not all terrorism is cursed; some terrorism is blessed. A thief, a criminal, for example feels terrorized by the police. So, do we say to the policeman, 'You are a terrorist'? No. Police terrorism against criminals is a blessed terrorism because it will prevent the criminal from repeating his deed. America and Israel exercise the condemned terrorism. We practice the good terrorism which stops them from killing our children in Palestine and elsewhere." (bin Laden, 2001a)

"Was De Gaulle a terrorist? Were those who worked to liberate their countries from occupation terrorists? We do not consider the West as an enemy but we believe Christian Zionism is criminal." (al-Zahar, 2005a)

"The one who says, 'We should fight against terrorism,' he is fighting against Islam. We know very well that USA meant no one else by the term 'terrorists' but Islam and Muslims and the one who wants to avoid terrorism is avoiding Islam." (al-Muhajiroun, 2004)

Martyrdom

Both Islam and Christianity have martyrs, individuals who have died for their faith. In Christianity, this is usually viewed as a passive act of resistance against persecution. In Islam, martyrdom also has the connotation of dying in battle, reflecting the different historical context of the religion's birth.

Like Christianity, Islam also strictly prohibits suicide. As a result, jihadis have sought to rationalize suicide operations as no different from fighting to the death. This is extremely controversial, even in jihadi circles. Indeed, jihadi leaders such as Zarqawi and bin Laden have been accused of turning Islam into a death cult and as such being heretics.

The rewards for becoming a martyr are many: painless death, posthumous prestige, instant paradise, intercession on behalf of family members, and of course, wedding with the proverbial 72 virgins. For a young man with no experience with the opposite sex, the latter cannot be a trivial inducement.

For jihadis, suicide operations are also extremely efficient and effective. A suicide bomber is the ultimate "smart bomb," capable of finding its target and overcoming possible obstacles. Moreover, a suicide attacker does not need a getaway plan, which is the most difficult stage of any terrorist operation and the most dangerous for the jihadi organization's members.

Finally, a suicide operation tends to generate more terror. It can occur in the most peaceful of settings against innocent victims. The fact that the attacker takes his own life conveys a deep sense of commitment to his cause, although the frequency of such attacks in Iraq and elsewhere is undermining the shock on which that sense of unique determination depends.

In sum, suicide operations are not only an extreme—and, most Muslims say, misguided—expression of faith, they are also a powerful military tactic.

> ". . . I'll die one death. Why shouldn't I die as a martyr?
> The martyr's spirit will go up very high, God will put it in the highest level
> He'll be flying with the birds of paradise, humming over the palaces
> He'll be with the purest of God's creation; His neighbors will be the prophets and their friends.
> I'll be able to see God as clearly as I can see the full moon
> Seven things that the martyr will get, can you tell me what they are?
> Your sins will be forgiven and your status will be very high
> You will get comfort in the grave and you will enjoy the resurrection
> You'll be crowned with respect and people far and near are going to respect you
> The virgins are waiting for my coming, kissing them is my illness and medicine . . . ." (al-Aslami, 2004)

> "My brothers! The ummah {Islamic community} that knows how to die a noble and honourable death is granted an exalted life in this world and eternal felicity in the next. Degradation and dishonour are the results of the love of this world and the fear of death. Therefore prepare for jihad and be the lovers of death. Life itself shall come searching after you." (al-Banna, undated(a))

> "The self-sacrifice operation, it is the Islamic way of life for those who resist.
> "Self-sacrifice operations in Muslim countries, it is part of the Islamic culture." (Mohammed, 2005)[20]

> "Martyrdom, according to our culture and thought, is the door through which one passes from false life to real life. It is the door through which one passes from mortal life to eternal life. It is the door through which one passes from a life of amusement, games, procreation and pride to a life of eternal bliss, continuous peace, happiness and bounty, where

---

[20] Omar Bakri Mohammed is a radical cleric and founder of the al-Muhajiroun organization who left the UK after blaming the British public for the July 7, 2005, bombings in London.

there are things that no eye has seen and no ear has heard, and no concern burdens the human heart." (Nasrallah, 2005)[21]

"In order to defend the homeland from the terrorist Crusader attack, there is a need for people who yearn for Paradise, and the shortest way to Paradise is death for [the sake of] Allah. Some of us should see the joyful and satisfied faces of the mothers in Iraq when they part from the fruit of their loins, who go off to the realms of honor, the realms of martyrdom. This is so that the enemy of the nation knows that safeguarding honor and the homeland is dearer than life, and that our mothers in Iraq, like our mothers in Palestine, [are willing] to sacrifice the fruit of their loins – but not their honor." (al-Rantisi, 2003)[22]

"Those who oppose martyrdom operations and claim that they are suicide are making a great mistake. The goals of the one who carries out a martyrdom operation and of the one who commits suicide are completely different. . . . The [person who commits] suicide kills himself for himself, because he failed in business, love, an examination, or the like. He was too weak to cope with the situation and chose to flee life for death.

   "In contrast, the one who carries out a martyrdom operation does not think of himself. He sacrifices himself for the sake of a higher goal, for which all sacrifices become meaningless. He sells himself to Allah in order to buy Paradise in exchange. Allah said, 'Allah has bought from the believers their souls and their properties for they shall inherit Paradise.'" (al-Qaradhawi, 2003b)

". . . [he] is not a suicide [bomber]. He kills the enemy while taking self-risk, similarly to what Muslims did in the past. . . . He wants to scare his enemies, and the religious authorities have permitted this. They said that if he causes the enemy both sorrow and fear of Muslims . . . he is permitted to risk himself and even get killed." (al-Qaradhawi, 2001a)

---

[21] This is an example of Shi'a jihadi thought justifying suicide operations. Hezbollah was the first Islamic organization to employ a suicide bomber, in November 1982. Hassan Nasrallah has been the Secretary-General of Hezbollah since 1992. He is credited with transforming Hezbollah into a modern fighting force, and he received a great deal of acclaim in the Arab world after the 2006 conflict between Hezbollah and Israel.

[22] Abd al-Aziz al-Rantisi assumed leadership of Hamas after the killing of Ahmad Yassin in March 2004. Al-Rantisi was killed by an Israeli airstrike in April 2004.

"What weapon can harm their enemy, can prevent him from sleeping, and can strip him of a sense of security and stability, except for these human bombs – a young man or woman who blows himself or herself up amongst their enemy. This is a weapon the likes of which the enemy cannot obtain, even if the U.S. provides it with billions [of dollars] and the most powerful weapons, because it is a unique weapon that Allah has placed only in the hands of the men of belief. It is a type of divine justice on the face of the earth . . . it is the weapon of the wretched weak in the face of the powerful tyrant." (al-Qaradhawi, 2003b)

"There is a widespread misconception, propagated by the Zionist enemy, that there are recruiters among the Palestinian fighters who look for martyrdom bombers. The opposite is true, the martyrdom bombers are the ones looking for the resistance factions in order to commit martyrdom operations.

"We are talking about hundreds of martyrdom bombers waiting in line to commit martyrdom operations. The factions' inability to supply enough operations for all of them is the only obstacle preventing them all from committing martyrdom operations." (Abu Zuhri and Shalhoub, 2004)[23]

"If someone prays honestly to God for martyrdom, God will deliver him to the abodes of martyrs even if he should die in his bed." (al-Salim, 2003)

"Testaments of Martyrs

"I am the Shahida Reem Saleh Riyashi. I hoped that the shredded limbs of my body would be shrapnel, tearing the Zionists to pieces, knocking on Heaven's door with the skulls of Zionists . . . .

"How often I spoke to my soul, 'O soul, if you loathe the Zionists, enemies of my religion, my blood shall be my path to march to Heaven. Since 8th grade I have striven, seeking people daily to guide, listen and help me . . . .

"How often I dreamed, how often I desired to carry out a Shahada-seeking [suicide] operation inside Israel, and by perseverance, and with Allah's grace, my wish was fulfilled as I wanted." (Riyashi, 2004)

---

[23] Sami Abu Zuhri is a prominent member and spokesman of Hamas. In 2006, Zuhri was caught attempting to smuggle more than $800,000 into the Gaza Strip. Faraj Shalhoub is a journalist who is considered to be an expert on Palestinian affairs.

"My dear mother, you who have cared for me, today I sacrifice my life to be your intercessor [on Judgment Day]. O my love and soul, wipe your tears, don't be saddened. In the name of Allah, I've achieved all that I've aspired. Don't let me see you sad on my wedding day with the Maidens of Paradise. So be happy and not sad, because in the name of Allah, after death is merciful Allah's paradise." (Abu Hafs, 2004)

"Going to God

I am going to God, mother
I am going to live in His mercy
My feet will lead (guide) me
God willing, to His orders and right path.
Don't be sad, sing and ululate.
God has chosen me
As a man, for I have lived every day
As a man that bought his religion and sold his whims.
Mother of my son, be hopeful and patient.
We will meet in heaven.
I will die for my nation to live.
I will be alive in heaven.
Just one push on the trigger and I'm over,
Thus disfiguring the face of the enemies.
May the faces of those who don't fear God be disfigured,
The faces of those who don't defend Him.
May the cowards never sleep.
It is shameful what is happening in Jerusalem.
Get up, coward, as a man,
And perform glorious acts. Don't fear.
Father, forgive my sins,
And feel proud of the son you'll meet in heaven.
For the principle we lived forI {sic} will die so that you may live by it, father." (al-Maarek, 2001)

"Angels of mercy, escort our souls to Heaven after we fulfill this duty of crushing the descendents of monkeys and pigs. Dear father and mother, blessings of honor and respect to you, while you escort me to the Maidens of Paradise as a martyr." (al-Takrouri, 2003)

Not all jihadis support suicide operations. Abu Muhammad al-Maqdisi, the cleric who converted al-Zarqawi to jihadism, has argued against this tactic.

". . . the martyrdom operations are an exceptional means, not a traditional, original means of Jihad operation. Similarly, I expressed my reservations about killing civilians, and attacking churches and Shiite mosques – if it is true that Al-Zarqawi is doing these deeds." (al-Maqdisi, 2005b)[24]

". . . but I am talking about matters, if the media really have any credibility, that we heard about that might have been chosen by Abu-Mus'ab [to be carried out]. I have some reservations about these, which include the expansive use of operations which we call jihadi, or which some may call suicide or martyrdom operations.

. . . .

"I took the middle path on this matter, as have our scholars, with regard to killing a Muslim who is being used as shield for the unbelievers. . . . The jurists permitted killing such shields out of necessity, i.e., if not killing them would cause greater harm to Islam and the Muslims, especially when the shields will inevitably be killed anyway. Our scholars [have set] conditions for this. . . . We have applied the jurists' opinion in operations in which a jihad fighter infiltrates a group of unbelievers and blows himself up, killing them and causing them great losses, and is killed himself. Killing the shield or killing another soul is the same thing, because both are souls that have immunity, and you are also a soul with immunity whose killing is forbidden. In any case, we thought that these operations were permissible [only] when necessary.

"There were those who disagreed with us on this matter. They thought that [suicide operations] were a conventional method [of attack] just as is the use of a weapon, such as a Kalashnikov [rifle], a pistol, or anything else. We say that it is not a traditional method, but an exceptional one, to be used only when necessary. We used to tell them that if the jihad fighter could kill the enemy with a Kalashnikov [rifle] or a pistol, he was then forbidden from blowing [himself] up—he is forbidden from resorting to this method. Six months ago . . . Six months ago, every day, we would read news in the newspapers and see on television tens of killed Iraqi civilian women and children, while no more than one or two of the American occupiers were killed. There must be reservations about this matter, and it must be reconsidered." (al-Maqdisi, 2005a)

---

[24] Abu Muhammad al-Maqdisi is an influential jihadi figure associated with militant Salafism and the argument that Arab rulers are infidels. He is also well known as an ideological mentor of al-Zarqawi, although the two disagreed publicly over al-Zarqawi's targeting of Shi'a.

And this was Zarqawi's response:

> "[Al-Maqdisi's attack] is a new arrow aimed at our hearts, except that this time it is not from the quiver of those [enemies] to whom I previously referred, but from a man who is one of this school [of ours] and a religious scholar. This was Sheikh Abu Muhammad Al-Maqdisi's article, 'Al-Zarqawi – Support and Advice: Hopes and Pains.'
>
> . . . .
>
> "The sheikh [Al-Maqdisi] mentions that I used to follow his view in disallowing suicide operations, and that I have now started to use them extensively in Iraq. To which I answer that this is not the case. Indeed, I maintained that they were not permissible when I was in Afghanistan during the Communist invasion . . . which was before I had met Al-Maqdisi. When I met him, my belief [on this issue] was in agreement with his. Then, when we got out of prison and I went to Afghanistan once again, I met Sheikh Abu Abdallah Al-Muhajir and we discussed the question of suicide operations, and Sheikh [Al-Muhajir] concluded that they should be permitted. I read a very valuable study by him on this question, and heard some recorded cassettes by him on this matter. Allah opened my heart to [accept] his conclusion.
>
> "Not only did I adopt the idea that [suicide operations] are permissible, but I see fit to advocate them as commendable." (al-Zarqawi, 2005e)

Women in Islam and Jihad

Women have played important roles in jihad operations, including suicide bombings in Israel, Jordan, and Chechnya. The Hezbollah attack that destroyed the Marine barracks in Lebanon in 1983 was carried out by a woman driving a truck loaded with explosives. Perhaps because of women's participation in jihad, jihadis often have a somewhat more positive view of the capacities of women than do non-violent Salafis such as Wahhabis. Although women are typically relegated to a supporting role in jihad, their assistance is both encouraged and appreciated. Nevertheless, the most important task of women is considered to be raising more jihadis.

> "As for the relation between the sexes, Islam has guaranteed to women a complete equality with men with regard to their sex; it has permitted no discrimination except in some incidental matters connected with physical capacity, with customary procedure, or with responsibility, in all of which the human status of the two sexes is not in question. Wherever the physical endowments, the customs, and the responsibili-

ties are identical, the sexes are equal; and wherever there is some difference in these respects, the discrimination follows that difference.

"In the spiritual and religious sphere, men and women are equal.
. . .

"Or again, in the sphere of possessing and administering money,
they are equal. . . .

"In the case of the law about a man getting double the share of a
woman in an inheritance, the reason is to be found in the responsibility which a man carries in life. He marries a woman and he undertakes
to maintain her and their children; he has to bear the responsibility of
the whole structure of the family. . . . So the question here is one of difference in responsibility, which necessitates a similar difference in the
law of inheritance.

"Or there is the case of men being overseers over women. . . . The
reason for this discrimination lies in physical endowment and in use
and wont in the matter of oversight. Because a man is free from the
cares of maternity, he can attend to the affairs of society over considerable periods and can apply to these affairs all his intellectual powers.
On the other hand, a woman is preoccupied for most of her life by
the cares of family. The result is that these responsibilities promote in
women a growth in the direction of the emotions and the sentiments,
while in men growth is promoted in the direction of reflection and
thought.
. . . .

"But the strongest point in Islam is the equality that it guarantees
to women in religion as well as in their property and earnings. Also,
it gives them the assurance of marriage only with their own consent
and at their own pleasure, without any compulsion or negligence;[25] and
they must get a dowry. 'And give them their stipulated price.' (4:28).
. . .

". . . . Islam declared war on the idea that a girl child was a disaster
and that she was better put away while she was still an infant; it was
implacably opposed to the custom of burying daughters alive, which
was current in the life of some of the Arabian tribes.
. . . .

"We must also remember this about Islam—and in its favor—that
the freedom that the materialistic West grants to women does not flow
from this noble and humane source; nor are its objectives the pure

---

[25] Arranged marriages are common in many parts of the Muslim world. The marriage of al-Wahhabi's daughter
to al Saud's son is an example from the past (see pp. 49–50).

objectives of Islam. . . . It is well to remember that the West brought women out of the home to work only because their men folk shrank from the responsibility of keeping them and caring for them although the price was the chastity and honor of woman. Thus and only thus were women compelled to work.

"It is to be remembered also that when women did emerge to work, the materialist West exploited the opportunity presented by a surplus of labor to pay them lower wages; thus employers were able to dispense with men in favor of women, who were cheaper to pay, because the men were beginning to raise their heads and demand their true value. So when women in the West came to demand equality with men, it was first and most essentially an equality of wages that they wanted, so that they might be able to eat and to support life. When they could not gain this form or equality they demanded the right of the franchise, so that they might have a voice to speak for them. And finally they demanded access to parliaments, so that they might have the necessary representation when their equality was being established." (Qutb, 1949, pp. 73–76)

"Beating is permitted [to the man] in the most limited of cases, and only in a case when the wife rebels against her husband. . . . The beating, of course, will not be with a whip, a stick, or a board. The beating will be according to what the Prophet said to a servant girl who annoyed him on a particular matter, 'If it were not for fear of punishment in the Hereafter, I would have beaten you with this miswak.'[26]

"Likewise, the beating must come only after admonishment, and expelling [the wife] from the bed [as is said in the Qur'an 4:34], 'Admonish them, leave them alone in their beds, and beat them.'

"He also said: 'Beating is not suitable for every wife; it is suitable for certain wives and for other wives it is not. There is a woman who cannot agree to being beaten, and sees this as humiliation, while some women enjoy the beating and for them, only beating to cause them sorrow is suitable. . . .

"The Prophet said about those who beat their wives: 'Those are not the best among you.' The respectable and honest Muslim man does not beat his wife, and his hand is not accustomed to beating. If [the husband] beats [his wife] he must beat her in the way of which we spoke. He must refrain from beating her in sensitive places or on her face." (al-Qaradhawi, 1977)

---

[26] Twigs commonly used as toothbrushes.

". . . My virtuous sisters. . . . A woman in the family is the mother, the wife, the sister, and the daughter. In society, she is the raiser of children, the proselytizer, and the Jihad fighter who, just as she protects her family from any possible aggression, she defends her society against any poisonous thoughts and intellectual and moral dissolution. And she is the soldier who carries her pack and her weapon on her back in preparation for any military attack. . . ." (Umm Badr, 2004)

"In general, women are not required to go for jihad but their exit with male Jihadis to cure the ill and the wounded and to fetch water for the thirsty is permissible. . . . Also it is permissible for women to fight directly in some situations. . . . Women must get permission from their guardians before going and must be accompanied by mahram [a male chaperone]." (Nasir al-Fahd, unknown, in al-Rasheed, 2007)[27]

"There are many ways a Muslim woman can participate in Jihad, both by accompanying the Mujahideen to the battlefield, and by staying behind:

. . . .

"1. Participation in the Actual Fighting

"While Jihad (or Qital) is generally waged by men, there is clear evidence of women's participation in Jihad – both during the times of the Prophet Muhammad (peace be upon him), and throughout Islamic history, up until this day.

. . . .

    "And coming to this very day and age, we have our beloved sister, Shaheedah Hawaa' Barayev, who was martyred recently in Chechnya during a solo Martyrdom Operation in which 27 Russians were killed and numerous others injured.

. . . .

    "A note for sisters wanting to participate in fighting these days:
    "By the Grace of Allah, The Most High, the situation in the Ummah is not that desperate yet, that sisters are called to fight. . . .

. . . .

"2. Supporting the Fighters in the Battlefield

"There are several ways in which Muslim sisters can support the Mujahideen on the battlefield directly. . . .

---

[27] Nasir al-Fahd was a Saudi supporter of al-Qaeda who issued several fatwas sanctioning violence. He was imprisoned in 2003 and renounced extremism in a well-publicized media event later that year.

. . . .

"Medical Support . . .

"In Chechnya itself, while Muslim women cannot travel with the Mujahideen, we see sisters working as nurses managing the meagre {sic} health resources available for the Mujahideen. . . .

. . . .

"Providing Weapons and Ammunition

"This is another area where sisters can help. One sister in her fifties from the UK carried weapons and ammunition for the Bosnian Muslims over mountains, as she knew the enemy would not suspect her.

"Encouraging the Mujahideen to Remain Steadfast

"Most notable in this aspect was the Prophet (peace be upon him)'s aunt. . . . When she got ready to participate in the battle of Uhud, she carried a spear (or dagger) with her. . . . [The Prophet] asked her what she would do with it. She said she will remain at the back of the army and use it to strike those Muslims who dared to escape from the battle—and this role she played very well. . . .

"3. Guard Duty and Protection

. . . .

"3. [sic] Encourage Loved Ones to Go for Jihad

. . . .

"It has to be said that men tend to listen more if they are told to be 'men' by women. So sisters, use whatever means Allah has given you within Islamic bounds, encourage all the Muslims you can to realize their duty to Allah and His deen. And very importantly, encourage other sisters as well, as it is they, with Allah's help, who mold the thought-process of their young sons – the future mujahideen of the Ummah." (Sister AI, 2001)

"The outfitting of fighters offers an opportunity for women, who cannot ride out in battle in the path of God. They can equip fighters with their money, their jewelry, and their property in order to reap the great reward. Women played an important role in the emergence of Islam and in various subsequent periods. Some of them cut their tresses or gave their jewelry as gifts. We recall the sister of the unique hero and martyr Abu Ja'far al-Yamani, who was killed in Chechnya. In his biography on the site http://www.qoqaz.com, we read: 'His sister sold her gold and outfitted him with her money. Where are the [other] women? Where are the men?'" (al-Salim, 2003)

"There are hundreds of female martyrdom bombers, who stream en masse and insist on participating in martyrdom operations. This is a unique phenomenon, reflecting the live spirit of Jihad among this people.

. . . .

"We see this stream of young men and of women seeking martyrdom. This people emphasizes its adherence to the option of martyrdom, especially, in light of the models of female martyrdom bombers.

"The Palestinian resistance, at times, purposely uses women in some operations that men cannot carry out, especially in high security areas, which male Palestinian Mujahideen cannot easily reach. This is why the Palestinian woman has an important role in the Palestinian resistance, and at times she may even have roles that the young male Palestinian Mujaheed cannot fulfill." (Abu Zuhri and Shalhoub, 2004)

"At this point, I would like to call attention to some obstacles in the hope of finding available means of reducing them or overcoming them so that they do not become a reason for tripping up the women's jihad. I will start, with God's help, to address these obstacles in general. . . .

"Lack of knowledge of the Sharia: This is a matter neglected by many of our women. . . . The first source for receiving knowledge is the Qur'an, so the female jihad fighter must always recite it and put effort and care into memorizing it. . . .

"Weakness of faith and holding this world dear: Here, we might see a Muslim woman crying in grief for her sisters in Iraq, for the female prisoners in Palestine, for the women who have lost their children in Chechnya, and for the widows of Afghanistan and other Muslim lands. We may hear her threaten their enemies and swear to succor their victims, but when faced with the moment of truth, they back down, holding on to their jobs and position that they find hard to let go of. . . .

"Neglect of preparations: 1) Psychological preparation: The female jihad fighter may feel apprehensive of fighting on the path of God with money, verbal support, or the sword. . . . 2) Military preparation: This is the problem for the majority of our women, and even many of our men. . . . A woman, if she is not a jihad fighter, must at least know how to use a weapon for defense. . . .

"A female jihad fighter must have good knowledge of the types of weapons and ammunition; how to disassemble, clean, and reassemble weapons; and how to use and aim them. This is what we will help you with in the upcoming episodes about the Woman's Camp.

"3) Physical preparation: It is important that the female jihad fighter should enjoy a high level of physical fitness. She should maintain her weight through moderation of food and drink, and by often fasting the voluntary fasts, and by exercising. . . .

"Lack of Awareness: We have found that some sisters have an incorrect understanding of jihad—that it is for men, not women; or that jihad is strictly carrying a weapon and direct confrontation. This is contrary to the truth, because a Muslim woman is a jihad fighter wherever and whenever she is; she is a jihad fighter when she finances the jihad, and she is a jihad fighter when she awaits her jihad fighter husband while raising his children in a manner that pleases God and his Prophet, she is a jihad fighter if she picks up a weapon to defend herself, she is a jihad fighter if she is patient and bears with her husband the jihad fighter who is on the path of God, and she is a jihad fighter when she supports the jihad by calling for it with her words, her actions, her convictions, and her prayers.

"It is true that jihad was made mandatory for men and women, and that a woman's jihad is to perform the major and minor pilgrimages [to Mecca—the Hajj and 'Umrah] but, when necessary, a woman goes forth for jihad as does a man, without the need for permission from her husband or other male relative because it has become mandatory, and mandatory religious commandments do not require permission." (Umm Badr, 2004)

"We give the good tidings to the Muslims that there are female mujahidin raised to face any possibility, after seeking the help of the Almighty God. We pray to God to protect them and increase their strength and steadfastness. . . .

"One of the examples in this respect is that an Arab sister in Kandahar asked her husband to swear by God that if he embarked on a martyrdom operation he would take her with him to help him in the jihad and attain martyrdom together in the cause of God. A bomb dropped by the patron of peace and defender of human rights killed both of them. May God gather them with the martyrs, amen." (al-Ayiri, undated, in Center for Islamic Studies and Research, 2003)

"Message Addressed to the Spouse of the Infidel Paul Johnson[28] From the Spouse of a Martyr in the Arab Peninsula:

"I heard that you appeared on television, acting innocent, and in all insolence wondering about your husband's crime. I believe that, in fact, he was one of the top criminals, even if he was not viewed as such in your blaspheming tradition, where criminals are considered innocent, and the innocent who defend their rights are considered criminals.

"What was the purpose of your husband's work on the Apache helicopters? Did you think that those planes fly over Afghanistan, Palestine, and Iraq to give away roses and candy to our children there? I bet you do know that they drop missiles and bombs over their heads, turning their streets and their homes into ash, with their burnt bodies lying on top.

"Do you consider his work decent and him innocent when he worked on this type of planes?

"Are you aware that my husband was killed before my eyes, and in his own country? Are you aware that those who killed him were security men hired to protect the colonialists and terrify and kill the local Muslims? The whole world spoke and was shaken when your husband was held hostage, but nobody said half as much when, three years ago and until this day, America – the country of justice and freedom – detained over 600 Muslims in Cuba. This is in addition to Muslim prisoners in Iraq, Pakistan, Saudi Arabia, Jordan, and other countries.

"Let it be known that our brothers who are being detained in your prisons, and those who your husband burned with his plane, are not alone. There are hearts that beat with love for them, just as you showed that you love your deceased husband and more. Muslim blood is more precious to us than the Ka'aba (the Muslim sacred stone in Mecca), whereas your husband's is that of a dog, for he was a blaspheming polytheist. . . .

"Mountains of bodies of his fellow countrymen will follow your husband's, until they leave the land of our Prophet, prayer and peace upon him, in humiliation.

"How can you speak of your damned husband's innocence, when you hear the Mujahideen's warnings to leave our land? . . .

---

[28] Paul Johnson, Jr., an American whose decapitated body was found in northern Riyadh on June 18, 2004, was a 49-year-old Lockheed Martin Corp. employee who worked in Saudi Arabia for more than a decade. The Falluja Squadron (in the Arabian Peninsula), which claims to have ties to al-Qaeda, claimed responsibility for kidnapping and beheading him.

"Surely you did not care when my husband was killed, or perhaps you didn't know. Even if you did know, you were probably happy because he got killed before he reached your husband and his people!!

"My consolation is that the Mujahideen were able to reach their goal with precision and slay your husband. I swear to God that I was extremely happy that day, for the true terrorist was killed, after having sucked the blood of our Muslim children." (Um al-Shahid, 2004)[29]

"So we organized our ranks adjacent to our men to support, succor, and aid them, and to encourage them, pray for them, raise their children, and prepare the [requirements of war]. We hope that God almighty, knowing the truth of our wills and the goodness of our deeds will choose us and take us as martyrs on His path.

"We shall stand covered in our veils and wrapped with our 'abbayas, with weapons in hand and our children in our arms, using the guidance of the Qur'an and the Prophet's tradition. . . . The blood of our husbands and the torn limbs of our children are offerings to bring us close to God so that He may facilitate martyrdom on His path for us." (Umm Badr, 2004)

Raising Mujahid Children

"This is perhaps the most important role women can play in Jihad. . . . The key is to start instilling these values in them while they are babies. Don't wait until they are seven to start, for it may be too late by then! Some practical tips that most sisters can implement without difficulty are as follows:

"1. Tell children bedtime stories of Shuhadaa {martyrs} and Mujahideen. . . .

"2. Give young children a lot of love and nurture a sense of security and confidence in them . . . don't scare them with threats of things such as policemen, monsters, jinn, and other things. . . . Instead, try to make them improve their behaviour by stressing how Allah, The Most Glorious, loves people who do good and how He can punish those who do bad if He wants to.

"2. {sic} Emphasize, while disciplining young children, that they are not to hit a Muslim, but rather forgive, and are only to get their anger out on the enemies of Allah who fight against Muslims. . . .

---

[29] Um al-Shahid/Shaid is a pseudonym ("Mother of a Martyr").

"3. Eliminate your television and video games completely if you can (these things mostly teach shamelessness, anarchy, and random violence). . . . In addition to the largely damaging content of TV in general, another of its negatives is the laziness and passiveness that it breeds, and the mental and physical loss that it contributes to. . . .

. . . .

"5. Only if you have acted upon items 3 and 4 above, it is a good idea to start your children young in terms of introducing them (through safe toys) to target-shooting. . . . This can be done through toy guns and toy military sets, as well as by engaging in sports that develop good hand-eye coordination, such as darts and archery. . . . play military games with them in a fun way, and get them interested in these (as opposed to other largely useless, but very popular games and sports), then that will insha'Allah be counted as Jihad in itself. . . .

. . . .

"7. Get your young children interested in Jihad by getting military books (preferably with pictures) and other similar books, CDs, videos, and by visiting web sites . . . and encourage them to become like these people at the least." (Sister AI, 2001)

". . . If young children can learn the names of all the Pokemon characters, surely they can learn some basic terminology related to Jihad." (Sister AI, 2001)

Killing Muslims

Killing Muslims is expressly forbidden in the Qur'an. For this reason, there has been great controversy over jihadi attacks that kill Muslims. The response of jihadis is that these Muslim casualties are "collateral damage" or "human shields" that cannot be avoided. Moreover, jihadis argue that many so-called Muslim casualties are really apostates and heretics who deserved to be killed. This is part of the rationale used by Sunnis in Iraq for attacking Shi'as. See Chapter Eight for a discussion of the Sunni-Shi'a conflict.

"One of the great principles of our faith is that we should not spill even a drop of Muslim blood unjustly, for the end of the whole world is less significant than the spilling of one Muslim's blood." (Abu Maysara, 2005a)[30]

"'The shedding of Muslim blood . . . is allowed in order to avoid the greater evil of disrupting jihad." (al-Zarqawi, 2005c)

"We heard from some Mujahideen during discussions on this matter that demonstrated that they did not care about casualties in the ranks of the general Muslims. They say that most of these casualties are from the sinful Muslims, those helping the occupation, or from the innovators whose belief was wrong. To others, whether right or wrong in their descriptions, all this talk is wrong, being impermissible originally, and should be avoided. No good scholars said the blood of people like this is permissible." (al-Hukaymah, 2006)

"The legitimacy of these [means] has been established even if [their use] results in the killing of a number of Muslims even if it is known that they are likely to be there at the time, for whatever reason. This is justified under the principle of Dharura [overriding necessity], due to the fact that it is impossible to avoid them and to distinguish between them and those infidels against whom war is being waged and who are the intended targets. Admittedly, the killing of a number of Muslims whom it is forbidden to kill is undoubtedly a grave evil; however, it is permissible to commit this evil – indeed, it is even required – in order to ward off a greater evil, namely, the evil of suspending jihad. To claim that [such means of war] are not permissible here, especially in light of the present form of fighting, means inevitably suspending jihad and stopping it – indeed, burying it alive and completely shutting the gate of jihad. . . .

"The Evil of Heresy Is Greater Than the Evil of Collateral Killing of Muslims

"Islamic law states that the Islamic faith is more important than life, honor, and property. Indeed, it is the most important of the five inalienable rights,[31] and their very basis, and safeguarding it takes precedence over safeguarding them. It should be noted that all of these inalienable rights can not be safeguarded except through assuring the observance of the Islamic faith. . . ." (al-Zarqawi, 2005c)

---

[30] Abu Maysara is the pseudonym of a spokesman for both al-Qaeda in Iraq and the Mujahideen Shura Council, a conglomeration of Iraqi insurgent groups. He often posts claims of responsibility for insurgent attacks.

[31] The five inalienable rights in Islamic law are religion, life, honor, property, and the right to procreate.

"God knows that we were careful not to kill Muslims, and we have called off many operations in the past to avoid losses . . . but we cannot kill infidels without killing some Muslims. It is unavoidable . . . .

". . . killing of infidels by any method including martyrdom operations has been sanctified by many scholars even if it meant killing innocent Muslims." (al-Zarqawi, 2005c)

"The reasons justifying the killing of the Muslims who were killed collaterally in the bombing[32] are too long to be expounded in this brief book. We cede to those who have discussed the question in detail. Let us list the overall reasons and basic issues of the question only.

"The presence of Muslims in the complexes is beside the basic principle, which is that the legal status of the complexes was that of abodes of unbelief. This is because they were protected by force and because the precepts of Islam did not apply to them. The person carrying out the operation did not know about the presence of Muslims, though that was possible, as happens in most of the operations of the mujahidin in Chechnya, Palestine, Afghanistan, and elsewhere.

"If their presence in the complex had been known, the operation still would not have been prohibited. At best, the Muslims in the complex would have been like human shields by means of which the unbelievers shielded themselves. Indeed, a human shield would have had a better status inasmuch as he would really be compelled, while the persons in question were not compelled to enter the unbelievers' complexes." (Center for Islamic Studies and Research, 2003)

"'Killing Muslims who are acting as a shield is not the most preferable option, but is necessary if you must kill them to get at the enemy. If you do not kill the Muslim shield, the enemy will kill the Muslims anyway.' . . . 'restoring the religion is more important than restoring the soul.' . . . 'My killing Muslims . . . is defending ourselves. The purpose of this is to defend the whole nation from the enemy.'" (al-Zarqawi, 2005e)

"Brother Muslim: Don't ever come close to the sites of vice and infidelity so that you won't get hurt." ("Al-Qaeda Warns Sunni Muslims," 2005)

"Those amongst you, who are working for our enemies the Blasphemers, beware. Leave them for the safety of your Religion first, and your

---

[32] On May 12, 2003, suicide bombers targeted Western residential compounds in the Saudi Arabian capital, Riyadh, killing 34 people, including eight Americans.

own safety, in case the Jihad people target those blaspheming companies, enemies of the Muslims and collaborators in the war against Islam. We warn you against approaching the Blasphemers in this area, or else you shall receive their fate. Al-Qaeda already issued a warning stating that it will target companies that are run by the Blasphemers; in particular, the airline and oil companies will be targeted." (al-Amer, 2004)

"I will also stress what my brother Ali said in his letter, that we have not raised the banner of jihad to kill believers. Sound minds, not to mention proofs from religious law, refute this charge against us.

"How could we leave, suffer hardships, face dangers and strife, and leave our country, an easy life, and safety, to go to Afghanistan, Chechnya, Bosnia, Somalia, Kashmir, and other Islamic lands? Why did we go there despite all the hardships and dangers?

"We went there to defend the honor, religion, and security of Muslims, to protect their lives, and to set our blood before their blood. Is it logical that we would ransom people far away with our blood, risk our necks for them, and then decide to terrorize our own people closest to us and shed their blood?" (al-Ayiri, undated, in Center for Islamic Studies and Research, 2003)

Killing Innocents

In response to the attacks on the World Trade Center in New York, the bombings in Madrid and London, and the wholesale killing of Shi'a in Iraq, differences have erupted between jihadis and other Muslims over the religious legitimacy of targeting innocent people. The response of the jihadis has been threefold: First, jihad requires attacking unbelievers; second, the targets are not innocent, because by voting and paying taxes, they support governments that have anti-Islamic policies; and third, under Islamic law, there is no such thing as an infidel civilian. The Shi'a fall into the category of "innocents," since Jihadis in Iraq do not regard them as Muslims.

"There is no such thing as an 'innocent' kafir, innocence is only applicable for the Muslims; do not say 'innocent' for the kafir, the most you can say for them is that they are 'victims.' The Muslim however, is innocent even if he engages to fight and conquer the kafir, because he is fulfilling the shari'ah." (al-Muhajiroun, 2004)

"Islamic history has no term for 'civilian' in the Western sense. This is a Western term. In our Islamic rules of war, one can be a 'combatant,' a 'non-combatant,' or 'protected by an agreement.' A person can be a combatant even if he does not carry a weapon. In other words, a person who came to wash and cook for the American soldiers in order to free them to fight – like the Nepalese – such a person is considered a combatant.

. . . .

"If they say that you have killed children and the prophet has spoken against doing that, you tell them, yes we know that the prophet has spoken against it. We never targeted kids, we have repented if we ever did that but you insist on the sin and the wrong. Tell them we do not need your advice. How can you speak on behalf of children and you are making them orphans and killed their fathers for being in Jihad? You have fought the faith of God while the Mujahidin have fought the enemies of God. You have killed the faith with your corrupt school curriculums that taught them loyalty to you and taught them against their faith and Jihad.

"All the Zionist people are combatants in the field of battle." (Yassin, undated(b))[33]

"[Bin Laden:] We kill the kings of the infidels, kings of the crusaders, and civilian infidels in exchange for those of our children they kill. This is permissible in law and intellectually.

"Q: So what you are saying is that this is a type of reciprocal treatment. They kill our innocents, so we kill their innocents.

"Bin Laden: So we kill their innocents, and I say it is permissible in law and intellectually, because those who spoke on this matter spoke from a juridical perspective." (bin Laden, 2001a)

"I agree that the Prophet Mohammed forbade the killing of babies and women. That is true, but this is not absolute. There is a saying, 'If the infidels killed women and children on purpose, we shouldn't shy way from treating them in the same way to stop them from doing it again.'" (bin Laden, 2001a)

"Many Islamic scholars have ruled in favor of the symmetry of revenge. The West has killed thousands of Muslim civilians, and so Muslims are allowed to kill Western civilians, and there should be no doubt." (Anonymous, 2005b)

---

[33] Yassin was head of Hamas until he was assassinated by the Israelis on March 22, 2004.

"Which religion considers your killed ones innocent and our killed ones worthless? And which principle considers your blood real blood and our blood water? Reciprocal treatment is fair and the one who starts injustice bears greater blame." (bin Laden, undated(a))

"The problem {of criticism for killing innocents} lies with the religious scholars. When they are asked to confront these [Mujahideen], to talk with them and respond to the evidence they present. [The Mujahideen] tell {how} the Prophet drove nails into and gouged out the eyes of people from the 'Urayna Tribe. They were merely a group of thieves who stole from sheep herders, and the Prophet drove nails into them and threw them into the Al-Hrara area, and left them there to die. He blinded them and cut off their opposite legs and arms. This is what the Prophet did on a trifling matter – let alone in war. What else could they do when a 1000 lb. bomb lands on a house or a shack belonging to poor people, and the world doesn't shed a tear, but cries only about the slaughtering? All they have is a knife." (al-Siba'i, 2005)

"There is no doubt that God has commanded us to target the unbelievers, and to kill them and fight them with every means that can accomplish this goal. Even if the means does not distinguish between the intended warring unbelievers and unintended women and children, as well as those among the unbelievers whose intentional killing is not permitted." (al-Zarqawi, undated(c))

"We used to start our day by watching a slaughter [beheading] scene, for it is no secret to the knowledgeable that it stimulates and appeases the contents of the chests. . . . Until the Mujahideen stopped for a while. . . . We are eagerly waiting for [the comeback of] these blessed operations. . . . By Allah, many of those who suffer from high blood pressure and diabetes have complained about the cease of these operations, for they were tranquilizing them. . . . Someone told me, and I believe he speaks the truth, that he does not eat his food until he has watched a beheading scene, even if it were replayed or old." (Anonymous, 2004b)

Beheadings and the killing of innocents provoked an interesting debate between Zarqawi, on the one hand, and Zawahiri and Maqdisi, on the other. It was particularly noteworthy since Maqdisi was Zarqawi's first jihadi "mentor." Zawahiri won the debate over televised beheadings, and they largely stopped. But Zarqawi prevailed on the killing of innocents (e.g., Shi'a), hence the sectarian conflict in Iraq.

"Among the things which the feelings of the Muslim populace who love and support you {Zarqawi} will never find palatable – also – are the scenes of slaughtering the hostages. You shouldn't be deceived by the praise of some of the zealous young men and their description of you as the shaykh of the slaughterers, etc. They do not express the general view of the admirer and the supporter of the resistance in Iraq, and of you in particular by the favor and blessing of God.

"And your response, while true, might be: Why shouldn't we sow terror in the hearts of the Crusaders and their helpers? And isn't the destruction of the villages and the cities on the heads of their inhabitants more cruel than slaughtering? And aren't the cluster bombs and the seven ton bombs and the depleted uranium bombs crueler than slaughtering? And isn't killing by torture crueler than slaughtering? And isn't violating the honor of men and women more painful and more destructive than slaughtering?

"All of these questions and more might be asked, and you are justified. However this does not change the reality at all, which is that the general opinion of our supporter does not comprehend that, and that this general opinion falls under a campaign by the malicious, perfidious, and fallacious campaign by the deceptive and fabricated media. And we would spare the people from the effect of questions about the usefulness of our actions in the hearts and minds of the general opinion that is essentially sympathetic to us.

. . . .

"And we can kill the captives by bullet. That would achieve that which is sought after without exposing ourselves to the questions and answering to doubts. We don't need this." (al-Zawahiri, 2005b)

"I say this and stress it, as I listen to and follow the rampant chaos occurring today in Iraq, the goal of which is to disfigure [the image of] jihad and its shining image through [the use of] car bombs, the emplacement of improvised explosive devices on main thoroughfares, and firing mortar rounds and such at streets and markets and other such places where Muslims generally congregate. The pure hands of the jihad fighters must be kept clean of the blood of immune souls, even if they are sinners or lechers. . . .

"One matter that is worth indicating is the necessity for caution against entanglement in selecting means [of warfare] that are improper for the jihad fighter, as part of the reactions to the crimes of the tyrants. . . . An example of this is when the jihad fighter crosses the lines set by the Sharia by kidnapping or killing a Muslim, citing non-Sharia excuses such as the claim that [the individual] was employed by the unbelievers, [when the victim was only employed] in a manner that cannot be regarded as supporting the infidels or assisting in doing harm to Muslims." (al-Maqdisi, 2004)

"We are certain that, in our fight against the armies of apostasy, we will be faced with strong condemnation from the naïve among the people of this nation. In their faulty reasoning, they ask, 'How can a jihad fighter fight against his brother, his cousin, and his tribesman?' Do they not realize that the Prophet started first his fight against those who would stand in the way of the religion [who were] of his people, even before he fought against the Byzantines,[34] and that the companions followed in his footsteps?. . .

. . . .

". . . would that our imams and our preachers, if they do not deploy themselves to support the meek, and if they do not dedicate their speech to fight the enemies of the faith, would stay their tongues from attacking the jihad fighters, and refrain from providing aid to the Crusaders and the apostates." (al-Zarqawi, 2005d)

Goals

One of the curious things about jihadism is the notable lack of articulated political or social goals beyond implementing shari'a law. The election slogan of the Muslim Brotherhood in Egypt, "Islam Is the Answer," seems to suffice for jihadis.

Even such jihad writers as Sayyid Qutb focus their analyses on the shortcomings of other ideologies rather than explicating how their philosophy would translate into government structures and economic and social policy. As one jihadi notes, referring to Abu Bakr Naji's "The Management of Savagery," it is as if they are not really interested in governing, but only in waging jihad (Wright, 2006, p. 56). Bin Laden's only evident policy impact on the Taliban was in persuading them to blow up the historically priceless Bamiyan Buddhas.[35]

This is not to say that jihadis have no goals at all and are merely nihilists. Bin Laden reportedly was recruited into jihadism by others who played on his outrage over the presence of U.S. forces in Saudi Arabia. As they have evolved, jihadi ambitions have become both concrete and clear, even if their global goal is far-fetched. The first

---

[34] See al-Asfar, undated.

[35] These were the largest bas relief statues in the world, created in the third century and on the UNESCO list of world historic treasures. There was a world outcry when the Taliban destroyed them in March 2001 at the urging of Osama bin Laden.

objective is to expel the United States from Iraq and establish an Islamic state there. The jihadis would then act to push the United States and the West out of all Muslim lands and undertake the overthrow of "apostate rulers." Along the way, Israel would be destroyed, as would, presumably, the Shi'a. Finally, after a period of global warfare, the Islamic caliphate would rule the world. What this caliphate would look like is unclear. Despite the sense of loss of the Ottoman caliphate, jihadis typically denounce the Ottomans as corrupt and decadent, so that is not their likely model. It seems that both the caliphate of the Salaf and the global caliphate the jihadis wish to create are shrouded in myth. Nonetheless, one jihadi writer has put forward a 20-year plan for achieving this goal, which began September 11, 2001 (Wright, 2006). This millennial vision is no less ambitious than the 20th century totalitarian movements that preceded jihadism.

> ". . . To you I say that, yes, al-Qa'ida does not have a political program that is compatible with the international order, simply because the international order does not recognize us as an independent Islamic state. It forces us to revolve in its orbit, to go along with its secular systems, and to be under its military control.
>
> "Al-Qa'ida refuses this absolutely, and believes that this international system must be removed from the region and defeated militarily first, then the Islamic state must be re-formed in accordance with the Islamic system. This means that we will control our destinies, that we will rule ourselves, and that we will control our own wealth. In other words, we will reorganize our lives in accordance with our fundamental principles. This is a real experiment that has existed for 1,300 years; the peoples of the East ruled themselves and lived according to their own systems before the Western presence in the region, so there is no barrier that should prevent the return and resurrection of these systems that are based on the Qur'an and the Prophet's tradition.
>
> . . . .
>
> "In other words, any political program will not succeed unless we can defeat the West militarily and culturally, and repel it from Muslim lands. At that time, it will not be difficult for the nation—with its great energies and vast wealth—to re-form its life in accordance with the fundamentals of Islamic Sharia. In fact, we will become the masters of the world because the economic destiny of the world will be tied to us and to the riches that the world needs, which we hold. All components of world domination are available to us, but we are yet to live free and

rule ourselves by ourselves, away from the West and its proxies." (Allah, 2003)[36]

"The goals of the world jihad movement in its war with the United States have been clear from the beginning. . . .

"A halt to all forms of support for the Jewish state that has usurped Palestinian land; ending the embargo on all Islamic peoples, and first among them the Iraqi people; withdrawal from all Muslim lands, and first among them the land of the two holy places; a halt to support for the tyrants whose rule oppresses Muslim peoples." (Seif al-Din al-Ansari, 2002d)

"Therefore, the main target of the jihad and the jihad fighters is to strike against the foundations and the structure of the Western colonial project—what may be called the 'world order'—or, in clearer terms, to defeat the Crusaders in the battle which has continued for more than a century. Their defeat means, simply, the cancellation of all forms of nation-statehood, leaving only the natural state accepted by Islam." (Allah, 2003)

"What I seek is what is right for any living being. We demand that our land be liberated from enemies. That our lands be liberated from the Americans. . . .

"Let us take an example of poultry. Let us look at a chicken, for example. If an armed person was to enter a chicken's home with the aim of inflicting harm to it, the chicken would automatically fight back." (bin Laden, 1998b)

"Liberating the Muslim nation, confronting the enemies of Islam, and launching jihad against them require a Muslim authority, established on a Muslim land, that raises the banner of jihad and rallies the Muslims around it. Without achieving this goal our actions will mean nothing more than mere and repeated disturbances that will not lead to the aspired goal, which is the restoration of the caliphate and the dismissal of the invaders from the land of Islam.

"This goal must remain the basic objective of the Islamic jihad movement, regardless of the sacrifices and the time involved." (al-Zawahiri, 2001)

---

[36] Louis Attiya Allah is the alias of a Saudi who is a leading al-Qaeda ideologue. His writings have appeared on the Internet since September 11, 2001, and since the killing of Sheikh Yousef al-'Ayyiri, Allah is probably the most popular al-Qaeda ideologue. He took the name "Louis" as a prank while entering the United States.

"Look! As grandsons of Muhammad, God's prayer and peace be upon him, we have returned determined to restore our caliphate. Although the conspiracy and deception continued for 13 centuries, from the emigration of our prophet, God's prayer and peace be upon him, to the downfall of the Ottoman Caliphate, we will continue our endeavor until we restore what has been lost and revive our state and caliphate. . . . The caliphate we are working to establish cannot be compared with any known man-made political system." (Ibrahim, 1984)

". . . The tendency of the Arab and Islamic world is to unite the street on the basis of Islam. If Europe, which has a history rich in internal wars and various ethnic groups, has united economically, legally, and politically, why can't a nation with a single culture, language, history, and religion unite under a single flag?!" (al-Zahar, 2005b)

"The establishment of a Muslim state in the heart of the Islamic world is not an easy goal or an objective that is close at hand. But it constitutes the hope of the Muslim nation to reinstate its fallen caliphate and regain its lost glory." (al-Zawahiri, 2001)

"Covert and open Islamic groups have been trying for decades to establish the Islamic state, and so far they have made no progress, not even a single step, in this area. [This], while Jihad for the sake of Allah has managed to establish blessed states and entities that defended the Muslims and succeeded in applying Islamic Shari'a law for certain periods. The state of Sheikh Muhammad bin Abd Al-Wahhab [Saudi Arabia] arose only by Jihad. The state of the Taliban in Afghanistan arose only by Jihad. The Islamic state in Chechnya arose only by Jihad. It is true that these attempts were not perfect and did not fill the full role required, but incremental progress is a known universal principle. Yesterday, we did not dream of a state; today we established states and they fall. Tomorrow, Allah willing, a state will arise and will not fall . . . ." (al-Sa'di, 2004a)[37]

"It will be the beginning of an all-out war between two camps: the powers of belief and the powers of global infidelity. The stage of total confrontation will begin immediately after the declaration of the Islamic state. . . . The means of the Islam state and its capacity to recruit and to make preparations will be great and immense. In par-

---

[37] Abu Abdallah al-Sa'di is an al-Qaeda–affiliated ideologue and contributor to al-Qaeda in the Arabian Peninsula's online magazine *Sawt al-Jihad (The Voice of Jihad)*.

ticular so, because at this stage there will be more than 1.5 billion Muslims. This will cast terror in their enemies and cause them to withdraw rapidly." (Hussein, 2005)[38]

"We once ruled the world and the day will come when, by god, we will rule the entire world. The day will come when we will rule the United States, the day will come when we will rule Britain, we will rule the whole world, [and all will live in peace and comfort under our rule] except the Jews. The Jews will not live in peace and comfort under our rule. Treachery will keep being their nature throughout history. The day will come when the whole world will rid itself of the Jews. . . ." (Mudeiras, 2005)

And sometimes the dreams of the future are an occasion for fantasy.

"Listeners! The Moslems in Denmark make up three percent [of the population], yet constitute a threat to the future of the Danish kingdom. It's no surprise that in Bitrab (the ancient name of Medina, a city in Arabia to which Mohammed emigrated) they were fewer than three percent of the general population, but succeeded changing the regime in Bitrab.
    "It's no surprise that our brothers in Denmark have succeeded in bringing Islam to every home in that country. Allah will grant us victory in their land to establish the [Islamic] revolution in Denmark. . . .
    "They [the Danes] will fight against their Scandinavian neighbors in order to bring the country into the territory of the revolution. In the next stage, they will fight a holy jihad to spread Islam to the rest of Europe, until it spreads to the original city of Medina where the two cities will unite under the Islamic flag." (Amira, 2005)

This statement (above) may reflect one source of the ethnic tensions that led to the Danish cartoon episode, which received widespread attention.

". . . It is high time that Rome had its cross uprooted and the city decked out for the arrival of the new conquerors, passing through Al-

---

[38] Fuoad Hussein is a Jordanian journalist and radical who has interviewed a number of al-Qaeda ideologues and other prominent jihadi thinkers.

Andalus[39] and the Pavement of the Martyrs {Balat al-Shuhada}[40] and Vienna[41] and Constantinople, to which we are yet drawn by a longing that grows in our breasts day by day. For our Prophet (who does not lie when he speaks, being the most truthful of speakers) did promise: 'God hath set aside for me the world, and I beheld its east and western lands, and the dominion of my Nation shall reach unto that which was set aside for me.'" (*Al-Jama'a*, 2004)

"Thus, Muslims can have only one goal: converting the entire humanity to Islam and 'effacing the final traces of all other religions, creeds and ideologies.'" (al-Ayerri, 2003)[42]

". . . Our call is to make the word of Allah the highest, and the Shari'a will rule the East and West of the earth, to wipe out unbelievers wherever they are and in any form." (*Highest Intuition*, 2005)

---

[39] Al-Andalus is the historical Islamic term for Spain, preserved in the present-day province of Andalucía. The author is recalling "unfinished work." (*Al-Jama'a*, 2004, fn4)

[40] Balat al-Shuhada is the village near Tours in France where the Muslim conquerors led by Abd al-Rahman al-Ghafiqi were halted by the Merovingian Charles Martel in 732 AD, marking the furthest point of Muslim expansion in western Europe. (*Al-Jama'a*, 2004, fn5)

[41] The Ottoman army was halted at the gates of Vienna in 1683, marking the furthest extent of Islam in eastern Europe. (*Al-Jama'a*, 2004, fn6)

[42] Yussuf al-Ayerri (also known as Abu Muhammad), a Saudi citizen, was one of Osama bin Laden's closest associates, dating back to the early 1990s. He was killed in a gun battle with security forces in Riyadh in June 2003.

CHAPTER FIVE

World View

The ideology of jihadism is accompanied by somewhat unique perceptions of various aspects of the world, its institutions, its history, and the motives of major players on the world scene. It is not possible to say whether the perceptions shaped the ideology or vice-versa. Certainly, some jihadi views are propaganda and deliberate distortions of reality. But other distortions are matters of deeply held belief. Either way, they tend to reinforce the jihadi totalitarian and conspiratorial mindset. It is also true that many jihadi views on certain issues are shared by a large number of non-jihadis—the Israel/Palestine conflict being the most prominent. However warped the jihadis' perceptions may be, they are based on a quite sophisticated knowledge of the West.

A Clash of Civilizations

Leaders in the United States and Europe go out of their way to deny the prospect of a clash of civilizations between Islam and the West, while jihadis earnestly seek such a conflict and portray it as inevitable.

> "It is true there will be a clash of civilizations. The argumentation is correct that there will be a clash between Islam and the infidels. There is no [example] of Islam and infidels, the right and the wrong, living together in peace." (Ba'asyir, 2005)

> "The war of cultures started long before the attacks and before Huntington and Fukuyama. This war existed since the existence of Infidels and Faithful. The crusades and the massacres against the Muslims by the Jews and Christians can be seen everywhere." (Abu-Firas, 2004, in al-Maqdisi, undated(b))[1]

---

[1] Abu Firas was a 10th-century Arab knight and poet who wrote a series of famous *habsiyahs* (prison poems) while imprisoned by the Byzantines.

Islam Under Threat

A frequently stated jihadi belief that falls into the category of both perception and propaganda is that Islam is under attack by the West in general and the United States in particular. This is a key tenet of the jihadis' ideology, because, as pointed out in the previous chapter, they assert that when Islam is defending itself, jihad is the personal obligation of every Muslim man, woman, and child. It is important to note that while jihadis cite many cases of Muslims being attacked (in the Philippines, Indonesia, Afghanistan, Iraq, and other areas), many of the attacks have been the result of provocations by jihadis themselves. Moreover, in some of the attacks, such as those in Bosnia, Kosovo, and arguably Iraq, the United States and the Europeans were on the side of the Muslims. Nonetheless, the jihadi argument that Islam is under assault taps into a deep feeling among Muslims that the West disrespects Islam, as evidenced by the Danish cartoon episode and the reaction to the September 12, 2006, speech of Pope Benedict XVI. This feeling is reinforced by jihadi authors' frequent drawing of explicit parallels between today and the Crusades.

> "Wherever you turn your gaze to Islam,
> You find it is as a bird with broken wings." (al-Salim, 2003)

> "The battle today cannot be fought on a regional level without taking into account the global hostility toward us." (al-Zawahiri, 2001)

> "We Muslims are besieged by many forces that want to uproot the Muslims under various pretexts – the pretext of terrorism, the pretext of fundamentalism, this pretext or that pretext. The goal is to fight this nation. They want to eradicate the nation of Islam." (al-Qaradhawi, 2005)

> "In short, the world is witnessing at the hands of Western civilization the most insolent and malevolent colonial barbarian attack known to history, whose leadership has devolved to a gang of Crusader would-be Zionists in the American administration. It is possible to say that these 'Third Crusader Campaigns,' if this expression is permissible, is a continuation in a malicious and organized form of the two campaigns that preceeded it – the first during the 11th and 12th Christian centuries, and the second which spanned from the 17th century until the middle of the 20th century." (al-Suri, 2005)

> "The Americans' intentions have also become clear in statements about the need to change the beliefs, curricula, and morals of Muslims to become more tolerant, as they put it. In clearer terms, it is a religious-

economic war. They want the believers to desist from worshipping God so that they can enslave them, occupy their countries, and loot their wealth." (bin Laden, 2004a)

"The sultan is mischievious.[2] He uses his intelligence services and his resources to lure the 'ulama. He offers to work with them to initiate reform. After the 'ulama fall in his hand, they become accustomed to seeing sins. They redefine the forbidden and the permissible." (Muhammad Surur and Zayn al-Abdin, unknown, in al Rasheed, 2007)

"Experience has taught us, and events have given us the knowledge, that the disease afflicting these {Middle} Eastern nations assumes a variety of aspects and has many symptoms. It has done harm to every aspect of their lives, for they have been assailed on the political side by imperialist aggression on the part of their enemies, and by factionalism, rivalry, division, and disunity on the part of their sons. They have been assailed on the economic side by the propagation of usurious practices throughout their social classes, and the exploitation of their resources and natural treasures by foreign companies. They have been afflicted on the intellectual side by anarchy, defection, and heresy which destroy their religious beliefs and overthrow the ideals within their sons' hearts. They have been assailed on the sociological side by lewdness of manners and morals, through the sloughing off of the restraints of the humanitarian virtues they inherited from their glorious, fortunate ancestors; while through imitation of the West, the viper's venom creeps insidiously into their affairs, poisoning their blood and sullying the purity of their well being." (al-Banna, undated(c))

"We stand before a military invasion armed with the newest military instruments and scientific technology, equipped with the most destructive strategic and security plans and policing devices; whereby, their tanks convey to us programs for social, religious, and cultural transformation comprised of methodologies for replacing the Islamic faith and fragmenting the popular elements of Arab and Muslim identity, programs for reshaping societies, intellectual and cultural elements, educational and research methodologies, and media programs." (al-Suri, 2005)

---

[2] Reference to the king of Saudi Arabia.

". . . the Zionist blueprint constitutes a danger to the entire Nation and not just the people of Palestine. Iraq was occupied because of a Zionist agenda that was placed on top of the American agenda. If Iran is hit this will happen as part of a Zionist agenda that has become an American agenda. Do not take the Zionist danger lightly because it does not menace only Palestine, Lebanon or the Ring States [surrounding Israel]. It is threatening all of you. The Western imperialist blueprint finds in American imperialism a tool to hit our Nation, wreck its unity and prevent its survival as a civilization." (Mish'al, 2005)[3]

"Our era is one of unparalleled ordeals and banishment for Islam. Exile and affliction have become the rule of the day. The entire world has become a battlefield. The hunt is on for those who hold fast to their faith and fight for it with word and with deed. The whole world has declared war on terror—read 'jihad'—and denounced all the forms of jihad that Muslims practice.

   "They have united against Islam. All of the infidel nations and their supporters have come together from near and far, banding together against the group that has, with God's aid, assumed the burden of a fierce, unflagging, brutal war against unbelief and the infidels to bring about the rule of God. They suffer no harm from traitorous, defeatist Muslims, nor from those who have sunk into the deep mire of this world, their foes in the infidel lands, or the fractious factions of apostates, falsifiers, and misguided heretics." (al-Salim, 2003)

"The western forces that are hostile to Islam have clearly identified their enemy. They refer to it as the Islamic fundamentalism. They are joined in this by their old enemy, Russia. They have adopted a number of tools to fight Islam, including:

(1) The United Nations.

(2) The friendly rulers of the Muslim peoples.

(3) The multinational corporations.

(4) The international communications and data exchange systems.

(5) The international news agencies and satellite media channels.

(6) The international relief agencies, which are being used as a cover for espionage, proselytizing, coup planning, and the transfer of weapons." (al-Zawahiri, 2001)

---

[3] Khalid Mish'al is the Hamas leader exiled in Syria.

"It should not be hidden from you that the people of Islam had suffered from aggression, iniquity and injustice imposed on them by the Zionist-Crusaders alliance and their collaborators; to the extent that the Muslims' blood became the cheapest and their wealth as loot in the hands of the enemies. Their blood was spilled in Palestine and Iraq. The horrifying pictures of the massacre of Qana,[4] in Lebanon, are still fresh in our memory. Massacres in Tajakestan, Burma, Cashmere, Assam, Philippine, Fatani, Ogadin, Somalia, Erithria, Chechnia and in Bosnia-Herzegovina took place, massacres that send shivers in the body and shake the conscience." (bin-Laden, 1996)

"My Muslim and Mujahid brothers, don't you see the Muslims being killed in Afghanistan and in Iraq?! Don't you see, on the television screens, the bereaved women crying out for the Muslims' help?! Don't you see the torn body parts of children, and their skulls and brains scattered . . . ?" (*Voice of Jihad*, 2004)

"Your [sic] are trying to divide us from each other with your dollars so that we forget our names and our memory in order to instill the evil you spread all over our land . . . so that our brother kills our brother, our father, our uncles. So that a son kills his father and his mother. Let me tell you: your hopes will be turned down, it will never happen. . . . We fear [only] Allah, the master of the universe who has shattered tyrants in times past and will do it [again] in the future.

"You come to us with your shame and ignorance. Allah will disgrace you, not welcome nor greet you." (al-Subh, 1998)[5]

"Q. What is the principle of Hudaybiyah [the covenant between {the} prophet Muhammad and the People of the Book]?

"A. Hudaybiyah means different things according to the legal situation. When Islam is strong, we come to the infidel's country, not to colonize but to watch over it so that the infidel cannot plan to ruin Islam. Everywhere, infidels conspire to ruin Islam. There is no infidel who wouldn't destroy Islam if they were given even a small chance. Therefore, we have to be vigilant.

"Q. What are the conditions for Islam to be strong?

---

[4] Qana is a village in southern Lebanon where, in April 1996, during fighting with Hezbollah, Israeli artillery struck a United Nations compound where hundreds of Lebanese refugees had taken shelter, killing 106 and injuring 116, along with four UN peacekeepers.

[5] Atallah Abu al-Subh is a columnist for *Al-Risala*, a weekly Hamas publication.

"A. If there is a state, the infidel country must be visited and spied upon. My argument is that if we don't come to them, they will persecute Islam. They will prevent non-Muslims converting to Islam." (Ba'asyir, 2005)

"Every Muslim is on one of the frontiers of Islam. Let him beware, lest Islam be attacked through him." (Shakir, undated, in Center for Islamic Studies and Research, 2003)[6]

"Every day we grow weaker and weaker. Every day America attacks us in another country, so what is preferable? That we act now while our veins still pulse, or that we wait until we see an American soldier arranging the worshipers' entrance into the mosque in Mecca . . . ?" (Yahyah bin Ali al-Ghamdi, 2004)

"A review of our current reality amid the neglect of God's laws—including jihad in the path of God—reveals the divisions, factionalism, and strife that have afflicted Muslims. This is nothing but a deviation from the true path and a failure to stand by the great creed. It has led to infidel hegemony over Muslim lands and an explosion of strife, division, and rancor among Muslims. This is what God has decreed for those who turn away from His laws and forget the fate He has spoken of in the Koran." (al-Salim, 2003)

"Muslims can never be defeated by others. We Muslims are not defeated by our enemies, but instead, we are defeated by our own selves." (Azzam, 1987)

History and Geopolitics of the Middle East

"If we look at the nature of the conflict between us and the West, we find that when they invaded our countries more than 2,500 years[7] ago they did not have a sound religion or ethics. Their motive was to steal and plunder. Our ancestors in Bilad al-Sham (Jordan, Syria, Lebanon, and Palestine) remained under occupation for more than 10 decades. We defeated them only after the mission of our Prophet Muhammad,

---

[6] Shaykh Ahmad Shakir was an Egyptian scholar and an expert in the oral traditions of the times of Mohammad (Hadith).

[7] The history described here is difficult to follow, but presumably he is referring to Alexander the Great, b. 356 BCE and d. 323 BCE.

may God's peace and blessings be upon him. It was the true commitment to Islam that reshaped the Arab character, liberated it from the pre-Islamic concepts, enlightened the hearts and minds, and released energies. Neither the Arabs nor anybody else could stand in the face of the battalions of faith at the time. The Persians, Tatarians, Turks, Romans, and Berbers collapsed in front of the shouts of God is great. We were the pioneers of the world. We rescued the people from worshipping people to worshipping the God of people, praise be to him." (bin Laden, 2004a)

"One of the Orientalists spoke truth when he said that had the Safavid[8] state not existed we [sic] in Europe would today be reading the Qur'an just as the Algerian Berber does. Yes, the hosts of the Ottoman state stopped at the gates of Vienna, and those fortifications almost collapsed before them [to permit] Islam to spread under the auspices of the sword of glory and jihad all across Europe. But these armies were forced to return and withdraw to the rear because the army of the Safavid state had occupied Baghdad, demolished its mosques, killed its people, and captured its women and wealth. The armies returned to defend the sanctuaries and people of Islam. Fierce fighting raged for about two centuries and did not end until the strength and reach of the Islamic state had waned and the [Islamic] nation had been put to sleep, then to wake up to the drums of the invading Westerner." (al-Zarqawi undated(a))[9]

"Why did the spread of the Islamic spirit come to a halt a short space after the time of the Prophet?

"Here again we must emphasize two historical facts:

"1. This halt was only partial, never complete; it never came to a complete stop on a particular day. It took place only in a limited sphere, that of politics. . . .

"2. The change that overtook the system and the development of politics—a partial change, as we have just said—was the product of an unfortunate mischance . . . .

---

[8] The Safavids were a dynasty uniting and ruling over Iran from 1501 until 1736. The Safavids were also in charge of establishing Shi'a Islam as the dominating religion in Iran (LookLex, an expansion of the *Encyclopaedia of the Orient*, online at http://www.i-cias.com/e.o/). Many historians believe that constant war between the Sunni Ottoman Turks and the Shi'a Safavid Empire in Persia so weakend both that the Ottomans were unable to capture Vienna and entered into a long period of decline, a decline that for the jihadis has lasted until the present.

[9] Zarqawi was making a historical argument against the Shi'a.

. . . .

"The first of these is to be found in the rise of Abbasid[10] state, with its reliance on elements newly converted to Islam. The attitude of these peoples to their new religion was never whole-hearted because of the national loyalties whose roots remained strong within them. As time went on, the Abbasid state deserted these elements on which it had been founded, and which were now beginning to acquire a tincture of Islam for others whose hearts were closed to Islam, Turks, Circassians, Dailamites and such like. So this dynasty continued to find its support in elements that were opposed to the spirit of Islam and to which it gave a favored position because it relied on them. . . .

"Then followed the destructive raids of the Mongols, bursting with savage ferocity on the Islamic world. Without delay Islam turned aside the force of the onslaught, swallowed it up, and assimilated it. Yet this was not accomplished without causing in the spirit of Islam itself a profound upheaval in which the practices and traditions of this religion were forcibly modified. . . .

. . . .

"As we trace the development further, in the West we find the disaster in Andalusia,[11] and in the East the disaster of the Crusades. In the first of these Islam was worsted, in the second it was victorious. But from that time to this it has had to contend with ferocious enemies of the same spirit as the Crusaders, enemies both open and hidden.

"But the final disaster to befall Islam took place only in the present age, when Europe conquered the world, and when the dark shadow of colonization spread over the whole Islamic world, East and West alike. Europe mustered all its forces to extinguish the spirit of Islam, it revived the inheritance of the Crusaders' hatred, and it employed all the materialistic and cultural powers at its disposal. Added to this was the internal collapse of the Islamic community, and its gradual removal over a long period from the teachings and injunctions of its religious faith." (Qutb, 1949, pp. 268–270)

---

[10] Abbasids (from *Encyclopaedia of the Orient* (http://www.unc.edu/awmc/encyclopediaoftheorient.html)): Caliphate dynasty ruling from 750 until 1258. The Abbasids claimed to descend from Abbas, an uncle of Muhammad. The Abbasids governed from Baghdad, a city founded by the second Abbasid caliph in 762, and from Samara during portions of the 9th century. The Abbasids took over from the Umayyads in 750 and stayed in power until the Mongols conquered Baghdad in 1258 and had the caliph killed.

[11] Islamic forces under General Tariq ibn-Ziyad invaded the Iberian peninsula in 711. The Muslims were expelled by Christian forces under Ferdinand and Isabella in 1492.

"Europe had always looked to Byzantium as a relic of the glory of ancient Greece and Rome and had regarded it as the fortress of Europe against Asiatic barbarism. Hence, with the fall of Constantinople[12] the gate was thrown wide open to the flood of Islam. In the centuries that followed, and which were filled with wars, the hostility of Europe to Islam was no longer a question of merely cultural importance; it was now a question of political import also. And this fact further increased the violence of that hostility." (Qutb, 1949, p. 271)

"As everyone knows, they [the quisling[13] Arab countries] entered the First World War on the British side and fought against the Ottoman caliphate. Britain rewarded them with imperialism—it gave Palestine to the Zionists, transferred the Arab's natural wealth to the West, and oppressed the Islamic peoples. The same holds true for their alliance with the United States against Iraq. They were rewarded for the Madrid Conference and the Oslo agreements. They are the allies of the United States and the children of Zion against the mujahidin in Palestine and Afghanistan, and we see their reward in the current straits of the quisling Arafat, the Egyptian quisling, the Saudi quisling . . . [ellipses as published]." (Abu Ayman al-Hilali, 2002)[14]

"This is a recurring war. The original crusade brought Richard [the Lionhearted] from Britain, Luis from France, and Barbarus from Germany. Today the crusading countries rushed as soon as Bush raised the cross. They accepted the rule of the cross." (bin Laden, 2001a)

"The United States, and the global Jewish government that is behind it, have realized that [government by] Islam is the popular demand of the nations of this region, which is considered the heart of the Islamic world. They have realized that it is impossible to compromise on these issues. Hence the United States has decided to dictate its wishes by force, repression, forgery, and misinformation. Finally it has added direct military intervention to all the foregoing methods.

"This policy, no matter how long it persists, is a short-term policy that will necessarily provoke repeated eruptions. However, what other alternative do the United States and Israel have? Allowing the fundamentalist movement any degree of freedom will shake the pillars of

---

[12] On May 29, 1453.

[13] Quisling: traitor. Coined in reference to Norwegian fascist politician and Nazi collaborator Vidkun Quisling.

[14] Abu Ayman al-Hilali is a Saudi member of al-Qaeda who served as an interpreter for bin Laden.

the pro-US regimes. Hence, a decision has been made to resort to the [repression by force] policy . . . . This provides a future guarantee for Israel's security. Nevertheless, history gives the lie to all such plans, for the Crusaders stayed in Greater Syria for 200 years but then had to leave even though they were a model of a settler occupation just like Israel today. Likewise communism was consigned to history and pursued by curses after 70 years of oppression, obliteration of identity, and population transfers." (al-Zawahiri, 2001)

". . . and at a time when our wounds have not yet healed in the aftermath of the Crusades against the Islamic world during the last century, and as a result of the Sykes-Picot agreement[15] between Britain and France that led to the partition of the Muslim world into pieces and disembodied limbs, and which the agents of the Crusaders still rule today, a new Sykes-Picot agreement looms: the Bush-Blair agreement, which is under the same standard and purpose. It is the standard of the Cross, and the purpose is to crush and rob our beloved Prophet's nation, peace and blessings upon him.

"The Bush-Blair agreement claims that it aims to destroy terrorism, but it is now clear to everybody, even the general public, that it seeks to destroy Islam." (bin Laden, 2003b)

"For a long time, the enemies [the Jews] have been planning, skillfully and with precision, for the achievement of what they have attained. They took into consideration the causes affecting the current of events. They strived to amass great and substantive material wealth which they devoted to the realisation of their dream. With their money, they took control of the world media, news agencies, the press, publishing houses, broadcasting stations, and others. With their money they stirred revolutions in various parts of the world with the purpose of achieving their interests and reaping the fruit therein. They were behind the French Revolution, the Communist revolution and most of the revolutions we heard and hear about, here and there. With their money they formed secret societies, such as Freemasons, Rotary Clubs, the Lions and others in different parts of the world for the purpose of sabotaging societies and achieving Zionist interests. With their money they were able to

---

[15] The Sykes-Picot agreement was a secret political agreement signed by Britain and France on May 16, 1916, near the end of World War I, to work together to divide up the territories of the Ottoman Empire and put them under British and French control—in effect, making them colonies. Under the League of Nations, these divisions were "mandates" under which Britain and France were to prepare the new nations for self-government, something that did not happen until after World War II.

control imperialistic countries and instigate them to colonize many countries in order to enable them to exploit their resources and spread corruption there.

"You may speak as much as you want about regional and world wars. They were behind World War I, when they were able to destroy the Islamic Caliphate, making financial gains and controlling resources. They obtained the Balfour Declaration,[16] formed the League of Nations through which they could rule the world. They were behind World War II, through which they made huge financial gains by trading in armaments, and paved the way for the establishment of their state. It was they who instigated the replacement of the League of Nations with the United Nations and the Security Council to enable them to rule the world through them. There is no war going on anywhere, without having their finger in it." (Hamas, 1988)

"As you may recall, the [Muslim] nation had made several attempts in the recent decades to resist the Zionist-Crusader alliance to liberate Palestine. The republics and kingdoms embraced several earthly religions in the region, like pan-Arabism, socialism, communism, democracy, and other doctrines. These material forces have proved beyond any shadow of doubt that they surrendered to the US-led Crusader-Zionist alliance. The people followed these forces for a long time only to find they are still at square one. We have had enough of chasing mirages." (bin Laden, 2004a)

"Since the collapse of the Soviet Union, one superpower has been leading the world: the United States. Students of history know that two powers have dominated the world in all ages, except in few eras mentioned in history and expositions, like the eras of Solomon, Dhu-al-Qarnayn, Al-Namrud, and Alexander. The fact that two powers checked each other in the world was a mercy from God to humanity. The Almighty said, 'And did not God check one set of people by means of another, the earth would indeed be full of mischief.'

. . . .

---

[16] "His Majesty's Government view with favour the establishment in Palestine of a national home for the Jewish people, and will use their best endeavours to facilitate the achievement of this object" (Balfour Declaration, 1917). As of February 14, 2008: http://www.mfa.gov.il/MFA/Peace%20Process/Guide%20to%20the%20Peace%20Process/The%20Balfour%20Declaration)

"We live in an unstable international situation or more correctly in a transitional period to which the rules applied in normal conditions do not apply. It also does not have the prerequisites to survive for long.

". . . The United States, which has become the uncontested sole superpower, is adapting to the situation. It got rid of the restrictions, which the conflict with the Soviet Union had imposed on it, and adopted a new policy. This policy is summed up in taking a direct approach to secure its interests in the world without regard to the interest of others, because it considers itself the sole power in the world and the world should adapt to what it wants." (Center for Islamic Studies and Research, 2003)

Colonialism

Since the time of the Prophet, the Middle East had been the province of empires and caliphates, based in Damascus, Cairo, Baghdad, and Istanbul. In the 19th century, the Arabs, restive under the control of the Ottoman Turks, sought their own nation. In World War I, the British and the French promised the Arabs independence for fighting on the allied side. Instead, they ended up dividing the territories of the Ottoman Empire into "mandates," which they ran.

In World War II, the Arabs were again promised independence, but many of them distrusted that promise, and a number looked to Nazi Germany as a possible liberator. With the advent of the United Nations, and under pressure from the anti-colonialist policy of the United States, the war-weary British and French withdrew, leaving the administrative boundaries of their mandates to become national borders. Jihadis such as Ayman al-Zawahiri argue that direct colonialism was replaced by "veiled" colonialism, under which puppet governments ruled the Middle East in the interest of one side or another during the Cold War. Thus, America was labeled colonialist as well.

"The Muslim countries range between those occupied by military armies that shed the blood of their people every day, violate their honor, and commit crimes that no Muslim would accept for his Muslim brother and countries colonized through agent local governments, which carefully carry out the plans of colonialism that the colonialists themselves are unable carry out.

"The Muslim countries, which are in this state, need the jihad more than water or food, because jihad is the shari'ah solution. It is the duty of every Muslim." (Center for Islamic Studies and Research, 2003)

"The governments in the Muslim lands are no more than flags put by the Crusaders before leaving to keep a watchful eye on the Muslims so

they don't have a government which brings back the glory of Islam."
(Mustafa, undated)[17]

"Colonialism is either direct or veiled.

. . . .

"The past century was the century of the direct colonization of the
Muslim countries, under which they languished for many years. This
was a time when the Islamic World had reached the highest degree of
ideological deviation, polytheism, and disregard for jihad. Colonialism
could not find any significant resistance in most countries, particularly
at the beginning.

"Toward the end of the colonialist era, the colonialist countries were
no longer able to bear the painful blows they received from the mujahidin in the colonized countries. . . .

"At this stage, Zionism intervened and put its touches on a colonialism that would ensure the interests of the colonialists and save them
from the predicament that they faced. . . . The colonialist plans did
not change. The colonialists changed the face of their policies. Why
could they not respond to the wishes of the resistance men and remove
their men with the blue eyes and the blond hair from their midst and
replace them with people of their kind who spoke their language and
wore lambskin over wolf hearts?

. . . .

"It is important to know that the colonialist enemy might give
up veiled colonialism and establish, through its armies, explicit colonialism when there is little fear of resistance or the agent leadership
could not achieve the interests of colonialism or had deviated—even
in a small way—from its hegemony. For this reason, the United States
chose to invade Iraq militarily and might choose to invade any Muslim
country near or far from Iraq at any time." (Center for Islamic Studies
and Research, 2003)

"Except for Israel, which is in fact a huge US military base, the United
States did not resort in the past to conspicuous and intensive military
presence to run its affairs in the Middle East until the second Gulf war
erupted. When that happened, the United States rushed to the region
with its fleets, its land troops, and air power to manage its own affairs
with its own hands under the shadow of its own guns.

---

[17] Abu Ibrahim Mustafa was the pseudonym of Nabil Sahraoui, the leader of the Algerian jihadi group Salafist
Group for Prayer and Combat (GSPC)—today, al-Qaeda in the Islamic Maghreb. He was killed by the Algerian
army in June 2004 after serving as leader for approximately one year.

"With this conspicuous US military presence, several new facts emerged including, first of all, the transformation of the United States from a mover of events from behind a veil to a direct opponent in its battle against the Muslims. Formerly, in both the Arab-Israeli conflict and in managing the internal affairs of other countries, the US administration used to portray itself as an impartial party, or at least as an indirect opponent that merely—as the US alleges—furthers the values of democracy, liberty, and Western interests. Now, however, the role of US power has become clear in attacking Iraq, defending the oil sources, and managing security affairs in some Arab countries." (al-Zawahiri, 2001)

"One of the most important tools to control countries of the world was the World Trade Agreement[18] project, which was the hanging rope for the economic independence of any state and its liberation from American hegemony." (Center for Islamic Studies and Research, 2003)

Globalization

"In light of globalization/Americanization, everyone agrees that the Arab and Islamic countries have submitted to US-Zionist hegemony. They remain colonies." (Abu Ayman al-Hilali, 2002)

"The {U.S.} strategy's key elements are as follows:

"• Economic globalization links the global economy to the United States for ultimate control over capital through the World Trade Organization, transnational corporations, the IMF, and the World Bank.

"• Political globalization entails direct political interference in various countries, the division of the world into geopolitical regions, the creation of a strategic framework based on vital interests, the imposition of economic sanctions on those who resist (under the pretext that they practice terror, human rights violations, and political despotism), and protection for the children of Zion and all of their allies through the veto weapon . . . [ellipses as published]

"• Educational globalization involves direct intervention in curricula to shape minds and raise people with US values. Egypt is a living example. USAID has given 90 billion pounds to the Egyptian regime over

---

[18] The World Trade Agreement was an agreement to liberalize trade among 123 countries. It was the culmination in April 1994 of the Uruguay Round of trade-liberalization negotiations, which also created the World Trade Organization to enforce the agreed-upon trade rules.

the last 25 years and $185 million to education since 1981, along with specialists, programs, and advice.

"• Cultural globalization imposes the United States' culture and way of life through US schools and restaurants . . .[ellipses as published]

"• Security globalization entails coordination between all international intelligence agencies to strike at anyone who lets himself be seduced by the CIA into attacking them.

. . . .

"The advocates of globalization/Americanization are not content with their own blatant corruption and atheism. They want to impose it by force on all humanity, including those who have accepted God's law and implemented it on their land like the Taliban movement. . . . This is what the infidel United States does with its definition of terrorism, peace, and justice. With its policies, it sets itself up as a rival to God in His magnificence, greatness, rule, and law.

"The United States is the enemy of God's faith and Muslims. It is fighting against them." (Abu Ayman al-Hilali, 2002)

"The Islamic nation is struggling against globalization, and it continues with its negative attitude towards Western rhetoric and explanations. The Westerners' rage increased once it became clear to them that [Muslims] could use the same computers that they did without espousing the same values. Against all their assessments, [Islamic] culture cannot be shattered by technology." (al-Qurashi, 2002a)

"My brothers, its easiest and the best translation that everybody can understand will be that the Koran is world order [preceding two words in English]. Allah sent the Koran to the world so that its order [preceding word in English] is enforced. There should be no other order, American or any other system, in the presence of the Koran." (Saeed, 2005)

Nationalism

The nation-state—a sovereign geographic and political unit based on shared ethnicity, language, or the history of its people—is a modern Western concept that evolved out of feudal structures such as monarchies. In the Middle East, the idea of the nation-state was imported along with the reality of colonialism, under which the mandated powers drew lines in the desert defining their domains. Even when ruled by empires, the people of the region had a sense of locality based on the principal cities:

Baghdad, Damascus, Jerusalem, and of course, Cairo, with its millennia-old continuity as a political entity.

The first "independent" Middle East states were monarchies, but by the 1950s, they were increasingly being replaced by republics waving the flag of new national identities—Egyptian, Syrian, Iraqi, Libyan. Even the surviving monarchies—Jordan and Saudi Arabia—worked to create a national ethos. But national identity based on geographic borders was always at odds with Arab ethnicity and language, and with Islam, which knew no such boundaries. To resolve this contradiction, the first Egyptian President, Gamal Abdul Nasser, pushed pan-Arab socialism and created the United Arab Republic by joining with Syria. (Pan-Arabism also had its antecedents in Europe, including pan-Slavism, which helped precipitate World War I.)

Pan-Arabism proved to be a chimera, but nation-states endured, despite being new and based on arbitrary boundaries. They gained solidity because they conferred legitimacy and power on local ruling elites. To this must be added the fact that the new Arab capitals were historic political centers. However, the success of these governments, measured by the living standards of most of their populace, has been meager. Not only are jihadis trying to exploit the resulting discontent, they are doing so by tapping into the popular feeling (despite the failure of Pan-Arabism) that all Arabs and all Muslims (i.e., Sunnis) are one nation.

> "Ejection of the occupier from Islamic lands means simply canceling all borders and all forms of nation-statehood created by the West. This means that when jihad is enjoined in, for example, Iraq, it will not stop at the colonial borders. It will not stop at the borders of Jordan and accept it as a separate entity, because there is no such entity as the state of Jordan in the Islamic concept. The jihadi movement in the Arabian Peninsula will not stop at the borders of the so-called Kingdom of Saudi Arabia, because that entity is an artificial one that has no legitimate or legal reality that would prevent the movement of the jihad outside of it to Yemen, for example, or the so-called 'Gulf States.' All of these forms of nation-states have no meaning or immunity that prevents their dissolution when the jihad moves." (Allah, 2003)

> "You are wrong if you think that it was only the Egyptian spy[19] who was slain. No, for among those who fell to that happy dagger were a mighty infidel tyranny and an idol [nationalism, Pan-Arab nationalism and patriotism] who is worshipped instead of Allah; did you not see this as he was slain?!
>
>   . . . .

---

[19] President Anwar Sadat of Egypt, who was assassinated on October 6, 1981.

"And these are the lessons we learned: The collapse of the national identities. When these are opposed to the Shari'a [Islamic religious law] or attempt to rival it, and when they cause division among people and [provide a basis for] allegiances, then these national identities should fall, and Arab nationalism {should be} first and foremost." (al-Shamari, 2004)

"People must be warned of the error of the claim by some leaders about the need to preserve the national fabric, national cohesion, or national unity. Not only is there a suspicion of infidel nationalism in this claim, it indicates that they have no understanding of God's habitual way of causing civilizations to rise and fall.

. . . .

"This is a view shared by not a few of the pious who do recognize the boundaries between the Islamic states, boundaries created by colonialism. In other words, the modern territorial state created by colonialists on the eve of the First World War had no attraction and still has none." (al-Zahrani, 2004)

"The bone of contention between us and them [secularists] is that while we define patriotism according to the creed of Islam, they define it according to territorial borders and geographical boundaries. For every region in which there is a Muslim saying: 'There is no god but Allah, and Muhammad is the Messenger of Allah,' is our homeland . . . . All Muslims in these geographical regions are our people and brethren: we are concerned about them, and share their feelings and sensitivities. Advocates of patriotism alone are not like this, since all that concerns them lies within a specific and narrowly defined region of the earth. This obvious difference is manifested whenever any nation desires to expand itself at the expense of others, for we would not approve of this at the expense of any Muslim nation. We only seek power so that we may all share it. But the advocators of fanatical patriotism see {a} problem in this; and as a result, bonds of amicable relationship are snapped, power is dispersed, and the enemy strikes out by pushing each one against the other." (al-Banna, undated(c))

United Nations

The Middle East has had extensive experience with the United Nations, from the partition plan that legitimized the establishment of Israel, to the refugee assistance organizations for the Palestinians, to the peacekeepers and the observer/monitors who have sought to stabilize the region.

"With respect to the United Nations, it is merely a Crusader-Zionist tool even though it might seek cover by offering some relief work. Which organization handed over Palestine to the Jews other than the United Nations? Which organization brought about the secession of East Timor other than the United Nations? Which organization justified the Iraq embargo and the killing of more than 1 million children other than the United Nations?" (bin Laden, 2004c)

"The talk about the United Nations as an independent party ruling the world is nonsense. Perhaps the United Nations was a body whose judgment was sought and accepted by the nations that established it, including the United States. However, today, it is a toy in the hands of World Zionism. The United States ignored the United Nations when it shyly opposed its invasion of Iraq. Three Crusader countries officially participated in the war with it, disregarding the UN resolutions.[20]

. . . .

". . . they [present Arab rulers] agree in their covenants to the legitimacy of the United Nations. All their covenants are a practical application of their joining these United Nations and membership in its idolatrous pact, which is not based on the choice of every covenanter, but is an imposition by the United Nations, to which they have agreed to grant legislative power to interdict and criminalize, to forbid and command. They have the right to fight anyone who refuses to enter it and sign its unbelieving terms. The least of them in terms of unbelief is their agreement not to discriminate between Muslim and unbeliever and to deny matters known to be necessary parts of religion; indeed, they have deemed them to be among the things that they have agreed among themselves to be crimes: for example, terrorism, under which head they have classified fighting by Muslims against unbelievers for a religious reason." (Center for Islamic Studies and Research, 2003)

". . . I pray to God—after having granted you success in destroying the dead, deaf, and mute false gods [ancient Buddhas of Bamiyan] – that He will grant you success in destroying the living false gods, the ones that talk and listen. God knows that those [gods] pose more danger to Islam and monotheism than the dead false gods. Among the most important such false gods in our time is the United Nations, which has become a new religion that is worshipped to the exclusion of God.

---

[20] There was no UN resolution against the invasion. The United States argued that UN Resolution 1441 was sufficient to authorize an attack on Iraq. It sought another, more explicit resolution but failed to obtain one.

The prophets of this religion are present in the UN General Assembly. . . . The UN imposes all sorts of penalties on all those who contradict its religion. It issues documents and statements that openly contradict Islamic belief, such as the International Declaration for Human Rights, considering all religions are equal, and considering that the destruction of the {Bamiyan} statues constitutes a crime . . . ." (bin Laden, 2001, in Cullison, 2004)

"The United Nations is a crusader's establishment that legislates for the humiliation of Muslims, the strikes on them, and their fragmentation. Its funds and the blood of everyone who works in it are sanctioned [allowed] to every Muslim." (Abu-Hafs al-Masri Brigades (Al-Qa'ida), 2004)

"After Europe endured the crushing miseries of war between its mosaic of peoples, certain Western thinkers arrived at the idea of world peace. This suggests that this is a Western idea that resulted naturally from European life. Certain Arab intellectuals who are capable only of copying and following imported this idea and popularized it in Arab and Islamic intellectual circles. It has not yet gained a foothold in the real world, however. Instead, it has remained a theoretical construct that has not prevented war or established peace.

"All of the institutions that have been founded to advance this goal were merely an obedient tool in the hands of powerful countries, which use them as another means of imposing their political agenda. The League of Nations failed to achieve any of the goals it was founded to achieve. The United Nations is nothing but a tool to domesticate Muslims and train them to submit gradually to the goals of the Zionist and crusader project. 'The modern age we live in confirms this truth to us. Suffice it to say that imperialism grew strong only through the treachery of international institutions' (Musa, 1984). This means that world peace as it is conceived of in the West is an 'idealistic' idea that political leaders exploit to lull their people into a stupor. Strong countries repeat the idea to rob others of their will to fight jihad.

"Most of the governments oppressing the Islamic community have participated in this deception. They popularized this myth through their official media with made-to-order intellectual products until 'peace' became the only strategic option. They abolished all alternatives so that they are no longer taken into consideration. They told people that any option other than peace is a form of recklessness, or even barbarism unworthy of civilized men. This well-planned brainwashing operation aims to undo the idea of the enemy and make the Islamic community easy prey." (Seif al-Din al-Ansari, 2002d)

". . . they [infidels] call something 'internationally banned,' 'contrary to legitimate international authority,' 'forbidden by international law,' 'in violation of the Charter of Human Rights,' or 'in violation of the Geneva Convention,' and so forth.

. . . .

"All these terms have no standing in Islamic law, because God Almighty has reserved judgment and legislation to Himself." (al-Fahd, 2003a)

Zionism

Even after the expulsion of the Jews from Palestine by the Romans in 70 CE, a small number of them always lived in the region, which was principally populated by Muslim Arabs, with a sizable number of Christian Arabs. But starting in the 1880s, increasing numbers of Jews emigrated to Palestine, most of them fleeing from oppression and violent pogroms promoted by Czarist Russia. This "return to Zion" movement was supported by the World Zionist Congress, which met for the first time in 1897. Zionism was one of the nationalist movements in Europe that sought to create ethnicity-based nation-states out of the prevailing Austro-Hungarian, German, Ottoman, and Russian Empires. (In the Balkans, this struggle precipitated World War I.) For the Jews, this movement faced the additional obstacle of their not having a homeland to begin with.

In 1917, Britain committed itself, under the Balfour Declaration, to bringing about a "national homeland" for Jews in Palestine. The British motives were a complex amalgam of good intentions, wartime diplomacy, and imperial interests. There had long been a genuine desire to respond to the aspirations of the Jews for a nation of their own (Britain had offered Uganda to them in 1908). The Balfour Declaration helped build support for Britain in World War I, particularly in the United States. (Germany was rumored to be contemplating a similar move.) Finally, Britain wanted to stymie French control of the area. It imagined establishing a protectorate over the Jewish homeland which would serve as a base from which to defend the Suez Canal.

When the Ottoman Empire was divided into mandates by the League of Nations, Britain got Palestine, which it soon divided into two parts, making everything west of the Jordan River Trans-Jordan. The rise of nazism between the wars increased the flow of Jews from Europe and led to rising tensions with the Arab population, and Arab riots against the Jews broke out in 1920 and 1929. Arab nationalism was also on the rise, and on the eve of World War II, the Palestinian Arabs revolted. To placate them, Jewish settlement was severely restricted. Subsequently, to secure Arab support during the war, the British promised independence after the war—which the Arabs believed included Palestine.

But after the Holocaust and the end of the war, the trickle of Jewish immigrants became a tidal wave. British forces tried to stop it, but in the face of growing violence, Britain decided that when its mandate expired in 1947 it would not seek its renewal. Thus the problem was dumped into the lap of the fledgling United Nations. The Security Council called for the partition of the Holy Land. Jewish leaders accepted the UN plan, but the Arabs did not. When the British mandate ended, Israel declared its independence. Its Arab neighbors attacked but were unable to defeat the Israeli forces. Hundreds of thousands of Palestinian Arabs fled the fighting and became refugees. In June 1947, a ceasefire was declared, and the resulting line between Israeli and Arab forces came to be known as the Green Line.

The end of the fighting left Jordan in control of the West Bank and the old city of Jerusalem. Syria seized the Golan Heights, and Egypt seized the Gaza Strip. These areas were retaken by Israel in the 1967 Six Day War, along with the Sinai Peninsula. This massive and decisive defeat of Egypt, Jordan, and Syria simultaneously (remembered by Arabs as "the catastrophe") seriously undermined the secular regimes and gave a boost to the Islamists. The capture of the Dome of the Rock in Jerusalem made the "liberation" of Palestine an issue for Muslims worldwide. In another war in 1973, Egypt regained part of the Sinai, and in the 1978 Camp David Accords brokered by the United States, it regained the rest of it for agreeing to peace with Israel. Under the accords, the Palestinian areas of the West Bank and Gaza were to become autonomous.

Israel, however, continued to occupy large areas of the Palestinian Territories, citing security concerns. Moreover, it began to build settlements on the occupied land. Israel's fears about security were exacerbated by attacks launched by the PLO, which was founded in 1964.[21] These attacks included the killing of Israeli athletes at the Munich Summer Olympics in 1972, aircraft and cruise-ship hijackings, and a three-year uprising (Intifada) which started in 1987.

In the Oslo Accords, in 1993, Israel and the PLO agreed on the establishment of a Palestinian Authority and a phased withdrawal of Israel from the West Bank and Gaza. This and subsequent efforts to move toward a peace agreement with Israel were resisted in a campaign of violence by extremists, principally the Islamist Hamas organization, which introduced the wholesale use of suicide bombings against civilians.

Hamas, an offshoot of the Muslim Brotherhood in Egypt, was founded in December 1987. It is a Salafist and jihadi organization—but rather than emphasizing the restoration of a universal Muslim caliphate, Hamas focuses on destroying Israel and establishing an Islamic state on the territory of Palestine. In 2001, following the

---

[21] "Founded in 1964 as a Palestinian nationalist umbrella organization dedicated to the establishment of an independent Palestinian state" (http://www.fas.org/irp/world/para/plo.htm).

failure of the Camp David negotiations, Hamas led a second Intifada with the acqui-escence of Yasser Arafat and the PLO. Israel responded to the accelerating suicide bombings by reoccupying the West Bank and Gaza.

After the death of PLO leader Yasser Arafat, another opportunity for a negoti-ated peace seemed to emerge, but in Palestinian elections in 2005, the corruption and ineffectiveness of the PLO caused its defeat. Hamas was elected to the control of the government, although PLO leader Mahmoud Abbas (aka Abu Mazen) retained the presidency. The United States, the European Union, and Israel refused to deal with the Hamas government and cut off all aid to Palestine, demanding that it reject terrorism, accept Israel's right to exist, and abide by previous agreements of the Pal-estinian Authority. However, contacts continued with Mahmoud Abbas.

Israel withdrew from Gaza unilaterally in 2005, and the struggle for control between Hamas and the PLO intensified. In 2007, Hamas routed PLO fighters and seized full control of Gaza. President Abbas labeled this a coup d'état and discharged the Hamas government. A government of technocrats has now taken its place, and a revived hope that a new opening for a negotiated peace has emerged.

> "The fact that must be acknowledged is that the issue of Palestine is the cause that has been firing up the feelings of the Muslim nation from Morocco to Indonesia for the past 50 years. In addition, it is a rallying point for all the Arabs, be they believers or non-believers, good or evil." (al-Zawahiri, 2001)

> "First of all, due to the colonialist, occupational, racist, and [plunder-ing] nature of Israeli society, it is, in fact, a military society. Anyone past childhood, man or woman, is drafted into the Israeli army. Every Israeli is a soldier in the army, either in practical terms or because he is a reservist soldier who can be summoned at any time for war. This fact needs no proof. Those they call 'civilians' are in effect 'soldiers' in the army of the sons of Zion.
>   "Second . . . as far as the people of Palestine are concerned, it [Israel] is a 'society of invaders' who came from outside the region – from Russia or America, from Europe or from the lands of the Orient – to occupy Palestine and settle in it . . . .
>   "Those who are invaded have the right to fight the invaders with all means at their disposal in order to remove [the invaders] from their homes and send them back to the homes from whence they came. . . . This is a Jihad of necessity, as the clerics call it, and not Jihad of choice." (al-Qaradhawi, 2003b)

> ". . . the amount of destruction done by Israel is much greater than the towers in New York." (Abu Firas, undated, in al-Maqdisi, undated(b))

"World Zionism, together with imperialistic powers, try through a studied plan and an intelligent strategy to remove one Arab state after another from the circle of struggle against Zionism, in order to have it finally face the Palestinian people only. Egypt was, to a great extent, removed from the circle of the struggle, through the treacherous Camp David Agreement. They are trying to draw other Arab countries into similar agreements and to bring them outside the circle of struggle." (Hamas, 1988)

"One of the most important objectives of the new Crusader attack is to pave the way and prepare the region, after its fragmentation, for the establishment of what is known as 'the greater State of Israel,' whose borders will include extensive areas of Iraq and Egypt, through Syria, Lebanon, Jordan, all of Palestine, and large parts of the Land of the Two Holy Places." (Osama bin Laden, 2003, in Hegghammer, 2006)

"Today it is Palestine, tomorrow it will be one country or another. The Zionist plan is limitless. After Palestine, the Zionists aspire to expand from the Nile to the Euphrates. When they will have digested the region they overtook, they will aspire to further expansion, and so on. Their plan is embodied in the 'Protocols of the Elders of Zion,'[22] and their present conduct is the best proof of what we are saying." (Hamas, 1988)

"The Zionist enemy cannot continue to bear the heavy costs of occupation. The Zionist entity cannot withstand a lengthy war. The Zionist entity does not bear a lengthy war of attrition. The Palestinian people, despite their losses, are capable of withstanding a long-term confrontation." (Khaled Mishal, undated)

"It is no longer a secret that the Zionists were behind the Nazis' murder of many Jews, and agreed to it, with the aim of intimidating them [the Jews] and forcing them to immigrate to Palestine. Every time they failed to persuade a group of Jews to immigrate [to Palestine], they unhesitatingly sentenced [them] to death. Afterwards, they would organize great propaganda campaigns, to cash in on their blood." (al-Rantisi, 2003)

"Hisham Sham'as: 'Israel should be completely wiped out, so the Palestinians will have a country to return to.'

---

[22] An infamous anti-Jewish fabrication by the Russian Secret Police in the 19th century used to justify pogroms against Jews, which ironically stimulated the first wave of Jewish immigration to the Holy Land.

"Mediator: 'If someone tells you this motto is unrealistic, how would you respond?'

"Hisham Sham'as: 'There is no such thing as unrealistic. Just as Israel . . . Just like Hitler fought the Jews – We are a great Islamic nation of Jihad, and we too should fight the Jews and burn them.'" (MEMRI, 2005)

"When we compare the Zionists to the Nazis, we insult the Nazis – despite the abhorrent terror they carried out, which we cannot but condemn. The crimes perpetrated by the Nazis against humanity, with all their atrocities, are no more than a tiny particle compared to the Zionists' terror against the Palestinian people." (al-Rantisi, 2003)

"The ingathering [of the Jews] from all corners of the earth on the land of Palestine is one of the signs of the Day of Judgment. . . . the goal of this ingathering is so that [it will be possible] to torment them, and ultimately to kill them, until the last of them is killed together with the false messiah." (Sheik al-Ghamdi, undated)

"The Western states tried for over two centuries to establish Israel. They considered its presence in the region a basic guarantee for serving the Western interests. Israel separates Egypt and Syria, the two major regions that for several years served as a wall of steadfastness against the Crusades and the Tartar conquests. Until this day they constitute a considerable human weight in the heart of the Islamic world.

"As for France, it has tried since the end of the 18th Century to establish Israel. Here are some examples:

"When Napoleon Bonaparte headed for Syria, following his invasion of Egypt, he failed to conquer Akko[23] in 1799. As a result, he issued his famous call to the Jews everywhere. His statement was distributed in Palestine as well as simultaneously in France, Italy, the German provinces, and Spain. This indicates that the issue was far greater than a local incident that Bonaparte faced, having failed to conquer the walls of Jerusalem. The statement said:

"'From Napoleon Bonaparte, the Supreme Commander of the Armed Forces in the French Republic in Africa and Asia, to the legitimate heirs of Palestine:

---

[23] Akko, or Acre, is in the Western Galilee district in northern Israel.

"'O Israelis; O unique people; the forces of conquest and tyranny have failed to deprive you of your origin and national existence, although they deprived you of the land of your ancestors.'

"'The neutral and rational observers of people's destiny, although they lacked the powers of prophets such as Isaiah and Joel, have realized the prophecies predicted by these prophets through their sublime faith; namely, that God's slaves (the word Israel in Hebrew means the slave of God) will return to Zion and chant. They will be overwhelmed with joy when they restore their kingdom without fear. Rise forcefully, O those expelled in the wilderness. You are facing a fierce battle waged by your people, after the enemy had considered the land inherited from the forefathers a booty to be divided among them as they wish.'" (al-Zawahiri, 2001)

"It brings us both laughter and tears to see that you have not yet tired of repeating your fabricated lies that the Jews have a historical right to Palestine, as it was promised to them in the Torah. Anyone who disputes with them on this alleged fact is accused of anti-Semitism. This is one of the most fallacious, widely circulated fabrications in history. The people of Palestine are pure Arabs and original Semites. It is the Muslims who are the inheritors of Moses (peace be upon him) and the inheritors of the real Torah that has not been changed. Muslims believe in all of the Prophets, including Abraham, Moses, Jesus and Muhammad, peace and blessings of Allah be upon them all. If the followers of Moses have been promised a right to Palestine in the Torah, then the Muslims are the most worthy nation of this." (bin Laden, undated(b))

Palestine

"The Islamic Resistance Movement [Hamas] believes that the land of Palestine is an Islamic Waqf[24] consecrated for future Moslem generations until Judgement Day. It, or any part of it, should not be squandered: it, or any part of it, should not be given up. Neither a single Arab country nor all Arab countries, neither any king or president, nor all the kings and presidents, neither any organization nor all of them, be they Palestinian or Arab, possess the right to do that." (Hamas, 1988)

"We do not and will not recognize a state called Israel. Israel has no right to any inch of Palestinian land. This is an important issue. Our

---

[24] A *waqf* is an inalienable religious endowment in Islam, typically devoting a building or plot of land for Muslim religious or charitable purposes.

position stems from our religious convictions. This is a holy land. It is not the property of the Palestinians or the Arabs. This land is the property of all Muslims in all parts of the world." (al-Zahar, 2005a)

"The US is unable to prevent the support of the Muslims from reaching Hamas because we do not receive the support of any country or organisation. We only have the donations we receive from Muslim individuals in every corner of the globe, and the US stands helpless with this type of aid.

"The US, however, can try to entice the Palestinian Authority against us, which is most troubling to us. We do not wish to enter into a civil internal war, for such a war is capable of wiping out the Palestinian existence and terminating the Palestinian cause in favour of the enemy. This was the reason we took the initiative to declare a temporary and conditional truce, with the aim of foiling the US-Zionist scheme." (al-Rantisi, undated)

"If I am killed there will arise a thousand like me." (Yassin, undated(a))[25]

"The effect of this humiliating limitation [Camp David Agreements[26]] was evident. After the peace treaty, Israel bombarded the nuclear reactor in Iraq, invaded southern Lebanon and placed an agent army there, occupied Dahlak island at the southern entrance to the Red Sea, increased its support for the secessionist movement in southern Sudan, and allied itself with Turkey to isolate Syria. It even suggested that Israel's security extends as far as Pakistan in the east, in a clear reference to the Pakistani nuclear program, which Israel considers a threat." (al-Zawahiri, 2001)

"Those who did not approve this accord [The Egyptian Israeli peace treaty] were nevertheless influenced by the fabrications made by those rulers [reference to Egyptian President Anwar Sadat] and said: 'The presence of the Jews on the land of Palestine has become an unavoidable reality that we must accept. The Ummah must now be prepared

---

[25] Ahmed Ismail Yassin was the founder and spiritual leader of Hamas, responsible for reviving and overseeing militant activity in the Gaza Strip. His title was "Supreme Guide." He was assassinated by Israel on March 22, 2004, following a suicide bombing that killed 10 Israelites and wounded 16.

[26] The Camp David Accords were signed by Egyptian President Anwar Sadat and Israeli Prime Minister Menachem Begin on September 17, 1978, following negotiations at Camp David. The two agreements were brokered by U.S. President Jimmy Carter and signed at the White House.

to deal with it!!' There are also those poor and defeated people who thought that this cursed accord will relieve their difficulties. The best of those people were crying: 'Land in exchange for peace.' All those people overlooked the fact that this is a matter of Kufr[27] and Iman[28] and that it is a trial from Allah to test His servants and to distinguish the wicked from the good, and to witness those who will give victory to the religion by sincerely fighting for Allah's Cause. . . ." (Sheikh Abu al-Waleed al-Ansari, undated)

"The establishment of a Palestinian state {The Palestinian Authority established in 1994 in the Oslo Accords is not a sovereign state} removed the issue from the hands of the confrontation states.[29] They established a state with an agent government headed by the most despicable agent in history: Yasir Arafat, who will receive what he deserves from God. The issue became secondary to the confrontation states. Attention was focused on the Palestinian state and its leadership. . . .

"When a Palestinian leadership assumed power and people started looking to it as the official mouthpiece of the Palestinian cause, the Palestinian leadership began playing its despicable historic role, which is to perpetuate colonialism and change the view and treatment of the usurping Israeli entity. It launched a peace process and established coexistence with Zionism as an established fact and as a neighbor with whom it must deal on this basis, even as it was killing Muslims everywhere and at any time." (Center for Islamic Studies and Research, 2003)

". . . the Zionists . . . who were not satisfied with all the treacherous deeds of the Palestinian Authority and with the repression of the Palestinian Mujahideen by Yasser Arafat and his [Palestinian] Authority in the days of the implementation of the Oslo Accords. The Jews were led by the repeated operations to bypass the collaborator [i.e. Arafat] and occupy the territories in order to punish the [Palestinian] Mujahideen by themselves. . . ." (Allah, 2004)

"Secularism completely contradicts religious ideology. Attitudes, conduct and decisions stem from ideologies.

---

[27] Kufr (kuffar) is an "infidel," a non-believer.

[28] Iman is a state of belief in God and other articles of faith, as well as actual demonstration of belief in practice and behavior.

[29] Neighboring Arab states that had declared their opposition to Israel.

"That is why, with all our appreciation for the Palestinian Liberation Organization – and what it can develop into – and without belittling its role in the Arab-Israeli conflict, we are unable to exchange the present or future Islamic Palestine with the secular idea. The Islamic nature of Palestine is part of our religion and whoever takes his religion lightly is a loser." (Hamas, 1988)

"We are against any economic cooperation with Israel. We want a local Palestinian economy so that others do not influence it. We want investment, but without kickbacks, bribes, and commissions. If we can make the interest rate zero in this economy, based on Arab, Islamic, and international investment, then this would be an achievement. We want to spread the culture of resistance. We want tourism, but tourism of a people that have dignity. We will change the names of the settlements to represent the martyrs who died attacking them. We will tell the tourists that the honest rifle was able to achieve victory." (al-Zahar, 2005a)

"The national interest demands that we not cooperate with Israel in the security, political, or economic sphere. Can we cooperate with the Zionist enemy against someone from among the Palestinian people, for example?! If so, what is the difference between us and anyone else? Is it conceivable for us to tie our weak economy to the Israeli economy – which the U.S. is helping with at least $3 billion a year – or should we link it with the economy of the Arab and Islamic peoples? . . . Should we buy a liter of gasoline from Israel at five shekels when we can buy it from Egypt for one shekel? The facts should lead us to cut off our relations with the Israeli enemy by all means. The question is whether to do this gradually or all at once. This will be determined according to the relationship between us and the Arab peoples. If such a direct relationship can be planned, it would be a crime to continue the relationship with Israel." (al-Zahar, 2005b)

"Imagine a people living over a limited area that is part of one of the world's big cities, yet despite siege and starvation they manufacture rockets. Some used to like {sic} down at these [Al-Qassam] rockets. But Sharon went down on his knees before them.[30] He feels their greatness and their effect, for they exceeded what is in the warehouses of our Arab and Islamic armies." (Mish'al, 2005)

---

[30] A reference to Israel's withdrawal from Gaza on September 12, 2005.

"Occupation always ended under pressure of force and resistance. This is the way people won freedom. . . . There is [sic] no people who won freedom without paying the price. Hence the Palestinian people are proceeding in accordance with the historical norms of popular uprisings and resistance of invading forces." (Mishal, undated)

"In truth, we [Hamas] are conducting the way of life of a religious state, and [what] our constitution [sets out] in matters of marriage, divorce, interpersonal relations, and commerce is based on the Islamic Shari'a. There are even many Islamic banks worldwide. What else is necessary in order to establish a religious state that [already] exists de facto in the home, the marketplace, the clinics, the schools, and everywhere else. It is a crime to portray us as a religious state in the sense connected to medieval European thought – when the religious state allied with the feudal [nobility], and collaborated with them in order to extort the poor and unjustly distribute resources in favor of the feudal [nobility] in Europe. This is why the people abandoned European feudalism – the religious state – and its allies, and became secular. We are not secular, and our state is not a religious state according to the European model. Our religion is completely different . . . ." (al-Zahar, 2005b)

"We [Hamas] are not a copy of the Taliban. . . . Among us, the percentage of educated women is higher than the percentage of educated men, and our leadership includes both men and women. We have political institutions that lead Islamic activities, and also women's organizations, student organizations, and institutions that provide services. Judge us according to what we [actually] are.

. . . .

"The Christians have lived in this land with full civil rights, and this is Islam's approach to them. They have had full civil rights, and there is no reason that they would not be entitled to participate [in the Hamas lists] as long as [they adhere to] Hamas' platform, which includes no corruption and no encouragement of corruption, no treason, and no collaboration with the enemy. The door is open not only to Christians, but to all independent factions and individuals who agree to the platform of reforms and resistance that we espouse. This is a platform that unites all those of Palestinian identity, within the country and outside it, Christians[31] and Muslims alike." (al-Zahar, 2005b)

---

[31] Christian Palestinians constitute 8.7 percent of the population of the West Bank and Gaza.

"He who claims there will be a lasting peace between us and the Jews is an infidel." (bin Laden, 2001a)

Democracy and Secularism

"There can be no doubt that one of the greatest dangers threatening the hegemony of Islam and Sharia rule in the community is the secularism that the United States will impose on the region by force. The crusaders have called for this secularism to be implemented throughout the Islamic world after the occupation of Iraq. By the will of God, they have never been closer to implementing their plan to move the Islamic world from dictatorship to democracy, which means swinishness in all areas of life.
. . . .

"One of the worst products of secularism is democracy, which abolishes the authority of the Sharia over society and opposes it in form and in content. The Most High said, 'The command is for none but Allah' [12:40]. Democracy says that the command is for none but the majority of the people.

"Secularism is about more than just democracy. Secularism involves the separation of religion and state. It operates on the principle, 'Render therefore unto Caesar the things which are Caesar's; and unto God the things that are God's.' They also call for hateful capitalism, the emancipation of women, equality between men and women, the equality of religions, and no differentiation between people on the basis of religion or creed. Secularism espouses absolute freedom—freedom of belief, freedom of worship, freedom of conduct, utterance, and action, freedom of knowledge, freedom in all things. The human being is transformed from a servant of God into a base animal. We see how they live today in the United States and in Europe—people in decay, unrestrained by any boundaries, serving only their desires, moved only by desire, opportunistic and ugly, driven only by self-interest, even at the cost of millions of human deaths. . . . We have here pointed out its main features. This great unbelief is what they are thrusting on the region as an alternative to Islam. Who stands ready to confront this unbelief? How can we stop its advance into the lands of Islam?" (al-Ayerri, 2003)

"Democracy is the vile fruit and illegitimate daughter of secularism, because secularism is a heretical school of thought that aspires to isolate religion from life or separate religion from state . . . and democracy is the rule of the people or the rule of the tyrants. But in any event, it is not the rule of Allah the Exalted, and it does not take the unswerving legislation of Allah into account at all unless it is first compatible with all the articles of the constitution, and then with the desires of the people, and even before that with the desires of the tyrants or the masses. . . ." (al-Maqdisi, undated(a))

"The arrival of democracy to the Muslim countries will constitute great corruption. Therefore, the Jihad warriors in Iraq must close ranks and swear allegiance to a general imam of the Muslims in Iraq to whom the rules of the Imama [imamate] apply, and who will be chosen by the Shura members, the Jihad warrior commanders, and the Ulema of the Muslims.

"But it is forbidden to hold general elections to choose the general imam or [to choose] members of the Shura council even in a country ruled by the laws of Islam, because these are the methods and ways of the infidel democratic regime, and [these methods] must not be associated with Islam.

. . . .

"Islam does not treat equally – either in this world or in the world to come – the wise and the ignorant, the Muslim and the infidel, the pious and the sinner. But the elected democratic regime treats all these as equal in the elections. . . ." (al-Sayf, 2004)

"First: Democracy is based on the idea that the people are the source of authority, including the legislative authority, through the selection of representatives of the people who act in their stead in the creation and adoption of laws. In other words, the legislator obeyed under democracy is mankind, not God. This means that, with regards to the creation of laws, and of permitting [certain actions] and prohibiting [others], man is deified, worshipped, and obeyed, not God. This is the essence of impiety, polytheism, and falseness because it contradicts the fundamentals of the religion, including the worship of one God—it involves making mankind God almighty's partner in the most divine of His authorities: ruling and lawmaking. God said: 'The decision rests with Allah only, Who hath commanded you that ye worship none save Him.' Yusuf: 40. And He said: 'nor does He share His Command with any person whatsoever.' Al-Kahf: 26. . . .

"Second: Democracy is based on the idea of freedom of religion and creed. Under democracy, a person has the right to believe whatever he pleases, to adopt the faith of his choice, and to revert to any religion whenever he wishes to do so, even if this apostasy leads to the abandonment of the religion of God almighty, to atheism, or the worship of [a false god] other than God. Beyond doubt, this is a matter that is in contradiction of many Sharia texts. A Muslim who reverts from his religion to disbelief shall be sentenced to death under Islam, as is set forth in the Hadith narrated by Bukhari and others: 'He who exchanges his religion, kill him.' [The hadith does not say] 'leave him be.'

. . . .

"Third: Democracy is based on the principle of considering the people to be the sole arbiter to whom all rulings and disputes must be submitted. If a dispute occurs between the governor and the governed, each of the two parties can threaten the other with recourse to the will of the people, so that the people may make a decision in the matter of their dispute. This is contrary to the rules of monotheism, which determine that the arbiter between disputing parties is God almighty, and no one else. . . .

"Fourth: Democracy is based on freedom of expression and speech, no matter what the expression is, even if it contains attacks and insults to God and the rules of the religion. In democracy nothing is sacred that cannot be addressed or insulted.

"Fifth: Democracy is based on the principle of separation of religion and state, politics, and life; 'What is God's is God's,' is reduced to worship at houses of worship. All other political, economic, social, and other aspects of life are the domain of the people. . . .

"Sixth: Democracy is based on the freedom to form groups and political parties, etc. regardless of the beliefs, thoughts, and moral standards of these groups. And this is not permissible under the Sharia. Among them is that this voluntary acceptance of the legitimacy of the impious parties includes an implicit satisfaction with disbelief, even if one does not explicitly say that one is satisfied with their freedom, the impiety, etc. . . .

"Seventh: Democracy is premised upon the acceptance of the opinion of the majority, and adoption of the wish of the many, even if the majority agrees to falsehood and open impiety. This is a wicked premise that must be rejected in its entirety, because what is right in Islam is what is in accordance with the Qur'an and the tradition of the Prophet, whether those who agree [with these sources of law] are many or few.

What is in contradiction of the Qur'an and the tradition is false, no matter if the entire population of the world support it. . . .[32]

"Among the things that attract attention and cause great wonder is that, no matter how poor the consequences that have been brought upon Muslims by experiments in democracy, which include weakness, disputes, separation, and conflict that have caused the larger group to splinter into many groups . . . Despite all of this and despite more that is shameful, there are people who still find democracy appealing. They defend it as though they were its progenitors. They love democracy in their hearts as the sons of Israel loved the [golden] calf in the past. . . ." (al-Zarqawi, 2005a)

"In this statement, we reveal some evidence of why democracy should be prohibited and why it stands in opposition to the religion of Allah:[33]

. . . .

"3.) The religion of Allah is complete, as are his Islamic laws comprehensive and complete. Therefore, casting ballots over his already known and established laws is considered to be among the worst of the forbidden acts. . . .

. . . .

"7.) Many people associate the concept of legitimacy with the idea of general elections, meaning that legitimacy is created by the people and not the laws of Allah. This is the greatest form of idolatry, the idolatry of democracy.

"8.) Democracy looks upon everyone as equals: the Muslim and the non-Muslim, males and females, the righteous and the evil, the educated and the ignorant. However, the laws of Allah do not look equally at all these groups. . . ." (al-Jaysh al-Islami fi Iraq, 2005)

"The fight for democracy and the democratic process in the Western world is rather a relative affair; or a gimmick to shore up the Western image. Interest or pressure groups are saturated with their vested interests; policies are being formulated by distinct and separate lobbying powers within parliament and among party stalwarts. In most cases, the locus of power has shifted to the Jewish Lobby. . . . Bribery financed and bogged down election campaigns, corruption decadence,

---

[32] As noted in Chapter One, there are many different understandings of the basic texts of Islam and no agreed mechanism for determining orthodoxy.

[33] This list has been edited to make it not redundant with the previous excerpt.

and amorality have had debilitating and deploring effects on, and influenced the complexion and outcome of elections." (al-Suri, 2005)

"Everyone must stop blaming the Taliban for things that in fact characterize the people of the West, who seek to turn the international community into a swamp of corruption and destruction, and to spread abomination and disease in the name of absolute freedom.

. . . .

"Three months ago, Sweden permitted men to marry men and women to marry women. Are these punishments the democracy that we want? Are these the laws that the Palestinian street looks forward to? Will we give homosexual and lesbian rights to a minority of emotional and moral perverts, or [will we {Palestinians} choose] the other law that awaits us? . . . We must choose the law we want: the law of the jungle, chaos, AIDS, and homeless people . . . or the law of justice and mercy that we so badly need?" (al-Zahar, 2005b)

"You politically criticize your rulers and talk of launching campaigns against them on the issue of rigging [elections] and other problems. For God's sake, straighten up. . . . These things happen because these drawbacks are inherent in the system. As long as this evil system remains in force, the evil will continue haunting the world." (Saeed, 2005)

". . . the most dangerous thing about the Greater Middle East plan launched by Bush, which deals with democracy and reform, is that it is a blackmail card against the regimes. The United States does not care about reform or democracy for us. The United States cares none whether it rides the saddle of democracy or dictatorship, provided that its interests are protected. It tolerates dictatorships that side with it and is angry with democracies if they oppose it. It is a card to blackmail the regimes. The United States knows that most of our regimes do not want change, reform, or democracy. The result—and we sample it in Palestine—is regrettably that in order to avoid the US wrath and sidestep change, reform and democracy, the regimes pay out of the Palestinian or Iraqi purse and pocket in order to avoid wrath or deflect pressures for reform at home {i.e., they support the United States on Iraq and the Israel/Palestine issue to avoid U.S. pressure for reform}." (Mish'al, 2005)

". . . Zionist organizations under various names and shapes, such as Freemasons, Rotary Clubs, espionage groups and others, which are all nothing more than cells of subversion and saboteurs. These organizations have ample resources that enable them to play their role in societies for the purpose of achieving the Zionist targets and to deepen the concepts that would serve the enemy. These organizations operate in the absence of Islam and its estrangement among its people. The Islamic peoples should perform their role in confronting the conspiracies of these saboteurs. The day Islam is in control of guiding the affairs of life, these organizations, hostile to humanity and Islam, will be obliterated." (Hamas, 1988)

"We should learn from the example of Algeria[34] that democracy is a fiction . . . designed to distract the energies of vigorous youth. . . . Algeria teaches us that the peaceful solution is a deficient one . . . and teaches us that hastiness for results causes reverses, and that progressing too soon from guerrilla warfare is a lethal mistake." (al-Sa'di, 2004b)

Natural Disasters

"The entire Islamic world overflowed with joy when Hurricane Katrina struck in America, which seemed to reel from the strength of the hurricane and went asking for aid from all the countries of the world. Broken and completely humiliated, George Bush, a fool who is being obeyed, announced his obvious incapability to deal with the wrath of Allah that visited the city of homosexuals.

"While Louisiana is trying to recover from the aftermath of Hurricane Katrina, another hurricane fiercely struck the state of North Carolina, on the Atlantic coast, but so far there have been no casualties or significant damage, as was expected. We hope that Allah will humiliate America with this hurricane to make it a lesson for whoever wants to listen.

"This is the end of the (Islamic) nation's weekly news summary from Sout Al-Khilafa." (Global Islamic Media Front, 2005a)

"I believe that the destructive hurricane [Katrina] which hit America, within its own house, was nothing but the result of a prayer of a father or a mother whose son was killed, or of a boy who became an orphan,

---

[34] In 1991, Algeria held an election which the Islamists won. The Algerian military voided the election, and an insurgency ensued in which jihadi groups were active. More than 100,000 people were killed in the violence. The major conflict has ended, but a few jihadi groups continue to fight, principally the Salafist Group for Preaching and Combat, which has ties to al-Qaeda.

or of a woman whose honor was violated on the lands of Afghanistan, Iraq or others." (al-Zarqawi, 2005e)

". . . Hurricane Katrina, which revealed to the entire world the great helplessness in dealing with the destruction caused by this hurricane, because of the tremendous attrition of the American army's resources in Iraq and Afghanistan. This hurricane has once again brought to mind the manifestations of racial discrimination among the American people . . . what is still to come will be even more terrible, Allah willing." (al-Zarqawi, 2005f)

"Musharraf addressed the nation last night. . . . He says that people should face the earthquake[35] with courage. I fear that these rulers are the reason for Allah's wrath. What were his words? He said face it courageously. O cruel people, how can you face Allah's wrath with courage? What kind of thinking is this?
    ". . . rulers and people need to eliminate this thinking and these beliefs in the anti-Allah. We need to bow before Allah, which will quell His anger. . . . There is no other solution if you want to save Pakistan from natural disasters and the enemies of Islam, India, the United States, all these cruel Jews, and the enemies of Allah." (Saeed, 2005)

"All praise to Allah he has his own plans. Maybe he is using us [victims of Kashmir earthquake] as an example, of a people who have not yet taken seriously the warning of Allah that our deeds are not good. We have been ignoring the cries of our brethren for too long now; we have not acted in time but Allah's warning has. This could happen to all of the Muslims tomorrow if we do not heed the warning. We will be proud to be the group of Muslims who sacrificed a generation for the good of others if Allah's warning works." (al-Marid, 2005)[36]

"Haven't they learned the lesson from what Allah wreaked upon the coast of Asia, during the celebration of these forbidden [things]? At the height of immorality, Allah took vengeance on these criminals.

---

[35] The major earthquake on October 8, 2005, in the Pakistan-administered disputed region of Kashmir.

[36] The concept of a wrathful God is also present in Judaism and among certain Christian fundamentalists.

"Those celebrating spent what they call 'New Year's Eve' in vacation resorts, pubs, and hotels. Allah struck them with an earthquake.[37] He finished off the Richter scale. All nine levels gone.

"Tens of thousands dead." (al-Munajjid, undated)

"To have the space shuttle crash in Palestine, Texas, with a Texas president and an Israeli astronaut, somebody might say there is a divine hand behind it." (al-Timimi, 2003b)

"There is no doubt that Muslims were overjoyed because of the adversity that befell their greatest enemy.

"The Columbia crash made me feel, and God is the only One to know, that this is a strong signal that Western supremacy (especially that of America) that began 500 years ago is coming to a quick end, God Willing, as occurred to the shuttle.

"God Willing, America will fall and disappear." (al-Timimi, 2003a)

"If we know that the hole in the ozone will weaken them, we would have worked hard on making it bigger." (Abu Firas, undated, in al-Maqdisi, 2004)

---

[37] The 2004 Indian Ocean earthquake, with a magnitude of 9.15, generated a series of lethal tsunamis on December 26, 2004, that killed approximately 230,000 people throughout the Indian Ocean basin.

CHAPTER SIX

Enemies

The jihadis have made no secret about who their enemies are—infidels in general, and Christians, Jews, apostate regimes, and Shi'ites in particular. This chapter focuses on how jihadis think about these enemies, with special emphasis on their views of the United States and the West. Chapter Eight discusses Shi'ites and Iran.

> "I say to the worshippers of the cross, to the sons of apes and pigs, the Jews, and to their lackeys, the infidels and apostates, in the East and the West – live in fear." (Abu Zubeida, undated)

> "The Americans, Jews, and the Crusader West are our enemies and they are combatants. They must be killed wherever they are caught. Arabs and Muslims who support them are considered to be like them and must be killed because they are apostates." (Abu-Hafs al-Masri Brigades (Al-Qa'ida), 2004)

> "All governments (adopting western democracy and/or members of the UN) in Muslim Land must be removed immediately. . . . Organizations such as the UN, IMF and World Bank are enemies to Islam and must be classified as enemy organizations." (Muslim Unification Council, 1999, policy statement, in Habeck, 2006)

Infidels

> "Jihad is waged to hurt the infidels. . . . Killing the infidels destroys them physically, taking spoils from them inflicts damage on their assets, and taking them captive or enslaving them injures their honor and morale. Such actions are viewed as deeds of righteousness. . . ." (al-Ali, 2006)[1]

---

[1] Hamed al-Ali is a Kuwaiti cleric who has provided both financial and ideological support for militant jihadism. He has issued fatwas in support of suicide attacks, explicitly including suicide airline crashes in the style of the

"The clash [between Islam and infidels] continues because of the deep-seated hostility between the two camps: 'for the unbelievers are unto you open enemies' [4:101]. This hostility is not a random state of affairs that results from personal considerations or temporary stands that depend on earthly calculations of profit and loss. It is an attitude toward Muslims that is firmly established in the souls of the infidels. It is automatically countered by hostility from Muslims toward the infidels. . . ." (Seif al-Din al-Ansari, 2002d)

"Dogs, like dogs, like other animals, are not assigned [religious] missions and commandments, and [religious prohibitions] are not forbidden them; they were created according to a particular nature, and they do not deviate from their nature. They are different from the infidel, who was created by Allah in order to worship Him and in order to believe in His monotheism, but who denied Him, and took other gods beside Him.

". . . the heresy of that infidel and his rebellion against the religion of Allah requires the permitting of his blood and [sanctions] his humiliation, and that his blood is like the blood of a dog and nothing more.

"What is said above is sufficient to cause the monotheist . . . to burn with desire for the blood of the infidel, to slaughter the enemy of Allah, and to cut him up into pieces. This is not strange at all." (Nasser al-Najdi, 2003a)

"Regardless of the norms of 'humanist' belief, which sees destroying the infidel countries as a tragedy requiring us to show some conscientious empathy and . . . an atmosphere of sadness for the loss that is to be caused to human civilization – an approach that does not distinguish between believer and infidel . . . I would like to stress that annihilating the infidels is an inarguable fact, as this is the [divine] decree of fate . . . ." (Seif al-Din al-Ansari, 2002c)

"There are two parties in all the world: the Party of Allah and the Party of Satan – the Party of Allah which stands under the banner of Allah and bears his insignia, and the Party of Satan, which includes every community, group, race, and individual that does not stand under the banner of Allah." (Qutb, undated(a))

9/11 attacks. He was implicated in involvement in a Kuwaiti terrorist cell in 2005 and was briefly arrested and designated a "terrorist facilitator" by the U.S. Treasury Department. Recently, he has spoken loudly against the threat of Shi'ites in general and Iran in particular.

"Several years ago, a sinful call arose, which unfortunately garnered support from some clerics and preachers of this religion, Islam . . . [a call] for the unification of the monotheistic religions. They flaunted an empty and false motto of 'religious harmony,' Christian-Islamic friendship, and uniting the three religions into a global religion' . . . .

"The call for the unification of the religions is a call for the abolition of religious differences among people: No more Muslim and infidel. All will come under the unity of human harmony. . . . This accursed call has ramifications that most certainly will shake Islam in the hearts of its people, leading them to the lowest of the levels of Hell. This call will lead . . . to presenting the infidels' schools of thought as correct, and to silence regarding them; to permitting conversion to Judaism and Christianity with no shame whatsoever; to the abolition of the vast difference between the Muslims and others – a difference underpinning the conflict between truth and falsehood; to the transformation of the religion of Islam into a religion like the other, false religions, into a religion that has no advantage over the other religions . . . ; to refraining from calling [people] to join Islam, because if the Muslim wants to do so, he must tell the truth about the infidels . . . .

"[This is] . . . a call to dismantle the pact among Muslims in all the corners of the Islamic world and to replace it with an accursed alternative harmony – the 'Harmony of the Jews and Christians.' This is, in truth, a call to Muslims to stop accusing Jews, Christians, and other non-Muslims of being infidels. . . ." (Siyami, 2004)

"The true goal of the People of the Book, whether Jews or Christians . . . is to lead Muslims astray from their religion to the religion of the People of the Book." (Qutb, undated(b))

"Are the Muslims enemies of the People of the Book [Jews and Christians], or do they exalt all the prophets, including Abraham, Moses, and Jesus? Are the Muslims indeed hostile to the Torah and the New Testament? The Muslims hold these books sacred, but have been demanding for 14 centuries that we provide the correct, original versions of these books, and it we [was] the Crusaders, who could not comply." (al-Zawahiri, 2005e)

". . . Our number-one enemy is the Jews and the Christians, and we must free ourselves to invest all our efforts until we annihilate them – and we are able do this if Allah allows us to do it – because they are the main obstacle to establishing the Islamic state." (al-Dosari, 2003b)

"Allah made annihilating the infidels one of his steadfast decrees. According to the [divine] natural law of alternating fortunes, Allah said: '[Allah will] obliterate the infidels' [Qur'an 3:141].

. . . .

"When we say that annihilating the infidel forces is a divine decree, it means that it is an immutable, valid law and a constant principle that does not change with time, place, people, and circumstances. As it existed in the time of Noah and Hud, so it exists in our time, and will exist also in the future. . . .

"As the decree of annihilation applies to the infidel forces in the previous nations, and none was saved from it, so will it apply to the infidel forces of our time, and none will be saved from it. That is, just as the country of Thamoud, the country of 'Aad, the country of Midian,[2] and other [countries] were annihilated, without a doubt the country of America and the country of the Jews will be annihilated. Moreover, all infidel countries will be annihilated, and with them all the pharaohs and the tyrants of the present time, whatever their elements of power and capability." (Seif al-Din Al-Ansari, 2002a)

"If they [the rulers or the government] don't take from the Qur'an laws [to live by] in their private and public lives and in the law with which they govern the land, are they infidels or not? . . . And if they are infidels . . . what is the difference between them and the Jews? And if they are like the Jews, then should we treat them and live with them as if they conquered our country and are governing us?" (Marwan Hadid, unknown, in McCants, 2006)

Christians

Muslims consider Jesus as one of their prophets, a very special one who will return on the Day of Judgment. However Jesus (Issa) is not a god to be prayed to—nor is he the son of God. This is considered *shirk* (denying that God has no partners) and polytheism.

"'From those, too, who call themselves Christians, We did take a covenant, but they forgot a good part of the message that was sent them: so we estranged them, with enmity and hatred between the one and the other, to the day of judgment. And soon will Allah show them what it is they have done' [5:14]." (al-Salim, 2003)

---

[2] These were ancient political entities which today would lie in parts of western Saudi Arabia, southern Jordan, Israel, and the Sinai.

"Christianity grew up in the shadow of the Roman Empire, in a period when Judaism was suffering an eclipse, when it had become a system of rigid and lifeless ritual, an empty and unspiritual sham. The Roman Empire had its famous laws, which still live as the origin of modern European legislation; the Roman public had its own customs and social institutions. Christianity had no need then—nor, indeed had it had the power—to put before a powerful Roman government and a united Roman public laws . . . rules and regulations for government or for society. Rather, its need was to devote its power to moral and spiritual purification; and its concern was to correct the stereotyped ritual and the empty sham of ceremonial Judaism, and to restore spirit and life to the Israelite conscience.

. . . .

"Accordingly, the Christian faith pushed to the uttermost limit its teachings of spiritual purity, material asceticism, and unworldly forbearance. It fulfilled its task in this spiritual sphere of human life, because it is the function of a religion to elevate man by spiritual means so far as it can, to proclaim piety, to cleanse the heart and the conscience, to humble man's nature, and to make him ignore worldly needs and strive only for holy objectives in a world of shades and vanities. But, it left society to the State, to be governed by its earthly laws . . . .

. . . .

"Hence arose that division between religion and the world in the life of Europe; for the actual truth inherent in the nature of things is this, that Europe was never truly Christian. Hence religion there has remained in isolation from the business and the customs of life from the day of its entry to the present day." (Qutb, 1949, pp. 20–24)

"The truth is that all spiritual religions—and Christianity most of all—are opposed equally to European and American materialism. . . . But Christianity, so far as we can see, cannot be reckoned as a real force in opposition to the philosophies of the new materialism; it is an individualist, isolationist, negative faith. It has no power to make life grow under its influence in any permanent or positive way. Christianity has shot its bolt so far as human life is concerned; it has lost its power to keep pace with practical life in succeeding generations, for it came into being only for a limited and temporary period, between Judaism and Islam." (Qutb, 1949, pp. 316–317)

". . . Allah recalled Jesus[3] because the Israelites had rejected him in spite of the clear signs he had brought. They had been disobeying God for centuries and, in spite of many a warning and admonition served to them, their national character was rapidly deteriorating. They had killed several Prophets, one after the other, and had grown so audacious as to demand the blood of any good man who ventured to invite them to the Right Way. In order to give them the last chance for turning to the Truth, God appointed among them two great Prophets, Jesus and John [John the Baptist] (God's peace be upon them), at one and the same time. These Prophets came with such clear signs of their appointment from Allah that only such people dared reject them as were utterly perverted and prejudiced against the Truth and were averse to following the Right Way. Nevertheless the Israelites lost their last chance also as they not only rejected their invitation but also had the head of a great Prophet like John cut off openly at the request of a dancing girl. And their Pharisees and Jurists conspired and sought to get Jesus punished with the death sentence by the Roman government. Thus they had proved themselves to be so obdurate that it was useless to give the Israelites any further chance. So Allah recalled His Prophet Jesus and inflicted on them a life of disgrace up to the Day of Resurrection.

"It will be useful here to bear in mind the fact that this whole discourse is meant to refute and correct the Christian belief in the Godhead of Jesus. . . ." (a'la Maududi, 2003)

"How can we permit the Catholic Pope's talk of a need to find meeting points and agreement between Islam and Christianity, so that there will be peaceful coexistence between the two religions and harmony between the two communities? Is it conceivable that there should be agreement and a meeting point with those who fabricate terrible falsehoods about Allah . . . claiming that Jesus, peace be upon him, is his son?!" (Siyami, 2005)

"Christians have thrown themselves at the feet of Jews, supporting them, serving them . . . one would be extremely surprised about their ignorance and lack of intelligence with respect to the beginning of their history that was marked by long periods of their persecution waged against them by the Jews. . . ." (al-Maqdisi, 1997, in McCants, 2006)

---

[3] Brought him back from earth.

Jews

The previous chapter contained excerpts from jihadi comments on the Israel/Palestinian issue. Muslims who support the Palestinians and oppose Israel often say that they are not against the Jews, but only Zionists. Jihadis make it clear that they hate the Jews.

> "The Jews are the objects of Allah's [promised] wrath, while the Christians deviate from the path of righteousness. . . . The Qur'an described the Jews as a nation cursed by Allah, a nation at which he was angry – some of whom he turned into apes and pigs. . . ." (Qari, undated)

> "With their spite and deceit, the Jews are still misleading this nation, and distracting her away from her Koran in order that she may not draw her sharp weapons and her abundant ammunitions from it. . . . [The Jews'] aim is clearly shown by the Protocols [of the Elders of Zion]. The Jews are behind materialism, animal sexuality, the destruction of the family and the dissolution of society. Principal among them are Marx, Freud, Durkheim and the Jew Jean-Paul Sartre." (Qutb, undated, in Haim, 1982, pp. 155–156)

> "The [Islamic] nation has also been promised victory over the Jews, as the Prophet Muhammad has told us: 'The Day of Judgment will not arrive until the Muslims fight the Jews and kill them. . . .' This Hadith also teaches [us] that the conflict with the enemy will be settled by killing and warfare, and not by disabling the potential of the [Muslim] nation for decades by a variety of means such as the deception of democracy." (bin Laden, 2003d)

> "My message to the loathed Jews is that there is no god but Allah [and] we will chase you everywhere! We are a nation that drinks blood, and we know that there is no blood better than the blood of Jews. We will not leave you alone until we have quenched our thirst with your blood, and our children's thirst with your blood. We will not leave until you leave the Muslim countries. . . ." (Abu-Jandal, 2006)

> ". . . the basic question I'd like you to answer is whether, in your opinion, there is no difference between Zionism as an ideological political movement and Judaism as a religion.

"Rami: I believe that the Jew is more dangerous than the Zionist. Why? Because the so-called settlers[4] . . . who are now fighting Sharon,[5] oppose Zionism even though they are Jewish. They even refuse to serve in the Israeli army. All the Jewish rabbinical schools belong to this Jewish stream, which does not even recognize Israel, because it wants Greater Israel, from the Nile to the Euphrates. They consider the Zionists to be infidels. The Orthodox Jews consider the Zionists to be infidels who violated the religion . . .[6]

. . . .

"As far as I'm concerned, Judaism is not a religion. Judaism is a criminal and dangerous mafia." (Rami, 2005)

"It is important for the Muslim to know the characteristics of the Jews that are mentioned in Allah's Book because it will be these characteristics that will initiate their downfall and humiliation. Some of these distinctive characteristics of the Jews are explained below:

"• They like to spread mischief and corruption on earth and strive hard to accomplish this, '. . . and they (ever) strive to make mischief on earth. And Allah does not like the Mufsidun (mischief-makers)' [5:64].

"• They have incurred the Curse and Wrath of Allah. The consensus opinion of the Imams of Tafseer regarding the people asserted in the verse, '. . . those who earned Your Anger' [1:7] is the Jews. . . .

"• They are people of indignity, disobedience and transgression as stated by Allah. . . .

"• They are people of cowardliness, dismay and weakness as described by Allah subhanahu wa ta'ala: 'They fight not against you even together, except in fortified townships, or from behind walls. Their enmity among themselves is very great' [59:14], '. . . and if they fight against you, they will show you their backs, and they will not be helped' [3:111]." (Sheikh Abu al-Waleed al-Ansari, undated)

The West

". . . the Crusader spirit . . . runs in the blood of all Occidentals. It is this that colors all their thinking, which is responsible for their impe-

---

[4] Israelis who have occupied settlements on the territory of the West Bank and Gaza captured in the 1967 War.

[5] When Prime Minister Sharon unilaterally evacuated Gaza in 2005, the settlers were forced to leave as well.

[6] This is not generally true of orthodox Jews but is so for some ultra-orthodox Jews.

rialistic fear of the spirit of Islam and for their efforts to crush the strength of Islam. For the instincts and the interests of all Occidentals are bound up together in the crushing of that strength." (Qutb, 1949)

"When we speak of the hatred of Islam, born of Crusading spirit, which is latent in the European mind, we must not let ourselves be deceived by appearances, nor by their pretended respect for freedom of religion. They say, indeed, that Europe is not as unshakably Christian today as it was at the time of the Crusades and that there is nothing today to warrant hostility to Islam, as there was in those days. But this is entirely false and inaccurate. General Allenby[7] was no more than typical of the mind of all Europe, when, entering Jerusalem during the First World War, he said: 'Only now have the Crusades come to an end.'" (Qutb, 1949)

"Despite the fact that the religious convictions that gave rise to European hostility to Islam have now lost their power and been replaced by a more materialistic form of life, yet the ancient antipathy itself still remains as a vital element within the European mind. . . . The spirit of the Crusades, though perhaps in a milder form, still hangs over Europe; and that civilization in its dealings with the Islamic world still occupies a position that bears clear traces of that genocidal force." (Asad, 1934, in Qutb, 1949, p. 273)

"The leadership of mankind by Western man is now on the decline, not because Western culture has become poor materially or because its economic and military power has become weak. The period of the Western system has come to an end primarily because it is deprived of those life-giving values which enabled it to be the leader of mankind.

"It is necessary for the new leadership to preserve and develop the material fruits of the creative genius of Europe, and also to provide mankind with such high ideals and values as have so far remained undiscovered by mankind, and which will also acquaint humanity with a way of life which is harmonious with human nature, which is positive and constructive, and which is practicable.

"Islam is the only System which possesses these values and this way of life.

"The period of the resurgence of science has also come to an end. This period, which began with the Renaissance in the sixteenth cen-

---

[7] The British commander in the Middle East during World War I.

tury after Christ and reached its zenith in the eighteenth and nine-
teenth centuries, does not possess a reviving spirit.

"All nationalistic and chauvinistic ideologies which have appeared in
modern times, and all the movements and theories derived from them,
have also lost their vitality. In short, all man-made individual or collective theories have proved to be failures.

"At this crucial and bewildering juncture, the turn of Islam and the
Muslim community has arrived—the turn of Islam." (Qutb, 1964)

"The average European . . . knows only one necessary religion—the
worship of material progress; the only belief that he holds is that there
is but one goal in life—the making of that life easier and easier. It is, as
the definition has it in significant terms, 'an escape from the tyranny
of nature.' The shrines of such a culture are huge factories and cinemas,
chemical laboratories and dance halls and power stations. The priests
of such a worship are bankers and engineers, cinema stars and indus-
trialists and aviators. The inevitable result of this state of affairs is that
man strives to gain power and pleasure. . . . On the cultural side the
upshot has been the evolution of a humanism with a moral philosophy
confined to purely pragmatic questions, in which the highest criterion
of good or evil is whether or not any given thing represents material
progress." (Asad, 1934, p. 282)

"Oh people of the West, don't be fooled by the lies of Blair and Bush
that you are free nations, for the only freedom that you have is the freedom to be slaves of your whims and desires. Your children are free to
be deprived of their childhood and their innocence. Your women are
free to be used as tools of business and entertainment, and all of you
as a whole are the slaves of con men and women who rule you. They
are your real enemies. If you only knew – they are the ones who drag
your countries to the pit of America's group of scavengers, who seek to
ravage the entire globe for the interests of a handful of gangsters and
corporate companies. Democracy, human rights, and freedom are all
but hollow illusions, with which they tranquilize inhabitants of the
human farms which they control.

"The Muslim world is not your backyard. The Muslim world is not
Germany, Japan, or South America. The honorable sons and daughters
of Islam will not sit down, watching you spread your evil and immorality and infidelity to our land. The honorable sons of Islam will not
just let you kill our families in Palestine, Afghanistan, Kashmir, the
Balkans, Indonesia, the Caucusus, and elsewhere. It is time for us to be

equals – as you kill us, you will be killed, as you bomb us, you will be bombed." (al-Sheik, undated)

"To the Muslims living in the West, anyone among you who can immigrate to the lands of Muslims let him do so. Anyone who cannot do so, let him be on his guard by living in the Muslims' areas, have enough food for himself and his family for one month, have the means to defend himself and his family, leave in the house enough money for one month or more, and pray more and seek the help of Allah.

"... The race is now between you, time, and the European countries that have refused to stop their attacks on Muslims. Do not blame us for what is going to happen. We apologize to you beforehand if you are to be among the dead." (Abu-Hafs al-Masri Brigades (Al-Qa'ida), 2004)

"The West ignores the power of faith. Western civilization, which is based on the information revolution, cannot distance the Muslims from the Koran. The book of Allah brings to the hearts of Muslims a faith deeper than all the utopian descriptions and than the [lies] of the tyrannical Western propaganda machine." (al-Qurashi, 2002a)

"If the leaders of the West really cared about the truth and transparency, they would not feign ignorance of decades of Western interference in Muslim affairs and the tyranny and oppression experienced by the people of Islam as a result of that interference. If Bush and Blair really cared about the freedom of the Iraqi people, they would not have propped up the tyrant Saddam for nearly two decades. If your leaders really respect (inaudible) the Muslims they would not be doing everything in their power to corrupt our religion and separate the Muslims from their faith while killing all those who refuse apostasy and humiliation. If your leaders really cared about your protection, they would have long since restored our security instead of continuing to rape, pillage and plunder the lands of Islam without so much as an ounce of shame or compunction." (Al-Qaeda, 2005)

"In addition, we must acknowledge that the west, led by the United States, which is under the influence of the Jews, does not know the language of ethics, morality, and legitimate rights.

"They only know the language of interests backed by brute military force. Therefore, if we wish to have a dialogue with them and make them aware of our rights, we must talk to them in the language that they understand." (al-Zawahiri, 2001)

"Q. In regard to the global condition, what kind of things can the West, especially America, do to make this world more peaceful? What kind of attitudes must be changed?

"A. They have to stop fighting Islam, but that's impossible because it is "sunnatullah" [destiny, a law of nature], as Allah has said in the Qur'an. They will constantly be enemies. But they'll lose. I say this not because I am able to predict the future but they will lose and Islam will win. That was what the Prophet Muhammad has said. Islam must win and Westerners will be destroyed. But we don't have to make them enemies if they allow Islam to continue to grow so that in the end they will probably agree to be under Islam. If they refuse to be under Islam, it will be chaos. Full stop. If they want to have peace, they have to accept to be governed by Islam." (Ba'asyir, 2005)

The United States

The United States has long been a target for Middle Eastern terrorists. Secular radical Palestinian groups and Shi'ite militants fighting against the U.S. presence and influence in Lebanon and Iran carried out aircraft hijackings; killed American passengers on flights and cruise ships; launched attacks on U.S. embassies and their personnel, including the seizure of the U.S. embassy in Teheran in 1979; blew up the U.S. embassy in Beirut twice; and destroyed the Marine barracks in which 280 men were killed in 1983.

Today's Middle Eastern terrorists are neither secular nor Shi'a, with the notable exception of Hezbollah. The Sunni jihadis came onto the scene after the Afghan war against the Soviet Union and the first Gulf War in 1989. Like their predecessors, they condemn U.S. support for Israel, but their indictment goes much further, to include American culture and an alleged determination to destroy Islam.

Osama bin Laden remains at the heart of this movement. In February 1998, he and several leading Muslim militants established the coalition called the World Islamic Front for Jihad Against Jews and Crusaders. He also issued a fatwa that constituted a formal declaration of war against the United States which went largely unnoticed in the Western press. A month after 9/11, he sent a letter to the American people. Excerpts from those documents are included in this section. Portions of numerous other communications from bin Laden since that time are also cited throughout this book.

In the jihadi debate over whether to engage the "near enemy" or the "far enemy," the United States is that "far enemy." Thus, while there are many references to the United States in this collection, we focus more extensively on jihadi perceptions of the "far enemy."

"I examined at length the history of Islam; I turned its pages; and I looked at the enemies of Islam, their wars against it, the Crusaders, and the idol-worshipers, in the East and the West, over more than 10 generations – and I found no enemy more hostile and abhorrent than America." (al-Fahd, 2003b)[8]

The following is from an open letter bin Laden sent to the American people shortly after 9/11 justifying his assault. Interestingly, it mentions a number of criticisms prominent in the United States and Europe that have nothing to do with Islam.

"(Q1) Why are we fighting and opposing you?

"(Q2) What are we calling you to, and what do we want from you?

"As for the first question: Why are we fighting and opposing you? The answer is very simple:

"(1) Because you attacked us and continue to attack us.

"a) You attacked us in Palestine . . . .

. . . .

"(a) . . . The creation and continuation of Israel is one of the greatest crimes, and you are the leaders of its criminals. . . . The creation of Israel is a crime which must be erased. Each and every person whose hands have become polluted in the contribution towards this crime must pay its price, and pay for it heavily.

. . . .

"(b) You attacked us in Somalia; you supported the Russian atrocities against us in Chechnya, the Indian oppression against us in Kashmir, and the Jewish aggression against us in Lebanon.

"(c) Under your supervision, consent and orders, the governments of our countries which act as your agents attack us on a daily basis; . . .

. . . .

"(d) You steal our wealth and oil at paltry prices because of you[r] international influence and military threats. This theft is indeed the biggest theft ever witnessed by mankind in the history of the world.

"(e) Your forces occupy our countries; you spread your military bases throughout them; you corrupt our lands, and you besiege our sancti-

---

[8] Al-Fahd, a Saudi Islamist, retracted his views on Saudi TV only a week after making this statement. This was a significant intellectual blow to al-Qaeda in the Arabian Peninsula.

ties, to protect the security of the Jews and to ensure the continuity of your pillage of our treasures.

"(f) You have starved the Muslims of Iraq, where children die every day. It is a wonder that more than 1.5 million Iraqi children have died as a result of your sanctions, and you did not show concern. Yet when 3000 of your people died, the entire world rises and has not yet sat down.

"(g) You have supported the Jews in their idea that Jerusalem is their eternal capital, and agreed to move your embassy there. With your help and under your protection, the Israelis are planning to destroy the Al-Aqsa mosque. . . .

. . . .

"Is it in any way rational to expect that after America has attacked us for more than half a century, that we will then leave her to live in security and peace?!!

. . . .

"(i) You are the nation who, rather than ruling by the Shariah of Allah in its Constitution and Laws, choose to invent your own laws as you will and desire. You separate religion from your policies, contradicting the pure nature which affirms Absolute Authority to the Lord and your Creator. . . .

"(ii) You are the nation that permits usury, which has been forbidden by all the religions. Yet you build your economy and investments on usury. . . .

"(iii) You are a nation that permits the production, trading and usage of intoxicants. You also permit drugs, and only forbid the trade of them, even though your nation is the largest consumer of them.

"(iv) You are a nation that permits acts of immorality, and you consider them to be pillars of personal freedom. You have continued to sink down this abyss from level to level until incest has spread amongst you, in the face of which neither your sense of honour nor your laws object.

. . . .

"(v) You are a nation that permits gambling in its all forms. The companies practice this as well, resulting in the investments becoming active and the criminals becoming rich.

"(vi) You are a nation that exploits women like consumer products or advertising tools calling upon customers to purchase them. You use women to serve passengers, visitors, and strangers to increase your profit margins. You then rant that you support the liberation of women.

"(vii) You are a nation that practices the trade of sex in all its forms, directly and indirectly. Giant corporations and establishments are established on this, under the name of art, entertainment, tourism and freedom, and other deceptive names you attribute to it.

"(viii) And because of all this, you have been described in history as a nation that spreads diseases that were unknown to man in the past. Go ahead and boast to the nations of man, that you brought them AIDS as a Satanic American invention.

"(ix) You have destroyed nature with your industrial waste and gases more than any other nation in history. Despite this, you refuse to sign the Kyoto agreement so that you can secure the profit of your greedy companies and industries.

"(x) Your law is the law of the rich and wealthy people, who hold sway in their political parties, and fund their election campaigns with their gifts." (bin Laden, undated(b))

"This means that the same America that fights against us in Egypt and backs Israel in the heart of the Islamic world is also leading the battle against us in Chechnya,[9] the Caucasus, and also in Somalia where 13,000 Somali nationals were killed in the course of what the United States alleged was its campaign to distribute foodstuffs in Somalia. In the name of food aid, the United States perpetrated hideous acts against the Somalis, acts that came to light only later. Detainees were tortured and their honor violated at the hands of the international coalition forces that allegedly came to rescue Somalia." (al-Zawahiri, 2001)

"How could they (the Americans) expect to have security if they continuously bring destruction and murder to our brothers and sisters in Palestine and Iraq? They are not entitled to any level of security any place in the world.

"As to their presence in the holy land (the land of the two holy Mosques) and in the entire Arabian Peninsula, it is forbidden, according to Allah's and his messenger's command." (bin Laden, 2004e)

---

[9] It is an article of faith among jihadis that the United States is materially assisting Russia in its war on Chechnya. In fact, the war has been a source of tension in the U.S.-Russian relationship, despite Russia's efforts to describe it as part of the "War on Terror."

"What takes place in America today was caused by the flagrant interference on the part of successive American governments into others' business. These governments imposed regimes that contradict the faith, values, and lifestyles of the people. This is the truth that the American government is trying to conceal from the American people.

"Our current battle is against the Jews. Our faith tells us we shall defeat them, God willing. However, Muslims find that the Americans stand as a protective shield and strong supporter, both financially and morally. The desert storm that blew over New York and Washington[10] should, in our view, have blown over Tel Aviv. The American position obliged Muslims to force the Americans out of the arena first to enable them to focus on their Jewish enemy. Why are the Americans fighting a battle on behalf of the Jews? Why do they sacrifice their sons and interests for them?" (bin Laden, 2001, in Cullison, 2004)

"The Americans will not allow any Islamic regime to assume rule in the heart of the Islamic world, unless it collaborates with them, as is happening now in Iraq." (al-Zawahiri, 2005e)

"America, have you ever tasted the taste of horror, sorrow, and pain? This is the taste that has been our lot for so long. This is the taste that has filled our stomachs, torn our guts, and burned our skin. This is routine for us, and is carried out by those you love [Israel]. . . ." (al-Subh, 2001)

"Our enemy is the United States, which was one of the two superpowers in the world and then became the sole superpower in this period in history. It sought to complete its domination of the world by imposing American culture, the values of American society, and aspects of the corrupt life in the United States. It also sought forcefully to impose a system on the countries of the world similar to the systems governments impose on individuals. It is moving earnestly to Americanize the entire world, particularly the Muslim World." (Center for Islamic Studies and Research, 2003)

"A target, if made available to Muslims by the grace of God, is every American man. He is an enemy of ours whether he fights us directly or merely pays his taxes." (bin Laden, 1998b)

---

[10] The 9/11 attacks.

"The ruling to kill the Americans and their allies—civilians and military—is an individual duty for every Muslim who can do it in any country in which it is possible to do it, in order to liberate the al Aqsa Mosque and the holy mosque from their grip, and in order for their armies to move out of all the lands of Islam, defeated and unable to threaten any Muslim. This is in accordance with the words of Almighty God, 'and fight the pagans all together as they fight you all together,' and 'fight them until there is no more tumult or oppression, and there prevail justice and faith in God.'

. . . .

"We – with God's help – call on every Muslim who believes in God and wishes to be rewarded to comply with God's order to kill the Americans and plunder their money wherever and whenever they find it. We also call on Muslim ulema, leaders, youths, and soldiers to launch the raid on Satan's U.S. troops and the devil's supporters allying with them, and to displace those who are behind them so that they may learn a lesson." (bin Laden, 1998a)[11]

"His fatwah said that all Americans must be killed wherever they can be found, because America deserves it. Therefore [according to bin Laden] if Muslims come across Americans, they have to attack them. Osama believes in total war. This concept I don't agree with. If this occurs in an Islamic country, the fitnah [discord] will be felt by Muslims. But to attack them in their country [America] is fine." (Ba'asyir, 2005)

"Therefore, I advise the youths to exercise their minds in the Jihad as they are the first ones upon whom Jihad is obligatory. . . . So know that targeting the Americans and the Jews by killing them in any corner of the Earth is the greatest of obligations and the most excellent of ways to gain nearness to Allah. Furthermore, I advise the youths to use their intelligence in killing them secretly." (bin Laden, 2003c)

"The United States, which, since the turn of the last century, has believed that it is the strongest, used that strength and power not to actualize justice and equality for the oppressed, but to besiege the[se] peoples, murder them, and spill their blood. It did not follow any

---

[11] Bin Laden's statement was signed by Sheikh Usamah bin-Muhammad bin-Ladin; Ayman al-Zawahiri, leader of the Jihad Group in Egypt; Abu Yasir Rifa'i Ahmad Taha, a leader of the Islamic Group; Sheikh Mir Hamzah, secretary of the Jamiat-ul-Ulema-e-Pakistan; and Fazlul Rahman, leader of the Jihad Movement in Bangladesh.

law, unless the law was passed to strengthen its hegemony and its power. . . .

"How much hatred has it stockpiled, and how many enemies has it gained? How many tortured people have burned American flags at every opportunity to express their rage? The US, with its think tanks and mighty research institutes, should have been ashamed of its hostility towards the nations and the peoples. . . ." (Hamad, 2001)

"[Khalil]: What about the major strike that you have been saying for long that you are planning to carry out against America?

"[Al-Ablaj]: I swear to you, my brother, that the strike is coming. As I said earlier, you don't use the winning card at any time. The strike must be well prepared. This means that it must be timed to occur when the giant starts staggering in his blood. At that time, he is ready for the fatal strike.

. . . .

"[Khalil]: Is it possible for you to target the US President and is it part of your plan to target senior US officials?

"[Al-Ablaj]: Brother: They have received advance fortifications [as published]. The truth is that I do not wish that Bush would be killed. I wish he would live to die a thousand times as he sees America collapses in front of his eyes. We want to kill him a thousand times every hour. We want the Americans to hang him and leave him dangling from their Statue of Liberty for being responsible for the destruction of their alleged civilization." (al-Ablaj, 2003a)

"In all the countries, except for rare cases, there are accomplishments in the area of preaching and Shari'a interests. Even in America, the head of unbelief and the greatest enemy of Islam and the Muslims, the centers of preaching are still open. But just because they exist does not mean that it is permitted to halt the Jihad against America while it kills the Muslims and occupies their lands, defends Israel, and preserves it [Israel] from its enemies. . . ." (*The Voice of Jihad*, 2004)

"And I say in emulation of those honorable ones: O people, America and its army are not too great for you [to defeat], for we have struck them, by God, time and again, and they have been defeated time and again. They are the most cowardly people when met [in battle]. It has become clear to us in our actions to defend against and fight the American enemy that he defends in battle mainly on psychological warfare waged by his massive propaganda machine. He also depends on dense aerial bombardment to hide the most important weaknesses he has, namely the American soldier's fearfulness, cowardice, and lack of a fighting spirit. If time were not short, I would tell you much about this, about things that are unbelievable that occurred during our fights with them in Tora Bora and in Afghanistan. I hope that God will facilitate some time for us to talk about this in detail." (bin Laden, 2003b)

"In short, the United States does not have the power that matches its international position and reputation. It depends mostly on the principle of deterrence. In deterrence, it mostly depends on the media with which it has fascinated the nations of the world. For years, American television exported American culture to the world, portraying the United States as the superpower that cannot be defeated. The magicians of the modern day pharaoh were the media people. 'They bewitched the eyes of the people, and struck terror into them: for they showed a great (feat of) magic.' [Koran verse]" (Center for Islamic Studies and Research, 2003)

"Every Muslim the minute he can start differentiating, carries hate towards Americans, Jews and Christians, this is part of our ideology.

"Ever since I can recall I felt at war with the Americans and had feelings of animosity and hate towards them." (bin Laden, 1998b)

"As for the war against the US, this war is not finished. And it will not be finished because the battle between us and the Americans is not a battle based on interests or personal differences but rather a battle between truth and falsehood – it is a conflict between the good and evil. America represents the head of this falsehood and the body of this evil, so the conflict against falsehood is ongoing and will remain as long as Jihad in the path of Allah remains and all of us know that (according to what the Prophet Muhammad (saws) has informed the Ummah) the Jihad will continue until the Day of Judgment." (Abu-Ghaith, 2002)

"Q. So it means that the fight against America will never end?

"A. Never, and this fight is compulsory. Muslims who don't hate America sin. What I mean by America is George Bush's regime. There is no iman [belief] if one doesn't hate America." (Ba'asyir, 2005)

Apostates

Jihadis, along with many other Muslims, consider apostates to be worse than infidels, because they once accepted the truth and then rejected it. Jihadis claim that all contemporary Arab and Muslim rulers are apostates and believe that according to the Qur'an, they should therefore be killed. Equally important, by labeling them apostates, jihadis are seeking to delegitimize established authority. The Qur'an calls for obedience to authority. Jihadis, particularly bin Laden, insist that the leaders are not true believers, they need not be obeyed, and indeed must be overthrown.

> "The Rulers of this age are in apostasy from Islam. They were raised at the tables of imperialism, be it Crusaderism, or Communism, or Zionism. They carry nothing from Islam but their names.[12] . . . It is a well-established rule of Islamic Law that the punishment of an apostate will be heavier than the punishment of someone who is by origin an infidel (and has never been a Muslim). . . . For instance, an apostate has to be killed even if he is unable to (carry arms and) go to war." (Faraj, 1979)

> "The disbelief of the apostasy now is more intense than the original disbelief; therefore, fighting the apostates is more worthy than was the fight against the earlier unbelievers." (al-Qaeda in Mesopotamia, undated)

> "After the fall of our orthodox caliphates on March 3, 1924,[13] and after expelling the colonialists, our Islamic nation was afflicted with apostate rulers who took over in the Moslem nation. These rulers turned out to be more infidel and criminal than the colonialists themselves. Moslems have endured all kinds of harm, oppression, and torture at their hands.
>
> ". . . But they (the rulers) did not stop there; they started to fragment the essence of the Islamic nation by trying to eradicate its Moslem identity. Thus, they started spreading godless and atheistic views among the youth. We found some that claimed that socialism was from Islam, democracy was the [religious] council, and the prophet – God bless and keep him – propagandized communism.

---

[12] In the Middle East, a person's name betrays his religious affiliation. Someone called George is always a Christian, someone called Muhammad is always a Muslim. The text of the Faridah here maintains that a person's name is the only indication by which one remembers that someone bearing a Muslim name is actually a Muslim.

[13] The Turkish revolution led by Kemal Atatürk, who sought to modify and secularize Turkey, abolished the caliphate on this date.

. . . .

"Colonialism and its followers, the apostate rulers, then started to openly erect crusader centers, societies, and organizations like Masonic Lodges, Lions and Rotary clubs, and foreign schools. They aimed at producing a wasted generation that pursued everything that is Western and produced rulers, ministers, leaders, physicians, engineers, businessmen, politicians, journalists, and information specialists." (*Manchester Document*, undated)[14]

"I no longer have a home whose shelter I can seek, for my homeland has been desecrated and set on fire.
O my nation, I am a bird who has seen a thicket, may I sing? Will I be blamed if I do?
Am I to blame if I present you with a fact; namely, that the rulers are our mortal enemies?
They are unbelievers; yet, they are called the servants and imams of Muslims.
They pretend to be our support, when, in point of fact, they are our disease and death.
The Crusaders' army has enveloped the universe, where are the pious, magnanimous, and audacious men?" (Hilalah, undated, in bin Laden, 2004a)

"The apostate and atheist regimes in the Muslims countries are . . . the 'Jews of the Arabs.' They represent shocking examples of lewdness, evil, and dedication to serving the enemies of Islam." (Bir, 2005)

"The rulers of the countries of Islam in this age are all apostate, unbelieving tyrants who have departed in every way from Islam. Muslims who proclaim God's unity have no other choice than iron and fire, jihad in the way of God, to restore the caliphate according to the Prophet's teachings." (al-Zahrani, 2004)

"They [apostate regimes] govern by ungodly laws, pay allegiance to the United States and the Crusader countries, turn for justice to the international body in all their cases, embrace the infidels and help them against the Muslims, turn against the religion, pursue the mujahidin, spread evil and atheism and defend them with troops and laws,

---

[14] The manual was located by the Manchester (England) Metropolitan Police during a search of an al-Qaeda member's home. The manual was found in a computer file described as "the military series" related to the "Declaration of Jihad."

and participate with the United States and the Crusader countries in their war against the honors, religion, people, and country." (Center for Islamic Studies and Research, 2003)

"What do you think about the [secular] rulers' polytheism? They made the United States a god. Does anyone doubt the fact that the rulers of the Muslim countries believe that the United States is the god? They abide by the orders that come from the United States. They obey the United States and also force the people of Muslim countries to do so. My brothers, this is what we call the polytheism of living gods that Allah does not tolerate in any case." (Saeed, 2005)

"The consensus of Islamic scholars has been that the right to govern, rule, or lead cannot be given to a Kafir. And if a ruler became a Kafir, he falls out of the fold of Islam, and his right to govern goes out with him. Alqadi Ayad, a respected classic scholar (may he have mercy from Allah) has said: 'If a ruler entered a state of Kufr and started to change what Allah has legislated, he loses the pledge given to him by Muslims, and he should be removed and replaced by a just Imam (a ruler who abides by the laws of Allah).'

"Therefore, we did not invent a Fatwa calling for disobeying or removing the Kafir ruler. This has been the consensus of Islamic scholars all along and it is what the Islamic laws mandate." (bin Laden, 2004e)

"The only way for corrective action is to remove the ruler as commanded by the laws of Islam. If he refuses to step down voluntarily, Muslims are obligated to remove him by force. This is what Allah and his messengers mandated." (bin Laden, 2004e)

"One may not make a [peace] treaty with an apostate, nor grant him safe passage or protection. According to Allah's religion, he has only one choice: 'Repent or be killed.'" (al-Zarqawi, 2005a)

Saudi Arabia

The House of Saud has ruled Saudi Arabia since the 1930s. Although it is the birthplace of fundamentalist Wahhabi Sunni Islam—the state religion—Saudi Arabia has long been a target of Islamic extremists seeking an even stricter interpretation, more akin to that of the Taliban in Afghanistan. However, jihadis have faced a difficult dilemma, for to physically attack the royal family and other Saudis would be widely regarded as a sin. This was amply proved during an attack by zealots on the Grand Mosque in 1979, which failed to spark a hoped-for uprising. Because of this dilemma, Islamic terrorists have generally focused on foreign targets in the kingdom.

Terrorist attacks in Saudi Arabia long antedate al-Qaeda. In addition to the attack on the Grand Mosque, fuel tanks were blown up in 1988. A U.S. military residence, the Khobar Towers complex, was hit by a truck bomb in 1996, killing 19 servicemen and wounding hundreds. The Saudi government blamed minority Shi'ites for both attacks, but some analysts believe this may have been done to deflect attention away from the growing threat of Sunni terrorism. Similarly, Saudi jails reportedly held hundreds of dissidents, and during the 1970s and 1980s, news of violent attacks was systematically suppressed.

Beginning in 2003, Saudi Arabia was hit by a wave of attacks by Sunni jihadis linked to al-Qaeda—attacks that could not be denied. Between 2003 and 2006, scores of terrorist incidents were carried out by a group that called itself "al-Qaeda in the Land of the Two Holy Places"—the jihadis do not recognize the legitimacy of the Saudi name. During this period, Saudi Arabia also became the Internet base for a virtual jihadi magazine, *al-Battar Training Camp*. Another important jihadi Internet document, "The East Riyadh Operation and Our War with the United States and Its Agents," contains an exegesis on jihadi philosophy to counter criticism for a bombing at the Vinnell Corporation compound in which 35 people, including some Muslims, died, and 200 were wounded. Excerpts from both of these web sites are used extensively in this book.

Saudi Arabia has long been a major focus of Osama bin Laden. A Saudi himself, of Yemeni extraction, he had a tense relationship with the Saudi royal family and in the 1980s left the country to wage jihad against the Soviet Union in Afghanistan, with Saudi support. He turned openly against the Saudi government and family when it permitted its territory to be used by U.S. forces deployed to liberate Kuwait from a takeover by Saddam Hussein. Bin Laden urged the formulation of an Arab or Muslim army instead. He feared that the U.S. troops would remain after the war, and they did. However, in 2001, those forces were relocated elsewhere in the Gulf region. Despite the fact that only 300 U.S. servicemen remain, bin Laden continues to rail against the U.S. military presence. He has also condemned the royal family for corruption, incompetence, oppression of jihadis, allowing infidels to live in the country with their own lifestyle, and failing to implement a stricter version of Islam. He claims that the unresponsiveness of the king to reformist entreaties (i.e., to form an even more fundamentalist government) has driven him to embrace violence.

The Saudi authorities have struck back hard against the jihadis. They claim that by the end of 2005, the security services had killed or captured all but one of the 26 men on their "Most Wanted" list, and that one was subsequently killed in Iraq.[15]

Nevertheless, Saudi Arabians reportedly continue to be a major source of financing for jihadis in Afghanistan and Iraq. Saudi Arabia is also the principal source of suicide bombers in the Iraqi insurgency and a base for training Saudi fighters for al-Qaeda in the Land of the Two Rivers. Saudi security services claim that they are not overly concerned about the return of these fighters after the war in Iraq, because most Saudi recruits are promptly martyred. However, those that survive are likely to be competent and battle-hardened.

"The kingdom [of Saudi Arabia] is the only country in the world that calls its people by the name of the ruling family." (al-Zahrani, 2004)

"One particular report, the glorious Memorandum Of Advice, was handed over to the king on Muharram, 1413 A.H. (July 1992), which tackled the problem, pointed out the illness and prescribed the medicine in an original, righteous and scientific style. It described the gaps and the shortcoming in the philosophy of the regime and suggested the required course of action and remedy. The report gave a description of:

"(1) The intimidation and harassment suffered by the leaders of the society, the scholars, heads of tribes, merchants, academic teachers and other eminent individuals;

"(2) The situation of the law within the country and the arbitrary declaration of what is Halal and Haram (lawful and unlawful) regardless of the Shari'ah as instituted by Allah;

"(3) The state of the press and the media which became a tool of truth-hiding and misinformation; the media carried out the plan of the enemy of idolising cult of certain personalities and spreading scandals among the believers to repel the people away from their religion. . . .

"(4) Abuse and confiscation of human rights;

---

[15] Among those killed were Yousuf al-'Ayiri and 'Abd al-'Aziz al-Muqrin, commanders of al-Qaeda in the Arabian Peninsula; they were killed by Saudi security forces in June 2003 and June 2004, respectively. Turki al-Dandani, another wanted Saudi, committed suicide during a pursuit by Saudi security forces on July 3, 2003. Saudi Sheikh Hamad al-Hamidi was arrested by Saudi security forces for supporting bin Laden. Issa al-'Awshan was killed by Saudi security forces in July 2004. Abdallah al-Rashud, a member of the Jurisprudent Committee of al-Qaeda in Saudi Arabia, died in June 2005. Salih al-Awfi, another commander of al-Qaeda in the Arabian Peninsula, was killed during a clash with Saudi security forces on August 18, 2005.

"(5) The financial and the economical situation of the country and the frightening future in view of the enormous amount of debts and interest owed by the government; this is at the time when the wealth of the Ummah {is} being wasted to satisfy personal desires of certain individuals!! while imposing more custom duties and taxes on the nation. (As the prophet said about the woman who committed adultery: 'She repented in such a way sufficient to bring forgiveness to a custom collector!!');

"(6) The miserable situation of the social services and infrastructure especially the water service and supply, the basic requirement of life;

"(7) The state of the ill-trained and ill-prepared army and the impotence of its commander in chief despite the incredible amount of money that has been spent on the army. The gulf war clearly exposed the situation;

"(8) Shari'a law was suspended and man made law was used instead;

"(9) And as far as the foreign policy is concerned the report exposed not only how this policy has disregarded the Islamic issues and ignored the Muslims, but also how help and support were provided to the enemy against the Muslims. . . .

. . . .

"Therefore it is very clear that the advocates of {the} correction and reform movement were very keen on using peaceful means in order to protect the unity of the country and to prevent bloodshed. Why is it then the regime closed all peaceful routes and pushed the people toward armed actions?!! which is the only choice left for them to implement righteousness and justice." (bin Laden, 1996)

"Each day, millions of people suffer from poverty and deprivation, while millions of riyals flow into the accounts of the heads of the [Saudi royal] family who wield power. In addition to all this, services are being scaled back, they are stealing lands, they forcibly impose themselves as 'partners' in businesses without giving any compensation, and so forth. The regime has gone beyond all this and has reached actions that clearly remove one from Islam." (bin Laden, 2004f)

"Should we talk about the unlawful confiscating of private properties and the rulers' obsession with building palaces? King Fahd has ordered the building of 'The Salam Palace' which cost SR 4 billions. What about Thahaban Palace? This one is on the Red Sea coast, 40 kilometers from Jeddah. If they put the country of Bahrain in its atrium, guests in the palace would not notice the presence on [sic] Bahrain there. Knowing that Bahrain is a 100 million square meters country with 1 million people living there, one can imagine how big the Thahaban Palace is? Does history know of a case that is more foolish than this one?" (bin-Laden, 2004e)

"Its [Saudi Arabia] prisons hold the oppressed who are subjected to insufferable tortures, and in it there are aggression and curses against Allah, insult to the religion, and contempt for the believers, [and all this] under the protection and patronage of the family of Saud, whose members simultaneously silence the reformists as well as those who call for virtue, and jail those who call on them to impose the law of Allah." (al-Dosari, 2003a)

"Thanks to God, some kindhearted people from the land of the two holy shrines (Saudi Arabia) and other countries were sending alms to the families of those widows and orphans {of suicide bombers} to ease their suffering and distress. Unfortunately, the conceited, arrogant prince, Abdallah Bin-Abd-al-Aziz, ordered that these well-doers be prevented from sending money to these families so that the martyrdom operations would stop. What kind of heart is that to issue such an order? Is it a heart of a human being, or is it a heart made of stone?" (bin Laden, 2004a)

"Riyadh rulers have decided to change the education curricula for fear of America. The adverse impact of these changes on both our religion and our culture is very obvious. As to the impact on religion, it is apostasy, as you know. The impact on our culture will be manifested in the new graduates of the new programs. New graduates will be friends and allies of America, they will learn to sell their national interest for personal gains, and they will learn to smile at the face of any American even though he occupies their land, robs their wealth, erases their identity, and imposes his western customs under the excuse of equal rights and United Nations Charter. This is a true of model of interfering in our domestic policies." (bin Laden, 2004e)

"The acts of disobedience [against Allah] committed by the regime are very grave. They are worse than merely grave offenses and mortal sins; they are so serious that those who commit such things are no longer Muslims." (bin Laden, 2004f)

American Presence in Saudi Arabia

"Since the American troops entered in such an immense number at the time of the Second Gulf War until today, American Crusader forces in the Land of the Two Holy Places have been increasing and settling in. Neighborhoods of Riyadh and Jedda are full of American housing complexes, and they have a large presence in the other cities.

"There has been an agreement between the client government of the Land of the Two Holy Places and the United States that these complexes should be a piece of American land. Americans in them have religious freedom and are not forbidden anything of their religion and their desires. The complexes have churches and bars; they have dance halls and mixed swimming pools and various kinds of unbelief and licentiousness. Shari'ah law is not imposed on them; indeed, they are not subject to the sovereignty of the government itself. The police, security forces, and organizations that command virtue and forbid vice do not enter them." (Center for Islamic Studies and Research, 2003)

"The crusaders were permitted to be in the land of the two Holy Places. . . . By opening the Arab peninsula to the crusaders the regime disobeyed and acted against what has been enjoined by the messenger of Allah (Allah's Blessings and Salutations may be on him), while he was at the bed of his death: (Expel the polytheists out of the Arab Peninsula); (narrated by Al-Bukhari) and: (If I survive, Allah willing, I'll expel the Jews and the Christians out of the Arab Peninsula); saheeh Aljame' As-Sagheer." (bin Laden, 1996)

"You Americans, you dared to implant your bases in the Arabian Peninsula. . . . You dared to hit Muslims in Afghanistan and Iraq from [bases in] the country of the two sanctuaries [Saudi Arabia].

"For what you have done, we will be following you. So watch out as you will see nothing from now on but our attacks as the real battle has just started." (al-Moqrin, 2004)[16]

"And every special thing to these crusaders from their communities [in Saudi Arabia], their bases, and means of transport, especially the western and American aviation companies [airlines], will be a direct target for our coming operations. . . ." (al-Qaeda in the Arabian Peninsula, 2004)

---

[16] Al-Moqrin was killed in Riyadh on June 18, 2004, during a government-sponsored raid in a downtown neighborhood.

In fact, there have been few operations since 2005.

"Those amongst you, who are working for our enemies the Blasphemers, beware. Leave them for the safety of your religion first, and your own safety, in case the Jihad people target those blaspheming companies, enemies of the Muslims and collaborators in the war against Islam. We warn you against approaching the Blasphemers in this area, or else you shall receive their fate. Al-Qaeda already issued a warning stating that it will target companies that are run by the Blasphemers; in particular, the airline and oil companies will be targeted." (al-Amer, undated)

"{We draw} attention to all the shari'ah violations and contradictions in totally depending on Western systems in the army. These include such abominations as allowing military law and not God to be the judge, the polytheist method of standing up for the royal anthem, and the military salute, which includes beating the ground with the feet and saluting the rank and not the one who carries it, and copying Western laws shamelessly. If a military rank were placed on a dog, you must salute it, because it is a 'royal decree,' as they call it. . . . Is this an army destined to strive in the way of God? Is this an army to be depended upon, after God, in dangerous and gloomy times?" (Center for Islamic Studies and Research, 2003)

"It is incredible that our country is the world{'s} largest buyer of arms from the USA and the area{'s} biggest commercial partners of the Americans who are assisting their Zionist brothers in occupying Palestine and in evicting and killing the Muslims there, by providing arms, men and financial supports." (bin Laden, 1996)

". . . the Kingdom of Saudi Arabia can fire Chinese-made strategic missiles at Israel, but the United States can control the missile after it is launched the same way it can control any American missile fired from Sultan Base.[17] The United States can guide this missile to hit any vital installation in Riyadh.

"The intention here is not to exaggerate the American strength. The United States can do this not because of its strength, but because of the subserviency of the leadership of Saudi Arabia. . . ." (Center for Islamic Studies and Research, 2003)

---

[17] It is not true that the United States can control these missiles.

"In the past, [Prince] Sultan [the Saudi defense minister] denied the presence of foreign forces on Saudi territory, and some people believed him. . . .

"In the past, they strongly denied their subserviency to the United States and stressed that their alliance with it was an alliance of mutual interests, and nothing more. . . .

"This is as far as words are concerned. As for deeds, there is much to say. The aircraft of the Crusader campaign took off from Saudi Arabia. They were supplied with fuel from bases in Saudi Arabia. The supreme command of the war was in the Sultan Base in Saudi Arabia.

. . . .

"The latest episode in their subserviency was their broad cooperation with the United States in pursuing the mujahidin in the world, collecting intelligence information about the mujahidin, and helping the United States arrest them. Because of information collected by the Saudi intelligence agencies, many mujahidin were arrested and many operations in the world and in the United States itself were foiled.

"Because of this despicable cooperation, the prisons in Saudi Arabia have become full of prisoners, held on charges of fighting with al-Qa'ida and Taliban against the United States or fighting with Khattab,[18] and recently on charges of attempting to infiltrate into Iraq to fight there. The shari'ah duty imposed on all the nation has become a punishable crime. They are doing all this to please the United States.

"No one reviewing ancient or modern history can find an example of agentry or treachery greater than this." (Center for Islamic Studies and Research, 2003)

"The crusader forces became the main cause of our disastrous condition, particularly in the economical aspect of it due to the unjustified heavy spending on these forces. As a result of the policy imposed on the country, especially in the field of oil industry where production is restricted or expanded and prices are fixed to suit the American economy, ignoring the economy of the country. Expensive deals were imposed on the country to purchase arms. People asking what is the justification for the very existence of the regime then?" (bin Laden, 1996)

---

[18] Ibn al-Khattab (born in Saudi Arabia in 1969, died March 20, 2002), more commonly known as Amir Khattab (also transliterated as Emir Khattab and Ameer Khattab) and Habib Abdul Rahman, was a Wahhabi warlord and financier working with Chechen militants in the first and second Chechen wars.

"Attiya Allah also discussed what might happen in the region were the Saudi regime to collapse. When asked 'Do you think that the Americans will leave us alone if the Zero hour arrives and the Al Saud regime is removed?' Attiya Allah responded:

"'No. They will not leave us alone. Initially, they will attempt to secure the sources of oil, in accordance to a long-existing plan. So they will not stand idly by. The question is: will they be able to do that in the event of a complete collapse of the regime and the ensuing rampant chaos? I strongly doubt that they will be able to do so if they are more entangled in the Iraqi quagmire than they are today, or if they are receiving strong blows inside America, because such strikes will cause them to lose their ability to concentrate." (Allah, 2003)

"Saudi Arabia is oil rich today. There was a time when they did not even have a piece of bread to eat. They accepted the belief of Allah being the only God. They corrected their deeds. Then, Allah blessed them with oil in their deserts. There is a lot of wealth in your deserts, but you are slaves. You cannot even drill oil without taking orders from the United States, reform your economies, or build your countries. Give up polytheism. Stop worshiping to the Bushes and bowing to the infidels. For God's sake, repent." (Saeed, 2005)

"One of the greatest places in which Jihad is a commandment applying to each Muslim individually is the land of the two holy places [i.e. the Arabian Peninsula]." (al-Dosari, 2003a)

"We have not conducted a single offensive operation; all operations that have taken place have been defensive operations. On the contrary, you will find that the brothers try as much as possible to avoid confronting the army and security forces. However, the government is escalating its war, and is trying to remove me and you and all Islamists. . . . I have taken upon myself an oath to purify the Arabian Peninsula from polytheists. We were born in and saw the light in this country, so we will fight the Crusaders and the Jews in it until we have repelled them or we are martyred. . . ." (Abu Hajer, 2003)

"We want to tell these demonic rulers [Tawaghit] and their rabble hangers-on, their black servants, their army, and their rabbis, monks, and agents: We did not take this path [of Jihad] because someone misled us or for the sake of some person.

. . . .

"We went forth to fight for the sake of Allah, and we saw the lands of the Muslims conquered and their holy places defiled by Jews, Christians, Shiites, and polytheists, and especially the land of the two holy places [i.e. the Arabian Peninsula], and so we undertook Jihad in it." (Ubay Abd al-Rahman al-'Utaybi, 2004)

". . . if the devils think that by killing a leader or two the battle is over they are foolish; how many people did the Islamic nation sacrifice during its fourteen centuries? The mujahideen have more blood to be shed." (Anonymous, undated(b))

"Clearly after Belief (Imaan) there is no more important duty than pushing the American enemy out of the holy land. No other priority, except Belief, could be considered before it; the people of knowledge, Ibn Taymiyyah, stated: 'to fight in defence of religion and Belief is a collective duty; there is no other duty after Belief than fighting the enemy who is corrupting the life and the religion. There is no preconditions for this duty and the enemy should be fought with one's best abilities.'" (bin Laden, 1996)

Debate has been particularly intense among Saudi jihadis over whether to attack the regime or the Americans living in Saudi Arabia—the "near or far" issue. However, in this case, the differences among the jihadis are over strategy rather than ideology.

"The people of jihad, those who love jihad, and those who are protective of the nation have become divided into two groups:

"1. People who believe that these invading forces who have sullied the land of the two holy sanctuaries must be struck, and that the Americans must be kept busy with their own problems and their own bases, so that they are too occupied to move forward to bombard Muslim lands and countries.

"2. Those who say that we must secure this base, this land, so that we may form armies in it and recruit the youth and collect support.

"We believe in the middle ground between the two. It is true that the enemy must be kept occupied with himself, and deprived [of] the chance for security because, as soon as he feels secure in his bases and his rear supply routes, we will have then granted him the chance to use these to strike against our brethren in various areas of the Islamic world. . . . Yet we must prepare for such a great effort in the best way possible. . . . We used to say: 'Wait! Allow us to prepare ourselves, and then we will strike against the Americans.'

"It is true also that these countries must be exploited, because they are the primary source of finances for most jihadi movements, and they offer a relative security and freedom of movement. . . . But we must balance between this and the fact that America is invading the Muslim world and is creating restrictions on jihadi movements, and even [non-jihadi] Islamic ones. . . ." (al-Muqren, 2003)

Criticisms of those not fighting the Saudi regime are both snide and contemptuous.

"Since our brothers in Al-Qa'ida are preoccupied with waging war on the Crusaders, and since it has become clear from their repeated communiqués that they are not attacking the internal security apparatus, we have decided to relieve them of this important [religious obligation] and to purge the land of the two holy places of the [Arab] agents, freeing [Al-Qa'ida] to purge it of the Crusaders. . . ." (al-Haramayn Brigades, 2003)

Those fighting the Americans reply:

"Perhaps the aim of the Mujahideen is to refrain from toppling the regime because the treasonous cover provided by the Saudi regime prevents America from striking a powerful blow to the entire country. That is one of the ideas that led the Mujahideen [to prefer] first of all neutralizing America, or paralyzing it, and only afterward turning to this regime and its ilk. I say this, even though I maintain that eliminating some members of the regime would be very useful and would make things easier for the Mujahideen without causing the regime's downfall.

. . . .

"The Mujahideen are waging a great ongoing war with the masters [the Americans], and the slaves [the Saudis] have no place in this battle. The slaps and kicks that harm the slave during the Mujahideen's battle against its master are of no consequence in light of his fate when his master is defeated. . . . The Mujahideen are warring with the masters, but we may soon see a little more attention directed toward these slaves. . . ." (Allah, 2003)

There are also excuses.

"We must understand that the situation in the land of the two holy places is deteriorating day by day for the Mujahideen and their financial sources, as well as regarding the secularization of the country and the attempt by the treacherous rulers to lead it to moral collapse, in accordance with the dictates of the White House." (Abu Hajer, 2003)

"When asked whether the attacks in Saudi Arabia 'caused Mujahideen shares to plummet' in Saudi society, he responded: 'That may have happened, but we must look at the matter with a broader view, and place these operations in the framework of the war of the Mujahideen against the whole Western-American plan. At certain stages of this war, the Mujahideen can think they require these operations, despite their high price in terms of morale.'" (Allah, 2003)

And bitterness.

". . . anyone who bears witness will recognize the abilities of the brothers in the Arabian Peninsula, their equipment, financial support, and abundant fighters. Yet now, we watch them instead sending martyrs to Shaykh Abu Musab [al-Zarqawi], so why aren't these brothers targeting the centers of the apostates and other supporters of the infidels [in Saudi Arabia]? We have witnessed the effectiveness of such acts from the operation against the Interior Ministry that took place in the Arabian Peninsula. We witness that after the operation, the [government] has scaled back the arrests and searches of the brothers' houses. So, I ask you to increase the number of these kinds of operations." (Sayyaf, 2005)

"I repeat that the people of the Hijaz are to blame and they come very short of defending all the Muslims. Why didn't they target even one oil pipe which is spread throughout the whole country for thousands of kilometers or the oil refineries, which is the most important factor for supplying the American military effort?

". . . [recent fighting] does not take away from how backwards the Saudis are carrying out their jihad . . . the planning and weakness is very obvious in their operations and it is clear the surrounding of these mujahideen was the work of a spy.

". . . [even though] their financial capabilities allow them to do their duties in a better way because other Muslims don't even get to eat their daily meals." (Anonymous, undated(b))

Since 2004, there has been a significant decline in jihadi attacks in Saudi Arabia. Jihadi activity seems focused on raising money and men and training for the conflict in Iraq.

Egypt

Because of its large population, its geographic location astride the Suez Canal, and its history, Egypt is the most important country in the Arab world, notwithstanding Saudi wealth. The Muslim Brotherhood was founded in Egypt, and some of the most influential jihadi writers (al-Banna, Qutb, al-Zawahiri) came from there.

Egypt became a protectorate of Great Britain in 1882 and then became nominally independent in 1922. However, British troops remained in the country, supporting the monarchy. King Farouk I was eventually overthrown by the army, and a republic was established in 1953.[19] Colonel Gamal Abdul Nasser emerged to lead the country under the flag of Arab socialism. He severely suppressed the Muslim Brotherhood, and its Qutb wing in particular. When he died and was replaced by General Mohamad Anwar el-Sadat, the Salafi Islamists hoped that the new government would institute an Islamic state. It did not, however, and once again they were suppressed. After Sadat was killed by jihadi terrorists (Jamaat al-Jihad), the Salafis once again were subject to a severe crackdown. Sadat's successor, General Hosny Mubarak, has also insisted on secular government but has slowly let the Islamists reemerge as long as they eschew violence. Some jihadis have condemned the renunciation of violence. In the legislative elections in fall 2005, the Muslim Brotherhood was not allowed to run as a political party, but individual members could do so as "independents." Good organization and popular antipathy toward the government enabled them to secure 20 percent of the seats in Parliament. Alarmed, the government cracked down before the upper-house (Shura) elections in 2007, arresting hundreds of Muslim Brotherhood members.

While the Brotherhood is gaining support, the jihadis in Egypt are weak. If an Islamist government should ultimately come to power, it is more likely to be akin to the Brotherhood than to al-Qaeda. The U.S. State Department has recently authorized formal contacts with the Brotherhood, suggesting that it is not regarded as a terrorist organization. Most of the excerpts in this section are taken from Ayman al-Zawahiri's *Knights Under the Prophet's Banner,* published as a memoir not long after 9/11. He was a central figure as well as an observer of jihadi operations in Egypt from the 1970s until the late 1990s.

---

[19] King Farouk I, the last ruling member of the Mohamed Ali dynasty, left Egypt for the last time on board the royal yacht Al-Mahrousa on July 26, 1952, following the Free Officers Revolution, which led to the declaration of the republic in 1953.

"The State (of Egypt in which we live today) is ruled by the Laws of Unbelief although the majority of its inhabitants are Muslims." (Faraj, 1979, p. 167)

"An analysis of the political situation in Egypt would reveal that Egypt is struggling between two powers: An official power and a popular power that has its roots deeply established in the ground, which is the Islamic movement in general and the solid jihad nucleus in particular.

"The first power is supported by the United States, the west, Israel, and most of the Arab rulers. The second power depends on God alone, then on its wide popularity and alliance with other jihad movements throughout the Islamic nation, from Chechnya in the north to Somalia in the south and from Eastern Turkestan in the east to Morocco in the west." (al-Zawahiri, 2001)

"Military secularism always claimed that it respected Islam. But this respect had only one meaning for it, namely, employing religious scholars to pour praise on it to justify its acts. Indeed, the military court based its judgment on a fatwa by Shaykh Jad-al-Haq, the mufti of Egypt and later on the Shaykh of Al-Azhar. It used his fatwa to massacre young fundamentalists." (al-Zawahiri, 2001)

"Any company owner can publish a paid advertisement demanding the cancellation of a law or an administrative decision. Any actor can criticize the laws pertaining to his profession. Any writer—such as Faraj Fawdah [who was killed by Muslim fundamentalists]—can object to and ridicule the shari'ah rulings. Any journalist can lambaste the government and object to its rules, decisions, and laws. The only one who cannot do this is the mosque preacher. This is because article 201 of the [Egyptian] penal code says: 'No one in a house of worship—even if he is a man of religion and is delivering a religious sermon—can say something that opposes an administrative decision or an existing law or regulation. Anyone who does this faces imprisonment and is fined 500 pounds. If he resists, the fine and imprisonment are doubled.'

"Further, the only people who are not allowed to form trade unions— a right that is guaranteed even to belly dancers in Egypt—are the religious preachers and scholars.

. . . .

"With the killing of Anwar al-Sadat [1981] the issue of jihad in Egypt and the Arab world exploded and became a daily practice. Confrontation of the regime, which was against the shari'ah and allied with

America and Israel, became a battle of continuous chapters that did not stop until today.

. . . .

"The government's response to these events [assassinating Sadat] was brutal in its intensity and method.

"The treadmill of torture and repression turned at full speed, writing a bloody chapter in the . . . modern history of the Islamic movement in Egypt. The brutal treadmill of torture broke bones, stripped out skins, shocked nerves, and killed souls. Its methods were lowly. It detained women, committed sexual assaults, and called men feminine names, starved prisoners, gave them bad food, cut off water, and prevented visits to humiliate the detainees. The treadmill of torture this time was different from previous ones in two ways:

"It turned and is still turning non-stop. It has devoured thousands of victims since the killing of al-Sadat. The shari'ah committee of the Lawyers Association estimated the number of grievances submitted from 1981 to 1991 at 250,000.

"One time the government released 5,000 repentant prisoners in a few days. How many are those who have not repented?

"In fact, the number of detainees in Egyptian prisons is not less in any case than 60,000. There is no way to contact them or to know their conditions in view of the tight security imposed on them by the government.

. . . .

"The Interior Ministry responded to us [killing of Sadat] by killing Dr. Ala Muhiy-al-Din in broad daylight in the street on 2 September 1990.[20] Muhiy-al-Din, may God bless his soul, was one of the leaders of the Islamic Group who advocated the dialogue with the government. He made this position known on several occasions. He raised the slogan of free dialogue, a policy that proved to be a total failure with our rulers.

"Muhiy-al-Din's killing was a clear signal to the Islamic Group that the call for dialogue will be punished by death and that the regime will not tolerate the existence of the jihad groups. In doing so, the regime was doing the logical thing. The jihad groups represented the most serious opposition to it. They were the most capable of recruiting and spreading among the Muslim youths. These groups also represented a serious threat to the policy of normalization with Israel, which will not

---

[20] This occurred nine years after Sadat was assassinated, and his murder was not the likely motive.

feel comfortable in Egypt so long as the threat of the Islamic groups exists.

. . . .

"The [Egyptian] regime had no choice but to turn the battle against the mujahid Islamic movement into an international battle, particularly when the United States became convinced that the regime could not survive alone in the face of this fundamentalist campaign. It was also convinced that this spirit of jihad would most likely turn things upside down in the region and force the United States out of it. This would be followed by the earth-shattering event, which the west trembles at the mere thought of it, which is the establishment of an Islamic caliphate in Egypt. If God wills it, such a state in Egypt, with all its weight in the heart of the Islamic world, could lead the Islamic world in a jihad against the West. It could also rally the world Muslims around it. Then history would make a new turn, God willing, in the opposite direction against the empire of the United States and the world's Jewish government." (al-Zawahiri, 2001)

"– The security measures taken by our regimes are such that the only way to confront them is to deploy an armed force with a considerable firepower and armor enough to enforce its control of the capital, wage battles, and remain steadfast for one or two weeks.

"– The Islamic movement possesses thousands of youths who are racing toward martyrdom, but these youths are not trained and lack combat experience.

"– The Islamic movement's infiltration of the Army will always be countered by purging operations. It is difficult for the Islamic movement to recruit a large number of officers in the Army without getting discovered, in view of the tight security measures within the ranks of the Armed Forces." (al-Zawahiri, 2001)

The moderating positions of the Muslim Brotherhood and the renunciation of violence by Islamic Jihad came as a blow to al-Zawahiri.

". . . MB {the Muslim Brotherhood} have regrettably committed several doctrinal mistakes. They issued statements, including a statement entitled 'Statement from the MB to the People.' They started speaking about a new fiqh [new jurisprudence] alien to the scholars of Islam and in which they equated Muslims with non-Muslims in all the material, moral, civilian, and political rights of citizenship.

"In a previous statement, the MB said they believe the Christians have the right to hold all the state's posts except the post of the President of the Republic. Why? In other words, the MB don't mind if the Egyptian Prime Minister is a Christian! Why not also a Jew? We do have Jews in Egypt. Or the issue is a political propaganda and not principles, as they claim?" (al-Zawahiri, 2001)

"The new legal research {the new jurisprudence mentioned above} . . . is nothing but the production of a strategic project of the Egyptian intelligence in which they began working two years ago in an attempt to eliminate the Jihadi ideology in Egypt, and was planned and supervised by the Chief of Religious Activity in the State Security Investigations.

. . . .

"No one can deny the practice of the Egyptian Ministry of Interior, which is programmed according to the strategy of the baton and the slaughtering in every detention center in Egypt in order to implement its strategic project. The frequent news conveyed to us from inside and outside the prisons tells us that anyone refusing the initiative or who is opposed to the modern research gets tortured and his relatives get denied the right of visitation, and he also gets transferred to remote prisons with maximum security . . . ." (al-Hukaymah, 2007)[21]

"Honourable brother [Aby Yasir, leader of the Egyptian Islamic jihad], I hesitated before writing to you, after hearing, in the media, about your announcement of {the} end to military operations. I listened and read comments in the media indicating that this latest initiative will put an end to disagreement between members of the group, in Egypt and abroad. The reviews added that the declaration demonstrates that the government's crackdown was successful.

"I remembered, after reading these reports, that we'd spoken about this issue earlier and that I'd written to you on the subject more than once but you never replied.

. . . .

---

[21] Muhammad Khalil al-Hukaymah, also known as Abu Jihad al-Masri (the Egyptian), is a member with disputed status within Egypt's Gama's al-Islamiyya (the Egyptian Islamic Group, or EIG). In an August 2006 video, he was introduced by al-Zarqawi as a prominent member of EIG, and he subsequently pledged EIG's allegiance to al-Qaeda. Other EIG leaders have downplayed al-Hukaymah's prominence and disavowed his pledge. His strategic writings include "A New Strategic Method in the Resistance of the Occupier," and he has recently appealed for support from Hamas and Fatah al-Islam in northern Lebanon.

"Let me begin by asking you if the media reports accurately reflect the situation and, if so, what are the details?

"There are many frightening thoughts going through my mind at present. Did you all agree on this policy [of non-violence]? What is the strategy vis-à-vis the government? Have you reached an agreement with the authorities? If so, what are the details? Why wasn't it publicised? Is the accord secret in some parts or entirely? Would the secret be known to the government but concealed from [the rest of Islamic Jihad]? If an agreement has taken place, what is the government permitting you to do?

"Furthermore, why was the declaration issued? Why was it frank on the withdrawal from the 'International Front' [the alliance with al-Qaeda][22] but silent on other issues?

. . . .

"Let me repeat, once more, that the declaration contradicts, for a large number of brothers, the principles on which Islamic Jihad was founded and its proud legacy. If one is to believe media reports and analyses, the initiative represents a serious setback . . . with your continuing silence giving me the impression you accept it.

"The experience of Hassan al Banna with the Egyptian government is still fresh in our minds. His end came after he chose to praise the despots and declare peace. They killed him as a present to the King! If making agreements with the authorities was productive, the Brotherhood would've benefited before you. Instead, members are still being imprisoned across Egypt.

"Beware of losing both in this world and thereafter. Your loyalty must be to God and His Prophet. Righteousness will be your salvation in this world and the next." (al-Zawahiri, 1999)

Pakistan

Al-Qaeda continues to be based in Waziristan and elsewhere along the Afghan border, despite U.S. and Pakistani efforts to eliminate it. President Pervez Musharraf has been the target of at least two assassination attempts by jihadis, possibly with the collaboration of elements in the army and intelligence services. Militant Islamists form a very vocal minority in Pakistan, but in parliamentary voting they have been stuck at about 20 percent of the seats. Since the devastating earthquake of 2005, Islamists have worked diligently to build support among the victims. The crushing of the

---

[22] Islamic Jihad was part of the original group that formed the World Islamic Front in 1998 together with bin Laden and other organizations.

jihadi rebellion at the Red Mosque was a blow to the extremists because it generated no substantial public support for them.

> "Musharraf wants a Pakistan without Islam. This is why they destroyed the Islamic schools, and they are inventing a new religion, which they composed for him in America. They call this fairy-tale 'enlightened moderation.'" (al-Zawahiri, 2005d)

> "The Pakistani government under the leadership of Musharraf contributed a frightening portion to the slaughter [of mujahideen in Afghanistan], since they killed tens of mujahideen on Pakistani land, and imprisoned hundreds and delivered them to the Americans. This occurred in the midst of the silence and bashful stupidity of the Muslim street in Pakistan, despite the cooperation that some of the righteous Pakistani brothers demonstrated in rescuing whoever they could from those who fled through Pakistan and Iran, and were able to spread out anew in the world and gather themselves after the crushing battles and the blind pursuit." (al-Suri, 2005)

> "Today, the Pakistani army plays the same role that the British Indian army used to play in the aggression against the Muslims in India, and in quelling the Muslim uprisings in the British colonies. Today, the Pakistani army operates as a private institution, serving the interests of Bush, and Musharraf pockets the reward. The Pakistani army has abandoned the mission of defending Pakistan, and is devoting itself to killing the Muslims in Waziristan, in defense of the American army." (al-Zawahiri, 2005d)

> "Remember brothers, by accepting their aid, you will lose your honour. You will become their slaves. They will ask [for victims of the Kashmir earthquake] you to follow their evil agenda. The UN, the US, and the EU are not the friends of humanity. They are the worst enemies of the Muslims. You should seek help from Allah only." (Makki, 2005)

> "Our prime minister [Shaukat Aziz] who was taught by Jews and trained by Christians, wants the nation to develop by having this interest-based economy and building up the foreign exchange reserves. Allah says, O Muslims! I have a different law to govern you than the one I have for Japan, the United States, and other infidels. What school did you go to? Where did you learn about the development? If you want to develop, you can do so by having the blessing from earth and the skies. How will you get those blessings? . . . Give up polytheism

and adopt the prophets' morality: wear Islamic dress, and abide by Allah's orders and laws. . . . Set up an Islamic system in Pakistan, it will progress." (Saeed, 2005)

Jordan

Jordan is a nation and monarchy that was created by the British after World War II as part of its League of Nations Mandate. After the signing of the Egyptian-Israeli Peace Treaty, Jordan also signed a peace treaty with Israel on October 26, 1994.

Jordan's most renowned jihadi terrorist was Abu Musab al-Zarqawi. He was a common criminal in a Jordanian jail in the 1980s, when he met Sheikh Abu Muhammad al-Maqdisi (aka al-Barqawi and al-Utaybi), a prominent Islamist cleric who became his "spiritual godfather" and mentor while they were both in prison (McGeough, 2004). After his release, Zarqawi became an active jihadi. Tried and sentenced to death in absentia by the authorities in Jordan, Zarqawi, operating from Iraq, masterminded a bloody suicide attack on three hotels in Amman on November 9, 2005. He was criticized for this by al-Maqdisi, who a year earlier had broken with him over the legitimacy of suicide attacks and the killing of innocents in Iraq (see Chapter Four). In response to the criticism, Zarqawi offered an extensive defense of his actions in an audio statement on November 18, 2005, a portion of which is excerpted below.

"The system of government in Jordan is a pagan and a Kafir system but the rulers of Riyadh were in alliance with King Hussain nevertheless. And because of this alliance, no one (in the Kingdom of Saudi Arabia) could criticize King Hussain or accuse him of being a Jewish agent, and if someone did, he would have been punished. But when King Hussain sided with Saddam when the later [sic] invaded Kuwait, King Fahd disowned him. As a result . . . documents and photographs proving that King Hussain was a traitor and a Jewish agent appeared everywhere in Riyadh. And that was true and he was what they described him to be. Likewise, Jordanian newspapers did not waste any time to fill their pages with photographs and documents proving that Riyadh rulers were British agents before they became American agents, and that was true as well." (bin Laden, 2004e)

"This act [helping the coalition forces in the second Gulf War] by Abdullah to aid the kafirs and pave the way for them to take Muslim lands and control the affairs of Muslims in their own land constitutes one of the ten causes of apostasy." (bin Laden, 2004e)

". . . the war has ups and downs, and as the days goes {sic} by, we will have more fierce confrontations with the Jordanian Government. The chapters of some of these confrontations have ended, but what is coming is more vicious and bitter, God willing." (al-Zarqawi, undated)

In November 2005, three hotels in Amman, Jordan, were struck by suicide bombers under the direction of al-Zarqawi. Fifty-four people were killed, including members of a wedding party.

"The al-Qa'ida Organization took this blessed step for the following reasons:

"1. The Jordanian government has publicly announced its unbelief, openly declared war against God and His Prophet, and rejected the Sharia and replaced it with artificial laws.

"2. The army of this regime has become the trusted guardian of the state of the Sons of Zion. How many jihad fighters, who wanted to enter the blessed land to fight against the brethren of monkeys and pigs, were killed by a treasonous bullet from behind, fired by a soldier of this treasonous regime?

"3. Its promotion of immorality and lechery, and its spreading of corruption. This country has become a swamp of vice and promiscuity. Any who have seen the hotels, nightclubs, discotheques, bars, and touristic resorts at Aqaba and the Dead Sea and such [may reach the same conclusion]. . . .

"4. This impious state has let loose the hand of the Zionist enemy, and has allowed it to infiltrate into Jordanian society economically, politically, and socially. The Jewish economic lords have grasped control of most companies, banks, factories, laboratories, etc. . . .

"5. The existence of secret American prisons in Jordan under the direct supervision of the Jordanian intelligence services. . . .

"6. As for the Iraqi issue, Jordan was and is yet a rear supply base for the American army. . . ." (al-Zarqawi, 2005j)

"Your [Jordan's King Abdullah II] star is fading. You will not escape your fate, you descendant of traitors. We will be able to reach your head and chop it off." (al-Zarqawi, 2005i)

CHAPTER SEVEN

"Prescribed for You Is Fighting . . . (2:216)"

"The battle has not stopped in the past 36 years. The fundamentalist movement is either on the attack or in the process of preparing for an attack." (al-Zawahiri, 2001)

Strategy

Jihadis are not mindless terrorists, killing for the sake of killing. They have thought through the use of terrorism to achieve their ends, as they have the tactics of martyrdom for inducing terror and defeating conventional military deterrence.

As we have seen, one of the jihadis' key strategic debates is whether they should attack the near enemy—local apostate regimes—or the far enemy—the United States and its allies. Faraj, in *The Neglected Duty*, designates the near enemy as most important (Faraj, 1979), but al-Qaeda has argued for attacking the far enemy, while al-Qaeda offshoots in Saudi Arabia and Iraq have emphasized the local adversaries. The war in Iraq has tended to obviate the distinction in practice, since many U.S. targets are so near at hand. Nonetheless, al-Qaeda continues to wage jihad in Saudi Arabia, Egypt, and Yemen, and the Algerian Salafist Group for Prayer and Combat (GSPC) has become al-Qaeda in the Islamic Maghreb.

Jihadi strategy also has another geographic dimension. A primary strategic goal is to seize territory that can be used as a base or a place in which to establish an Islamic state. There are three major candidates: Saudi Arabia, the Caucasus, and Iraq. Iraq is discussed in Chapter Eight; the strategic value to jihadis of the other two regions is described below.

Al-Qaeda's strategic concept also focuses on "broadening the front." In the United States, the discussion about counterterrorism and homeland security often focuses on the dilemma of trying to protect everything. Jihadi strategy seeks to exploit that dilemma. At the same time, there is little in jihadi writings about specific targets such as sports stadiums or shopping malls, which are of great concern to U.S. authorities.

Jihadis regard themselves as an elite vanguard. They see the concept of a vanguard leading the people as having roots in the Qur'an, but ironically, they also draw on Western concepts of a revolutionary vanguard developed by communist and fascist strategists. Jihadis have learned that to make such an approach work, they must mobilize the masses—a lesson which, again ironically, they learned from secular anticolonial national-liberation struggles.

The Near Versus the Far Enemy

"Al-Qa'ida follows a clear strategy. The choice to target the United States from the beginning was a smart strategic choice for the global jihad movement. The struggle with the United States' hangers-on in the Islamic region has shown that these hangers-on cannot keep their tyrannical regimes going for a single minute without US help. This is why we must strike the head. When it falls, it will bring down the rest. The choice to target the United States is understood and accepted throughout the Islamic community because everybody knows the crimes the United States has committed against Islam and Muslims. This is what ensures popular sympathy and support." (al-Qurashi, 2002b)

"In the wake of the USSR's collapse, the United States monopolized its military superiority to dictate its wishes to numerous governments and, as a result, has succeeded in imposing security agreements on many countries. In this way the power of the governments that are affiliated with the United States grew in the sphere of pursuing the mujahidin in many countries. Doubtlessly this had an impact on the fundamentalist movement. Still this has been a new challenge that the jihadist movement confronted with methods that can reduce its impact. It did this by turning the United States into a target." (al-Zawahiri, 2001)

"The Islamic movement and its jihad vanguards, and actually the entire Islamic nation, must involve the major criminals—the United States, Russia, and Israel—in the battle and do not let them run the battle between the jihad movement and our governments in safety. They must pay the price, and pay dearly for that matter.

"The masters in Washington and Tel Aviv are using the regimes to protect their interests and to fight the battle against the Muslims on their behalf. If the shrapnel from the battle reach their homes and bodies, they will trade accusations with their agents about who is responsible for this. In that case, they will face one of two bitter choices: Either personally wage the battle against the Muslims, which means that the battle will turn into clear-cut jihad against infidels, or they reconsider their plans after acknowledging the failure of the brute and violent confrontation against Muslims.

"Therefore, we must move the battle to the enemy's grounds to burn the hands of those who ignite fire in our countries." (al-Zawahiri, 2001)

"To begin by putting an end to imperialism is not a laudatory and not a useful act. It is only a waste of time. We must concentrate on our own Islamic situation: we have to establish the Rule of God's Religion in our own country first, and make the Word of God supreme. . . . There is no doubt that the first battlefield for jihad is the extermination of these infidel leaders and to replace them by a complete Islamic Order." (Faraj, 1979, p. 193 in 1986 trans.)

"[Khalil] Does this mean there are differences within your organization between a current that calls for focusing on striking at the United States and another current that calls for striking at the Arab states that are allied with America?

"[Al-Ablaj] Dear brother: The Arab states will not witness harm or aggression; only the US and Israeli targets and those who protect these colonialist interests [will be targeted]." (al-Ablaj, 2003a)

"As regards giving priority to striking these [apostate] states {rather} than to striking America, the answer is no. The strikes against America have their time. Crushing and devastating strikes against America will come at the suitable time. In other words, after wearing it out with injuries our strike must be a knockout. This is how a strike ought to be." (al-Ablaj, 2003a)

"My view is that we should do bombings in conflict areas, not in peaceful areas. We have to target the place of the enemy, not countries where many Muslims live." (Ba'asyir, 2005)

"Even if people disagree today regarding which of these two groups – the apostate traitor agents [i.e. the Arab governments] or the colonialist enemies [i.e. the Americans] – is more worthy to wage Jihad against, there need be no disagreement that Jihad is the solution for dealing with both of them." (MEMRI, 2003)

Secure Base

". . . {The} jihadist movement needs an arena that would act like an incubator where its seeds would grow and where it can acquire practical experience in combat, politics, and organizational matters. The brother martyr for this is how we think of him—Abu-Ubaydah al-Banshiri, may he rest in peace, used to say: 'It is as if 100 years have been added to my life in Afghanistan.' {Al-Banshiri drowned in Lake Victoria in 1996.}" (al-Zawahiri, 2001)

"The problem of finding a secure base for jihad activity in Egypt used to occupy me a lot, in view of the pursuits to which we were subjected by the security forces and because of Egypt's flat terrain which made government control easy, for the River Nile runs in its narrow valley between two deserts that have no vegetation or water. Such a terrain made guerrilla warfare in Egypt impossible and, as a result, forced the inhabitants of this valley to submit to the central government and be exploited as workers and compelled them to be recruited in its army.

. . . .

"The jihad movement must adopt its plan on the basis of controlling a piece of land in the heart of the Islamic world on which it could establish and protect the state of Islam and launch its battle to restore the rational caliphate based on the traditions of the prophet.

"Armies achieve victory only when the infantry takes hold of land. Likewise, the mujahid Islamic movement will not triumph against the world coalition unless it possesses a fundamentalist base in the heart of the Islamic world. All the means and plans that we have reviewed for mobilizing the nation will remain up in the air without a tangible gain or benefit unless they lead to the establishment of the state of caliphate in the heart of the Islamic world.

. . . .

"If the successful operations against Islam's enemies and the severe damage inflicted on them do not serve the ultimate goal of establishing the Muslim nation in the heart of the Islamic world, they will be nothing more than disturbing acts, regardless of their magnitude, that could be absorbed and endured, even if after some time and with some losses." (al-Zawahiri, 2001)

"Igniting the fire in the Arabian Peninsula is expected to be one of the keys to the great change, because the Arabian Peninsula is the heart, and any change in the Arabian Peninsula affects the other parts of the Islamic body." (Allah, 2003)

"The liberation of the Caucasus would constitute a hotbed of jihad (or fundamentalism as the United States describes it) and that region would become the shelter of thousands of Muslim mujahidin from various parts of the Islamic world, particularly Arab parts. This poses a direct threat to the United States represented by the growing support for the jihadist movement everywhere in the Islamic world. If the Chechens and other Caucasian mujahidin reach the shores of the oil-rich Caspian Sea, the only thing that will separate them from Afghanistan will be the neutral state of Turkmenistan. This will form a mujahid Islamic belt to the south of Russia that will be connected in the east to Pakistan, which is brimming with mujahidin movements in Kashmir. The belt will be linked to the south with Iran and Turkey that are sympathetic to the Muslims of Central Asia. This will break the cordon that is struck around the Muslim Caucasus and allow it to communicate with the Islamic world in general, but particularly with the mujahidin movement.

"Furthermore the liberation of the Muslim Caucasus will lead to the fragmentation of the Russian Federation and will help escalate the jihad movements that already exist in the republics of Uzbekistan and Tajikistan, whose governments get Russian backing against those jihadist movements.

"The fragmentation of the Russian Federation on the rock of the fundamentalist movement and at the hands of the Muslims of the Caucasus and Central Asia will topple a basic ally of the United States in its battle against the Islamic jihadist reawakening.

"For this reason the United States chose to begin by crushing the Chechens by providing Western financing for the Russian Army[1] so that when this brutal campaign against the Chechen mujahidin is completed, the campaign can move southwards to Afghanistan either by the action of former Soviet republics that are US agents or with the participation of US troops under the guise of combating terrorism, drug trafficking, and the claims about liberating that region's women." (al-Zawahiri, 2001)

---

[1] The claim that the United States is helping Russia against the Chechen rebels has no basis in fact but is commonly believed by jihadis.

Expanding the Battlefield

"We must also understand that the al-Qa'ida Organization has adopted a strategy in its war with the Americans based on expanding the battlefield and exhausting the enemy, who spread his interests over the globe, with successive and varied blows. The average strikes before 11 September was one every two years. However, after the blessed Manhattan Operation, the rate increased to two operations per year. Expanding the battlefield has invaluable benefits. The enemy, who needed to protect his country only, realized that he needed to protect his huge interests in every country. The more diversified and distant the areas in which operations take place the more exhausting it becomes for the enemy, the more he needs to stretch his resources, and the more he becomes terrified." (Center for Islamic Studies and Research, 2003)

". . . Our enemies are incapable or confused about opening several fronts. They thought the battle would be easy: Weak regimes and peoples that have been absent from the scene for years. So the planners thought the battle would be easy and opened multiple fronts at the same time. . . ." (Mish'al, 2005)

Deterrence

"Deterrence: This principle is based on the assumption that there are two sides [fighting] that seek to survive and defend their interests – but it is completely eliminated when dealing with people who don't care about living but thirst for martyrdom. While the principle of deterrence works well [in warfare] between countries, it does not work at all for an organization with no permanent bases and with no capital in Western banks, that does not rely on aid from particular countries. As a result, it is completely independent in its decisions, and it seeks conflict from the outset. How can such people, who strive for death more than anything else, be deterred?" (al-Qurashi, undated)

"Jihad and martyrdom operations are our strategic weapon against the enemy. Martyrdom is the general rubric for all of our doctrinal, intellectual, political, economic, and military programs . . . [ellipses as published]" (Abu Ayman al-Hilali, 2002)

"Just as they're killing us, we have to kill them so that there will be a balance of terror. This is the first time the balance of terror has been close between the two parties, between Muslims and Americans, in the modern age. American politicians used to do whatever they wanted with us." (bin Laden, 2001a)

"Ali Safuri, Islamic Jihad Leader: [through interpreter] It [suicide bombings] achieves for us the balance of terror. The balance of terror is important. When my countryman sees that Apache circling in the sky, he becomes scared. But also for them, when an operation takes place in Afula, the man in Tel Aviv becomes too scared to even sleep at his home. Such is the balance of terror." (Safuri, 2002)

". . . if there is an arrest or individuals are killed in a house raid, there must be an unexpected action that directs a strike of deterrence . . . [accompanied by] a media announcement that the strike is because of the arrest or the killing of brother and so-and-so . . . we make it clear that we will not stop targeting the people of tyranny; rather, their practices cause us to do more and make our operations more vicious." (Naji, 2004)

"Militarily, the 11 September raid is a great threat to the United States' current military standing. The asymmetric strategy that al-Qa'ida is pursuing entails the use of means and methods that the defender cannot use, recognize, or avoid. They rendered the United States' tremendous military superiority useless and reduced the effectiveness of US military deterrence internationally. The proliferation of the 'martyrdom bomb' and its expansion beyond Palestine to US targets has thrown off US calculations and caused the United States' sense of security to evaporate." (al-Qurashi, 2002b)

"For example, on war against the US. The most important thing is not killing, but terrorizing. Irhaab (terror) is wajib [obligation], while qotl (killing) is sunnah [meritorious]." (Ilyas, 2005)

Morale

"When the state of steadfastness and refusal is a comprehensive state among peoples and nations, it drives us to an important point I may characterize as instilling despair in the enemies that their military and security wagers will pay off. This is the point we wager on. We are not wagering on balancing the scales of power today with our enemy. We are betting on making our enemies despair of conquering us by their superior power or breaking our will and imposing defeat on us. This bringing of the enemy to the point of despair is a necessary thing. Allah was truthful: 'Today those who did not believe in your religion have despaired' [Koranic verse]. If the moment of despairing is reached, it is the crucial moment after which the enemies' forces retreat." (Mish'al, 2005)

"The enemy can be patient but cannot persevere. We, with our faith, creed, and love for meeting Allah, can persevere until the enemy collapses, even if this takes decades or centuries." (Abu-Hafs al-Masri Brigades (Al-Qa'ida), 2004)

Political Strategy

"The Islamic movement is not a substitute for the Islamic community; it is the vanguard that goes ahead of it. The ultimate goals of the Islamic change project—the caliphate—are too large for any group, no matter how capable, to achieve in isolation from the community." (Seif al-Din al-Ansari, 2002d)

"The jihad movement must come closer to the masses, defend their honor, fend off injustice, and lead them to the path of guidance and victory. It must step forward in the arena of sacrifice and excel to get its message across in a way that makes the right accessible to all seekers and that makes access to the origin and facts of religion simple and free of the complexities of terminology and the intricacies of composition.

"The jihad movement must dedicate one of its wings to work with the masses, preach, provide services for the Muslim people, and share their concerns through all available avenues for charity and educational work. We must not leave a single area unoccupied. We must win the people's confidence, respect, and affection. The people will not love us unless they felt that we love them, care about them, and are ready to defend them." (Zawahiri, 2001)

"The jihad movement must be eager to make room for the Muslim nation to participate with it in the jihad for the sake of empowerment [al-tamkin]. The Muslim nation will not participate with it unless the slogans of the mujahidin are understood by the masses of the Muslim nation.

"The one slogan that has been well understood by the nation and to which it has been responding for the past 50 years is the call for the jihad against Israel. In addition to this slogan, the nation in this decade is geared against the US presence. It has responded favorably to the call for the jihad against the Americans.

"A single look at the history of the mujahidin in Afghanistan, Palestine, and Chechnya will show that the jihad movement has moved to the center of the leadership of the nation when it adopted the slogan of liberating the nation from its external enemies and when it portrayed it as a battle of Islam against infidelity and infidels." (al-Zawahiri, 2001)

"The interest in understanding the rules of the political game and the political reality of the enemies and their fellow travelers and then mastering disciplined political action through sharia politics and opposing this reality is not less than the importance of military action." (Naji, 2004)

"In the absence of this popular support, the Islamic mujahed movement would be crushed in the shadows, far from the masses who are distracted or fearful, and the struggle between the Jihadist elite and the arrogant authorities would be confined to prison dungeons far from the public and the light of day. This is precisely what the secular, apostate forces that are controlling our countries are striving for. These forces don't desire to wipe out the mujahed Islamic movement, rather they are stealthily striving to separate it from the misguided or frightened Muslim masses. Therefore, our planning must strive to involve the Muslim masses in the battle, and to bring the mujahed movement to the masses and not conduct the struggle far from them." (al-Zawahiri, 2005b)

"The aim which motivates the enemies is a material aim. . . . Their principle absolutely does not submit to any moral value; rather, all the other principles are subordinate to it – friendship or enmity, peace or war – and are all determined according to self interest."

. . . .

"Therefore, we should formulate our military and political plans after properly understanding and appraisng the ceiling of interest which limits the action of each one of our enemies and work to widen the gap of interests between hostile factions. Therefore, the map of interests must be clear in the minds of our leaders of action." (Naji, 2004)

Oil

Jihadis have been of two minds about the role of oil in their designs. They recognize its strategic importance but early on were unsure whether to attack oil facilities or preserve them for themselves. Secondary debates focus on whether oil workers are legitimate targets and whether tactics should vary according to who owns the facility—Muslims or non-Muslims. In Iraq, the insurgency has conducted a campaign of sabotage of oil pipelines that limited oil production to about the same levels as those that existed before the war, but it is now increasing.

> "The presence of the USA Crusader military forces on land, sea and air of the states of the Islamic Gulf is the greatest danger threatening the largest oil reserve in the world. The existence of these forces in the area will provoke the people of the country . . . and push them to take up armed struggle against the invaders occupying the land; therefore spread of the fighting in the region will expose the oil wealth to the danger of being burned up. . . . I would like here to alert my brothers, the Mujahideen, the sons of the nation, to protect this (oil) wealth and not to include it in the battle as it is a great Islamic wealth and a large economical power essential for the soon to be established Islamic state, by Allah's Permission and Grace." (bin Laden, 1996)

> "You have to realize that our enemy's biggest incentive in controlling our land is to steal our oil. So, do not spare any effort to stop the greatest robbery in history. This (oil and other resources) is the treasures [sic] of our current and future generations. They (the west) plot with their allies and puppets in the area to buy our oil at a very low price. All products have gone up in prices several folds except oil itself, which is the basic component of the whole industry. Oil prices do not reflect market reality. . . . A fair price for oil at the present time is a minimum USD 100.00."[2] (bin Laden, 2004e)

> "I call upon the mujahideen to focus their attacks on the stolen oil of the Muslims. Most of its revenue goes to the enemies of Islam, and most of what they leave is plundered by the thieves who rule our countries. This is the greatest theft in the history of humanity. The enemies of Islam are consuming this vital resource with unparalleled greed. We must stop this theft any way we can, in order to save this resource for the sake of the Muslim nation.

---

[2] While this may seem unremarkable now, at the time, oil was priced at $31.67 a barrel—F.O.B. cost of crude oil imports in December 2004 (data from the U.S. Energy Information Administration).

"If the only way to repel these thieves is by killing them, they should be killed without honor." (al-Zawahiri, 2005d)

"Various oil interests can be targeted including oil fields, oil facilities, and seaports for oil exportation. The Islamic jurisprudence regarding killing should be observed when targeting individuals who are affiliated with the oil industry. It is prohibited to kill someone only to manipulate the oil prices. A whole independent and permissible reason should exist for killing him.

"Targeting oil facilities depends on who the owner is. The fundamental rule stipulates the inadmissibility of sabotaging the oil interests that the Muslims possess even though they are in the hand of atheists. The inviolability of the property depends on who the owner – and not the usurper – is. It is a duty to salvage such property from the infidels, not to sabotage it.

"However, it is permissible to sabotage Muslim property if there is no hope that the Muslims will derive benefit from it or if the damage that is inflicted on the infidels outweighs the benefits that the Muslims expect to get."

"It is strange that they want to dictate democracy and Americanize our culture through their jet bombers. Therefore, what is yet to come is even more malicious and devilish. The occupation of Iraq is a link in the Zionist-Crusader chain of evil. Then comes the full occupation of the rest of the Gulf states to set the stage for controlling and dominating the whole world. For the big powers believe that the Gulf and the Gulf states are the key to controlling the world due to the presence of the largest oil reserves there." (bin Laden, 2004a)

Tactics

"Dragging the masses into the battle requires more actions which will inflame opposition and which will make the people enter into the battle, willing or unwilling, such that each individual will go to the side which he supports. We must make this battle very violent, such that death is a heartbeat away, so that the two groups will realize that entering this battle will frequently lead to death. That will be a powerful motive for the individual to choose to fight in the ranks of the people of truth in order to die well, which is better than dying for falsehood and losing both this world and the next." (Naji, 2004)

"If they say that by your attacks on Jews and Americans you have weakened the Arab regimes and damaged their economy, demolished development projects, scared away investors and tourists, you tell them yes, and this is exactly what we want. . . . You are foolish, do you think we care about anything more than destroying and ending these bad and rotten regimes? The economy and development will come after the establishment of God's law.

"If they say that by your attacks in Istanbul, you have embarrassed the moderate Muslims in Turkey and pushed them to the American and the European side, you tell them we want to embarrass those that sell their religion, praise Ataturk and their secularism made them deny their religion and criticize Jihad and build coalition with the enemy to fight terror. In recent history, Turkey has always worked hard to please Europe so it can join the crusaders coalition and has always been close to the Americans and Jews.

"If they say that your terror was used to put pressure on the Arab regimes to implement reforms that are in the direction of secularism and changing curriculums for the benefit of globalization culture and love and brotherhood with the western infidels, you say yes, embarrassing those regimes is the ultimate goal of our jihad, we want to show their lies and make them stop hiding behind Islam while they opened their doors to secularism and the infidels in secret. They are still implementing reforms in curriculums to get closer to the infidels of the east and the west. Now they are doing openly what they used to do in secret and they are fighting the people of faith, the faith that feeds Jihad to please their American masters. The first step in defeating these regimes is embarrassing them.

"If they say that you started the fire of hatred between the west and the Muslims and you started the cultural war and you made them refuse the Hijab in their public schools, you tell them yes, and this is our duty as Muslims to cut the ties between Muslims and their enemies. Refusing the Hijab in schools is a blessing for our girls that will purify them from mixing with corrupt culture and bad curriculum. This will wake up the Muslims and make them aware of the hatred of those infidels toward Islamic traditions that could encourage Muslims to create alternative Muslim schools. The war on Hijab is also a war on Islam." (Firas, undated, in al-Maqdisi, 2004)

"These are the thousands of young people who have traveled to the land of jihad and joined the ranks of the mujahidin. Some of them are participating directly in battle. Others are still in training. Others have spread out in the cities waiting to play their role in the war at the right time and place. They are always ready to do their part.

"This group is highly disciplined and organized. They are the long arm of the jihad community. The enemy calls them 'sleeper cells.' In reality, they are cells of wakefulness and awareness. This is why the enemy cannot and will not discover them until they carry out their missions with God's protection." (al-Amili, 2002)

"The rate of operations escalates in order to send a living, practical message to the people, the masses, and the enemy's low-ranking troops that the power of the mujahids is on the rise. . . . Therefore, when we plan our operations, we should begin with small operations and then (undertake) larger ones, and so forth – even if we are capable of undertaking the largest (operations) from the very beginning – just as the al-Qaeda organization arranged operations to ignite confrontation. . . ." (Naji, 2004)

"For those who study the theory of fighting the enemy in the Muslim countries which are not occupied directly by emeny, we find that we will fight them in these countries in order to have some political pressure and psychological break down until they leave our countries. The fight will not be to eliminate them, and as long as it is like that, the reality and our interests support the idea of having a small operation every month against the enemy that will cause much more damage than one big operation every one or two years." (al-Hukaymah, 2007)

"As for operations in the form of waves, that is suitable for groups whose military bases and defensive positions are impregnable, but remote from the site of the operations. Likewise, it is suitable for groups that want to send a message to the enemy that waves of fear and paying the price for its actions will never end, and that the cessation of operations for a period of time does not mean this is a permanent stoppage, such that the enemy may do whatever it wishes with the Muslim masses; rather, we are preparing for another wave of operations which will fill their hearts with fear and this fear will have no end. . . ." (Naji, 2004)

"Regarding the American army, the mujahidin have tested it in many fields. The mujahidin gained experience in fighting the biggest power in the world then, the army of the Soviet Union. Whoever was engaged in the two wars can confirm that there is no comparison between the two armies. The United States superiority is in its air power only, and air power, as everyone knows, cannot decide a war." (Center for Islamic Studies and Research, 2003)

"Air power can be neutralized in many fields. It is useless in jungle warfare, as in the Philippines. Therefore, it withdrew quickly after it tried to attack the mujahidin in the Philippines. Tunnels in mountains are also very effective in reducing the effects of air power in a war. Air power is ineffective in urban areas, unless there are important installations or bases for ground forces." (Center for Islamic Studies and Research, 2003)

"Economic jihad involves three issues:

"– Military operations that aim to protect the economy of Muslims or take spoils from the enemy

"– Military operations that aim to inflict damage on the enemy's economy whether or not they target the sources of the economy

"– Boycotts, propaganda, or similar non-military operations against the enemy's economy." (al-Anzi, 2006)

Battlefield Lessons from Afghanistan

"1. Converting the military force to small units with good administrative capabilities will save us from heavy losses at one hand, and also help in controlling all the fronts with the least possible number of personnel. In addition, converting the people to armed militias will render the mission of the enemy impossible. Large military groups are a problem administratively. They would occupy a large land area, which would make hiding from aerial detection or air bombardment difficult.

"2. The idea of the Corolla vehicles {Toyota pickup trucks} was one of the best and they proved efficient with a capability in maneuver and deceit. They went through unusual operations throughout the duration of the battle with the Americans. We were joking that if the Japanese had seen the vehicles in action, they would have used them for marketing advertisements. . . .

"3. We agreed with the Taliban to stop firing all anti-airplane guns, because on the one hand, these planes were outside the range of the guns, and on the other hand, the firing would disclose the location of the guns and expose them to attack. . . . It is noteworthy to mention that SAM-7 missiles were never useful.

. . . .

"4. Administrative Affairs.

. . . .

"Horses and Motorcycles. Horses took the place of cars in transporting administrative things. The Abu Obaida Camp had three motorcycles which the brothers used in the previous days and which had proved their usefulness. It was a very successful idea that the Americans did not notice, and they did not fire one missile against them, even though they were moving around, lifting the wounded and transporting food and water . . . .

. . . .

"7. . . . Regarding trenches, we say that fighting in open areas without aerial cover or good air defenses is a big gamble and the fighter should be camouflaged under a difficult terrain. Buildings in cities act as a hindrance to the plans of the enemy, which also applies to planted areas.

"These [trenches] help in hiding the location, and facilitates the operations of traps for any ground attack unit. Our second advice is to train on reconnaissance, traps, and raiding operations and to work in small groups, and avoid by all means working in large groups.

"8. It is important to choose the appropriate field and prepare it to engage the ground enemy as soon as it advances and falls into the trap area. This will take away all the capabilities of the air forces and keep them outside the conflict until the engagement line is cut. As we said, the American soldier is qualified to perform cinematic roles only and the enemy will lose his heaviest casualties in these traps.

"9. It is impossible to win against the people no matter what the enemy possesses in weaponry, technical capabilities, and advanced technology. Victory over the United States is very possible and easy beyond the imagination of many. It has several components; the most important is the elimination of the hypocritical forces fighting on behalf of the American soldier. This group is weak militarily, shaken psychologically. It is mercenary, without any cause; its representation in the war was {a} trifle.

. . . .

"10. Good communications, for the enemy works on cutting lines of communications and causing disruption which could be very harmful.

"That is why it is very important to have alternatives to advanced technology, down to old-fashioned couriers." (al-Adel, 2003)

Targeting

"As for America's allies, they will be targeted by the assassination of the heads of the regimes, security officers, a number of presidents, and kings; this is in addition to the assassination of security officials such as intelligence officers who will be forming in their country a kind of a mafia. . . ." (Anonymous, 2005a)

". . . the most important jihadi target in this phase is attacks against tourists. They regard the Muslim countries as their back yard, and import with them their moral dirt." (al-Suri, 2005)

"Types of Targets within the Cities:

"1. Targets with an ideological aspect: The use of force is not recommended at the beginning of a military jihadi operation against religious ideological targets except in some cases such as:

"• Christianization of pure Islamic communities, like what happened in Yemen, in Iraq, and in Saudi Arabia – specifically in Riyadh – where Bibles were recently distributed to residences. Hunting down and killing whoever is responsible for performing such an act is a good thing. These people's identity is known to the Mujahideen, and we ask God to facilitate the task of going after them.

"• Undercover spying operations under any disguise, even if it was religious. Dealing with spiritual and religious Islamic figures, even if they were spies, should be done in a way to avoid a violent reaction from Muslims who were misled by those agents. Hitting them will only glorify and make symbols out of them. May God's anger fall upon them.

"• One of the exceptions also is publicity exercised by certain religious figures such as ministers, priests and rabbis, in which they attack Islam and Muslims. . . .

"• One other exception is a financial, military or moral mobilization of ideological figures (Jews and Christians) against Muslims.

"2. Economic targets: The goals of hitting those targets are to create a disruption in the stability required for moving the economic sector towards progression. This was accomplished by hitting the petroleum wells and pipes in Iraq, which kept foreign companies away from touching the oil, or at least created an absence of security and stability needed to steal the Muslims' wealth. Another goal is to withdraw or force the withdrawal of foreign capitals [sic] from the local market. The economic powers present on the site of conflict have been badly affected. As a result of the blessed strikes in Madrid, for instance, the entire European economy suffered. That was a double strike to the economy of the governments of the Crusaders, the Jews or the apostates. . . .

"Human targets sorted by level of importance:

"1. The Jews: They are divided in grades with respect to importance: American and Israeli Jews are first targeted, then British Jews, then French Jews, and so on . . . .

"2. The Christians: The grades of importance are as follows:

- Americans
- British
- Spaniards
- Australians
- Canadians
- Italians

"The above categories are divided into sections with respect to importance:

- Financial, economic, and businessmen, as money is of the essence in this era.
- Diplomats, politicians, intellectuals, analysts and political missions.
- Scientists and experts.
- Military commanders and soldiers.
- Tourists, and recreational groups, and every person who has been warned by the Mujahideen not to enter Muslim territories.

"3. The apostates: They are graded as follows:

"• Whoever is close to the Jewish and Christian Governments is considered one of the most important targets, such as Hosni Moubarak and the rulers of the Arab Peninsula and their advisors.
"• Seculars and modernists who spread corruption within the believers, and mock religion. Those bastards are considered the hypocrites of the fifteenth century.
"• Spies and investigators, as they are the shields and the fences of the Jews and Christians and they are the striking hand for the apostate rulers." (*Manchester Document*, undated)

"You know that the United States offered great prizes for whoever would kill those engaged in jihad in God's cause. God willing, we within the Al-Qa'ida Organization are committed to offering a prize amounting to 10,000 grams in gold to whoever would kill the occupier Bremer, his deputy, the commander of the US troops, or his deputy in Iraq.

. . . .

". . . whoever kills Kofi Annan, the head of his mission to Iraq, or his representatives, like Lakhdar Brahimi, will have the same prize, which is 10,000 grams of gold. There will be a prize of 1,000 grams of gold for whoever kills a military figure or civilian from the veto masters, such as the Americans or British, and 500 grams of gold for whoever kills a military figure or civilian from the slaves of the General Assembly in Iraq, such as Japan and Italy. In view of the security circumstances, the handing over of the prizes will be at the nearest possible opportunity, God willing. Whoever is killed after killing one of the soldiers of occupation, the biggest prize will be for us and for him. We pray that God would grant us martyrdom for His sake.

"As for the smaller prize (the gold), it will be for his heirs, God willing." (bin Laden, 2004c)

Raids

The principal attacks perpetrated by jihadis have been well covered in the media. This section conveys what the jihadis themselves say about several of these events. The word "raid" is used because that is how jihadis frequently term their attacks, drawing upon the language of the Qur'an. It reflects the strategy of besieging and wearing down the enemy, which has its roots in the tribal desert warfare that long preceded the time of the Prophet.

"Yesterday, London, and Madrid. Tomorrow, Los Angeles and Melbourne, Allah willing. And this time, don't count on us demonstrating restraint or compassion." (al-Qaeda, 2005)

"Initially, I would like to remind you of the defeats of some of the superpowers at the hands of the jihad fighters. I remind you of the defeat of the former Soviet Union, of which there are no more than traces remaining after grueling combat with the Afghans and their other Muslim supporters with the aid of God. Also, I remind you of the defeat of the Russians at the hands of the Chechens. The jihad fighters there set the most magnificent examples of sacrifice; the Chechen jihad fighters, with help from their Arab brothers and supporters, broke the arrogance of the Russians and cost them losses after losses, causing their withdrawal after the first war. The Russians returned once again with American support, and Russia is still being dealt huge losses from a small group of believers, whom we ask God to support.

"I also remind you of the defeat of the American forces in the year 1402 of the Hegira [1983 AD], when the Israelis swarmed into Lebanon. The Lebanese resistance sent a truck full of explosives to the headquarters of the American forces, the Marines, in Beirut, killing more than 240 of them. To hell and the worst of fates.

"Then, after the second Gulf War [Translator: Desert Storm; to most Arabs, the first Gulf war was the Iran-Iraq war], America inserted its armies in Somalia, where they killed 13 thousand Muslims there. Then the lions of Islam from among the Afghani Arabs leapt to face them, and they joined the battle on the side of their brothers there. They rubbed the nose [of the American forces] in the mud; they killed some of them and they destroyed some of their tanks and downed some of their helicopters. America and her allied then fled into the night, praise and gratitude to God!

"During this period, the young men of the jihad prepared improvised explosive devices to be used against the Americans in Aden. When they exploded, the cowards fled in less than 24 hours. In the year 1415 of the Hegira [1995 AD], an explosion in Riyadh killed four Americans. This was a clear message that shows the objection of the locals to America's policy of supporting the Jews and occupying the land of the two holy places.

"In the following year, another explosion took place in Khubar that killed 19 and wounded more than 400. After that, the Americans were forced to move their major centers from the cities to bases in the desert. After that, in the year 1418 of the Hegira [1998 AD], the jihad fighters openly threatened America,[3] that they must stop helping the Jews and leave the land of the two holy places [sic]. The jihad fighters were able, with the blessing of God, to slap America mightily twice in East Africa. The enemy rejected the warning and the Mujahideen managed, through the grace of Allah, to deliver two tremendous blows in East Africa.[4] Then America was warned again, without response. So God

---

[3] The threat was bin Laden's "Declaration of War Against the Americans Occupying the Land of the Two Holy Places."

[4] The attacks on the U.S. embassies in Nairobi, Kenya, and Dar es Salaam, Tanzania, in 1998.

granted success to the jihad fighters in a great martyrdom operation; the America destroyer USS Cole was destroyed in Aden. This was an echoing blow to the American military. This operation also had the effect of exposing the proxy status of the Yemeni government, like the other countries in the region." (bin Laden, 2003b)

The 9/11 Attacks

Osama bin Laden initially refused to take responsibility for the 9/11 attacks. This left the door open to a variety of conspiracy theories in which Jews, Christians, and the CIA were blamed for them. Once it became clear that al-Qaeda was responsible for the 9/11 attacks, a flood of justifications and self-congratulations spewed forth from jihadi sources. The principal sentiment was that the jihadis were no longer helpless—9/11 had empowered them. More recently, the attacks have been recast as a trap to lure the United States into attacking and awakening the Muslim people.

> "The Crusaders and Zionists know with certainty that what happened in New York and Washington occurred at the hands of radical Zionists or Christian movements, but because they saw an Islamic awakening in Afghanistan and they were fearful of the implementation of the Sharee'ah, in that Emirate. They feared that this could spread to the surrounding nations and so they went forth with this terror campaign[5] in which they used all sorts of internationally prohibited weaponry such as cluster bombs, bunker busters and others, killing thousands of civilian men, women and children." (ash-Shu'aybi, undated)

> "Al-Qa'ida planned, acted, and executed, and the martyrs went off to their Lord. The others withdrew, God willing, and no evil befell them. The world changed entirely in two hours. The defeated [Muslims] continue to ask themselves to this day, 'Could al-Qa'ida really have done this? Or was it just a Jewish deception?' This question did not result from a shortage of information. If that were the case, they could be excused for asking. The tragedy is that our leaders' minds have long ago fallen prey to a psychology of weakness." (Seif al-Din al-Ansari, 2002d)

The following is a memo of instructions allegedly written by the lead 9/11 hijacker, Mohamed Atta.

> "The last night

---

[5] The attack on the Taliban regime in Afghanistan.

"1. Commit yourself to death and renew the intention.

- Shave excess body hair and apply perfume.
- Take a shower.

"2. Learn the plan thoroughly from all angles, and anticipate the enemy's reaction or resistance.

"3. Read the at-Tawba ['Repentance'] and the Anfal ['Spoils of War']. [Chapters nine and eight of the Quran]. Consider what is meant by them, and what God promised the faithful by way of enduring bliss for the martyrs.

. . . .

"7. Cleanse your heart and purify it from blemishes. Forget that what is called the worldly kingdom for the time of play is past. The appointment with the truth has arrived. How much time in our lives have we wasted.

. . . .

"8. Let your breast be glad, for what lies between you and your wedlock in heaven is but mere moments, from whence you will begin a happy and pleasant life and eternal bounty with the prophets and the virtuous and the worthy martyrs, who will make good company. We ask God for his grace, and be optimistic, for he [the Prophet] loved optimism in everything.

. . . .

"12. Bless (yourself, baggage, clothes, knife, tools, ticket, passport, all of your papers) {This is done by speaking Koranic verses into the hands and then running the hands over the items to be blessed}.

"13. Check your weapon before departure, and before leaving, (let one of you sharpen his blade, that the one he sacrifices will be glad).

"14. Fit your clothes closely upon yourself, for this is the way of the worthy salaf (early Muslims), may God be pleased with them. They used to fit their clothes tightly upon themselves before battle. Then fit your shoes closely and wear socks that stay in place in the shoes and do not come down.

. . . .

"15. Do not leave your apartment unless you have performed ablutions, because the angels will seek forgiveness for you and make invocations for you as long as you are in a state of purity. Read what God the Most High said: 'Do you think We created you in vain?' [Surat al-Mu'minun].

"The Second Phase

. . . .

"All of their equipment and their money and technology be of no avail and will not harm you, unless by God's consent. Believers fear them not. Rather, it is the people of the Devil who fear them who at base like the fraternity of Satan. . . .

"Also, do not appear agitated or nervous. Be joyous and happy, glad and confident within because are undertaking an act that God loves and that pleases Him. Hence you will pass a day, God willing, with the women of Paradise:

"Smile, young man, in the face of destruction,

"For you are passing into perpetual paradise

"The Third Phase

"As you mount the [airplane], as soon as you take a step and before you enter it, pray and recall that it is an attack for God's sake, and as the Prophet said, 'There is more blessing in an attack or undertaking for God's sake than there is in the world and what is in it.'

"Then every one of you must get ready to carry out his role in the way that is pleasing to God, and must clench his teeth as the early Muslims—God have mercy on them—used to do before the fray in battle.

"At the moment of the confrontation, strike like heroes who do not want to return to the earthly world. Acclaim God's greatness [Allah Akbar], for this will strike fear into the hearts of the infidels. God the Most High said: 'Strike above the necks, and strike off their fingertips.'

"Know that the Gardens of Paradise have been adorned for you with their most beautiful decorations and the women of Paradise dressed in all their finery call for you, follower of God, to approach. If God gives to one of you the favor to slaughter then dedicate it to his father and mother for you are obligated to them. Do not disagree [among yourselves] and listen and obey. If you slaughter, then loot the one you have killed, for this was one of the ways of al-Mustafa [the Prophet]. . . .

"Then [two words missing] prisoners, make them prisoners and then kill them as God the Most High said, 'No prophet should have prisoners until he has thickened the land [with blood].'" . . .

"Do not forget to take spoils, even if it is only a cup of water to quench yourself or your brothers if it is available. Then when the promised moment of truth comes and Zero hour arrives, cleave your [one word missing] and open your breast welcoming death for God's sake, always recollecting [God]. Either end in prayer if possible seconds before [hitting] the target, or let your final words be: 'There is no God but God, and Muhammad, His Messenger.' After that, God willing, we will meet in the highest heaven, with God's will." (Atta, undated)

"UBL: We were at (inaudible) when the event took place. We had notification since the previous Thursday that the event would take place that day. We had finished our work that day and had the radio on. It was 5:30 p.m. our time. I was sitting with Dr. Ahmad Abu-al-(Khair). Immediately, we heard the news that a plane had hit the World Trade Center. We turned the radio station to the news from Washington. The news continued and no mention of the attack until the end. At the end of the newscast, they reported that a plane just hit the World Trade Center.
    "Shaykh: Allah be praised.
    "UBL: After a little while, they announced that another plane had hit the World Trade Center. The brothers who heard the news were overjoyed by it." (bin Laden, 2001b)[6]

"UBL: (inaudible) we calculated in advance the number of casualties from the enemy, who would be killed based on the position of the tower. We calculated that the floors that would be hit would be three or four floors. I was the most optimistic of them all. (inaudible) due to my experience in this field, I was thinking that the fire from the gas in the plane would melt the iron structure of the building and collapse the area where the plane hit and all the floors above it only. This is all that we had hoped for.
    "Shaykh: Allah be praised.
    . . . .
    "UBL: The brothers, who conducted the operation, all they knew was that they have a martyrdom operation and we asked each of them to go to America but they didn't know anything about the operation, not even one letter. But they were trained and we did not reveal the

---

[6] Introduction to the transcript : "In mid-November, Usama Bin Laden spoke to a room of supporters, possibly in Qandahar, Afghanistan. These comments were video taped with the knowledge of Bin Laden and all present."

operation to them until they are there and just before they boarded the planes.

"UBL: (inaudible) then he said: Those who were trained to fly didn't know the others. One group of people did not know the other group (inaudible)." (bin Laden, 2001b)

"I say to you, as Allah is my witness: We had not considered attacking the towers, but things reached the breaking point when we witnessed the injustice and tyranny of the American-Israeli coalition against our people in Palestine and Lebanon – then I got this idea.

"The events that had a direct influence on me occurred in 1982, and the subsequent events, when the US permitted the Israelis to invade Lebanon with the aid of the American sixth fleet.

"In those critical moments, I was overwhelmed by ideas that are hard to describe, but they awakened a powerful impulse to reject injustice and gave birth to a firm resolve to punish the oppressors. As I was looking at those destroyed towers in Lebanon, I was struck by the idea of punishing the oppressor in the same manner and destroying towers in the US, to give it a taste of what we have tasted and to deter it from killing our children and women." (bin Laden, 2004d)

"Why is the world surprised?! Why were millions of people astounded by what happened to America on September 11? Did the world think that anything else would happen? That something less than this would happen?!

"What happened to America is something natural, an expected event for a country that uses terror, arrogant policy, and suppression against the nations and the peoples, and imposes a single method, thought, and way of life, as if the people of the entire world are clerks in its government offices and employed by its commercial companies and institutions." (Abu Gheith, 2002)

"The fact is that the United States is part of the realm of war[7] and has concluded no agreement with Islam. This has Sharia ramifications that are well-known in the jurisprudence of jihad, and they settle the question [of the legitimacy of 9/11] definitively. They place the raid [9/11] atop the list of lawful deeds that evoke no doubts from an Islamic vantage point. Muslim scholars are agreed that that realm of war that

---

[7] Islamic theology divides the world into the realm of Islam and all else, which is the realm of war.

does not pay tribute to Islam is open to all forms of harm." (Seif al-Din al-Ansari, 2002d)

"The raid [9/11] was purely religious in nature. The mujahidin's stated aims were to strike the enemy in order to expel him from the Arabian Peninsula in keeping with the prophet's order: 'Expel the polytheists from the Arabian Peninsula.' This slogan had been forgotten, but it calls for the unification of all the scattered Muslims and mujahidin to restore the caliphate and reunite the community. The enemy surely realized this. He [President Bush] confirmed the religious nature of the raid when he declared a crusade against the mujahidin in particular and against the community in general." (al-Amili, 2002)

"The raid coincided with a rising tide of popular hostility toward the United States, once the model for the free world and a model of democratic values. This issue brought together Islamic popular forces with other forces in the world opposed to the United States. Opposition to globalization/Americanization began to spread. This became clear in the many demonstrations that the United States itself witnessed, as well as Europe and South Africa. There is a genuine popular rejection on all levels (intellectuals, environmentalists, pacifists) to US policy." (al-Qurashi, 2002b)

"The raid showed just how fragile is the supposed coexistence of Muslims and crusaders. As soon as the event took place, all of the West's vaunted values collapsed. What emerged were feelings of hatred and racist practices against everything Islamic, revealing that the crusaders' worldwide policy of connivance aimed only to contain and absorb Muslim abilities.

   "The blessed raid also sparked tension between the community and its traditional enemies, thus helping to restore the true Jewish and crusader enemy in the community's conscience after it had been all but erased by subjugation to the peace policy of lambs." (Seif al-Din al-Ansari, 2002d)

"As soon as the first real crisis hit the United States in the form of the September attacks, the United States embraced the opposite of all the principles it espouses: such as respect for freedoms and human rights. The detention camp at Guantanamo, which the United States wanted to use to terrorize Muslims, was a shameful stain on US 'democracy.' The unjust arrests that affected thousands of members of the Muslim community in the United States, and which violated the detainees' most basic civil rights, forever sullied the rosy image that the United States painted of itself. The US model for justice became arrest without a specific charge, a refusal to disclose the names of detainees, pressure and torture, claims without proof, widespread monitoring of telephone conversation and e-mail, the disclosure of individual bank accounts, and secret military courts that try cases by presidential order and do not allow defendants to appeal their sentences (including death sentences)." (al-Qurashi, 2002b)

"The blessed raid came to achieve this goal—to break the barrier of fear. It came to give Muslims tangible proof: This the United States that everyone fears has been trampled by the mujahidin. . . . A small group destroyed symbols meant to last for eternity, and they did so with an operation that surprised everyone. They made the terror that the United States inspires a thing of the past. . . . After 11 September everything is possible." (Seif al-Din al-Ansari, 2002d)

"They destroyed the idols of America; they struck the Department of Defense at its very heart, and they seriously wounded the US economy. They rubbed America's nose in the dirt, and they wallowed its pride in the mud. The skyscrapers of New York collapsed and, with them, something much larger and more important collapsed: The myth of the great America collapsed; the myth of democracy collapsed; it became clear to people that America's moral standards are dismally low; the myth of America's national security collapsed; the myth of the CIA collapsed, praise and gratitude to God." (bin Laden, 2003b)

"By the grace of God, the 11 September raid destroyed the superpower myth, the myth of an invulnerable continent guarded by two great oceans, the Atlantic and the Pacific.
    "The power and significance of the raid on the US enemy lay not only in the loss of life and property, but also in the political message that the raid sent to the freedom-loving downtrodden who yearn for freedom, dignity, and pride. . . . It struck a sudden blow at the pagan god of the age—the United States—from an unexpected direction. . . . But the blow struck at its heart and came from people the enemy saw as lacking ideas, will, or ability." (Abu Ayman al-Hilali, 2002)

"With this raid {9/11}, al-Qa'ida established a model of a proud Islamic mentality. This outlook does not view anything as impossible. By embracing the principle of initiative and action over reaction, preparing the next move before finishing the current move, and avoiding reactions that might upset the plan, al-Qa'ida set an example for other Islamic movements." (al-Qurashi, 2002b)

"Al-Qaeda's 9/11 attacks were carried out to force the Americans to expose the truth regarding their acts and intentions. There was the declaration of Bush, the son, regarding his crusade. . . . He began with an invasion of Afghanistan, and afterwards Iraq. From the point of view of Al-Qaeda's leaders, this is considered a success of the first stage of their plan, aiming to lure Washington to attack the Islamic Ummah, in order to waken it up from its sleep and lethargy. The Al-Qaeda leaders believe that the U.S.'s responsiveness to provocation was a strategic mistake made by the Jewish-Anglo-Saxon pact led by the Americans." (al-Ali, 2006)

"If it is correct to give it a name, then the new war that began successfully in New York and Washington should be called World War Three because of the great changes and widening fissures it has caused in the enemy edifice." (al-Amili, 2002)

Assassination of Anwar Sadat
Ayman al-Zawahiri, who had to flee Egypt after Sadat was assassinated, gives a dispassionate analysis of the consequences.

"The events of the rebellion of Dhu-al-Hujjah 1401 Anno Hegira, corresponding to October 1981 AD, focused on two fronts:
"The first front was the attack on al-Sadat and the upper echelons of his regime during the military parade on 6 October and the attempt to kill the largest number of officials and seize the radio building [in Cairo]. Activity on this front succeeded in killing Anwar al-Sadat but the upper echelons of the regime escaped and the attempt to seize the radio did not succeed.
"The second front was the armed uprising in Asyut and the attempt to seize the city. The uprising started two days after the assassination of al-Sadat; in other words, after the army succeeded in controlling the country and securing the regime. This attempt succeeded in seizing some police centers. But the government summoned the Special Forces, which started pounding the resistance positions of the brotherly young mujhahidin who were forced to leave these centers after running out of ammunition.
"The armed rebellion in Asyut was doomed to fail. It was an 'emotional' uprising that was poorly planned. The rebellion occurred two

days after the assassination of al-Sadat and was based on an unrealistic plan to seize Asyut and then advance northward toward Cairo, disregarding any figures about the enemy's strength and materiel.

"Thus the 1401 Hegira (1981) uprising ended with a fundamental gain—the killing of al-Sadat. The attempts that followed it were not successful because of poor planning and insufficient preparation." (al-Zawahiri, 2001)

Attack on a French Oil Tanker

The jihadis' penchant for exaggerating the effects of their operations is evident in the following excerpt. Thousands of tankers ply the Persian Gulf and Arabian Sea at any one time. This attack took place on October 6, 2002, off the eastern coast of Yemen, and did not sink the vessel (the MV *Limburg*). The attack was similar to the bombing of the USS *Cole* on October 12, 2002, in which suicide bombers rammed a small boat full of explosives into the side of the target ship. The effect was to briefly raise insurance rates.

"After the United States and its Christian allies had assumed that they had suppressed the hazard of the mujahideen and secured their strategic, military, and commercial interests in the region and deluded themselves and their people domestically, and the world internationally. ...Attacking a commercial target of this size, at this time, under these circumstances, and in this way has more significance and meaning. For it means:

"1) All the military, security, and political, etc., efforts that America and its allies have done to protect their strategic interests in this area have been futile.

"2) The mujahideen by the grace of God, no longer have restraints on action and are capable of surprising their enemy and [carrying out] attacks that are decisive, lethal, and strategic and in the appropriate time and place they determine." (al-Qaeda al-Jihad, Political Bureau, 2002)

Madrid Train Bombings

On March 11, 2004, jihadis bombed three train stations in Madrid, killing 191 people. This was one day before the Spanish general election. The Socialist party upset the conservatives in the election and within weeks withdrew Spanish troops from Iraq.

This was foreshadowed in a jihadi document found by Norwegian intelligence before the event.[8] It is excerpted below.

> "Therefore we say that in order to force the Spanish government to withdraw from Iraq the resistance should deal painful blows to its forces. This should be accompanied by an information campaign clarifying the truth of the matter inside Iraq. It is necessary to make utmost use of the upcoming general election in Spain in March next year.
>
> "We think that the Spanish government could not tolerate more than two, maximum three blows, after which it will have to withdraw as a result of popular pressure. If its troops still remain in Iraq after these blows, then the victory of the Socialist Party is almost secured, and the withdrawal of the Spanish forces will be on its electoral programme." (Media Committee for the Victory of the Iraqi People, 2003, in Lia and Hegghammer, 2004)

> "The Death Brigades penetrated into the European Crusader heartland, and struck a painful blow at one of the foundations of the Crusader coalition. This is part of a settling of old accounts with Crusader Spain, the ally of the U.S., in its war against Islam . . . ." (Abu-Hafs al-Masri Brigades of Al-Qa'ida, 2004)[9]

Killing of Paul Marshall Johnson, Jr.

The perpetrator of this raid, Abu Hajer, also known as Abdulazia Issa Abdul-Mohsin al-Muqrin, was killed by Saudi security forces when he attempted to dispose of Johnson's body.

> "Al-Mujahideen received accurate information on the presence of an American who could be a good target for a kidnapping operation. . . . This worm has been working for 10 years serving the crusaders military forces in the land of the two Holy Mosques, participating directly on the war against Muslims. . . .
>
> "Once we received initial observatory information then the next stage of confirmation and follow-up started and then we drew the plans to execute the operation on Saturday 24/4/1425H {May 14, 2004} before sunset. The plan required the use of Saudi police clothes and vehicles and other things. We set up a checkpoint at the service road on the south side of Airport Rd. . . . Four cooperative individuals and loyal to

---

[8] This document apparently was not made available to Spanish authorities, who initially blamed the attack on the Basque terrorist organization ETA.

[9] This claim is likely bogus.

their religion in the security apparatus donated the clothes and police vehicles, we ask God to reward them and help them to use their capabilities to serve Islam and al-Mujahideen.

"When the target arrived at the checkpoint, he was stopped, arrested, drugged and then was taken in a private car to the kidnapping station. His car (Camry) was burnt by a locally made burning bomb (Molotov).

. . . .

"Al-Mujahideen declared that they would kill the hostage within 72 hours unless the Saudi government releases all the Muslim prisoners in its custody. The ignorant Saudi government declared through the Americanized Adel al-Jubair that it would not accept the mujahideen demands because it will not negotiate with the terrorists. It did not realize that al-Mujahideen do not negotiate with the tyrants and have no desire to do so except having their demands literally implemented. Upon the expiration of the time period given, al-Mujahideen implemented their promise and killed the hostage. A report was issued showing the photos of the hostage killed. Thanks to God." (al-Muqrin, 2004b)

Assassination of Theo Van Gogh

On November 2, 2004, Dutch filmmaker Theo Van Gogh was attacked on the street in Amsterdam by a young Dutch Muslim, Mohammed Bouyeri, who objected to a short film on Islam that Van Gogh produced, called *Submission*. Van Gogh was shot, and his throat was slit. The Dutch public was horrified, not only at the deed, but that it could happen in the tolerant Netherlands, which had opened its arms to Muslim immigrants. A backlash developed, leading many Dutch to question the special steps that had been taken to accommodate Muslims in Dutch society.

The writer of the film's scenario was Hersi Ali, a Somali woman who, while serving as a translator in the social welfare agency, had seen firsthand the brutality inflicted on Muslim women in the name of Islam. The film recounted four stories of abuse. At the time of the killing, Ali was a member of the Dutch parliament. She now lives in the United States.

"I take complete responsibility for my actions. I acted purely in the name of my religion . . . .

"I can assure you that one day, should I be set free, I would do the same, exactly the same.

". . . {Referring to Van Gogh's mother} I don't feel your pain. I have to admit that I don't have any sympathy for you. I can't feel for you because you are a nonbeliever." (Bouyeri, 2005, in Rennie, 2005)

"Hersi Ali is a Somalian Member of the Dutch parliament and a 'former Muslim' as she says. This means that she is an apostate who renounced the Hanafi religion. This criminal did what no infidel has done [worse]. She started by heavily attacking the Islamic religion . . . and contributed in reflecting a bad image of Islam by writing the scenario of a movie called 'Submission' . . . directed by the deceased Theo Van Gogh, killed by one of the Muslim young men in Holland, to avenge Islam and Muslims.

. . . .

"Therefore, I am urging all the decent spears that are capable of cutting off that head, to not relinquish from doing so. This is an open invitation to every decent human being, protective of Islam and Muslims. Just picture that the one who is defaming the image of Islam is or as a matter of fact was a Muslim. I appeal to all the swords of righteousness to find a quick solution to the problem of this whore who stirred a commotion [discord] against the Islamic Community in Holland, and gave a bad image of Islam, requesting the Dutch to put more restraints on the Muslims there." (SITE, 2005a)

Attacks in London

In a statement to Europe on April 15, 2004, Osama bin Laden offered a truce with the Europeans if they would end their attacks on Muslims, stop intervening in Muslim affairs, and halt support of U.S. policies in the Islamic world. It was rejected by all the European countries, including Great Britain. Al-Zawahiri justified the attacks in London by saying that bin Laden had offered Europe a truce that the British refused to accept.

"The latest raid on the Crusaders' homes was the blessed raid on London, which was a slap in the face to British Crusader arrogance, after the mujaheed lion of Islam, Sheikh Osama bin Laden, may Allah protect him, had offered the peoples of the West a truce, if they leave the countries of Islam, but their arrogance drove them to crime, and their conceited foreign secretary, Jack Straw, said that these proposals should be treated with contempt. So let them pay the price of their government's filth and arrogance." (al-Zawahiri, 2005d)

"As long as Britain remains in a state of hatred and disbelief, then terrorizing it is a duty because it has appropriated the responsibility of fighting and wounding the Muslims and stealing their natural resources. Also, it supports America, the Jews, the Arab oppressors, and everyone else who is fighting against Islam in the new crusader

war against so-called terrorism in Afghanistan, Iraq, and against the
mujahideen everywhere . . ." (Algerian Salafist Group for Prayer and
Combat, 2005)

A prominent jihadi cleric, Atu Basir al-Tartusi, condemned the London bombings on the grounds that Muslims are bound not to attack territory where they enjoy
sanctuary.

> "[The London bombings] intended to kill Muslims, children, women,
> old men, and other innocents whose inviolability is protected by the
> Sharia . . . mass transit cannot be devoid of these categories of people.
>
> "Reciprocity [in attacking the enemy] is not always permissible . . . if
> we did this, then the passion for remedy and revenge has overwhelmed
> the Sharia-based judgment, and this is impermissible.
>
> "Under the banner of excessive enthusiasm and the passion for
> revenge, I often notice a sense of condescension and mockery toward
> the issue of the covenant and the assurance of protection [for Muslims
> in Britain], to the point where there are those who speak of the neces-
> sity for safeguarding and respecting the covenant and the assurance of
> protection as an object of derision and mockery. They do this despite
> the strong emphasis of the Sharia on the sacredness of the covenant and
> the assurance of protection. . . ." (al-Tartusi, 2005).

But this was not the general view.

> "The Muslims should use against the UK every means possible,
> approved by the Prophet . . . including destroying their houses and
> terrorize them. . . . Allah, May you destroy the United Kingdom and
> the United States and their allies; kill them and do not leave them a
> remain. May Allah humiliate the UK, and terrorize it . . . . Show us
> in the U.S., the UK, and their allies, your might and wonders of your
> power, like you did with Pharaoh . . . ." (Anonymous, 2005b)

> "We do not rule out the possibility that it was done by the intelligence
> agency of another Western country hostile to Britain. We do not rule
> out countries . . . or some Zionist Americans who wanted to over-
> shadow the G-8 summit. But at the same time, we do not rule out the
> Al-Qa'ida organization.

. . . .

"If Al-Qa'ida indeed carried out this act, it is a great victory for it. It rubbed the noses of the world's eight most powerful countries in the mud.[10] This victory is a blow to the economy . . . ." (al-Siba'i, 2005)[11]

"As for the beggar-scholars {mainstream Islamic leaders} who gathered outside the British parliament to demonstrate their support for Blair, and to attack the martyrdom-seeking mujahideen, I say to them: Why did you not gather outside the British parliament when the embargo killed a million children in Iraq? Why did you not gather outside the British parliament when the mosques in Afghanistan were bombed with worshippers inside? Why did you not gather outside the British parliament when the Zionist missiles killed Sheik Ahmad Yassin, Allah's mercy upon him. Why did you not gather outside the British parliament when the crusaders' bombers pulverized women and children in Falluja? Why did you not gather outside the British parliament when America desecrated the holy Koran? The beggar-scholars who issue fatwas in line with the head of the Anglican Church say that the response to the crimes of Bush and Blair cannot be to attack civilians. Our answer to them is that treatment in kind is just." (al-Zawahiri, 2005c)

"The blessed London raid is one of the raids that the Qaeda Al-Jihad organization had the honor of carrying out against the British Crusader arrogance, as well as the British Crusader aggression towards the Muslim nation for more than 100 years, against Britain's historic crime of establishing Israel, and against the ongoing crimes of the English perpetrated against Muslims in Afghanistan and Iraq.

. . . .

"Therefore, those of us from Al-Qaida's Committee in Northern Europe declare that the Muslim blood that has been – and is still being shed – will not be in vain and we swear to almighty Allah that we will sacrifice our souls and dead bodies for this religion, in order to raise the flag of the mujahideen, and to preserve the souls of the Muslims in the same way that our brothers in Britain have done previously {the

---

[10] The attacks in London occurred at the time of the G8 meeting in Scotland.

[11] Hani al-Siba'i is an Egyptian and an alleged leader of Egyptian Islamic Jihad. He was convicted in absentia on terrorism charges in Egypt and was granted political asylum in the United Kingdom.

London attacks}.[12] Allahu Akhbar, and the honor goes to Allah, his prophet, and the mujahideen." (Al-Qaida's Committee in Northern Europe, 2005)

The Jordan Hotel Bombings

On Wednesday, November 9, 2005, suicide bombers attacked three hotels in Amman, Jordan. At one hotel, the bomb was detonated at a wedding party, resulting in a severe public backlash. The following are excerpts from a series of communications from Abu Musaab al-Zarqawi, who was writing under a pseudonym. In the first, he is proud of the operations but soon seeks to justify them. As noted earlier, Zarqawi was a Jordanian who had been sentenced to death in absentia for previous terrorist acts in Jordan. (See the discussion of Jordan in Chapter Six.)

Immediately after the attack, al-Zarqawi issued this communiqué:

> "In these blessed days, in which the lions of monotheism are fighting against the might of the Crusader infidel and the treachery of the Shiites on the lands of Mesopotamia, and write sagas of pride in times of desperation and displacement. A small group of the lions of the best and most honorable of brigades, the al-Barra' bin-Malik Brigade, launched itself to support the religion and elevate the Word of Monotheism in a new attack against some of the dens that have been implanted in the land of the Muslims in Amman. After studying the targets and reconnoitering them, execution sites were selected at some of the hotels that the tyrant of Jordan had converted into a back yard for the enemies of the religion: the Jews and the Crusaders, and a place of iniquity for the nation's apostate traitors . . ." (Abu Maysara, 2005b)

When public reaction was negative, he tried to explain:

> "After the blessed attack conducted by the heroes of the nation, the lions of the al-Barra' bin-Malik Brigade, against some of the dens of evil in Amman, we committed to explain to Muslims some of the reasons the jihad fighters targeted these dens, so that all may know that we did not target [the dens] until after we had determined that they were centers for waging war against Islam and for supporting the Cru-

---

[12] "NOTE: In the wake of the 7/7 bombings in London, many purported extremists groups have issued apparent communiques or claims of responsibility. Typically, it is difficult – if not impossible – to determine the authenticity of such documents. By contract, this message on behalf of 'Al-Qaida's Committee in Northern Europe' was authenticated and distributed by the same online authority responsible for Abu Musab al-Zarqawi and Al-Qaida's Jihad Committee in Iraq. Thus, the presumed credibility of this statement is comparatively higher" (Al-Qaida's Committee in Northern Europe, 2005).

sader's presence in Mesopotamia and the Arabian Peninsula, and supporting the presence of the Jews in Palestine.

"After a not inconsiderable period of time during which the targets were reconnoitered from the inside and information was collected in a painstaking investigation, these specific hotels were selected for many reasons, including the fact that they had become the favorite work locations for intelligence services, especially those of America, Israel, and some Western European countries, with the participation of the intelligence services of Egypt, the Palestinian Authority, Saudi Arabia, and Jordan. [These locations contained] the secret war-rooms from which the battles of the so-called 'War against Terrorism' are commanded. . . .

"They also became the safe rear headquarters where the apostate Shiite government and their guests lived and met after the jihad fighters turned Baghdad into a blaze that burns them, even inside their 'Green Zone'. . . ." (Abu Maysara, 2005b)

When the Jordanians demonstrated against him:

"This is a message to the Muslims in Jordan: We would like to assure you that we are among the people who care most for your safety. How could this not be the case, when you are more beloved to us than our selves and our sons? . . .

"As for the image that this traitorous regime painted that you are the victims of the jihad fighters, that is all falsehood. May God protect us from ever spilling your blood. If we wanted to kill innocents, as this apostate regime claimed, we would not have risked our men to cross the security cordons around those hotels of iniquity. If we wanted to spill your blood, God forbid, it would have been simpler by far to have those martyrs blow themselves up in public places where hundreds of people congregate and present such easy targets, such as the Hashimiyah Square, the al-'Abdali complex, or commercial centers, such as the Safeway, etc.

. . . .

"As for the Muslims who were killed in this operation, we ask God to have mercy on them and to forgive them. We swear that it was not they that we intended; we did not, and will not, consider targeting them for even a moment, even if they are sinners and lechers. This assumes that the explosion went off near to them, because the martyr brothers targeted halls that hosted a meeting for the intelligence officers of some Crusader nations and their proxies. The harm that befell the killed [Muslims] was due to the collapse of parts of the secondary ceiling on top of them as a result of the force of the explosion. It should be clear that this was an unintended and unexpected occurrence. . . ." (al-Zarqawi, 2005i)

"It was agreed that explosive vests would be used in order to strike with precision at the targets, and to cause greater damage. At the time of execution, brother Abu-Khubayb attacked the leaders of unbelief and atheism with [weapons that] sent them to their fates. . . ." (Abu Maysara, 2005c)

"He {the driver of the car from Iraq} had two explosive belts. . . . He made me wear one and he wore the other and taught me how to use it, how to pull and control it. He said we would carry it out in hotels in Jordan. We hired a car and went to the hotel.

". . . He {Rishawi's husband Ali Hussein Ali Shamari} took a corner {of the Radisson ballroom}, and I took a corner. . . . There was a wedding in the hotel, children, women and men. My husband carried it out. I tried to carry it out, but it did not explode. I went out. The people started running and I ran away with them." (Sajida Rishawi, 2005)

CHAPTER EIGHT

Iraq and Afghanistan

Iraq

The major events in Iraq over the past five years are widely known. Therefore, rather than loosely organizing the excerpts in this chapter by subject matter, we take a more chronological approach, inserting explanatory material in footnotes.

It is noteworthy that some jihadis saw the U.S. invasion of Iraq as an opportunity. Statements about the inevitability of the United States losing the war are undoubtedly self-serving propaganda, but that was small comfort as events unfolded in the direction the jihadis anticipated. The following excerpts, most of which are taken from correspondence between al-Zarqawi and al-Zawahiri, paint a picture of an insurgency struggling to get traction until early 2004, when al-Zarqawi decided to attack the Shi'a in order to solidify support among the Sunnis. This correspondence also reveals al-Zawahiri's and others' hesitation to adopt an anti-Shi'a strategy, but their ultimate acceptance of al-Zarqawi's approach. Sunni insurgent leaders subsequently engaged in an intense debate about this issue, as well. Zarqawi seems to have prevailed by deeds rather than words. His death and the "surge" seem to have eased the violence.

> "Saddam himself was a thief and an apostate, of course. But the solution to the {sic} Iraq's problem should have never been taking Iraq out of the hands of a local thief to put it in the hands of a global thief." (bin Laden, 2004e)

> "The enemies of God are aware that this war is a turning point in the world, that it is a choice between an absolute control of the infidel West, its culture, and way of life and the Islamic renaissance which is coming, God willing. Therefore, Bush said at the national council for the development of democracy that the failure of democracy in Iraq will encourage terrorism in the world and constitute a threat to the Americans. British Prime Minister Tony Blair said that what is going on in Iraq today will define relations between the Islamic world and

the West. He said that this is the basic battle at the beginning of the 21st century and added: We are at a point where the failure in Iraq will be a disaster for the entire West."[1] (al-Zarqawi, 2004c)

Before the Invasion

"But if war is at the gates, is the triumph of this Crusader oppressing aggression certain? I don't think so. I think that the West's arrogance will lead it to its sure end if it is determined to act with aggression and terror against the Islamic nation, and that its first defeat will be in Iraq.

". . . In order for Iraq to achieve the great, longed-for victory, it must prepare all the strength it can for this battle. The most important qualities of strength are: being helped by Allah, and truly and faithfully relying on Him.

"Iraq does not need the Arabs' {states} help. The Arabs are helpless right now, and they think that the smartest thing for them to do is surrender. They cannot help themselves. How, then, will they help Iraq? 'Those whom you call besides Him have no power to help you, nor can they help themselves' [Koran 7:197].

. . . .

"Another quality of strength is that our people in Iraq [should] be united despite their various traits. All of you are in the target's bull's-eye. The bombs and the fire [that will be dropped on you] will not differentiate between you. Be one hand and one heart, as the hand of Allah is with the collective. 'Allah loves those who fight in His cause arrayed in serried ranks, as though they were a strong wall . . . .' [Koran 61:4]." (al-Rantisi, 2002)

"Another quality of strength is that the Iraqis will have an army of martyrs. The enemies of Allah and the enemies of this people are cowards. They crave life, while the Muslims crave martyrdom. The martyrdom operations that shock can ensure that horror is sowed in the [enemies'] hearts, and horror is one of the causes of defeat. There is no other way than to establish thousands of squads of martyrs, in a secret apparatus, who, from now, have at their disposal the capability, as well as thousands of sophisticated explosive belts, with powerful explosive [capacity] to cause great damage." (al-Rantisi, 2002)

---

[1] While we found statements by Blair that were not inconsistent with this interpretation, we could not find any literal quotations that matched this statement.

"Another quality of strength is will, free of all weakness or hesitation, and this is one of the qualities of our brothers in Iraq . . . . If the Crusaders fail to break the will of the resistance of the Iraqi people – and fail they will, by Allah's will – the only thing they will gain from their aggression is tears. . . . Ultimately, the battle is a battle of wills. We must be convinced that we must win it. The first stage of defeat is disappointment, despair, and pessimism. I maintain that Allah has freed the Iraqi people of these dangerous ills." (al-Rantisi, 2002)

After the Fall of Baghdad

". . . there should be no dialogue with the occupiers but the dialogue with weapons, this is our obligation today, and this is for what we should strive." (bin Laden, 2004b)

". . . I say, having sought help from God, that the Americans, as you know well, entered Iraq on a contractual basis and to create the State of Greater Israel from the Nile to the Euphrates and that this Zionized American Administration believes that accelerating the creation of the State of [Greater] Israel will accelerate the emergence of the Messiah." (al-Zarqawi, 2004b)

"As you know, God favored the [Islamic] nation with jihad on His behalf in the land of Mesopotamia. It is known to you that the arena here is not like the rest. It has positive elements not found in others, and it also has negative elements not found in others. Among the greatest positive elements of this arena is that it is jihad in the Arab heartland. It is a stone's throw from the lands of the two Holy Precincts and the al-Aqsa [Mosque]. We know from God's religion that the true, decisive battle between infidelity and Islam is in this land, i.e., in [Greater] Syria and its surroundings. Therefore, we must spare no effort and strive urgently to establish a foothold in this land." (al-Zarqawi, undated(a))

"You, the mujahideen: there is now a rare and golden opportunity to make America bleed in Iraq, both economically and in terms of human losses and morale. . . . Don't miss out on this opportunity lest you regret it." (bin Laden, 2004, in Hegghammer, 2006)

"America wanted to enter Iraq for its own reasons – not in order to disarm it of weapons of mass destruction or in order to save the Iraqi people from the hands of Saddam. They [the Americans] announced that they would enter Iraq even if Saddam left. The U.S. launched [a war] because it wanted to destroy Iraq's military power so as to clear the way for Israel, for its weapons and arsenal, and so that no one with these weapons will remain in the region except for Israel . . . ." (al-Qaradhawi, 2003a)

Problems

The insurgency in Iraq got off to a slow start, and al-Zarqawi and his jihadis had a difficult time training, organizing, and motivating the Iraqis. The jihadis came to increasingly depend on recruiting foreign fighters.

> "Most of them {Sunni fighters} have little expertise or experience, especially in organized collective work. Doubtlessly, they are the result of a repressive regime that militarized the country, spread dismay, propagated fear and dread, and destroyed confidence among the people. For this reason, most of the groups are working in isolation, with no political horizon, farsightedness, or preparation to inherit the land. Yes, the idea has begun to ripen, and a light whisper has arisen to become noisy talk about the need to band together and unite under one banner. But matters are still in their initial stages. With God's praise, we are trying to ripen them quickly.
>
> . . . .
>
> "Their numbers {of foreign fighters in Iraq} continue to be negligible as compared to the enormity of the expected battle. We know that the convoys of good are many, that the march of jihad continues, and that only confusion over the banner and a muffled reality keep many of them from [answering] the call to battle. What prevents us from [calling] a general alert is that the country has no mountains in which we can take refuge and no forests in whose thickets we can hide. Our backs are exposed and our movements compromised. Eyes are everywhere. The enemy is before us and the sea is behind us. Many an Iraqi will honor you as a guest and give you shelter as a peaceable brother. As for making his house into a base for launching [operations] and a place of movement and battle, this is rarer than red sulphur. For this reason, we have worn ourselves out on many occasions sheltering and protecting the brothers. This makes training the green newcomers like wearing bonds and shackles, even though, praise be to God and with relentless effort and insistent searching, we have taken possession of growing numbers of locations . . . ." (al-Zarqawi, undated(a))

> "1 – We are striving urgently and racing against time to create companies of mujahidin that will repair to secure places and strive to recon-

noiter the country, hunting the enemy – Americans, police, and soldiers – on the roads and lanes. We are continuing to train and multiply
them. As for the Shi'a, we will hurt them, God willing, through martyrdom operations and car bombs.

. . . .

"3 – This will be accompanied by an effort that we hope will intensify
to expose crippling doubts and explain the rules of shari'a through
tapes, printed materials, study, and courses of learning [meant] to
expand awareness, anchor the doctrine of the unity of God, prepare the
infrastructure, and meet [our] obligation." (al-Zarqawi, undated(a))

". . . Jihad here {Iraq} unfortunately [takes the form of] mines planted,
rockets launched, and mortars shelling from afar. The Iraqi brothers still prefer safety and returning to the arms of their wives, where
nothing frightens them. Sometimes the groups have boasted among
themselves that not one of them has been killed or captured. We have
told them in our many sessions with them that safety and victory are
incompatible, that the tree of triumph and empowerment cannot grow
tall and lofty without blood and defiance of death, that the [Islamic]
nation cannot live without the aroma of martyrdom and the perfume
of fragrant blood spilled on behalf of God, and that people cannot
awaken from their stupor unless talk of martyrdom and martyrs fills
their days and nights. The matter needs more patience and conviction.
[Our] hope in God is great." (al-Zarqawi, undated(a))

". . . we have been waiting until we have weight on the ground and
finish preparing integrated structures capable of bearing the consequences of going public so that we appear in strength and do not suffer
a reversal. We seek refuge in God. Praise be to God, we have made
good strides and completed important stages. As the decisive moment
approaches, we feel that [our] body has begun to spread in the security vacuum, gaining locations on the ground that will be the nucleus
from which to launch and move out in a serious way, God willing."
(al-Zarqawi, undated(a))

". . . So where are we? Despite few supporters, lack of friends, and
tough times, god has blessed us with victories against the enemy. We
were involved in all the martyrdom operations – in terms of overseeing,
preparing, and planning – that took place in this country except for
the operations that took place in the north. Praised be to Allah, I have
completed 25 of these operations, some of them against the Shi'a and

their leaders, the Americans and their military, the police, the military, and the coalition forces. There will be more in the future, god willing. We did not want to publicly claim these operations until we become more powerful and were ready for the consequences. We need to show up strong and avoid getting hurt, now that we have made great strides and taken important steps forward. As we get closer to the decisive moment, we feel that our entity is spreading within the security void existing in Iraq, something that will allow us to secure bases on the ground, these bases that will be the jump start of a serious revival, god willing." (al-Zarqawi, 2004a)

"There is no doubt that the Americans' losses are very heavy because they are deployed across a wide area and among the people and because it is easy to procure weapons, all of which makes them easy and mouth-watering targets for the believers. But America did not come to leave, and it will not leave no matter how numerous its wounds become and how much of its blood is spilled. It is looking to the near future, when it hopes to disappear into its bases secure and at ease and put the battle-fields of Iraq into the hands of the foundling government with an army and police that will bring the behavior of Saddam and his myrmidons[2] back to the people. There is no doubt that the space in which we can move has begun to shrink and that the grip around the throats of the mujahidin has begun to tighten. With the deployment of soldiers and police, the future has become frightening." (al-Zarqawi, undated(a))

"O nation of Islam, O my nation: We are pained by the strange humili-ation and the utter silence with which you deal with the great battle and confrontation in this age {Iraq}. Where are the heroes, the lions, and the youths of Muhammad, May God's peace and blessings be upon him? Where are the Islamic ulema? Why have you deviated from the right path, stopped leading the marchers, surrendered to vain desires, and kept sitting complacently on the ground? Where are the Koranic struggles? Where are the stories of the outstandinbg {sic} and splendid men and the legacies of the ulema and mujahidin? Can anyone of you not revive them?" (al-Zarqawi, 2004b)

"I could swear by God that you {Zarqawi} are asking about us and our situation in here; the morale has weakened and lines of the Muja-hidin have become separated due to some leaders' actions, God does

---

[2] The Myrmidons of Greek myth were known for their loyalty to their leaders. The word "myrmidon" later came to mean "hired ruffian," according to the Oxford English Dictionary.

not accept such actions, and that will delay the victory. We do have big mistakes where some of us have been discarded.

"To conclude what has happened with us, he {another unknown jihadi leader} said either you carry out a martyr operation or go back to your family. After, we were told this was an order from the Sheik {al-Zarqawi}. Indeed, some of the brothers had returned back, some were recorded as martyred and the rest were hanging around and did not know what to do, besides they were humiliated and immorally treated. . . . We have brothers that were tortured and jailed. They are harmless and nobody is meeting with them or asks about them. It is unlike the case in Fallujah where you used to come and visit us, and we enjoyed your party. The situation has changed dramatically and that is not acceptable to God. . . .

"The most important issue here is, do not hear from just one side, even if that person was close to you. But hear from all sides so the facts will become clear to you.

"We have leaders that are not capable of being good leaders. We are not accusing them without reason but we have tested them and found them incapable.

"Thank God, Sheik, please test those who are underneath you. Some of them are in a rush, some are unfair and some have other issues.

"My last request to you Sheik is that I need to meet with you to share a lot of unknown issues. And, to be honest with you, I really do not trust anyone anymore that says he is coming from your side." (al-Qusaymi, 2005)

"Sons of Islam, men of belief, Allah almighty has opened an opportunity for Jihad in Iraq. Recall those who followed the path of Jihad and martyrdom: the path of glory, and not of humiliation; of pride, and not of subjection; of paradise, and not of hell. . . . Where are those striving to defend their religion? Where are the lovers of virgins in paradise? Where are the seekers of the Garden of Eden? Where are those desiring martyrdom, seeking to become near the Prophet and to please the Merciful? Where are the lovers of martyrdom?" (al-Qaeda in the Arabian Peninsula, 2005)

"Shik Zafer Al-Abidi: Just as the enemy recruited thirty-five of the world's countries to occupy Iraq, we have the right and the honor (to recruit) Arab fighters. We are connected by the destiny of our Arab identity and Islam. But the (Arab volunteers) do not have a leading role. They had the honor of participating, but most of the fighting was carried out by Iraqis, and of Falluja in particular.

"Journalist: . . .

"We are fighting the Jihad for the sake of Allah in Al-Khaldiya, Falluja, and Ramadi. The entire world, George Bush and others, say we support Saddam Hussein. We are not fighting for Saddam Hussein." (al-Abidi, 2005)

"We {Saudi Volunteer} have come to support our Muslim brothers in Iraq. We are not foreigners. A foreigner is someone who does not belong to our religion and people – those occupiers." (Anonymous, 2005c)

". . . anyone who attempts to distinguish between Iraqis and non-Iraqis with regards to jihad in the cause of Allah and helping to determine the destiny of the nation, then he would be mistaken. The true foreigner is the one who runs away from the land of courage and rests with the oppressors who toss him their scraps and leave him to sip at the remnants of their drunken binges. . . . May Allah be our witness, we say to you that the fingernail of any foreign mujahid who is fighting in Mesopotamia beyond Shaykh Abu Musab al-Zarqawi – may Allah protect him – is worth more than a country full of those who follow al-Sistani, al-Jaafari, al-Hakim, al-Sharastani, and Chalabi. . . . anyone who forsakes his own country and comes to Mesopotamia in order to declare jihad in the cause of Allah and who remains steadfast in the Muslim homeland is superior to any Iraqi who runs away from battle, delivering himself into the hands of the oppressors and attempting to distinguish between the Iraqis and the non-Iraqis." (al-Baghdadi, 2005)

Sunni Versus Shi'a

The sectarian war in Iraq is perhaps the most historically important development to emerge from the U.S. invasion, one that may shape the politics of the Middle East for decades to come. Despite centuries of conflict between these sects, going back to the earliest days of Islam, and the oppression of the Shi'a under Saddam Hussein, this sectarian clash was not necessarily inevitable. Sunni and Shi'a lived together amicably for long periods in Islamic history, but the deliberate strategic decision of al-Zarqawi to provoke war with the Shi'a changed all that.

From the very outset of the insurgency, al-Zarqawi evidenced hatred of the Shi'a, but he also realized that attacking them would have the additional advantage of provoking retaliation, which would then mobilize the Sunni. To begin killing Shi'a, he had to delegitimize them as authentic Muslims. At the outset, al-Qaeda ideologist al-Zawahiri strongly criticized this strategy and urged cooperative efforts in fighting the insurgency. However, by the end of 2004, bin Laden had accepted al-Zarqawi's policy and made him head of al-Qaeda in Iraq. Subsequently, there was additional push-back from insurgent Sunni clerics,[3] but al-Zarqawi was undeterred, and sectarian war continued to escalate.

In the following excerpt, he begins by making a case against the Shi'a:

> "These [Shia's have been] a sect of treachery and betrayal throughout history and throughout the ages. It is a creed that aims to combat the Sunnis." (al-Zarqawi, 2004b)

> ". . . They, i.e., the Shi'a, have declared a secret war against the people of Islam. They are the proximate, dangerous enemy of the Sunnis, even if the Americans are also an archenemy. The danger from the Shi'a, however, is greater and their damage is worse and more destructive to the [Islamic] nation than the Americans, on whom you find a quasi-consensus about killing them as an assailing enemy.
>
> . . . .
>
> "They have befriended and supported the Americans and stood in their ranks against the mujahidin. They have spared and are still sparing no effort to put an end to the jihad and the mujahidin." (al-Zarqawi, undated(a))

> "Their {Shi'a} Ghunusi religion (one based on special personal enlightenment) {rather than the revealed world of Allah} veils itself with lies and covers itself with hypocrisy, exploiting the naïveté and good-heartedness of many Sunnis. We do not know when our [Islamic] nation will begin to learn from historical experience and build on the testimony of the empty eras. The Shi'i Safavid state was an insurmountable obstacle in the path of Islam. Indeed it was a dagger that stabbed Islam and its people in the back." (al-Zarqawi, 2004b)

> "Shaykh-al-Islam Ibn-Taymiyah was right in his description of these people {Shi'ites} when they repudiated the people of Islam. He said: This is why they cooperated with the infidels and the Tartars against the Muslim masses. They were the main cause of the invasion of Muslim countries by Genghis Khan, king of the infidels. They also were the cause behind Hulegu's invasion of Iraq, capture of Aleppo, and plunder of Al-Salihiyah, by their viciousness and cunning.

---

[3] Following Zarqawi's September 2005 declaration of war on the Shi'ite community, other pro-resistance Sunnis, including Sheikh Zakariyah Muhammad Isa al-Tamimi of the Higher Committee for Dawa, Guidance, and Fatwa, condemned his tactics.

"They plundered Muslim soldiers as they passed through on their way to Egypt in the first conquest attempt. They robbed Muslims on highways. Some of them cooperated with the Tartars and Franks against Muslims. They felt depressed by Muslim victories.

"When the Muslims conquered the coast of Acre and other places, some of them (Shi'ites) backed the Christians against the Muslims, according to the stories related by some of them. These are just a few examples of their doings." (al-Zarqawi, undated(b))

Zarqawi then makes strategic arguments.

"Our fighting against the Shi'a is the way to drag the [Islamic] nation into the battle. We speak here in some detail. We have said before that the Shi'a have put on the uniforms of the Iraqi army, police, and security [forces] and have raised the banner of preserving the homeland and the citizen. Under this banner, they have begun to liquidate the Sunnis under the pretext that they are saboteurs, remnants of the Ba'ath, and terrorists spreading evil in the land. With strong media guidance from the Governing Council and the Americans, they have been able to come between the Sunni masses and the mujahidin. I give an example that brings the matter close to home in the area called the Sunni Triangle – if this is the right name for it. The army and police have begun to deploy in those areas and are growing stronger day by day. They have put chiefs [drawn] from among Sunni agents and the people of the land in charge. In other words, this army and police may be linked to the inhabitants of this area by kinship, blood, and honor. In truth, this area is the base from which we set out and to which we return. When the Americans disappear from these areas – and they have begun to do so – and these agents, who are linked by destiny to the people of the land, take their place, what will our situation be?" (al-Zarqawi, undated(a))

"They {Shi'a} pose a danger not only to Iraq, but to the whole region. If the Shi'a have influence over Iraq, or if they obtain some kind of autonomy in southern Iraq, they will be so much closer to extending their influence. After all, they exist in considerable numbers in Saudi Arabia, Kuwait, and Bahrain. If these Shi'a get organized and if their initiatives get support from countries that sponsor them – Iran, Syria, and Lebanon – it will mean that they have reached advanced stages in their 50-year plan. . . ." (al-Neda, undated)

"These in our opinion are the key to change. I mean that targeting and hitting them in [their] religious, political, and military depth will provoke them to show the Sunnis their rabies and bare the teeth of the hidden rancor working in their breasts. If we succeed in dragging them into the arena of sectarian war, it will become possible to awaken the inattentive Sunnis as they feel imminent danger and annihilating death at the hands of these Sabeans.[4] Despite their weakness and fragmentation, the Sunnis are the sharpest blades, the most determined, and the most loyal when they meet those Batinis (Shi'a), who are a people of treachery and cowardice. They are arrogant only with the weak and can attack only the broken-winged. Most of the Sunnis are aware of the danger of these people, watch their sides, and fear the consequences of empowering them.

. . . .

"The solution that we see, and God the Exalted knows better, is for us to drag the Shi'a into the battle because this is the only way to prolong the fighting between us and the infidels.

. . . .

"If we are able to strike them with one painful blow after another until they enter the battle, we will be able to [re]shuffle the cards. Then, no value or influence will remain to the Governing Council or even to the Americans, who will enter a second battle [along] with the Shi'a. This is what we want, and, whether they like it or not, many Sunni areas will stand with the mujahidin. Then, the mujahidin will have assured themselves land from which to set forth in striking the Shi'a in their heartland, along with a clear media orientation and the creation of strategic depth and reach among the brothers outside [Iraq] and the mujahidin within." (al-Zarqawi, undated(a))

Zarqawi gives bin Laden, who evidently has reservations about attacking the Shi'a, a polite brush-off.

"You, gracious brothers [al Qaeda], are the leaders, guides, and symbolic figures of jihad and battle. We do not see ourselves as fit to challenge you, and we have never striven to achieve glory for ourselves. All that we hope is that we will be the spearhead, the enabling vanguard, and the bridge on which the [Islamic] nation crosses over to the victory that is promised and the tomorrow to which we aspire. This is our vision,

---

[4] Sabeans, also referred to as Sabian Mandaeans, follow a pre-Islamic faith and are a religious minority in Iraq and neighboring countries. In recent years, they have endured forced conversion and murder in Iraq (Crawford, 2007).

and we have explained it. This is our path, and we have made it clear. If you agree with us on it, if you adopt it as a program and road, and if you are convinced of the idea of fighting the sects of apostasy [Shi'a in Iraq], we will be your readied soldiers, working under your banner, complying with your orders, and indeed swearing fealty to you publicly and in the news media, vexing the infidels and gladdening those who preach the oneness of God. On that day, the believers will rejoice in God's victory. If things appear otherwise to you, we are brothers, and the disagreement will not spoil [our] friendship. [This is} {sic} a cause [in which] we are cooperating for the good and supporting jihad." (al-Zarqawi, undated(a))

And less politely . . .

"1 – {There are two choices} We fight them {the Shi'a}, and this is difficult because of the gap that will emerge between us and the people of the land. How can we fight their cousins and their sons and under what pretext after the Americans, who hold the reins of power from their rear bases, pull back? . . .

"2 – We pack our bags and search for another land, as is the sad, recurrent story in the arenas of jihad, because our enemy is growing stronger and his intelligence data are increasing day by day. By the Lord of the Ka'ba, [this] is suffocation. . . .

"I come back and again say that the only solution is for us to strike the religious, military, and other cadres among the Shi'a with blow after blow until they bend to the Sunnis. Someone may say that, in this matter, we are being hasty and rash and leading the [Islamic] nation into a battle for which it is not ready, [a battle] that will be revolting and in which blood will be spilled. This is exactly what we want, since right and wrong no longer have any place in our current situation." (al-Zarqawi, 2004b)

Bin Laden ultimately tries to have it both ways, condemning the idea of declaring the Shi'a to be infidels but promoting Zarqawi to the leadership of al-Qaeda in Iraq.

"We do not declare [Muslim] people collectively to be infidels and do not consider the killing of Muslims to be permissible. If some Muslims are killed during the operations of the mujahideen, we pray for Allah's mercy upon them. This is to be considered accidental manslaughter,

and we ask Allah to forgive us for it, and we bear responsibility for it.
. . ." (bin Laden, 2004f)

"The warrior commander [and] honored comrade Abu Mus'ab Al-
Zarqawi and the groups who joined him are the best of the community that is fighting for the sake of the word of Allah. Their courageous
operations against the Americans and against the apostate Allawi government have gladdened us . . . .

"We in the Al-Qa'ida organization very much welcome their union
with us. This is a tremendous step on the path to the unification of the
efforts fighting for the establishment of a State of Truth and for the
uprooting of the State of the Lie . . . .

"Know that the warrior comrade Abu Mus'ab Al-Zarqawi is the
commander [Amir] of the Al-Qa'ida organization in the land of the
Tigris and the Euphrates, and the comrades in the organization there
must obey him." (bin Laden, 2004g)

But push-back against attacking the Shi'a arises from Zarqawi's "mentor," Abu
Muhammad al-Maqdisi, and others.

". . . I [go] according to the school of Sheikh Al-Islam ibn Taymiyya,
who did not declare ordinary Shiites as non-Muslims [takfir al-shi'a]
. . . Hence, it is forbidden to equate them with Jews and Christians in
fighting and in similar things.

"It is forbidden to equate the ordinary Shiite with the American in
warfare. Even if our Sunni brothers in Iraq have many justifications . . .
this does not justify blowing up mosques. . . . Permitting the blood of
the Shiites is a mistake in which Jihad fighters had best not become
entangled. I have expressed reservations in this matter in particular
because the bombings are taking place in the mosques, because this
is the sectarian Fitna [civil strife] for which the occupier has yearned.
. . ." (al-Maqdisi, 2005a)

"The number of Iraqis killed in suicide operations has become a tragedy for Iraq's people . . . the mujahideen (holy fighters) must revise their
tactics and I must stress that I have reservations about these actions."
(al-Barqawi, 2005)

And Zawahiri again tries to reason with Zarqawi.

"This subject {the position on the Shi'a} is complicated and detailed. I have brought it up here so as not to address the general public on something they do not know. But please permit me to present it logically:

. . . .

"I assert here that any rational person understands with ease that the Shia cooperated with the Americans in the invasion of Afghanistan, Rafsanjani himself confessed to it, and they cooperated with them in the overthrow of Saddam and the occupation of Iraq in exchange for the Shia's assumption of power and their turning a blind eye to the American military presence in Iraq. This is clear to everybody who has two eyes.

"People of discernment and knowledge among Muslims know the extent of danger to Islam of the Twelve'er school of Shiism.[5] It is a religious school based on excess and falsehood whose function is to accuse the companions of Muhammad {of heresy} in a campaign against Islam, in order to free the way for a group of those who call for a dialogue in the name of the hidden mahdi who is in control of existence and infallible in what he does. Their prior history in cooperating with the enemies of Islam is consistent with their current reality of connivance with the Crusaders.

. . . .

"We must repeat what we mentioned previously, that the majority of Muslims don't comprehend this and possibly could not even imagine it. For that reason, many of your Muslim admirers amongst the common folk are wondering about your attacks on the Shia. The sharpness of this questioning increases when the attacks are on one of their mosques, and it increases more when the attacks are on the mausoleum of Imam Ali Bin Abi Talib, may God honor him. My opinion is that this matter won't be acceptable to the Muslim populace however much you have tried to explain it, and aversion to this will continue.

"Indeed, questions will circulate among mujahedeen circles and their opinion makers about the correctness of this conflict with the Shia at this time. Is it something that is unavoidable? Or, is it something {that} can be put off until the force of the mujahed movement in Iraq gets stronger? And if some of the operations were necessary for self-defense,

---

[5] "Those who believe that the third son was the rightful ruler of Islam are called the 'Twelvers,' because they believe that there were 12 Imams. . . . The Twelvers are by far the largest group of Shiite Muslims, because the Iranians are Twelvers. Perhaps eighty percent of the Shiis are Twelvers. Twelvers constitute ninety percent of the modern population of Iran and fifty-five to sixty percent of the population of Iraq. Twelver Shiites are the majority in Iran, Iraq, Azerbaijan and also have substantial populations in Turkey, Pakistan, Lebanon, Syria, India, Afghanistan and Bahrain" (http://www.GlobalSecurity.org).

were all of the operations necessary? Or, were there some operations that weren't called for? And is the opening of another front now in addition to the front against the Americans and the government a wise decision? Or, does this conflict with the Shia lift the burden from the Americans by diverting the mujahedeen to the Shia, while the Americans continue to control matters from afar? And if the attacks on Shia leaders were necessary to put a stop to their plans, then why were there attacks on ordinary Shia? Won't this lead to reinforcing false ideas in their minds, even as it is incumbent on us to preach the call of Islam to them and explain and communicate to guide them to the truth? And can the mujahedeen kill all of the Shia in Iraq? Has any Islamic state in history ever tried that? And why kill ordinary Shia considering that they are forgiven because of their ignorance? And what loss will befall us if we did not attack the Shia? And do the brothers forget that we have more than one hundred prisoners – many of whom are from the leadership who are wanted in their countries – in the custody of the Iranians? And even if we attack the Shia out of necessity, then why do you announce this matter and make it public, which compels the Iranians to take counter measures? And do the brothers forget that both we and the Iranians need to refrain from harming each other at this time in which the Americans are targeting us?" (al-Zawahiri, 2005b)

In the midst of this debate, U.S. Marines routed al-Qaeda from its redoubt in the town of Tal Afar on the Syrian border.

"The battles in Tal-Afar are commanded by the Mujahideen brothers of Al-Qaida in the Land of the Two Rivers and the Mujahideen rely on Allah alone for support. They convey that the Cross Worshipers have received a big blow and are tasting the humiliation at the hand of the Mujahideen. Martyrdom operations are ongoing at Tal-Afar; in addition to planting explosive devices, and luring the enemy into street fights avoiding civilian casualties between Muslim women and children. We withdrew from some neighborhoods just for this purpose alone; you have received from the Mujahideen news that relieves the Muslim chest, this is by the grace of Allah." (al-Zarqawi, 2005g)

The battle of Tal Afar was, in fact, a total defeat for al-Qaeda and thus prompted the open declaration of war set forth below. Tal Afar has since been periodically re-infiltrated and reliberated.

"The Organization of al-Qa'ida in Mesopotamia has decided the following: First, because the government of the grandson of Ibn-al-

'Alqami[6] and servant of the Cross Ibrahim al-Jaafari has declared all-out war against the Sunni people of Talla'far, followed by al-Ramadi, al-Qa'im, Samarra', and Rawah, in the pretense of returning rights and destroying the terrorists, the organization has decided to announce all-out warfare against all Shiites in Iraq, wherever they may be found, tit for tat, for it is you who started this [sic].

"Take care, for we swear that we shall offer you no mercy. . . .

". . . From this moment on, each person who is proven to be affiliated with the National Guard, the police, or the Army, and whoever proves to be an agent or spy for the Crusaders, will be killed." (al-Zarqawi, 2005f)

And Zarqawi tries to intimidate any dissenters.

"The sons of the tribes are among the pillars of the jihad. These tribes had the honor to support the jihad and those who wage it. Nevertheless, we warn the tribes that each tribe, group, or association found to be involved in helping the Crusaders and their apostate servants, we swear by He who sent Muhammad that we will target them as we target the Crusaders, and we shall remove them from their milieu and disperse them, for there are but two camps – the camp of righteousness and its followers and the camp of corruption and its mob." (al-Zarqawi, 2005f)

"Sunna: has your son's blood become so cheap that you sell it for such a paltry sum?! Has the dignity of your women become so slight?! Woe unto you; were you not informed that many of your pure and spotless sisters in the Sunni community of Tel'Afur were violated, their chastity slaughtered, and their wombs filled with the sperm of the Crusaders and their brothers the hateful Rafidites!?[7] Where is your religion?! And where your chivalry, your ardor, and your manliness?" (al-Zarqawi, 2005f)

However, the insurgent clerics refuse to be intimidated.

"[Statements] like [Al-Zarqawi's] dangerous declaration fulfill the most dangerous aspirations of the occupier to tear the country asunder and ignite fitna (internal strife) among the people. [These statements] also provide the interim government with what it needs – the rallying of

---

[6] Ibn-al-'Alqami was an Iraqi Shiite vizier who capitulated to the Mongol invaders.

[7] "Crusader-Rafidites" refers to "Americans-Shi'ites." It is used derogatorily by Sunni extremists.

the Iraqi public around it, now that it has lost everything owing to its terrorist policy. . . .

"We call upon Abu Mus'ab Al-Zarqawi to retract these threats since they damage the image of Jihad, jeopardize the success of the plan of Jihad and resistance in Iraq and lead to further bloodshed of innocent Iraqis." (Association of Muslim Scholars in Iraq, undated)

". . . the above does not necessarily mean that we justify and permit the sectarian war in Iraq, in which people are killed because of their name, identity or sect regardless of their opinions or actions . . . for not all the Shi'ites in Iraq – neither elite nor masses – are infidels. Moreover, not all the Shi'ites fight with the invaders and collude in their plot, and [not all of them] participate in the murder of Sunni Muslims and in the aggression against their honor and the holy places. Consequently, we cannot generalize by fighting [them] and killing [them] all indiscriminately, without considering what the texts of the Shari'a permit or prohibit. . . .

"Furthermore, despite the black history of the Shi'ites, which is full of treason and conspiracy against the nation and its people on many occasions, [we] do not know of any highly regarded ulama of Islam who have issued a fatwa permitting the killing of any Shi'ite merely because he is Shi'ite." (al-Tartousi, undated)

"We strongly reject Al-Zarqawi's ideas and regard them as a crime which aims to [undermine] the unity of Iraq and to generate internal sectarian strife among the people of the united homeland. . . . The party that targets Shi'ites in [their] mosques is the same party that targets Sunnis, assassinates ulama, preachers and imams of the mosques, and targets innocent civilians." (Mustafa of Tikrit, undated)

Zarqawi complains about his critics, but his attacks continue. With Shi'a attacks on Sunnis, the sectarian war he hoped to create took on a life of its own.

"We do not understand why this ferocious campaign against Mujahideen is occurring at the present time. This is exactly what the cross worshippers and their collaborators want to see. They want to stop the spread of Jihad that has already started to dismantle their dreams. They {Association of Muslim Scholars} . . . will be well advised to aim their arrows in the direction of the brothers of swine and Apes and those who promote 'National Islam.'" (al-'Qaeda in the Land of the Two Rivers, 2005b)

Ultimately, al-Qaeda Central sends Zarqawi a scathing letter enumerating his "defects" and instructing him to back off on violence and focus on "good deeds" that will attract more popular support. He is threatened with being replaced if he does not.

"What am I commanding you to do . . . ?

"If you were to ask am I commanding you to abandon the matter that you are in? My response: No, not necessarily, which means that it is not required, although it is a possibility if you find at some point someone who is better and more suitable than you . . .

"Therefore, it is incumbent on you to mend your flaws in many things. It is not sufficient that you have with you a shar'ia council and groups of guys who lack expertise and experience no matter who they are. On the whole, I will advise you on a number of measures in this arena:

"– That you abstain from making any decision on a comprehensive issue (one with a broad reach), and on substantial matters until you have turned to your leadership; Shaykh Usamah and the Doctor . . . and their brothers there, and consulted with them . . . .

". . . embracing the people and bringing them together and winning them over and placating them and so forth . . . my brother, is a great way towards victory and triumph that is not lesser than military operations. . . .

". . . however, [you should do this] with gentleness, gradual open mindedness, while overlooking and being quiet about many of their mistakes and flaws, and while tolerating a great deal of harm from them for the sake of not having them turn away and turn into enemies on any level.

"– Paying attention to the class of religious scholars and shaykhs in Iraq in particular, and in the world as a whole, and respecting them as a whole, and not opposing any of them, no matter what, and no matter what errors they made in shaping the hearts of the public . . . .

"The long and short of the matter is that the Islamic theologians are the keys to the Muslim community and they are its leaders. This is the way it is, whether you like it or not. Thus, we address them with utmost kindness in word and speech, and we demonstrate respect and reverence for them in phrasing, in order to be {in} harmony with them and with the public behind them, which are the masses of the Muslim nation. . . .

"You must incline yourself to this, and be humble to the believers, and smile in people's faces, even if you are cursing them in your heart, even if it has been said that they are 'a bad tribal brother,' and what you have to . . . Among the most crucial of things involved is exercising all caution against attempting to kill any religious scholar or tribal leader who is obeyed,[8] and of good repute in Iraq from among the Sunnis, no matter what . . . .

"The important thing is to keep your reputation and that of the mujahidin pure, especially your organization, and to gain peoples' affection and love, and to strive for it. . . .

"Let us not merely be people of killing, slaughter, blood, cursing, insult, and harshness; but rather people of this, who are unopposed to mercy and gentleness . . . .

"Thus anyone who commits tyranny and aggression upon the people . . . and drives people away from us and our faith and our jihad and from the religion and the message that we carry, then he must be taken to task, and we must direct him to what is right, just, and for the best. Otherwise, we would have to push him aside and keep him away from the sphere of influence and replace him and so forth, for this is an important matter. . . . You need to look deeply within yourself and your character . . ." (Atiyah, 2006).

For some, the clash between Sunni and Shi'a is so painful that they retreat into denial.

"I don't think that Abu Musab al-Zarqawi exists as such. He's simply an invention by the occupiers to divide the people." (al-Kalesi, 2005)

A Week of Ramadan
In Islam, fighting is normally suspended during Ramadan; however, al-Qaeda called for continued attacks (al-Aamer, 2004).

"Your brother from the military division of Al-Qaida Organisation in the land of the Two Rivers, on Monday, Ramadan 21st 1426, corresponding to October 24, 2005, successfully detonated an explosive device targeting a Crusaders patrol, completely destroying a Hummer killing all Crusaders on board, by the grace of Allah.

. . . .

"Your brother from the military division of Al-Qaida Organisation in the land of the Two Rivers, on Tuesday, Ramadan 22nd 1426, corresponding to October 25, 2005, attacked Police retractors patrol in

---

[8] In early 2007, al-Qaeda began a campaign of assassinating tribal leaders who were cooperating with the coalition forces.

the area of Al-Mansour, the four road junction, during sunset 'Iftar,' killing three apostates, by the grace of Allah.

. . . .

"Your brother from the military division of Al-Qaida Organisation in the land of the Two Rivers, on Tuesday, Ramadan 22nd 1426, corresponding to October 25, 2005, a sharp shooter, gunned down three apostates police in the area of Al-Mathnah neighbourhood at Mosul, by the grace of Allah.

. . . .

"Your brother from the military division of Al-Qaida Organisation in the land of the Two Rivers, on Tuesday, Ramadan 22nd 1426, corresponding to October 25, 2005, detonated an explosive device inside the home of Crusaders spy at Baquba, by the grace of Allah.

. . . .

"Your brother from the military division of Al-Qaida Organisation in the land of the Two Rivers, on Wednesday, Ramadan 23rd 1426, corresponding to October 26, 2005, detonated an explosive device targeting Crusaders Humvee at Baquba, destroying the vehicle and killing four crusaders on board, by the grace of Allah.

. . . .

"Your brother from the military division of Al-Qaida Organisation in the land of the Two Rivers, today, Ramadan 24th 1426, corresponding to October 27, 2005, setup a tight ambush targeting an apostates patrol from the puppet army. The Mujahideen commenced the fight by detonating an explosive device followed up by automatic weapons fire, destroying two of their vehicles and killing all on board, by the grace of Allah.

. . . .

"Your brother from the military division of Al-Qaida Organisation in the Land of the Two Rivers, today, Ramadan 24th 1426, corresponding to October 27, 2005, successfully detonated an explosive device targeting a crusaders patrol, destroying one of their Hummers and killing all on board, by the grace of Allah.

. . . .

"Your brother from the military division of Al-Qaida Organisation in the land of the Two Rivers, Today, Ramadan 24th 1426, corresponding to October 27, 2005, assassinated General Shwqui, the head of the Al-Ibah Khanah police station, during his visit to in the area of Al-Toa'mah in Durrah, by the grace of Allah." (al-Qaeda in the Land of the Two Rivers, 2005c)

Looking Ahead

". . . it is my humble opinion that the Jihad in Iraq requires several incremental goals:

"The first stage: Expel the Americans from Iraq.

"The second stage: Establish an Islamic authority or amirate, then develop it and support it until it achieves the level of a caliphate – over as much territory as you can to spread its power in Iraq, i.e., in Sunni areas, is in order to fill the void stemming from the departure of the Americans, immediately upon their exit and before un-Islamic forces attempt to fill this void, whether those whom the Americans will leave behind them, or those among the un-Islamic forces who will try to jump at taking power.

"There is no doubt that this amirate will enter into a fierce struggle with the foreign infidel forces, and those supporting them among the local forces, to put it in a state of constant preoccupation with defending itself, to make it impossible for it to establish a stable state which could proclaim a caliphate, and to keep the Jihadist groups in a constant state of war, until these forces find a chance to annihilate them.

"The third stage: Extend the jihad wave to the secular countries neighboring Iraq.

"The fourth stage: It may coincide with what came before: the clash with Israel, because Israel was established only to challenge any new Islamic entity.

"My raising this idea—I don't claim that it's infallible—is only to stress something extremely important. And it is that the mujahedeen must not have their mission end with the expulsion of the Americans from Iraq, and then lay down their weapons, and silence the fighting zeal. We will return to having the secularists and traitors holding sway over us. Instead, their ongoing mission is to establish an Islamic state, and defend it, and for every generation to hand over the banner to the one after it until the Hour of Resurrection." (al-Zawahiri, 2005b)

"The cries from the infidel leaders and their supporters have changed from threatening tones to screams of agony and pain due to their predicament in Mesopotamia. Their new religion, 'democracy,' is taking its last breaths after its deception was revealed and the mujahideen attacked it. Now, we witness how their soldiers who used to spread fear across the whole world are losing control over the entire country [of Iraq] and groups of the faithful are able to attack them every day." (Abu Abdelrahman al-Iraqi, 2005)

"Things may develop faster than we imagine. The aftermath of the collapse of American power in Vietnam—and how they ran and left their agents—is noteworthy. Because of that, we must be ready starting now, before events overtake us, and before we are surprised by the conspiracies of the Americans and the United Nations and their plans to fill the void behind them. We must take the initiative and impose a fait accompli upon our enemies, instead of the enemy imposing one on us, wherein our lot would be to merely resist their schemes.

". . . This is the most vital part. This authority, or the Sharia amirate that is necessary, requires fieldwork starting now, alongside the combat and war. It would be a political endeavor in which the mujahedeen would be a nucleus around which would gather the tribes and their elders, and the people in positions, and scientists, and merchants, and people of opinion, and all the distinguished ones who were not sullied by appeasing the occupation and those who defended Islam.

. . . .

"Therefore, I stress again to you and to all your brothers the need to direct the political action equally with the military action, by the alliance, cooperation and gathering of all leaders of opinion and influence in the Iraqi arena. I can't define for you a specific means of action. You are more knowledgeable about the field conditions. But you and your brothers must strive to have around you circles of support, assistance, and cooperation, and through them, to advance until you become a consensus, entity, organization, or association that represents all the honorable people and the loyal folks in Iraq. I repeat the warning against separating from the masses, whatever the danger." (al-Zawahiri, 2005b)

"If you continue the same policy of aggression against Muslims, God willing, you will see horror that will make you forget what you saw in Vietnam.

. . . .

"They are repeating with regard to Iraq the same claims and lies they uttered about Vietnam.

"Did they not tell you that they would train the Vietnamese people so that they would run their own affairs themselves, and that they were defending freedom in Vietnam?" (al-Zawahiri, 2005c)

"I say to him {President Bush}: You pathological liar, you were lying when you entered Iraq, you are lying when you are being defeated in Iraq, and you will be lying when you leave Iraq. You entered Iraq under the pretext of WMDs, you are being defeated in Iraq under the pretext of achieving freedom and security, and, Allah willing, you will soon be leaving Iraq under the pretext that your mission is accomplished. But you will leave behind dozens of thousands of dead, wounded and crippled." (al-Zawahiri, 2005e)

"The ultimate goal of the Mujahdeen after the occupiers leave, is establishing an Islamic Emirate that will be the start to defend Islam and Muslims; a step on the way to revive the Caliphate. In Iraq we should not forget that al-Quds [Jerusalem] is nearer than a stone's throw from Baghdad. If the Islamic Emirate is established in Iraq, Allah willing, it could go through the Jordanian betrayer entity to be at the Palestinian borders, and Allah willing, the Mujahdeen from inside Palestine and outside should be united. Then it will be the big conquest and the greatest victory." (al-Hukaymah, 2006)

"No doubt that the general scenery in the region is becoming critical, and will end with a conflict, as we have mentioned before when we explained the Safawi[9] and crusader projects, or the Farsi-Western struggle to control this important part of the world, with what it has of strategic differences. Inevitably, a conflict will occur sooner or later. . . . Therefore, [America] will cause more devastation in a new war. It is a culture which does not know anything but destruction." (al-Ali, 2007)

"It's very clear that the most idiotic American project across history, which was called 'the Great Middle East,'[10] has fallen on its face and is on its first step on the way to its evil goals. There is no question in that now, the question is, what will follow this failure?" (al-Ali, 2007)

By the time of this writing, violence had dropped dramatically in Iraq. Sunni militias fought al-Qaeda, which had retreated to the region near Mosul, where it continued to try to incite sectarian conflict.

Afghanistan

Before the Afghan war, relations between Osama bin Laden and Mullah Omar were not always smooth, and after the war, there were recriminations about bin

---

[9] A Sunni term for Iranian Shi'ites.

[10] The Greater Middle East Initiative of the Bush administration, which seeks to spread democracy in the region.

Laden's impetuousness. Most jihadi comments on the war generally fall into two categories: The first is analyses of what happened when the Taliban were routed. The
second focuses on the present situation, including claims of a resurgent Taliban and
al-Qaeda.

"The strangest thing I have heard so far is Abu Abdullah's {pseud-
onym for bin Laden} saying that he wouldn't listen to the Leader of the
Faithful when he asked him to stop giving interviews. . . . I think our
brother [bin Laden] has caught the disease of screens, flashes, fans, and
applause . . . .

. . . .

"You {bin Laden} should apologize for any inconvenience or pressure
you have caused . . . and commit to the wishes and orders of the Leader
of the Faithful on matters that concern his circumstances here . . . .

"The Leader of the Faithful, who should be obeyed where he reigns,
is Muhammad Omar, not Osama bin Laden. Osama bin Laden and
his companions are only guests seeking refuge and have to adhere to
the terms laid out by the person who provided it for them. This is
legitimate and logical." (Abu Mosab al-Suri and Abu Khalid al-Suri,
1999, in Cullison 2004)

"When I came here the first time it was because of a desire to revive the
Muslim spirit and an attempt at rescuing the children and the powerless. The British attacked Afghanistan before Osama bin Laden was
here, Russians came here before me and now the Americans. We pray
that god will defeat them just like he did their allies before them. We
ask God to give us the power to defeat them as we did others before."
(bin Laden, 2001a)

"The US would have invaded Afghanistan even if there was no Osama
and this is a FACT. The reason for the invasion of Afghanistan was
to remove the Islamic law and impose a puppet secular government
on the people of Afghanistan. A government with Sharia law was not
acceptable to America." (Hakimi, undated)

"{The jihadi experience in Afghanistan was} a tragic example of an
Islamic movement managed in an alarmingly meaningless way . . . .
Everyone knew that their leader (bin Laden) was leading them to the
abyss, and even leading the entire country to utter destruction but they
continued to carry out his orders faithfully and with bitterness." (Abu
Walid al Masri, undated, in Wright, 2006)

"From the beginning, the organization's leaders prepared for all possibilities, and especially the worst ones, readying appropriate alternatives. In the war in Afghanistan, they wisely withdrew fighting formations, removed equipment and stockpiled it in the mountains, and prepared for a long guerilla war. Abroad, jihad cells spread out in various countries, each preparing to carry out its mission according to a plan with no room for improvisation or confusion. The success of this jihad planning put fear in the hearts of Americans everywhere. Warnings of impending jihad attacks have taken a murderous toll on the nerves of the US masses, who do not understand why their vast military apparatus has failed to stop these attacks." (al-Qurashi, 2002b)

"We don't want to repeat the mistake of the Taliban, who restricted participation in governance to the students and the people of Qandahar alone. They did not have any representation for the Afghan people in their ruling regime, so the result was that the Afghan people disengaged themselves from them. Even devout ones took the stance of the spectator and, when the invasion came, the amirate collapsed in days, because the people were either passive or hostile. Even the students themselves had a stronger affiliation to their tribes and their villages than their affiliation to the Islamic amirate or the Taliban movement or the responsible party in charge of each one of them in his place. Each of them retreated to his village and his tribe, where his affiliation was stronger!!" (al-Zawahiri, 2005b)

"The Arab and Western media are responsible for distorting the image of the Arab Afghans[11] by portraying them as obsessed half-mad people who have rebelled against the United States that once trained and financed them. This lie was repeated more frequently after the Arab Afghans returned to Afghanistan for the second time in the mid-1990s in the wake of the bombing of the US embassies in Nairobi and Dar es Salam.

"According to the leader of the Egyptian Al-Jihad Organization, the purpose of the distortion campaign against the Arab Afghans is clear and obvious, namely, the wish of the United States to deprive the Muslim nation of the honor of heroism and to pretend to be saying: Those whom you consider heroes are actually my creation and my mercenaries who rebelled against me when I stopped backing them." (al-Zawahiri, 2001)

---

[11] This is the name given to the Arab volunteers who focused the fight against the Soviet forces in Afghanistan and then became members of al-Qaeda.

"This message, which was prepared in a hurry, aims at providing our people in the Arab region with a clear picture, from the [battle] field, of the reality of the American enemy and its fighting tactics, and we will use layman's language and refrain from using military terminology.

. . . .

"The American soldier is not fit for combat. This is the truth that the leaders of the Pentagon know, as much as we and everyone who was engaged with them know. The Hollywood promotions will not succeed in the real battlefield. Therefore, the American commanders tend to use the air forces and missile bombardment to vacate the ground from any resistance, paving the way for the advance of the American phonies.

. . . .

"We differ completely from our enemy in the psychological fight. While our enemy depended on creating lies about itself, magnifying its power [by saying that] it will not be defeated and the war will not exceed a week as it has sweeping power which can make miracles, and its program depended on terrorizing the competitor because of the Crusaders' hopelessness in their deteriorating fighting level, we were working on bonding every one with his God and his relation with Him, and He is mighty, strong and keen." (al-Adel, 2003)

"What did they accomplish in Afghanistan? They removed the Taliban government from Kabul, and it settled in the villages and mountains, where the real power of Afghanistan lies. Northern Afghanistan and Kabul have become a scene of chaos, pillaging, looting, defiling [women's] honor, and drug dealing, which have flourished under the American occupation. Then they held elections, which resembled a masquerade more than anything, since the country's periphery is controlled by highway bandits and warlords, since the international committees monitoring the elections – or rather, those who bear false witness – could not cover more than ten voting districts, even if they wanted to. Transferring the ballot boxes takes 15 days, under the control of the warlords and highway bandits, and then under the control of the occupation forces, and since any resistance, or anything resembling resistance or opposition, is met with bombardment, missiles, the burning of villages, and the killing of hundreds." (al-Zawahiri, 2005e)

"The mujahideen gathered from all countries of the world alongside the Emir of the Believers [Mullah Omar] together with those of pure intentions. They united to fight this new global Crusader alliance and their hypocritical lackeys, mercenaries, and highway bandits, such as [Afghan President] Hamid Karzai, [Afghan General] Dostum, [former Afghan minister] Fahim, and others. Allah be praised, these operations hardly ever cease in Afghanistan's provinces, causing the Americans and their allies to lose sleep. The proud Afghan people fights for its faith.[12] Allah willing, this will be the end of America and its allies in Afghanistan, and its grave will lie with the graves of the invaders, such as the English and the Russians." (Atallah, undated)

"This is what they have accomplished to this day in Afghanistan. In Kabul, their [allies] are terrified, and their president cannot leave his office. If he goes to Kandahar, he faces assassination attempts. If his plane lands in Gardez, missiles catch up with it. Forged elections . . . Crusader forces led by America taking blows on a daily basis . . . An almost complete media blackout . . . Pakistani collaboration . . . Despite all this, America was forced to admit the strength of the resistance it faces, and to admit that the Taliban is still the strongest force in Afghanistan.

"Brothers, I tell you – and the Crusaders and their apostate collaborators cannot refute it – that were it not for the continuous support the Pakistani army gives the Americans, they would have left a long time ago – and they will leave soon, Allah willing." (al-Zawahiri, 2005d)

"The United States lost the battle in Afghanistan. It has achieved nothing worth noting beyond the murder of innocent civilians. The real rulers of Afghanistan are the Taliban and al-Qa'ida. We find sufficient proof of this in the fact that the head of this fabricated state is guarded and defended by Americans. They do not trust the mujahid people—or even mercenaries—because they know well that vengeance awaits the traitors. This is the fate that befell Karzai's deputy. The United States, Karzai, and the international alliance are part of a historical and political farce . . . [ellipses as published]" (Abu Ayman al-Hilali, 2002)

"East and South Afghanistan are now an entirely an open field for the mujahideen. The hypocrites have shut themselves off within the districts' capitals and the Americans hide in their trenches and refuse to come out to face the Mujahideen, although the Mujahideen provoke them with shelling and shooting and by cutting off the roads around them.

---

[12] Recent news reports state that the Taliban fighters are being paid twice what the Afghan army receives.

"Their defense focuses on aerial bombardment that wastes US money only generating dust.

"In Kabul, the Americans and the peacekeeping forces are burnt by the shells of the Mujahideen and they anticipate martyrdom operations at any time, Allah willing." (al-Zawahiri, 2004b)

"The provinces under Taliban control are Paktika, Paktiya, Zabul, Uruzgan, Helmand, Ghazni, Kandahar, but if we declare the emirate, the American occupiers will bomb innocent civilians and we do not want our brothers to be in any further suffering.

". . . The Taliban are in full control of the Pashto, Persian and other ethnic groups are with them. Afghan people and all the world has understood the fact that Americans are not our or anyone's friends nor are they humanity's friends. America has no proper plan to govern Afghanistan, only the Taliban can maintain law and order in this country and establish a government here." (Hakimi, undated)

"In Muslim Iraq, the Mujahideen have foiled US plans after the feebleness of the interim government was exposed. America's defeat in Iraq and in Afghanistan has become a question of time, Allah willing. In both countries, the Americans are locked between two fires. If they stay, they will bleed to death, and if they retreat, they will lose everything." (al-Zawahiri, 2004b)

These boasts have increasingly become true. As of this writing, the United States is taking more casualties in Afghanistan than in Iraq.

CHAPTER NINE

Operations

The role played by al-Qaeda as an organization in the jihadi movement is no longer clear. There is little doubt that it has become more decentralized, with al-Qaeda "franchises" in Iraq and Saudi Arabia. Other groups (some of which may not really exist) have appropriated the al-Qaeda name, and still others are simply inspired by bin Laden. Algeria, Chechnya, Palestine, Lebanon, Indonesia, and the Philippines have their own homegrown jihadi organizations, some of which are affiliated with al-Qaeda.

Some observers believe that al-Qaeda Central is still functioning on the Afghan-Pakistan border and is a source of financing, planning, and propaganda. They also point to the fact that key members of several terrorist plots have taken the obligatory trip to Pakistan and to the existence of an official media organization (the Global Islamic Media Front, GIMF) that publishes statements of bin Laden and al-Zawahiri, as well as other jihadi communications. Others view al-Qaeda and the entire jihadi movement as more of a virtual organization—a network that consists of small cells linked by the Internet via nodes such as web pages, chat rooms, and blogs, many of which are now password-protected. Whatever their configuration, the jihadis must carry out basic organizational tasks such as public and internal communication, training, recruitment, and propaganda. Increasingly, many of these activities are carried out over the Internet.

This chapter focuses on the jihadis' organizational activities and the crucial role of the Internet in them.

> "The organization continues to exist and I bring glad tidings to the Muslims that the organization is operating with higher energy and more determination to retaliate for the blood of the killed innocents. The Al-Qaida organization is not childish or a fragile organization which can be destroyed easily as some people may think especially as we know who we are fighting and we know that one day the entire world will confront us and fight against us and this is what happened. Our organization has been built on this fact." (Abu Ghaith, 2002)

Finances

"Money is surely the foundation of jihad. One of the greatest boons to the mujahidin and to jihad occurs when a group of people in the community, or the entire community, collects donations and sends them to those who have left to fight. This has a tremendous influence that all can see. This practice has thrown the world's unbelievers into confusion. They have frozen the accounts of the mujahidin and hemmed in those who help them. But the mujahidin continue along their path: 'Neither those who oppose them or betray them can harm them.'" (al-Salim, 2003)

"Some army leaders say, 'Money is the nerve of war.' This has become truer as time passes and life becomes incomparably more complex and costly. The business of jihad is no exception. Each organized jihad operation that bears fruit requires generous financing. It usually requires months or even years of preparation and careful work to ensure that the enemy suspects nothing. Al-Qa'ida realized this early. As a result, over the years it developed a complex financial network to provide funds for its needs. This has led several respected experts to state that neither the CIA nor Britain's MI6 has ever encountered an international financial network as complex as the one al-Qa'ida constructed. Making matters even more difficult for hostile intelligence services, the network is divided into numerous parts that are usually connected to each other only by the thinnest of threads.

"According to reports by strategic institutes, al-Qa'ida's requirements to conduct training and operations inside and outside of Afghanistan are probably about $50 million annually. If this estimate is correct, then it's hardly odd that the organization includes a few financial specialists and pays great attention to training in finances and business, putting significant effort into its transnational investments." (al-Qurashi, 2002b)

"If the rich kept themselves from their pleasures for a single day, if they stopped spending their money on luxuries for one day and gave it instead to the mujahidin—who are dying from the cold, losing their feet in the snow, suffering from a shortage of rations and ammunition to defend and replenish themselves—if the rich would take one day to spend money on the Afghan mujahidin, their money would, God willing, move the jihad much closer to victory." (Azzam, undated, in al-Salim, 2003)

"When we begin administering some of the regions (by permission of God) financial reserves will rush in upon us from charitable giving. . . . Likewise, there is money obtained from financial institutions which we will plunder from what the authorities of the regimes of apostasy have left behind when they leave these regions. . . . Naturally, there will be disbursements (of money) and rights (given to) the people; acts of injustice necessitate the granting of these rights before everything else. However, through good planning and the proper handling of these revenues it is possible for us to store them for the needs of Islamic activism which will arise. At this time, let those who are firmly rooted in knowledge among the people tawhid and jihad give religious justification for and explicate the details of how to spend the money on tribal leaders among the people and the like for uniting them in order that they may give their allegiance to our administrations." (Naji, 2004)

Recruitment

Recruiting jihadi fighters is a complex process that involves both the Internet and personal contact and persuasion. Internet web sites, chat rooms, and blogs can be viewed as the marketing phase of jihadi recruitment. This phase creates awareness, shapes perceptions, and stimulates interest. The personal contact is the sales phase, where the recruit is persuaded to take a decisive step. There is a great deal of literature about the sociology and psychology of this process. This section contains examples, first-person accounts, and commentary on recruitment.

"I invite you to the first day of the month of the great swearing of an oath of loyalty to the commander of the Muslim armies, Sheikh Osama bin Laden, and to the commanders of the global jihad: Sheikh Ayman Al-Zawahiri, Emir of the Believers Mullah Muhammad Omar, and Abu Mus'ab Al-Zarqawi, and to all the jihad fighters.

"Oh God, you need this oath of loyalty, the oath of death for Allah that will terrorize the infidels and earn the jihad fighters in particular, and the Muslims in general, reward in the world to come . . . .

"Moreover, for this oath of loyalty to death it is not necessary for you to die now – but in the near future, the very near future, Allah willing, we must all join this blessed convoy, particularly since we have sworn an oath of loyalty." (Global Islamic Media Front, 2005c)

"In the Name of God

Preliminary Registration for Martyrdom Operations

I _____, child of _____,
born 13_____ [Islamic calendar], the City of:
_____ proclaim my preparedness for carrying out martyrdom operations:

_____ against the occupiers of the holy sites [referring to Najaf, Karbala, and other places in Iraq].

_____ against the occupiers of [Jerusalem].

_____ for carrying out the death sentence of the infidel Salman Rushdie.

Also, I would like to become an active member of the Army of Martyrs of the International Islamic Movement. Yes ___, No ___

Contact telephone:

Applicant's address:

Applicant's signature:" (Rodriguez, 2004)[1]

". . . {prison} is the perfect recruitment and training grounds for radicalism and the Islamic religion." (Umar, undated)

"Asked {by al-Majallah} if the decision of Al-Qa'ida to recruit foreigners {U.S. and European citizens} among its ranks has achieved its aspired goals, he {al-Ablaj} said: 'Yes, it has and it has already yielded fruit. Work is continuing.'" (al-Ablaj, undated)

"Many people claim to fight jihad and want to inflict harm on the enemy. But few of these people have sufficient courage to overcome the material and moral obstacles to carry out their claims. A Muslim may want to join a jihad group or organization, especially one on the level of al-Qa'ida, but when he gets the opportunity, he finds himself reviewing his calculations and connections with this world. At the last

---

[1] "An expatriate Iranian who alerted Insight Online to this 'job posting' said that while recruitment of young suicide killers has been going on for many years . . . this is the first time that such groups have circulated application forms and done so publicly" (Rodriguez, 2004).

moment, he pulls out. He cannot overcome the first barrier. If he does manage to overcome it, he finds himself facing a second barrier—the barrier of exile. In most cases, he must leave his job, his profession, his family, and his tribe to join the ranks of the mujahidin. Very, very few people have the courage needed to overcome this second barrier.

"If he overcomes this successfully, he will find himself facing a third barrier—joining the battle in deed and in act, rather than in word. This is the highest summit of Islam. When they overcome these three barriers—and the heroes of the raid {9/11} overcame them success-fully—they find themselves facing the last barrier. They must offer their souls to their Creator and place their lives in His hands. They race to their Maker, crying, 'We have hurried to Your side, our Lord, that You might be pleased.' Then they have risen up to the summit of jihad, which is martyrdom in the path of God to aid His faith and inflict harm on His enemies. They were only able to overcome these obstacles with unique courage. This is the power of the divine that overcomes all barriers." (al-Amili, 2002)

". . . In the organization, colors and races dissolve. There are no foreign-ers among us. We are all brothers, believers, and have a close relation-ship. There is no problem in these brothers [US and European citizens] reaching the rank of a leader in a group, although we often sense that they seem to shy away from anything that gives them the title of leader over their brothers. Their hearts yearn for God and paradise and they see the position of leader as a trust and a big responsibility. As for the expertise they acquired in various fields, they did so under our instruc-tions." (al-Ablaj, undated)

As part of their crackdown on jihadis, the Saudi security forces arranged for a number of captured terrorists to talk to the media about the experience of being recruited. It is not known whether these statements were coerced.

"1. They told me: Join us and you will enter paradise. My friend replied: And if I go to hell, who will help me then?

"2. They used to assure us that the attacks and bombings were designed to drive the idolaters from the Arabian Peninsula. Then they said: We want to overthrow the state because it is an infidel state! Then they said: We wish to establish an Islamic state with Mecca at its center. Later they changed their style and said: We wish to implement the prophet's Hadith 'and they will reform what other people have spoiled.' We do not know what they will say in the future.

"3. My ambition was to become an engineer, but they ruined my ambition with stories of jihad and the houris of paradise who would be waiting for us. They told us that at the end of times we would be the victorious sect and all the others would collapse and vanish!

"4. I love jihad. Every believer loves jihad, but we chose the wrong path.

. . . .

"6. My experience started with cellular telephone text messages about jihad, followed by telephone conversations, and then meetings with the shaykhs of misguidance. After joining the cell and residing in hideouts and guesthouses and experiencing a sense of loss, we sat and cursed our country's religious scholars. . . .

. . . .

"9. They do not debate anything with the members but tell them: Carry out the orders. We want you to attain martyrdom and go to paradise.

"10. They tell you: It is your duty as a good son to your parents to go and carry out jihad. If you are killed, then you will be a martyr and intercede for them in heaven. Therefore you do not now need to ask their permission to do what you are doing.

"11. They told us we were permitted to lie to our parents and forbade us to reveal the organization's secrets.

"12. One recruiter and evil guide told me: If you do not go to Iraq to carry out jihad, then you are a sinner. I replied: Why, Shaykh, do you not go yourself along with Abd-al-Rahman and Ahmad? He responded angrily: If we go to carry out jihad there and die, who will prepare the young men here? I believed him.

. . . .

"15. Saudi youths are targets because many of them are truthful, pious, and ready to help others without hesitation.

"16. I thank God that I was arrested before I could hurt other Muslims.

. . . .

"23. Among the methods we used in the organization: I recruited a 16-year-old and I used this method to convince him: We love the homeland more than any others do. Anyone who blows himself up in an operation is a patriot and a martyr who helps to liberate the homeland from the infidels who occupied it with the help of a society that has sold its country and resources to the occupiers." (al-Zaydan, 2005)

Jihadi recruiters are not above using the threat of force.

"I was recruited by a close friend of mine . . . . He used to work in terrorist operations, and he asked me to join him on these operations but I couldn't. He subsequently tried to kill me several times." (Terrorist #3, 2005)

"I wouldn't do it, I told him {the recruiter} that I wasn't interested, that I'm an orphan living with my mother, and that my father died in 1984. I have no brothers or sisters, and I support my mother. He told me: 'I don't care about these things. I will kill you and your mother.' You understand? He threatened me. I had to work with them." (Terrorist #4, 2005)

A recruitment pitch.

"It was God's will for me that, in years past, I was a supervisor at a number of summer centers, and I lived among the youth at summer centers for several years. Because of my close knowledge of a number of those youths, my knowledge of the sincerity of their intentions, and their protectiveness of Islam, I find that this is an opportunity to send a message to every youth who has participated, or is currently participating, in summer centers. My message is also addressed to my brothers the supervisors and administrators of summer centers . . . .

"O youth of the summer centers: Are you satisfied that the enemies who are murdering our brethren in Iraq, Afghanistan, and Palestine are safe in our lands while you still live? . . .

"Will you not awaken, o youth of Islam, and rise from your stupor? This, by God, is a Crusade against the nation. If you do not take the God-decreed position of jihad against the enemy, you will only experience more humiliation, subjugation, and insult that ill-befit you, the youth of Islam.

. . . .

"Will you not rise, o youth of Islam, to succor your religion and to protect your nation? Are the Christians more protective of their faith [than you are of yours], so that they come as fighters, carrying the [standard of the] Cross on our lands? Are the Christian women and their prostitutes more courageous than you, so that they have come to invade the lands of Islam, leaving their families and property behind?

Can you not see, o youth of Islam, that the war today is a Crusade, and among the major events of the era? Any who stays behind is a loser who has deserted his religion and his nation. . . . even if he pretends that he is a defender! Can you not smell the perfume of Paradise and the sweet scent of the martyrs who have departed this world in defense of their religion and their nation, expending their lives in the path of God in defense of the nation and in combat against the Cross and its agents?"

". . . Those who made out of [the Muslim] lands a theater of war are their traitorous rulers who made of the land a safe base for the soldiers of the Cross and their commanders.

"Do not accept humiliation for your faith; fight them upon your lands and eject them from them. . . ." (al-Oshan, 2004)

A response.

". . . and we view jihad and martyrdom as mandatory for the nation, and a source of its dignity, as well as a pillar of its strength and stability. But, as we chanted and preached, we had no idea that the sacrifice must be made against our brothers—the men of the security forces! Or that our sacrifice would involve killing tens of Muslims to exact revenge upon but a few of the polytheists! We did not think that our jihad would require the breaking of promises made by the people of Islam! . . .

"The matters that we are called upon to address are grave and dangerous, for they involve excommunication of the state and declaring the people to be unbelievers, followed by an announcement of rejection of the state and the people, breaking promises and commitments, and spilling of much blood. In the course of this, many Muslims will inevitably be used as shields, and will be killed. Battles will be enjoined against Muslim security officers . . . .

"These important issues require a large number of jurists, as well as specialized studies and research to be conducted by numerous juristic committees who will be charged with studying the matters and making decisions. How can we deal with these issues of import without recourse to jurists? By dealing with a few persons who are yet students . . . ?" ("From Youth of the Summer Camps," 2004)

Suicide Bombers

"Moderator: How are the martyrdom bombers selected? How are they recruited and prepared mentally, and morally?

"Faraj Shalhoub: I want to talk about recruiting, before I talk about the selection. . . . They are committed even before they reach the fighting stage. They are committed to their cause and draw their belief in it from the mosque.

. . . .

"They volunteer for martyrdom and self-sacrifice for the cause, and the first to be selected are the most believing, whose conviction is the deepest, because they have the greatest chance of persevering to the very last minute.

"The second point is that (the volunteer) must be physically and, in general, capable of carrying out the mission skillfully. A third issue is the human factor and I want to mention this in a nutshell. (The volunteer) cannot be a child of a single parent who provides for the family. This is why most volunteers for martyrdom operations are not married.

"There is also another group of criteria on which we have no time to elaborate, but those mentioned are the main ones.

"Moderator: Let's talk about the physical issue you already mentioned. Doesn't the martyrdom bomber only push a button on the explosive belt and explode? Is there more to it than that? Does he need physical and military preparation for his martyrdom?

"Faraj Shalhoub: Absolutely. The mental preparation and morale building are on {a} high level, even though most of those volunteering to commit martyrdom operations have already come a long way in mental and morale preparation. As for the physical aspect, some Palestinian factions active in the field of martyrdom have special committees for training and special committees for selection.

"During the first stage of training, there is an emphasis on physical training, as written in special booklets of their military wings. There is a need for physical training because a martyrdom operation, whether the storming of a settlement or an explosion, requires physical strength so the Mujaheed can reach the final stages of the operation.

"Moderator: And special military training . . .

"Faraj Shalhoub: It also requires morale {sic} preparation and so, he spends some time in religious ritual and intensive spiritual preparation until he reaches a certain level of conviction that pushes him [to] commit martyrdom, regardless of the fact that his mental readiness was high to begin with.

"Moderator: Meaning, in the last stages before committing the martyrdom operation?

"Faraj Shalhoub: This comes following his decision to commit martyrdom. The volunteers are those who initiate and accept upon themselves to commit a martyrdom operation." (Abu Zuhri, 2004)

Media

Jihadis are media-savvy. Their communications strategy uses broadcast media primarily for propaganda purposes and the Internet for narrow-casting.

Terrorist operations are planned for maximum media exposure. Unusual targets and mass casualties are ways to generate coverage. But jihadis in Iraq are not content with that approach. For propaganda purposes, they create their own videos of virtually every terrorist attack, often at great risk to themselves and their operations. These videos are not only made available to broadcast networks such as al-Jazeera, they are posted on web sites as well.

Not surprisingly, jihadi sensitivity to the requirements of the media extends to their strong reaction to what they regard as hostile media. Al-Jazeera, for example, is widely considered in the United States to be pro-terrorist, but from the jihadi perspective, it is considered a mouthpiece of the West. Such reaction is part of the jihadis' general view that mainstream media are controlled by their enemies. Their principal strategy in response is to exploit the Internet, with key strategists sometimes offering detailed advice on how to structure the message.

". . . I say to you: that we are in a battle, and that more than half of this battle is taking place in the battlefield of the media. And that we are in a media battle in a race for the hearts and minds of our Umma. And that however far our capabilities reach, they will never be equal to one thousandth of the capabilities of the kingdom of Satan that is waging war on us." (al-Zawahiri, 2005b)

"Unite, O Muslims of the world, behind the Global Islamic Media Front.[2] Set up squadrons of media jihad (holy war) to break Zionist control over the media and terrorize the enemies." (Saladin, undated, in Billah, undated)

---

[2] The Global Islamic Media Front (GIMF), heir to the "Global Front for Fighting Jews and Christians" set up by Osama bin Laden in Afghanistan in 1998, presents itself as the hub for al-Qaeda propaganda on the Internet.

"The Front does not belong to anyone. It is the property of all Muslims and knows no geographical boundaries. All IT and communication experts, producers and photographers . . . are welcome to join." (Billah, undated)

"We must get our message across to the masses of the nation and break the media siege imposed on the jihad movement. This is an independent battle that we must launch side by side with the military battle.

. . . .

"At {sic} attempt to spread news of the mujahidin provides the mujahidin with a popular base of media support.

- It sows optimism among the community so that Muslims know that the path of pride and dignity lies through jihad and martyrdom.

"Methods include:

"• Forums and chat in the Internet.
"• Mailing lists that contain a large number of addresses to distribute news of the mujahidin.
"• Printing out news from Internet sites, copying them, and distributing them to relatives and friends.
"• Using gatherings to distribute or read news of the mujahidin.
"v Placing news in mosques and other public places such as schools and ATMs.
"• Sending short mobile phone messages, which bring a reward from God. You can also use Internet sites that allow free SMS-messaging.
"• Printing out news and distributing it to scholars, students, preachers, and imams to exert a positive influence on them." (al-Salim, 2003)

"Al-Ramadi is surrounded and the attack on it is very severe, so it is not at all easy to send a tape outside of Al-Ramadi . . . not to mention the fact that the American forces are looking for these two soldiers, so that they can retrieve them, and if they did it would be a huge victory for the Americans on their Hollywood-like screens. Therefore, it was an act of military wisdom to slaughter the hostages and not to risk the exposure of their location even if it was at the expense of a victory in the media for the mujahidin." (Global Islamic Media Front, 2005b)[3]

---

[3] According to the Foreign Broadcast Information Service (FBIS), an announcer also reported on the beheading of two American "soldiers," saying that the United States refused to cooperate and release female Muslim captives in the enemy's jails after Zarqawi's group had given them 24 hours to do so. He quoted Abu-Maysarah al-Iraqi,

"In the media, the United States has failed to market its crusade. The US propaganda machine has been unable to defeat feelings of hatred toward the United States. It has not even managed to dispel the doubts within the United States. The immensity of the Western propaganda apparatus did not prevent its defeat at the hands of Shaykh Usama. The cameras of CNN and other Western media dinosaurs undertook the task of filming the raid {9/11} and sowing fear in its aftermath. It didn't cost al-Qa'ida a cent. Moreover, the 'terror' tapes that CNN showed later demonstrated the mujahidin's increased capabilities and endeared them to the Islamic community. Al-Jazirah's exclusive video-tape of Shaykh Usama and other leaders brought the network world-wide notoriety and carried the voices of the mujahidin to the Islamic community and the entire world at no cost. By way of contrast, one should note that many revolutionary organizations in the past took hostages merely for the sake of airing their message. Today, the international media is in a race for scoops on the latest statements by the mujahidin. The mujahidin have also put the Internet to work, using it effectively to deliver their voices and points of view to hundreds of thousands of Muslims." (al-Qurashi, 2002b)

"The U.S. enemy, unable to gain the upper hand over the mujahedin on the battlefield, has since Sept. 11 been trying to gag the world media. . . . The more the United States tries to stifle freedom of expression, the more determined we will become to break the silence. America will lose the media war, too." (al-Qaeda, undated, in Kelley, 2002)

". . . Seemingly, the [Munich Olympics] operation failed because it did not bring about the release of the prisoners, and even cast a shadow of doubt on the justness of the Palestinian cause in world public opinion. But following the operation, and contrary to how it appeared [at first], it was the greatest media victory, and the first true proclamation to the entire world of the birth of the Palestinian resistance movement." . . . "In truth, the Munich operation was a great propaganda strike. Four thousand journalists and radio personnel, and two thousand commentators and television technicians were there to cover the Olympic games; suddenly, they were broadcasting the suffering of the Palestinian people. Thus, 900 million people in 100 countries were witness to the operation by means of television screens. This meant that at least

the official spokesperson of the group, as saying that "the soldiers were killed in a manner to soothe the hearts of the believers," and that they were "slaughtered according to the technique of the prophet's companions," which would mean that they were beheaded.

a quarter of the world knew what was going on in Munich; after this, they could no longer ignore the Palestinian tragedy. . . . The September 11 [operation] was an even greater propaganda coup. It may be said that it broke a record in propaganda dissemination. . . . With few exceptions, the entire planet heard about it." (al-Qurashi, 2002a)

"Media-friendly styles and ideas that would incite the jihad resitance . . . First: on the substance and message content: Emphasize and highlight all topics in the following chapters:

"1. Call attention to the body of Quranic textual material . . .

"2. Call to attention the body of Fatwas . . .

"3. Bring to attention the body of anecdotes and narratives from the Prophet's biography, Islamic history and provocative war stories . . .

"4. Emphasize and play up the history of the Crusade expeditions . . .

"5. Intensify and highlight contemporary colonial Crusade expeditions . . .

"6. Emphasize and feature anecdotal history of aggression and destruction . . .

"7. Emphasize and highlight the history of modern day conspiracies against the Islamic world . . .

. . . .

"13. Stay vigilant and alert to contemporary American cultural invasion operatives . . .

. . . .

"15. Feature and disseminate a culture of militarism . . .

. . . .

"17. Feature and disseminate atrcocities perpetrated at the hands of American campaigns . . .

. . . .

"21. Mail messages of admonition to personalities that cooperate with Zionist and American expeditions." (al-Suri, 2005)

Hostile Media

"What is the sickness from which the mujahidin are suffering?
    "The media have squawked and the brains of the false gods (taghut) have screeched out all the obfuscation they have. They have tried with

all their power and more to mar the reputation of the mujahidin and to dry up the pure spring of the Islamic call and veil its gleaming light. They have been no exception to and will not be an exception to what every tyrant does in every age. Among the charges they have heaped on the mujahidin is that they are mentally ill.

"This is exactly what the polytheists said to the prophets and messengers: 'We say nothing, but that one of our gods has smitten thee with some evil.' (Koran 11:54). Even so not a Messenger came to those before them but they said, 'A sorcerer, or a man possessed!' (Koran 51:52). This is the device of someone who has no other device, the means of someone for whom all other means have failed.

"A group of troublemakers has said strange and terrible things—belittling jihad, marginalizing, demeaning, postponing, delaying, and finally demolishing it. They hide this behind glittering posters and gripping titles, claiming that the community has suffered enough wounds, is not ready for jihad, does not have sufficient power, and lacks the right upbringing. They say that those who set off to take part in the jihad left behind orphans and widows. They engage in false rumors, defeatism, mockery, and abuse." (al-Khudayr, undated)

"However, in the face of hostile media it is difficult to create an operation which justifies itself . . . for the stage in which the hostile media is active, there is no way to justify the operations save by issuing published statements. Statements through audio or visual media prepare everyone for the operations before they are undertaken – without specification, naturally – and they are justified afterwards through a powerful, rational, sharia-based justification, which the addressed class heeds. These statements should be communicated to all of the people, not just to the elite. Most of the statements should include our general goals which are acceptable to the people, even if they are not stated explicitly: We fight in order to get rid of the enemies of the Umma and their agents who have destroyed the beliefs of the countries and plundered their wealth and made us into their servants. As everyone can see, they are clearly destroying everything." (Naji, 2004)

"But this effect {negative reaction to Jihadi attacks} is temporary and will disappear if, for example, the Mujahideen strike another blow in America. Then sympathy will return to what it was in the past, and may even increase." (Allah, 2003)

"I was very saddened to see some people affiliated with the Islamic call and learning among those who defiled our honor, attacked us, and hurled the vilest epithets against us. We received insults and abuse.

. . . .

"Let everyone who has uttered a word against us in any form whatever—journalist, student, preacher, or scholar—know that he is a helper against us wittingly or unwittingly. Yes, he is a helper in the injustice against us, the spilling of our blood, and the delivery of us to these wrongdoers. Let each one of you fear God, for your words are only increasing the wrongdoer in his wrongdoing and further depriving the wronged of his rights." (al-Ayiri, undated, in Center for Islamic Studies and Research, 2003)

"The media of this age is explicit evil;
For, by its hands, news is falsified.
And by its hands, all vices are true,
And by its hands, ideas are distorted.
And with it, fire is set high in roaring blaze,
And with it, doubts are raised into blurring dust!" (Bir, 2005)

"Aljazeera, enough of attempts to please the Crusaders and . . . (Shia) leaders.

"You claim that your motto is to open the floor for all opinions . . . so why is your channel a mouthpiece for the Americans?

"Why don't you report news of the mujahidins (fighters) as it is and why this premeditated attempt to harm the image and reputation of the mujahidins?" (al-Qaeda in the Land of the Two Rivers, 2005a)

The Internet

As discussed in the previous section, the Internet is often used for proselytizing and building up virtual like-minded communities. But it is also used for tactical and operational purposes. Off-the-shelf encryption is essentially unbreakable, offering terrorists secure communications for plotting attacks. To prevent interception of non-encrypted messages, al-Qaeda developed an electronic "dead drop." In addition, the Internet is being used to wage electronic jihad and provide training and instruction. The terrorists who were responsible for the London train bombings are believed to have made extensive use of Internet training and possibly communication.

To fight against Internet jihad, governments are shutting down web sites and trying to track URLs and web addresses. However, jihadis have created password-protected sites. They hop from one web address to another and hijack unsecured servers, some belonging to U.S. businesses. Nevertheless, official efforts are apparently paying off to some extent. According to one jihadi, the only place where it is safe to operate jihadi Internet sites is Iraq (al-Faqih, 2005).[4]

> "We strongly urge Muslim Internet professionals to spread and disseminate news and information about the jihad through e-mail lists, discussion groups and their own Web sites . . . . The more Web sites, the better it is for us. We must make the Internet our tool." (al-Qaeda, in Kelley, 2002)

> "In this day and age, where electronic advances are quite sophisticated and the power of communication and knowledge is applied to the Internet and the Satellite television stations, both are powerful engines for communicating with the public at large . . . . Let us not forget that large scale publication expenses are exorbitantly high and exceed the budgets and capabilities of most organizations, not to mention the inconceivable option of disseminating a particular jihadist ideology. The answer to overcome that difficulty lies in the Internet and the Satellite television stations that have and are visiting the critical mass of households, rich and poor." (al-Suri, 2005)

> "This is the Internet that Allah operates in the service of jihad and of the mujahedoun,[5] and that has become [a tool in service of] your interest – such that half the mujahedoun's battle is waged on the pages of the Internet, which is the only outlet for passing announcements to the mujahedoun." (MEMRI, 2005b)

> ". . . I used my cellular telephone to record the assassination of a foreigner, on the grounds that he was an infidel. I would then add rousing words and slogans to the pictures, post them on the Internet, and send them as messages to others as an achievement made by our cell." (al-Zaydan, 2005)[6]

> "It's brilliant . . . it's possible {with encryption} to send a verse from the Koran, an appeal for charity and even a call for jihad and know it will not be seen by anyone hostile to our faith, like the Americans." (Jabril, undated, in Kelley, 2002)

---

[4] Any decrease in open web sites has in all likelihood been eclipsed by the increase in password-protected sites.

[5] Variant spelling of mujahideen (holy warrior).

[6] It is unknown whether these statements were made under duress, but they provide insight into jihadi media operations.

"Electronic Jihad

"This term has gained widespread usage to describe those who help the jihad through the Internet. . . . We focus on two Internet projects—forums and hacking.

"The first project: forums

"One should select appropriate subject threads that discuss jihad and try to advance it. Forums can be used for distributing articles. Existing articles may need to be republished and articles in progress may need further preparation.

"Subject threads can be divided into the following areas:

"• Incitement to jihad and its virtue, especially at the current stage.
"• Defense of the mujahidin and their honor from all who would seek to harm them.
"• Ideological consciousness-raising for jihad.
"• Scholarly support and studies in Islamic law about jihad.
"• Keeping track of secular and heretic opponents of jihad and exposing them to shame." (al-Salim, 2003)

"The second project: Hacking

"This is real electronic jihad using the language of strength. It involves attacks by groups and individuals. Whoever dedicates himself to this project gives himself over fully to jihad. His efforts focus on destroying American sites that oppose jihad and the mujahidin, as well as sites that belong to Jews, secularists, defeatists, the foes of the mujahidin, evil forums, and rumor-mongers.

"If someone does not possess these skills but would like to learn them, his intention is sound. This harms the enemy. Let us wage jihad, even if it is electronic jihad." (al-Salim, 2003)

"Name: J.A.M., 23 years old.

"[correspondent] On what charge were you sent to jail? Tell us about life within the cell.

"[J.A.M.] I was charged with membership of the organization, embracing takfiri ideology, and showing sympathy to the perpetrators of the Al-Muhayya bombing[7] in which many innocent people were

---

[7] "A truck-bomb attack on the Al-Muhayya residential compound in Riyadh on 08 November 2003 killed 17 people (among them five children). The attack demonstrated that foreigners of Arab origin, who comprise much of the managerial classes, are more vulnerable than American military installations. Abdulaziz al-Muqrin is believed to have organized the attack. Observers did not rule out the possibility the terrorists targeted the mostly-

killed. I was one of the people who posted news about this bombing on the Internet and described it as a great victory, using slogans and images that showed the destruction it had caused.

. . . .

"[correspondent] Were all the news reports that you posted on the Internet factual?

"[J.A.M., smiling] I want to confess: Most were lies, 'fabrications' so to speak, about the mujahidin's heroic feats. I also posted false reports about the security forces and about the bombings. I used to lie and disseminate false rumors on the site. The man in charge of Al-Qal'ah web site was pleased with me.

. . . .

"[J.A.M.] I used to alter the religious rulings that Shaykh Ibn-Baz issued, may he rest in peace. I did this to ruin his prestige. I used to make his rulings read as if he prohibited martyrdom operations and called them suicide operations even if they occurred in Palestine. I used to post their photographs on the Internet under banners calling them 'establishment ulema.'

"[correspondent] Could you tell us 'frankly' how the enemies exploited your zeal and used you as tools to serve their own aims?

"[J.A.M.] It is enough to say that many of the locations that hosted the jihadist web sites and supplied them with links to transmit news about the terrorist operations were operated by Jewish companies.[sic] A user who is skilled at Internet use should be aware of this. Indeed these companies provided the jihadist web sites with space free of charge. They wanted to achieve their aims through us. Furthermore most of the people in charge of those Internet sites are anonymous persons. I have ascertained that they are agents who use young men like us to destroy Islam." (al-Riyad, in al-Zaydan, 2005)[8]

"Oh Mujahid brother, in order to join the great training camps you don't have to travel to other lands. Alone, in your home or with a group

---

Arab housing compound by mistake, assuming it was inhabited by Westerners. Several years earlier, a US company had housed its American and European employees there. The attack was one of the few predicted by the American intelligence in advance. Washington had reported that there was 'an immediate terrorist threat in Saudi Arabia' and that 'the terrorists planning the attacks are moving into the operational phase.' Saudi and US cooperation on intelligence provided indications of an imminent attack, but not a specific location" (GlobalSecurity.org, undated).

[8] It is unknown whether these statements were made under duress or whether the reference to Jewish companies is an attempt by Saudi security forces to discredit jihadi Internet operations or a conspiracy theory of J.A.M. resulting from intellectual distortions of jihadi anti-semitism.

of your brothers, you too can begin to execute the training program. You can all join the Al-Battar Training Camp."⁹ (*al-Battar Training Camp*, 2004)

"The basic idea is to spread military culture among the youth with the aim of filling the vacuum that the enemies of the religion have been seeking to expand for a long time. Allah willing, the magazine {*al-Battar Training Camp*} will be simple and easy, and in it, my Muslim brother, you will find basic lessons in the framework of a military training program, beginning with programs for sports training, through types of light weapons and guerilla group actions in the cities and mountains, and [including] important points in security and intelligence, so that you will be able . . . to fulfill the religious obligation that Allah has set upon you . . . ." (Mansour, 2004)

Training

Training jihadis has become very difficult with the loss of the base in Afghanistan, though some simple camps are said to exist on the Afghan-Pakistan border. As a result, the Internet has become the central means for conveying the jihadis' accumulated knowledge on how to conduct terrorist operations. (Of course, the insurgencies in Iraq, Chechnya, and Afghanistan also offer significant learning-by-doing experience.)

A truly incredible volume of training material is available on the Internet. It includes material prepared for the Afghan war against the Soviet Union, such as the 7,000-page, ten-volume work prepared by al-Qaeda, as well as more contemporary compilations of instructional material. This section provides samples of such material relating to physical training, assassination, kidnapping, spying, and resisting torture and interrogation, as well as commentary by jihadis on the training process. The excerpts are drawn from materials widely distributed via the Internet, so they do not contribute to the dissemination of terrorist tradecraft. They are included here to convey the scope and nature of jihadi attitudes and thinking about some quite horrible and violent activities, not to improve jihadi skill sets.

". . . military training is an obligation in Islam upon every sane, male, mature Muslim, whether rich or poor, whether studying or working and whether living in a Muslim or non-Muslim country." (Azzam Publications, undated)

---

⁹ *Al-Battar Training Camp* was an online magazine that recruited and motivated youth and promoted the teachings of jihad. The web site is now defunct. Issue 20, October 2004, was the last issue.

"We can be sure that al-Qa'ida placed special emphasis on forming the mujahid vanguard that is the backbone of the jihad operation. This is what has produced such stunning results on all levels. The average mujahid from al-Qa'ida is better trained and prepared for his mission than any other fighter.

"On the theoretical level, al-Qa'ida spared no effort to develop the various military theories needed to advance jihad capability. The complete jihad encyclopedia that the organization prepared for all of the mujahidin during the first Afghan jihad covered all the details of armed combat. It set a major precedent. It consists of some 7,000 pages (10 volumes) and is considered an unparalleled primer for the mujahid on the hardships of jihad. It discusses military tactics, security, intelligence, light weapons, first aid, explosives, hand grenades, armor, weapons manufacturing, topography, and so forth.

"After the first Afghan jihad, the Islamic community still faced tremendous challenges on various battlefields: Palestine, Central Asia, the Balkans, the Caucasus, Kashmir, the Philippines, and so forth. Al-Qa'ida was the standard bearer of the world jihad movement. It provided a new theoretical basis to improve the training and combat skills of the mujahidin. They published a separate section on special forces operations. It includes chapters on preparing identity documents, setting up military camps, living quarters, concealing communications and movement, buying and delivering weapons, member security, security planning, and so forth.

"The training camps provided the best possible jihad preparation for fighting tyranny. They split the training course into three levels—basic, advanced, and special. Training was provided to tens of thousands of mujahidin to gain God's favor, aid His faith, and help the wretched of the earth. No organizational tie to al-Qa'ida was required. Only a small number of them with exceptional faith and mental, psychological, and physical ability were approached and asked to join al-Qa'ida. The purpose went beyond preventing infiltration. No organization, no matter what its capabilities, has succeeded in infiltrating al-Qa'ida. No one can join simply because he wants to. The leadership extends membership on the basis of a great deal of accurate information. This is what has allowed al-Qa'ida to recruit the cream of the jihad elite, which is positively reflected in the organization's jihad operations." (al-Qurashi, 2002b)

"The basis of all Jihad training is something that can be done in every country of the World: physical training. This requires little or no equipment and is something that one can fit round one's daily routine. This comprises four main areas: stamina, strength, speed and agility.

. . . .

"It is better to go to the gym with another brother if possible, or go at a time when there are as few women as possible. Public gymnasiums are generally un-Islamic places with loud music and improperly dressed men and women. Such an atmosphere is not befitting for the training of a Mujahid.

. . . .

"It is vital to join a martial arts club as part of the training for Jihad. . . . It is preferable to join clubs that emphasise on street-fighting and self-defence such as kung-fu styles rather than tournament fighting. You would never use high or flying kicks in a real fight. . . .

. . . .

"The majority of the time spent in Jihad is learning to cope with harsh, physically and mentally demanding living conditions. . . .

". . . The best way to learn these skills is to go camping into the outdoors with a small group of brothers. . . . The best training is to take some tents, food and water and warm clothes in a rucksack and go on treks lasting 2–3 days at a time. . . . Learn how to purify water, make wudu[10] and istinja[11] in cold water, attend to the call of nature in the outdoors, cook or heat food out in the open, making different types of knots with ropes, setting up tents and other similar activities. Learning how to start and maintain a fire in all conditions, wet or dry, with and without lighting instruments is one of the most important survival skills.

. . . .

"There are many firearms courses available to the public in USA. . . . Some of them are only meant for security personnel but generally they will teach anyone. . . . keep your opinions to yourself. . . . You are going there to train for Jihad, not call people to Islam.

. . . .

"Although sometimes it is difficult to obtain comprehensive military training in one's home country, it is very easy to do plenty of background reading using freely-available books and CDs, before one actually goes abroad.

---

[10] *Wudu* is the partial ablution performed before offering prayers, in which one washes the parts of the body that are generally exposed to dirt or dust.

[11] *Istinja* means cleaning one's private parts by using clean water and earth, after passing urine and stool.

"The US Army has produced a number of military field manuals on CD on all topics from light weapons, tanks and artillery to mines, military fieldcraft and combat medicine. The full set is available on CD for less than US$100 and many field manuals are also available on the Internet." (Azzam Publications, undated)

". . . The mujahid Shaykh Yusuf al-Ayiri said, 'A mujahid should be sufficiently fit physically to jog for 10 kilometers without stopping over a period of 70 minutes, at worst. He should be able to infiltrate a neighborhood in a city and run 3 kilometers in at least 13.5 minutes. He should be able to sprint 100 meters in 12–15 seconds. He should be able to march without long stops for at least 10 hours. He should be able to march while carrying up to 20 kilograms for at least four hours. He should be able to do more than 70 push-ups in a single session without stopping. He should be able to do 100 sit-ups in a single session without stopping. He should be able to crawl on his stomach for 50 meters in under 70 seconds. In order to develop his endurance, he should perform exercises with variations. This involves marching, marching quickly, jogging, running, and sprinting. The mujahid begins by walking for two minutes, then walking quickly for two minutes, then jogging for two minutes, then running for two minutes, then running quickly for 100 meters before returning to a walk. He should repeat this exercise without stopping 10 times.'" (al-Salim, 2003)

". . . get the [infidel] and crush his head in your arms, so you can wring his throat, so you can whip his intestines out. That's why you are doing training, to rip the people to pieces. Forget wasting a bullet on them, cut them in half!" (al-Masri, undated)

"Swimming and Horsemanship

"Learning to swim and ride on horseback will benefit the mujahid in the future, for swimming is one of the most important forms of physical training. Horsemanship has not lost its usefulness, especially in the lands where jihad is fought. We find the following saying of the prophet in Al-Bukhari: 'Immense good remains tied to the forelocks of horses until the Day of Resurrection—the reward and the blessing.' Horses are still used in the present in jihad in Chechnya, Afghanistan, and Iraq." (al-Salim, 2003)

"Characteristics of Members that Specialize in the Special Operations

. . . .

". . . Good training on the weapon of assassination, assault, kidnapping, and bombing (special operations).

. . . .

". . . Tranquility and calm personality (that allows coping with psychological traumas such as those of the operation of bloodshed, mass murder). Likewise, [the ability to withstand] reverse psychological traumas, such as killing one or all members of his group. [He should be able] to proceed with the work.

. . . .

"We note that special operations include assassinations, bombing and demolition, assault, kidnapping hostages and confiscating documents, freeing prisoners." (*Manchester Document*, undated)

". . . if anyone, Muslim or non-Muslims, approaches you offering training of this type {jihad} in the UK, it is a trap, you should stay away from that person and warn other people against that person because he might be an undercover agent. British National Intelligence MI5 does employ 'practising' Muslims to live amongst Muslims as agent provocateurs and entice them into traps such as these. Generally, these agents are amongst the most popular and influential members of the community. The Muslims are fooled by them because they fail to check up their background (where they came from, their history etc.) One can obtain almost any type of military training in some countries of the World, legally, so there is no need to risk going to prison for years just for learning how to use a single firearm illegally." (Azzam Publications, undated)

Kidnapping

"Kidnapping:

. . . .

"Secret Kidnapping: The target is kidnapped and taken to a safe location that is unknown to the authorities. Secret kidnapping is the least dangerous. Such was the case of the Jewish reporter Daniel Pearl, who was kidnapped from a public place, then transferred to another location. . . .

"Public kidnapping: This is when hostages are publicly detained in a known location. The government surrounds the location and conducts negotiations. The authorities often attempt to create diversions and attack the kidnappers. That was the case of the theater in Moscow, and the Russian officers' detention by Shamil Basayev and the Mujahideen brothers. A counter terrorism officer once said: 'There never was a successful kidnapping operation in the world.' This saying was intended to discourage the so-called terrorists. History is full of facts proving the opposite. Many operations by the Mafia, or the Mujahideen were successful. . . .

. . . .

"• Execution of the abduction: The abductors' roles vary, based on the location of the kidnapping operation. They are grouped in three categories: A) Protection group whose role is to protect the abductors. B) The guarding and control group whose role is to seize control of the hostages, and get rid of them in case the operation fails. C) The negotiating group whose role is extremely important and sensitive. In general, the leader of this group is the negotiator. He conveys the Mujahideen's demands, and must be intelligent, decisive, and determined.

"• Negotiations: The enemy uses the best negotiator he has, who is normally very sly, and knowledgeable in human psychology. He is capable of planting fear in the abductors' hearts, in addition to discouraging them. Kidnappers must remain calm at all times, as the enemy negotiator will resort to stalling, in order to give the security forces time to come up with a plan to storm the hostages location. The duration of the detention should be minimized to reduce the tension on the abducting team. The longer the detention is, the weaker the willpower of the team is, and the more difficult the control over the hostages is. . . . In case of any stalling, starting to execute hostages is necessary. The authorities must realize the seriousness of the kidnappers, and their dedicated resolve and credibility in future operations.

. . . .

"• Combating teams will use two attacks: a secondary one just to attract attention, and a main attack elsewhere.

. . . .

"• Watch out for the ventilation or other openings as they could be used to plant surveillance devices through which the number of kidnappers could be counted and gases could be used.

"• Do not be emotionally affected by the distress of your captives.

"• Abide by Muslim laws as your actions may become a Da'wa [call to join Islam].

"• Avoid looking at women.

. . . .

"Security measures for secret kidnapping:

. . . .

"• Look for listening or homing devices that VIPs often carry on their watches or with their money. VIPs could have an earpiece microphone that keeps him in touch with his protection detail.

"• Everything you take from the enemy must be wrapped in a metal cover and should only be unwrapped in a remote place far from the sheltering group.

. . . .

"• It is imperative to not allow the hostage to know where he is.

. . . .

"How to deal with hostages in both kidnapping types:

. . . .

"• Separate the young people from the old, the women and the children. The young people have more strength, hence their ability to resist is high. The security forces must be killed instantly. This prevents others from showing resistance.

. . . .

"• Do not approach the hostages. In case you must, you need to have protection, and keep a minimum distance of one and a half meters from them.

"• Speak in a language or dialect other than your own, in order to prevent revealing your identity.

"• Cover the hostage's eyes so that he cannot identify you or any other brothers.

"• Wire the perimeter of the hostage location [with alarms or explosives] to deny access to the enemy." (*al-Battar Training Camp*, 2004)

Assassination

"For example, when attempting to assassinate an important target – a personality, it is necessary to gather all information related to that target, such as:

"a His name, age, residence, social status

"b His work

"c Time of his departure to work

"d Time of his return from work

"e The routes he takes

"f How he spends his free time

"g His friends and their addresses

"h The car he drives

"i His wife's work and whether he visits her there

"j His children and whether he goes to their school

"k Does he have a girlfriend? What is her address, and when does he visit her?

"l The physician who treats him

"m The stores where he shops

"n Places where he spends his vacations and holidays

"o His house entrances, exits, and the surrounding streets

"p Ways of sneaking into his house

"q Is he armed? How many guards does he have?" (*Manchester Document*, undated)

"Assassinations Using Cold Steel

"A. Assassinating with a knife: When undertaking any assassination using a knife, the enemy must be struck in one of these lethal spots:

"From the Front:

"1. Anywhere in the rib cage.

"2. Both or one eye.

"3. The pelvis (under a target's navel)

"4. The area directly above the genitals.

"From Behind:

1. The axon (back of the head).

2. The end of the spinal column directly above the person's buttocks.

. . . .

"Assassination Using Hands:

"1. Choking.

"2. Poking the fingers into one or both eyes and gouging them.

"3. Grab the testicles by the hand and twist and squeeze.

"4. Grab the rib case with both hands and squeeze." (*Manchester Document*, undated)

"Al-Awsad {chat room} (user number 1):

"Once a week, a group of American 'dogs' come near us on the sea front. I have been following them for a long time and am interested in your suggestions for ways to get rid of them secretly.

"Salam (user number 2):

"If they arrive in a private car, put a large amount of sugar in the gas tank of the car. Then, you can ambush them on the way back because the car will get stuck in the way. You will have many options to get rid of them. You can run them over on the road, after they abandon the broken down car. You can put a trap on the beach if they tend to do a lot of walking. If you have people with you and 4 cars, you can stop them at a certain point on the road, at a traffic light for example, block them from all directions and burn them in their cars using a Molotov cocktail.

. . . .

"Al- Awsad (user number 1):

"Thank you all very much, but I would like to get rid of them quietly.

. . . .

"Saafalaha (user number 5):

"Why be discrete {sic}? Let them serve as an example for others like them. Let the Americans understand that they are not safe in Muslim countries. Burning their car is excellent or you could shoot all of them. The country is filled with weapons." (Hamas web site discussion, 2002)

Intelligence

"We have already penetrated US institutions. What is coming is worse. I cannot go into any more details because the matter is very sensitive." (al-Ablaj, undated)

"An Important Question: How can a Muslim spy live among enemies if he maintains his Islamic characteristics? How can he perform his duties to Allah and not want to appear Muslim?

"Concerning the issue of clothing and appearance (appearance of true religion), Ibn Taimia – may Allah have mercy on him – said, 'If a Muslim is in a combat or godless area, he is not obligated to have a different appearance from [those around him]. The [Muslim] man may prefer or even be obligated to look like them, provided his action brings a religious benefit of preaching to them, learning their secrets and informing Muslims, preventing their harm, or some other beneficial goal.'

". . . It is noted, however, that it is forbidden to do the unlawful, such as drinking wine or fornicating. There is nothing that permits those." (*Manchester Document*, undated)

". . . 'prevention security' ["Denial and Deception"], '. . . is intended to spread false information to mislead the enemy . . .' 'The mujahideen know which information to say, which to keep, and what false information to spread to fool the enemy . . . They know what they are doing, and they have information channels that they can use to spread any information they want to spread . . . .'" (Center for Islamic Studies and Research, undated)

"C. Gathering Information Through Recruitment {of agents}. . . .

"There are a number of motives that might entice an uncommitted person to take part in intelligence work. These motives are:

1. Coercion and entanglement
2. Greed and love for money
3. Displaying courage and love of adventure
4. Love of amusement and deviance
5. Mental and political orientation
6. Fear of being harmed

"The Organization may use motives No. 2, 3, 5, and 6 in recruitment.

. . . .

"Recruitment Stages: Suppose the Islamic Organization, with its modest capabilities, wants to obtain information about an important target (important personality, building, camp, agency, ministry). It has to do the following:

"1. Finding the Agent: In this stage, the Organization picks the suitable person for supplying the information. The Organization learns about that person: His financial condition, his family status, his position regarding the government, and his weaknesses and strengths.

"2. Evaluating the Agent: In this stage, the agent is placed under continuous observation to learn the times of his departure to and return from work, the places he visits, the individuals he meets, and his social interaction with those that he meets in coffee shops, clubs, etc.

"3. Approaching the Agent: After gathering information about him, a relationship with him is developed under a certain cover, such as:

"a. Family connection and tribal relations.

"b. Developing a friendship with him in the club, coffee shop, and workers union. The [recruiting] brother develops the friendship as if it were unpretentious and unplanned. The relationship should develop naturally and gradually in order not to attract the target's attention.

"Important Note: In case the first brother fails to develop a friendship with the target, another brother takes over after learning from the first about the target's weaknesses (motives that can be exploited) such as his love for money, opposition to the government, love for adventure, or display courage.

. . . .

"5. Testing the Agent {spy}: In this stage, the agent is assigned certain tasks in order to test his ability, loyalty, and dependability. The agent does not know that the Organization already has the sought information. If the information supplied by the agent does not match the Organization's existing information, then the agent may be an unreliable source of information or may be trying to mislead the Organization. During the testing stage, the agent should remain under careful observation to spot all his movements.

. . . .

"7. Treating the Agent: The brother who manages the agent should possess the qualifications of a perfect spy, a psychiatrist, and an interrogator. There are two points of view on treating the agent:

"First Point of View: Maintaining a strong personal relationship with the agent. This technique provides the agent with the motivation that entices him to take chances in order to please his friend with the information. However, this technique has disadvantages. The barriers between the agent and his superiors are removed, and the agent may ask for many things that were not agreed upon.

"Second Point of View: The person managing the agent treats him roughly and pushes him to the limits for the purpose of getting as much information as possible. This technique uses harshness, cruelty, and threats in order to keep the agent constantly active. I believe that the Islamic Military organization can combine the two techniques. The agent may be treated in a careful Islamic manner, while the managing brother appeals to the agent's conscience and his Islamic association with the work for majestic Allah's religion. He lures the agent with money and gifts, and uses cruelty and kindness when appropriate." (*Manchester Document*, undated)

Tips for Traveling

"• Don't wear short pants that show socks when you're standing up. The pants should cover the socks, because intelligence authorities know that fundamentalists don't wear long pants . . .
"• If a person, for example, wears a T-shirt or a shirt that has the drawing of a spirit—that is, a bird, an animal, etc.—don't cut off the head [the Islamic tradition frowns on the depiction of living beings]. Either wear it with the drawing, or don't wear it at all. Morover {sic}, you should never carry any item of clothing in your suitcase where the pictures have been tampered with, or where the head of the animal or bird has been cut off.
"• Don't wear clothes made in suspect countries such as Iran, Pakistan, Iraq, Libya, Sudan, North Korea, Cuba, etc.
"• Underwear should be the normal type that people wear, not anything that shows you're a fundamentalist.
"• A long time before traveling—especially from Khartoum—the person should always wear socks and shoes, to get rid of cracks [in the feet that come from extended barefoot walking], which take about a week to cure . . . .
"• If the mission requires wearing a chain, you should show it by opening the top buttons of the shirt.
"• Never use the perfumes used by the brothers [fundamentalists].
"• You should differentiate between
    a) Perfume used only after shaving—'After Shave' is written on the bottle. This type is used only on the chin and nowhere else.
    b) Perfumes—marked 'Lotion'—that are placed anywhere on the clothes, on the head, behind the ears, etc.
"• You should use the type of perfume for the underarms that usually comes in the shape of a soap ball. You should never use any other type of normal perfume under the arms.

"• You should differentiate between men and women's perfume. If you use women's perfume, you are in trouble." ("Tips for the Traveling Terrorist," 2004)[12]

Weapons

The Internet is also awash in instructions on weaponry, firearms, explosives, poisons, and booby traps. As in the section on training, the following excerpts cover only well-known (but sometimes startling) techniques.

> "One of the most celebrated counter-measures is the RPG (rocket propelled grenade) missile that targets armoured military vehicles and which, God permitting, is capable of destroying them . . . when the missile strikes it in a certain way . . . for the RPG missile, costing tens of dollars, can destroy a 100 million dollar tank! And two of them can destroy two tanks! There is simply no relation between the volume of loss, and the effort or cost expended to achieve this loss. The fact of the matter is that counter-measures in general, and RPGs in particular, are a blessing granted by God to guerrilla fighters
>
> . . . .
>
> "One such counter-measure is the SAM 7 missile, examples of which the mujahideen demonstrated at the 'Badr of Riyadh.'[13] These are effective counter-weapons against helicopters. [This reputation is not harmed by] some cases of failure when employed against jet aircraft, for mujahideen in Chechnya have recorded many instances where they were indeed able to down sophisticated jet aircraft by use of SAM-7 rockets." (Jamestown Foundation, 2004)[14]

Improvised explosive devices (IEDs) are the most common cause of death and injury in Iraq. They have a long history of use by terrorists in general and jihadis in particular.

---

[12] The "tips" are from a computer hard drive found in Afghanistan that purportedly belonged to al-Qaeda.

[13] "The attack by al-Qaeda on the al-Muhayya compound in Riyadh on 8 November 2003, in which SAM and RPG missiles were employed. A total of 18 were killed and 120 injured during the assault. The term 'Badr' comes from the Battle of Badr fought in March 624, the first of the significant battles fought by the Prophet" (Jamestown Foundation, 2004, fn5).

[14] In the section entitled "Lessons of the Afghan War," the writer states that the SAM-7s were useless against jet aircraft.

"Explosives are believed to be the safest weapon for the Mujahideen . . . [Using explosives] allows them to get away from enemy personnel and to avoid being arrested. An assassination using explosives doesn't leave any evidence or traces at the operation site. In addition, explosives strike the enemy with sheer terror and fright. (*Manchester Document*, undated)

"Booby Traps:

"These consist of creative, innovative methods aimed at planting anti-personnel and anti-vehicle explosive charges, and the enemy is blown up as a result of normal movement without paying attention to what is around him. Booby traps are considered one of the best ways to execute an assassination operation against enemy personnel because we have gotten a long distance away from the site of the incident without leaving any evidence or trace enabling the enemy to know who were the perpetrators.

"However, a brother should not be allowed the opportunity to work with setting booby traps until after he has mastered the use of explosives and has successfully worked in the electrical and mechanical fields, because the first mistake a brother makes could be his last mistake.

. . . .

"We will now touch on various simple types of booby traps to make it easy for the brother to comprehend . . . .

"1. The charge goes off when the door opens . . . . If we want to kill the target, we put [the booby trap] over the door; if we want to cut off his legs or bring about permanent injuries to various parts of the body, we put it in the vicinity of the door.

. . . .

"4. Booby-Trapping a Car:

"Close the electrical circuit and cause the explosion when the ignition key is turned to start the car. It is possible to use the car battery when setting this type of trap. Explosives placed in locations inside the car, in the back or front, cause the explosion to be centered inside the car.

. . . .

"7. It is also possible to booby trap a car by connecting two wires from the battery. One of the blasting cap wires makes contact with the wire connected to the battery, and the other wire connects to the line and is also connected to the fan. The wire connected to the battery does the same thing. When the ignition key is turned, the blade rotates, and the two sides connect, closing the circuit.

"8. There are very many things one could use in a very simple way to set a trap, like: shoes, bed etc." (*Manchester Document*, undated)

"Revolver:

. . . .

". . . It is preferable for assassinations because the empty shells are kept inside, making it difficult for investigators to determine the location from which the pistol was fired. It also makes it difficult to determine the type of pistol used.

. . . .

"Assassinations with Poison: We will limit [the discussion] to poisons that the holy warrior can prepare and use without endangering his health.

"First – Herbal Poisons:

"A. Castor Beans:

"The substance Ricin, an extract from Castor Beans, is considered one of the most deadly poisons. .035 milligrams is enough to kill someone by inhaling or by injecting in a vein. However, though considered less poisonous if taken through the digestive system, chewing some Castor Beans could be fatal. It is a simple operation to extract Ricin, and Castor Beans themselves can be obtained from nurseries throughout the country. . . .

. . . .

"Second – Semi-alkaline substances: They are highly solvent in alcohol.

"A. Tobacco:

"There is enough nicotine in three cigarettes to kill a person. Sixty to 70 milligrams of pure nicotine will kill a person within an hour if eaten.

. . . .

"Poisoning from Eating Spoiled Food:

"Since .000028 grams will kill a person, this poison is absolutely lethal. After consumption, the symptoms appear in 12 to 36 hours. They include dizziness, headaches, constipation, difficulty swallowing and speaking, fluids coming from the nose and mouth, and lack of muscle coordination. It results in death from respiratory failure. If it is received in the blood stream, death is very swift and almost without symptoms.

"How to Prepare Spoiled Food:

"Fill a pot with corn and green beans. Put in a small piece of meat and about two spoonfuls of fresh excrement." (*Manchester Document*, undated)

Weapons of Mass Destruction

The great nightmare is a jihadi attack on the United States with weapons of mass destruction (WMD)—in particular, nuclear weapons. There is no question that various jihadi sources have expressed their desire for them, and there is evidence that al-Qaeda was experimenting with chemical and biological agents in Afghanistan during the Taliban regime. Convicted al-Qaeda wannabe Jose Padilla claimed to have planned an attack with a "dirty bomb"—a bomb that uses nuclear isotopes in a conventional explosive device to disperse radioactive material over a wide area.

In 2005, al-Qaeda chief propagandist Mustafa Setmariam Nasar, also known as Abu Musab al-Suri, posted a 15-page document entitled "Biological Weapons." It showed "how the pneumonic plague could be made into a biological weapon." Based on U.S. and Japanese biological weapons programs from World War II, it showed "how to inject carrier animals, like rats, with the virus . . . how to extract microbes from infected blood . . . and how to dry them so that they can be used with an aerosol delivery system" (Coll and Glasser, 2005).

Bin Laden has hinted that he has nuclear weapons, al-Zawahiri has claimed to have actually acquired them, and others have said that al-Qaeda has access to chemical and biological agents. However, there is no objective evidence that al-Qaeda or any other jihadi group in fact has such weapons.

Nonetheless, jihadi ideologists have developed a variety of arguments to explain how using such weapons can be justified under Islamic law—the most quaint being reference to military weapons of the Middle Ages.

"a) The enemy started thinking about these {biological} weapons before WWI. Despite their extreme danger, we only became aware of them when the enemy drew our attention to them by repeatedly expressing concerns that they can be produced simply with easily available materials . . .

"b) The destructive power of these weapons is no less than that of nuclear weapons.

"c) A germ attack is often detected days after it occurs, which raises the number of victims.

"d) Defense against such weapons is very difficult, particularly if large quantities are used . . .

"I would like to emphasize what we previously discussed—that looking for a specialist is the fastest, safest, and cheapest way [to embark on a biological- and chemical-weapons program]." (al-Zawahiri, 1999, in Cullison, 2004)

"HM: Some Western media claim that you are trying to acquire chemical and nuclear weapons. How much truth is there in such reports?

"OSB {Osama bin Laden}: I heard the speech of American President Bush yesterday (Oct 7). He was scaring the European countries that Osama wanted to attack with weapons of mass destruction. I wish to declare that if America used chemical or nuclear weapons against us, then we may retort with chemical and nuclear weapons. We have the weapons as deterrent.

"HM: Where did you get these weapons from?

"OSB: Go to the next question." (bin Laden, 2001b)

"Nuclear Warfare Is the Solution for Destroying America

"In the name of Allah the most merciful. Thus, you are not mistaken in reading this text. This is the only way to kill the greatest possible number of Americans.

. . . .

"Even though the Americans have bombs possessing enormous power, Al-Qaeda is even more powerful than they, and it has in its possession bombs which are called 'dirty bombs,' and bombs with deadly viruses, which will spread fatal diseases throughout American cities.

. . .

"The coming days will prove that Kaedat el-Jihad [the Al-Qaeda organization] is capable of turning America into a sea of deadly radiation, and this will prove to the world that the end is at hand. . . . Yes, we will destroy America and its allies, because they have used their power for evil against the weak." (Abu Shihab El-Kandahari, 2002)

"(Khalil) Why are you afraid to disclose the strategic biological, chemical, or nuclear weapons you have and will you use them if you have them?

"(Al-Ablaj) Is there a sane person who discloses his secrets? Brother, the strategic weapons are not just remove the pin and strike. If such was the case, then it would have been available and would have been carried out before the blessed strike {9/11}. The matter needs time. Such a massive strategic weapon is bound to have reactions commensurate with its size. It must therefore be used at a time that makes the crusader enemy beg on his knee that he does not want more strikes and that he will withdraw into himself and occupy himself with his misfortune with the tails of shame, failure, and disgrace between his legs and licking his wounds after the utter defeat." (al-Ablaj, undated)

"They have contacted us, we sent our people to Moscow, to Tashkent, to other central Asian states and they negotiated, and we purchased some suitcase {nuclear} bombs."[15] (al-Zawahiri, undated(b))

The following is an introduction to an article posted on an Islamic web site that purports to provide nine lessons on how to build a nuclear weapon. It covers the history of nuclear science, radioactivity, nuclear source materials, the concept of critical mass, constructing nuclear weapons, and radium. It would not be possible to construct a fission weapon by using these "instructions," and, in any case, the obstacles to doing so are formidable. However, it does demonstrate continuing jihadi interest in obtaining nuclear weapons. The article appeared in Arabic and was taken down after a few days.

"Perhaps nuclear weapons represent a technology of the 1940s. However, the Crusaders – the allies of Satan, Allah's curse be upon them – insist upon depriving the Jihad fighters of the right to [have] these weapons. But now the Jihad fighters have acquired technological skills that enable them, with Allah's help, to understand this [nuclear weapons] technology. Thus, they are able to make a major leap forward in producing this kind of strategic weapon, even in the kitchens of their homes.

. . . .

"I shall begin, with Allah's help, with a number of lessons, starting with the clarification of the idea, until we reach the [stage of] experimentation and implementation, with the support of Allah's might." (Jihad Fighter No. 1, 2005)

---

[15] There is no available evidence that this is true. However, al-Zawahiri himself went to the Caucasus and Central Asia at some time during the 1990s; he was arrested by Russian authorities there and spent six months in jail before being released. According to Federal Security Service of the Russian Federation (FSB) spokesman Sergei Ignatchenko, al-Zawahiri was arrested by Russian authorities in Dagestan in December 1996 and released in May 1997.

Rationale for WMD

". . . A certain learned brother — may God grant him success — someone who writes over the internet and styles himself 'Brother of the One Who Obeyed God,' has asked me about the legal status of using weapons of mass destruction. The following is the text of the question . . .

"'Peace be with you and God's mercy and blessings!'

"'Everyone knows what has been published in the media about al-Qa'ida's intention to strike America with weapons of mass destruction. . . .'

"'What then is the legal ruling on their use by Muslims engaged in jihad?'

"'If one upholds their permissibility, are they permissible unconditionally?'

. . . .

{Answer} "If the infidels can be repelled from the Muslims only by using such weapons, their use is permissible, even if you kill them without exception and destroy their tillage and stock.

"All this has its foundation in the Prophet's biography, the Prophet's sayings about jihad, and the pronouncements of scholars, may God have mercy on them.

. . . .

"Point One: When they say 'weapons of mass destruction,' they mean nuclear, biological, and chemical weapons. They hold that using any of these weapons is a violation of international law. If one state should strike another with tons of 'conventional' bombs, killing tens of thousands, [p6][sic] this use of weapons would be allowed internationally. If another state should use a small number of so-called weapons of mass destruction, killing only a few hundred, this use of weapons would be forbidden internationally. Thus it is evident that they do not wish to protect humanity by these terms, as they assert; rather, they want to protect themselves and monopolize such weapons on the pretext of 'banning them internationally.'

. . . .

"If people of authority engaged in jihad determine that the evil of the infidels can be repelled only by their means, they may be used. The weapons of mass destruction will kill any of the infidels on whom they fall, regardless of whether they are fighters, women, or children. They will destroy and burn the land. The arguments for the permissibility of this in this case are many. . . .

". . . For example, with regard to America at this time, the matter of striking her with these weapons is permissible . . . . This is because God has said: 'And if you chastise, chastise even as you have been chastised.' (Koran 16:126)." (al-Fahd, 2003a)

"If a bomb was dropped on them [i.e. the Americans] that would annihilate 10 million and burn their lands to the same extent that they burned the Muslim lands – this is permissible, with no need to mention any other proof. Yet if we want to annihilate a greater number, we need further evidence.[16]

. . . .

"The first piece of evidence is 'texts that prove it is possible to carry out a surprise nighttime attack on the polytheists even if their offspring will be harmed by it.'
"The second piece of evidence is 'the texts that prove it is permissible to burn the land of the enemy . . .'

. . . .

"The third piece of evidence is 'the texts that prove that it is permissible to strike the enemy with a catapult and with similar things that annihilate them.' On this, Sheikh Hamed wrote: 'The clerics have agreed that it is permissible to strike the enemy with a catapult and similar things. It is known that the stone of the catapult does not distinguish between women and children and others; it is also [known] that it destroys any building or other thing that stands in its way. 'This constitutes proof that it is permissible to destroy the land of the infidels and to kill them – in the event that the Jihad requires this and in the event that the men of influence from among the Mujahideen think so. . . .'" (Ibn Hamed, undated)

"Q. How about using nuclear weapons by Muslims, is it justified?
"A. Yes, if necessary. But the Islamic Ummah should seek to minimalize [the intensity of the fighting]. Allah has said in verse 8 chapter 60 that we should equip ourself with weapon power—that is an order—but preferably to scare and not to kill our enemy. The main goal is to scare them. If they are scared they won't bother us, and then we won't bother them as well. But if they persist, we have to kill them. In this way, Prophet Muhammad sought to minimalize the fighting." (Ba'asyir, 2005)

---

[16] The following "evidence" is not factual but consists of references to the Qur'an and Sunnah.

"It {using nuclear weapons} would also prove that Al-Qa'idah is very popular all over the Islamic world." (al-Qandahari, 2002)

Diplomacy

For committed jihadis, diplomacy, with its inevitable compromise, is inherently heretical. Under their black-and-white worldview of jihad, one cannot compromise the truth or accept any measure of falsehood. To do so would be a sin. Similarly, peace with infidels is considered a snare and a delusion, a trick to rob jihadis of their manhood and thwart the effort to bring Islam to the world and recreate the caliphate.

This does not, however, mean that jihadis cannot engage in a truce with infidels. This is specifically allowed by the Qur'an. But such a truce can remain in place for only two years. Osama bin Laden offered the Europeans a truce in the first of the excerpts below.

> "Moreover, the examining of the developments that have been taking place, in terms of killings in our countries and your countries, will make clear an important fact; namely, that injustice is inflicted on us and on you by your politicians, who send your sons – although you are opposed to this – to our countries to kill and be killed.
>
> "Therefore, it is in both sides' interest to curb the plans of those who shed the blood of peoples for their narrow personal interest and subservience to the White House gang.
>
> . . . .
>
> "Based on the above, and in order to deny war merchants a chance and in response to the positive interaction shown by recent events and opinion polls, which indicate that most European peoples want peace, I ask honest people, especially ulema, preachers and merchants, to form a permanent committee to enlighten European peoples of the justice of our causes, above all Palestine. They can make use of the huge potential of the media. . . .
>
> "The door of reconciliation is open for three months of the date of announcing this statement."[17] (bin Laden, undated)

"Some may think that the absence of international and regional support for Jihad, in contrast to past support for the [Palestinian] resistance, is a weak point [for the Jihad movement]. Yet the opposite is true. This fact exempts the mujahedeen from the need to offer any concessions, or to

---

[17] This is the "truce" mentioned by al-Zawahiri in justifying the bombings in London on July 7, 2005 (see p. 225). Under the jihadi interpretation of Islam, "truces" may be undertaken with infidels, but not a permanent peace.

continually lower the threshold of their demands so that it leads to a fall – as happened to many resistance organizations that succumbed to the pitfalls of treachery and subjugation, and lost their principles. . . ." (al-Qurashi, 2002a)

"If I fall as a martyr in the defense of Islam, my son Muhammad will avenge me, but if I am finished politically and I spend my time arguing with governments about some partial solutions, what will motivate my son to take up my weapons after I have sold these weapons in the bargains' market?" (al-Zawahiri, 2001)

"Allah commanded fighting so that there will be no Fitna [internal strife] and so that the religion will be all for Allah. It is forbidden for a Muslim to agree to concessions and to evade the obligation incumbent upon him [in exchange for] a pinch of religion, a pinch of Shari'a law, and a pinch of religious ritual.

"On the contrary: The obligation according to the Shari'a as it is written in the Qur'an is that the religion will be all for Allah, and it is not possible to stop the fighting if part of the religion is for Allah and another part is for someone else." (*Voice of Jihad*, 2004)

". . . When the creed of enmity toward the infidels faded and the call sounded for tolerance and coexistence, its supporters combined animosity toward the mujahidin with a desire to reduce the people's acceptance of the mujahidin and their leaders. The message of coexistence and the internal front is best described as: 'Mercy for the infidels and cruelty toward the mujahidin.'" (al-Salim, 2003)

"My son, they will talk to you about peace, do not listen to such calls, because although I once believed them I am still living in a tent." (bin Laden, 2004a)

". . . The Jews and the Americans made up this call for peace in the world. The peace they're calling for is a big fairy tale. They're just drugging the Muslims as they lead them to slaughter. And the slaughter is still going on. If we defend ourselves, they call us terrorists." (bin Laden, 2001a)

"America knows only the language of force. This is the only way to stop it and make it take its hands off the Muslims and their affairs. America does not know the language of dialogue!! Or the language of peaceful coexistence!! America is kept at bay by blood alone . . . ." (Abu Gheith, 2002)

"Jihad and the rifle alone: no negotiations, no conferences, and no dialogues."[18]

---

[18] This is an oft-cited slogan. See the Introduction in Azzam, 1987.

CHAPTER TEN

Conclusion

As we attempt to come to grips with the incomprehensible, it is natural to reformulate it in concepts that are familiar and that resonate meaningfully in our culture. Thus jihadis are labeled madmen, fanatics, or evil-doers. While they may be these things, such words offer no insight as to how to deal with them.

In contrast, studying the self-portrait painted by the jihadis themselves suggests a number of conclusions that may offer practical guidance on how to respond to the jihadi movement.

It is a commonplace to say that jihadism reflects a struggle within Islam over how to cope with modernity. However, we in the West are not exactly innocent bystanders. The popular grievances that jihadis exploit—the aftereffects of colonialism, corrupt and ineffective governments, the suffering of the Palestinians—all have linkages to past or present Western policies. This means that the susceptibility of Muslim populations to jihadi blandishments can be impacted by Western, and in particular, U.S. policies.

The Israeli-Palestinian conflict is perhaps the most important case in point. If it were resolved, would jihadism end? No, but the jihadis would have a much harder time villainizing the West. Could the United States bring about such a resolution? No, not without the full support of the parties involved. But sincere and energetic peacemaking efforts would greatly strengthen America's political positions in the Middle East, as would high-level expression of concern over the plight of ordinary Palestinians.

For all the bravado and braggadocio of jihadi statements, it is difficult to escape the suspicion that the jihadis are nowhere near as powerful as they try to make themselves appear. They routinely exaggerate the importance of their exploits in order to mythologize them. Iraq is no exception; actual al-Qaeda attacks there are estimated to be only a small fraction of the insurgency, though they are typically high-profile. This is not to diminish the importance of al-Zarqawi's role in provoking a sectarian conflict, but that role has now taken on a life of its own.

The Internet offers another example. It is awash in jihadi web sites, and there is little question that it is being exploited for training, fundraising, recruitment, and coordination. Yet again, when browsing the blogs and chat rooms, one gets the impression that what is being witnessed is largely a form of "fantasy jihad." It is not comforting to see so many obviously educated young Muslims playing the game, but their participation does not mean that each log-on represents a sleeper cell.

Many of the jihadi statements in this book would achieve their desired effect if they exaggerated the threat and provoked an American overreaction. Such overreaction is a principal strategic objective of jihadi "raids." It makes the jihadis appear more powerful and threatening, which attracts recruits and enhances the message that the success of jihad is inevitable. One of the most useful things the U.S. government could do is tone down its rhetoric and bring the risk the jihadis pose into proportion.

Jihadis have substantial weaknesses that can be exploited. The most important is their lack of a secure base. The loss of Afghanistan was a severe blow to al-Qaeda, and its retreat into the mountains of the Hindu Kush has not provided much more than a refuge. The strategic objective of the battles in Iraq, Somalia, Chechnya, and elsewhere is to create an "Islamic state," reestablishing a secure base for expanding jihad, not only in the region, but throughout the world.

At present, jihadi bases are confined to regions along the Afghan-Pakistan border and certain areas of Iraq. These so-called "safe zones" do not, however, provide a base for conducting complex campaigns against the West, the development of weapons of mass destruction, or the raising of a jihadi army to threaten the region. The top-priority strategic military objective of the United States in the war against the jihadis must be to prevent the establishment of such a base and the destabilization, if not the elimination, of those refuges that exist.

A second major weakness is the propensity of jihadis to indulge in divisive doctrinal and strategic disputes. Jihadis are extremely sensitive to criticism from other Muslims and obsessive about justifying their actions by referring to the Qur'an and Hadith. They slander and threaten each other over such issues as takfir (excommunication), al-wala' wa al-bara' (loyalty and disavowal), the preeminence of the Verse of the Sword, suicide bombings, killing Muslims, the apostasy of the Shi'a, and the definition of the true Salafi orthodoxy. All of these differences can and should be exploited by targeted information and disinformation campaigns. The United States and its friends in the Middle East can cooperate in carrying out such programs. The conspiratorial mentality of jihadis will facilitate success against them. It is also possible to strengthen networks among moderate Muslims who can push this debate and counter the doctrine of jihad.[1]

This leads to a third weakness: the ignorance about Islam of the population targeted for jihadi recruitment, as well as of many rank-and-file jihadis. Even those who may have memorized some or all of the Qur'an do not necessarily understand all of its meanings. Ironically, the answer to jihadi interpretations may well be more public

---

[1] The principal argument against Western support for anti-jihadi groups is that this would discredit them. Effective anti-jihad groups, even without Western support, will face such charges anyway.

exposure to the Qur'an. Since illiteracy is so high in the Middle East, television, video, and audio programming should be emphasized. The most famous television personality in the Arab world is Hamdi Kandl, who has a religious program that is neither jihadi nor Salafist. The fact that any Muslim can be an Imam should encourage moderate Muslim programming.

Fourth, jihadi dependence on the Internet can also be exploited. The anonymity of the web can be used to stimulate rifts among jihadis, create false web sites, teach flawed tradecraft, and disseminate counterpropaganda.

Despite the extreme difficulties of bringing even a semblance of democracy to Iraq, democracy is the only ideology that is seen by jihadis as a real threat. But after the unfortunate success of Islamists at the polls in Egypt and the Palestinian territories, the United States has backed off of its pro-democracy efforts. It needs to redouble its commitment and develop a differentiated strategy to promote not only democracy, but also democrats. This does not mean blindly insisting on elections, regardless of the circumstances, but rather, pressing for human rights, rule of law, and especially, civil society. In this connection, one of the most telling jihadi concerns is the threat they see in groups such as Rotary, the Lions, and other civil-society organizations.

The question of a differentiated policy also applies to the American approach to secular Muslim groups and non-jihadi Islamist political organizations. The former are most likely to share American values and prove to be genuine democrats. The Islamists, however, are in the ascendancy, and perhaps our focus should be on encouraging Islamic democracy, which could well call for more-differentiated Islamic parties. It is certain that we should not equate democracy with secularism, for that is a losing proposition in today's Islamic world. Caution is required, because even relatively moderate Islamist movements can have jihadi elements and values. Nonetheless, the United States deals with the moderately Islamist government in Turkey and should be prepared to deal with others in the future. The best prescription for the West would appear to be to support the secularists and dialogue with the Islamists to encourage their evolution in more moderate directions.

One of the most compelling arguments made by jihadis and other Islamists in seeking popular support is that existing Middle East regimes are corrupt and ineffective. This they attribute to political systems that fail to embrace shari'a law. There is not much that outsiders such as the United States can do about corruption, but they, along with the international financial institutions, can reward government programs that are clean and withhold economic support for the individuals and programs that are corrupt. Western governments can also crack down on international corporations that participate in corruption by enforcing their commitment to the Organisation for Economic Co-operation and Development (OECD) Anti-Bribery Convention—which is now honored mostly in the breach.

There is greater opportunity in promoting more-effective government. The United States and other aid donors need to place greater emphasis on programs that enhance the capacity of government to deliver its services and not leave the field to the Islamists. Hamas, Hezbollah, and the Muslim Brotherhood have built their political support as much by operating health clinics as by propagating their ideology. If the United States can train capable and effective military personnel in the Middle East, it can try to do the same with bureaucrats and service providers, particularly providers of health and education.

It seems clear from the testimony of the jihadis that repression can work in controlling immediate threats. At least three generations of jihadis have been jailed or driven from Egypt. But could the United States both condone repression and promote democracy? The quandary is magnified by the fact that the principal target of repression is often the secular, or moderate Islamist, rather than jihadi groups. And this kind of repression can frequently help create extremists.

It is not inconsistent for the United States to both encourage vigorous pursuit of jihadi terrorists who advocate the violent overthrow of their governments and promote lawful and humane treatment for groups and individuals once they are apprehended. Nor is it hypocritical for the U.S. government to use its influence to protect the secular and moderate Muslim opposition. The evident strategy of some governments in the Middle East appears to be to repress that opposition so that their publics (and the United States) will be confronted with a choice of supporting either the regime or the Islamists. The U.S. government needs to make a particular effort to safeguard the secular opposition and encourage moderate Muslims' political activity.

The jihadis may believe that by successfully provoking sectarian conflict in Iraq, they have found a strategy that they can replicate elsewhere in the region to create turmoil and catapult themselves into a leadership position among the Sunnis. There are Shi'a and other non-Sunni minorities in most other Arab countries, although in much smaller numbers than in Iraq. Jihadi attacks on those minorities could provoke a cycle of violent reaction and counterreaction that could undermine legitimate authority. To this must be added the possibility that Iran or Shi'ites in Iraq are not only likely to back their co-religionists, they may even encourage them to use violence for their own purposes.

The United States needs to encourage its Sunni friends in the region, particularly in Saudi Arabia, to reach out to their minority communities to strengthen positive relationships that can withstand such jihadi tactics.

The root emotion that seems to drive jihadism is humiliation. The response of the West must be based on a foundation of respect, not for jihadis, but for other Muslims. Every aspect of U.S. policy and action must be informed by the need to demonstrate such respect. This includes our diplomacy, our assistance programs, our cultural exchanges, and the behavior of our military personnel. Too often, U.S. public diplomacy efforts are aimed at telling the Muslim world what good people we are, when the focus should be on what good people we think they are.

One underused resource in developing such an effort is the American Muslim community. Even jihadis have admitted that the U.S. government has imposed no impediments to preaching Dawa and seeking converts to Islam. However, since 9/11, the U.S. Islamic community has felt under pressure from suspicious federal and local authorities and has, in effect, kept its head down. In the immediate aftermath of 9/11, the Bush administration visibly reached out to American Muslim leaders. It is necessary to find ways to continue that dialogue. One objective of such an effort should be to encourage American Muslims to enter into the "war of ideas" with the jihadis.

The fanaticism that fuels violent jihad is difficult, if not impossible, for the outsider to grasp. Yet it has existed among political and religious groups throughout much of history. It has been described as a fire in the mind whose radiance attracts followers like moths to a flame (Billington, 1980). For jihadis, it is a force from God.

However, the most notable aspect of the first-person accounts of jihadi "raids" is the remarkable lack of affect in the storytellers: ". . . we found a Swedish infidel. Brother Nimr beheaded him." ". . . we found a restaurant, so we ate breakfast and rested. Then we went up to the first floor and found some Hindu dogs, so we slaughtered them." There is no passion in these hearts of darkness. There is no divine spark. There is oblivion, a nothingness.

Understanding this enemy is crucial to devising effective strategies and defenses and to waging the war of ideas that underlies jihadism. The point of departure must be their own words and actions. These provide an essential basis upon which we can prevail in this struggle. Going deeper into the minds of jihadi leaders, one finds empty souls obsessed with death. Comprehending that is an essential step in defeating them.

References

Abu Ghaith, Sulayman, Audio interview, June 24, 2002, trans. Jihad Unspun (JUS), "Jihad for the Sovereignty of Allah Alone," June 24, 2002. As of October 19, 2006:
http://www.jihadunspun.com/BinLadensNetwork/interviews/iwag02.html

Abu Gheith, Suleiman (Sulayman Abu Ghaith), "In the Shadow of Lances," Center for Islamic Research and Studies (CISR), 2002, trans. MEMRI, "'Why We Fight America': Al-Qa'ida Spokesman Explains September 11 and Declares Intentions to Kill 4 Million Americans with Weapons of Mass Destruction," Special Dispatch Series, No. 388, June 12, 2002. As of February 14, 2008:
http://memri.org/bin/articles.cgi?Page=archives&Area=sd&ID=SP38802

Abu Hafs, Mu'min Rajab Rajab, Video prepared before suicide attack on December 7, 2004, trans. Itamar Maracus and Barbara Crook, "A Self-Portrait of Suicide Terrorists," Palestinian Media Watch, March 2, 2006. As of February 14, 2008:
http://www.pmw.org.il/Latest%20bulletins%20new.htm

Abu-Hafs al-Masri Brigades (Al-Qa'ida), "The Mujahidin's Roadmap," *Internet Haganah*, July 1, 2004, trans. FBIS, GMP20040702000032. As of February 6, 2008:
http://internet-haganah.us/harchives/002292.html

Abu Hafs Al-Masri Brigades of Al-Qa'ida, Statement (purported), *Al-Quds Al-Arabi* (London), March 12, 2004, trans. Yigal Carmon, MEMRI, "The Alleged Al-Qa'ida Statement of Responsibility for the Madrid Bombings: Translation and Commentary," Inquiry and Analysis Series, No. 166, March 12, 2004. As of February 5, 2008:
http://memri.org/bin/articles.cgi?Page=archives&Area=ia&ID=IA16604

Abu Hajer, Interview, "An Interview with One of the 19 Most Wanted," *The Voice of Jihad*, Issue 2, October 2003, pp. 22–26, trans. RAND, March 2008. As of March 24, 2008:
http://ia340919.us.archive.org/0/items/ozoooS/s02.pdf

Abu-Hilalah, Yusuf, Poetry, in Osama Bin-Laden, Audio, Al-Jazirah TV, ISRC, January 4, 2004. As of February 14, 2008:
http://www.why-war.com/news/2004/03/04/fulltext.html

Abu Jandal, Adham Ahmad Hujyla, Video prepared before suicide attack on December 7, 2004, published on Hamas web site in February 2006, trans. Itamar Marcus and Barbara Crook, "A Self-Portrait of Suicide Terrorists," Palestinian Media Watch, March 2, 2006. As of February 14, 2008:
http://www.pmw.org.il/Latest%20bulletins%20new.htm

Abu Khubayb and Abu Zubayr, "The Slandered Jihad," trans. Institute of Islamic Information and Education (III&E), undated. As of March 7, 2006:
http://www.iiie.net/1/content/view/124/44/

Abu Maysara, "The Crest of the Summit of Islam," Department of Indoctrination, Issue 1, trans. MEMRI, "The Iraqi Al-Qa'ida Organization: A Self-Portrait," Special Dispatch Series, No. 884, March 24, 2005a. As of February 14, 2008:
http://memri.org/bin/articles.cgi?Page=archives&Area=sd&ID=SP88405

————, "A Statement from al-Qa'ida Organization on the Amman Attack," November 10, 2005b, trans. RAND, March 2008. As of March 25, 2008:
http://haganah.us/hmedia/10nov05-AQI_claim/alfirdaws-t7868-amman-claim_2.html

————, "A Statement from al-Qa'ida Organization in the Euphrates Taking Responsibility for the Amman Bombing," November 10, 2005c, trans. RAND, March 2008. As of March 25, 2008: http://jameed.net/2005/11/10/412/

————, "A Statement from al-Qa'ida Organization on the Details of al-Ansar Attack on Amman (Friday)," November 11, 2005d, trans. RAND, March 2008. As of March 25, 2008: http://lahdah.com/vb/showthread.php?t=15822

Abu Shihab El-Kandahari, "Nuclear Warfare Is the Solution for Destroying America," December 26, 2002, trans. J. R. Nyquist, "The Nuclear Fatwa: Translation of Text," February 2003. As of February 14, 2008:
http://www.jrnyquist.com/nuclear_fatwa.htm

Abu Zubeida, Video, undated, trans. MEMRI, "Messages by Al-Qaeda Operatives in Afghanistan to the Peoples of the West: The Crusaders Will Not Be Safe from Allah . . . We Will Strike Their Vital Enterprises," Special Dispatch Series, No. 992, September 23, 2005. As of February 14, 2008:
http://memri.org/bin/articles.cgi?Page=archives&Area=sd&ID=SP99205

Abu Zuhri, Sami, and Faraj Shalhoub, Debate, Al-Majd TV, July 8, 2004, trans. MEMRI, "On the Recruitment and Training of Palestinian Suicide Bombers," TV Monitor Project, Clip No. 117, July 8, 2004. As of October 23, 2006:
http://memritv.org/Transcript.asp?P1=117

Al-Aamer, Sheikh Aamer Bin Abdallah, "Men of Jihad, This Is Your Festive Season," Editorial, *The Voice of Jihad*, Issue 27, 2004, trans. MEMRI, "Al-Qa'ida Internet Magazine Sawt Al-Jihad Calls to Intensify Fighting During Ramadan – 'The Month of Jihad,'" Special Dispatch Series, No. 804, October 22, 2004. As of February 14, 2008:
http://memri.org/bin/articles.cgi?Page=archives&Area=sd&ID=SP80404

Al-Abidi, Shik Zafer, Interview, Al-Arabiya TV, November 24, 2005, trans. MEMRI, "The Battle of Falluja – Iraqi and Arab Mujahideen Speak to Al-Arabiya TV," TV Monitor Project, No. 946, November 24, 2005. As of January 23, 2008:
http://memritv.org/transcript/en/946.htm

Al-Ablaj, Abu-Muhammad, Email to Mahmud Khalil and questions from news correspondent, Al-Majallah, World News Connection (WNC), "Transcript: Al-Qa'ida Training Official Threatens to Clip Wings of US Eagle," June 22, 2003a. As of February 14, 2008:
http://www.why-war.com/news/2003/06/22/alqaidat.html

————, Internet interview with Mahmud Khalil, London, *Al-Majallah*, September 21, 2003, trans. World News Connection (WNC), "Transcript: Al-Qa'ida's Abu-Muhammad al-Ablaj on Bin Ladin, Weapons, US Targets," September 21, 2003. As of February 14, 2008:
http://www.why-war.com/news/2003/09/21/alqaidas.html

————, In answer to Al-Majallah questions through email, undated, World News Connection (WNC), "Qaeda Position on Recruiting Europeans, Americans," August 3, 2003b.

As of February 14, 2008:
http://www.why-war.com/news/2003/08/03/qaedapos.html

Al-Adel, Saif, "Message to Our People in Iraq and the Gulf [Region] Specifically, and to Our Islamic Ummah in General: The Islamic Resistance Against the American Invasion of Qandahar and Lessons Learned," March 2003, trans. Aimee Ibrahim, *Al-Qaeda's Advice for Mujahideen in Iraq: Lessons Learned in Afghanistan*, Alexandria, VA: Intel Center/Tempest Publishing, LLC, v1.0, April 14, 2003. As of February 14, 2008:
http://www.intelcenter.com/Qaeda-Guerrilla-Iraq-v1-0.pdf

Al-Ali, Hamed bin Abdullah, "Warning of the Implementation of Iran's Designs in Iraq and on the Sunni Muslim People," trans. SITE Institute, March 2006.

————, "What to Expect After the Coming War?" trans. SITE Institute, March 2007.

A'la Maududi, S'Abul, Commentary 28 (Qur'an 9:29), *The Meaning of the Qur'an*, 1967a, trans. Muhammad Akbar Muradpuri, Pakistan, Islamic Publications (Pvt.) Ltd., 4th ed., August 2003.

————, Commentary 67 (Qur'an 9:60), *The Meaning of the Qur'an*, 1967b, trans. Muhammad Akbar Muradpuri, Pakistan: Islamic Publications (Pvt.) Ltd., 4th ed., August 2003.

————, Commentary 51 (Qur'an 3:55), *The Meaning of the Qur'an*, Muradpuri, Pakistan: Islamic Publications (Pvt.) Ltd., Vol. 1., 4th ed., August 2003, p. 246.

A'la Maududi, Sayyeed Abdul, Address, April 13, 1939, trans. *Jihad in Islam*, Lahore, Pakistan: Islamic Publications (Pvt.) Ltd. As of February 14, 2008:
http://www.islamistwatch.org/texts/maududi/maududi.html

Al-Amer, Sheikh Amer Bin Abdullah, undated, *Al-Battar Training Camp*, Editorial, Issue 13, 2004, trans. SITE Institute, "Al Battar Issue No. 13," July 23, 2004. As of October 16, 2006:
http://siteinstitute.org/bin/articles.cgi?ID=publications5404&Category=publications&Subcategory=0

Al-Amili, Abu Sa'd, "Learning Lessons from the Raids on New York and Washington," 2002, trans. FBIS, "Book Commemorating September 11 'Raid,'" Majallat al-Ansar Publications, September 1, 2002, GMP20031027000226. As of February 14, 2008:
http://www.why-war.com/files/qaeda_celebrate_911.html

Al-Ansari, Sheikh Abu al-Waleed, "The Termination of "Israel"—A Qur'anic Fact," trans. Abu al-Waleed al-Hamawi, undated. As of February 14, 2008:
http://www.missionislam.com/nwo/termination.htm

Al-Ansari, Seif al-Din, *Al-Ansar*, Issue 16, August 24, 2002a, trans. MEMRI, "An Al-Qa'ida-Affiliated Online Magazine: On the Importance of Jihad as a Means of Destroying the 'Infidel Countries,'" Special Dispatch Series, No. 418, September 4, 2002. As of February 14, 2008:
http://memri.org/bin/articles.cgi?Page=archives&Area=sd&ID=SP41802

————, "Allah Will Torment Them by Your Hands," *Al-Ansar*, August 24, 2002b, trans. MEMRI, "Contemporary Islamist Ideology Authorizing Genocidal Murder," Special Report, No. 25, January 27, 2005. As of February 14, 2008:
http://memri.org/bin/articles.cgi?Page=archives&Area=sr&ID=SR2504

————, *Al-Ansar*, Issue 16, August 24, 2002c, trans. MEMRI, "An Al-Qa'ida-Affiliated Online Magazine: On the Importance of Jihad as a Means of Destroying the 'Infidel Countries,'" Special Dispatch Series, No. 418, September 4, 2002. As of February 14, 2008:
http://memri.org/bin/articles.cgi?Page=archives&Area=sd&ID=SP41802

————, "The Raid on New York and Washington: A Generic Description," trans. FBIS, "Book Commemorates September 11 'Raid,'" Majallat al-Ansar Publications, September 1, 2002d, GMP20031027000226. As of February 14, 2008:
http://www.why-war.com/files/qaeda_celebrate_911.html

Al-Anzi, Abd-al-Aziz Bin Rashid, "The Religious Rule on Targeting Oil Interests," Center for Islamic Research and Studies, trans. Open Source Center, Washington, D.C., March 2006.

al-Asfar, Banu, *The Byzantines*, undated. See "Sha'n al-Jadd ibn-Qays," al-Islam.com, As of April 1, 2008:
http://sirah.al-islam.com/SearchDisp.asp?ID=2447&Offset=0&Scope=all&SearchLevel=QBE& SearchText=%C3%87%C3%9D%C3%8A%C3%8A%C3%87%C3%A4&SearchType=root

Al-Aslami, Hamad, "Al-'Ayna,' Poem, *Al-Battar Training Camp*, Issue 7, March 2004. Northeast Intelligence Network Translation. As of February 14, 2008:
http://www.homelandsecurityus.com/battar7.asp

Al-Ayerri (al-Ayiri), Shaykh Yussuf, "The Future of Iraq and the Arabian Peninsula After the Fall of Baghdad," Center for Islamic Research and Studies, trans. Amir Taheri, "Al-Qaeda's Agenda for Iraq," *New York Post*, September 4, 2003. FBIS, "Future of Iraq, Arabian Peninsula After the Fall of Baghdad," GMP20030929000003, August 1, 2003. As of February 14, 2008:
http://www.benadorassociates.com/article/544

Al-Aziz, Abd al-Qader bin Abd, Pamphlet, undated, trans. Reuven Paz, The Project for the Research of Islamist Movements (PRISM), "Islamic Legitimacy for the London Bombings," Occasional Papers, Vol. 3, No. 4, July 2005. As of February 14, 2008:
http://www.e-prism.org/images/PRISM_no_4_vol_3_-_Islamic_legitimacy.pdf

Al-Baghdadi, Abu Hamza, Video, September 21, 2005, trans. Global Terror Alert, "Video of Abu Hamza al-Baghdadi from 'Al-Qaida's Jihad Committee in Mesopotamia' (Abu Musab al-Zarqawi)," September 21, 2005. As of February 14, 2008:
http://www.globalterroralert.com/pdf/0905/zarqawi0905-14.pdf

Al-Banna, Sayyed Hassan, *Letter to a Muslim Student*, 1935, trans. Leicester, United Kingdom: The Islamic Foundation/FOSIS, ISBN 0860372588, September 1995. As of February 14, 2008:
http://www.pks-anz.org/Files/eBook/Letter%20to%20a%20Muslim%20Student.pdf

————, "Peace in Islam," *Shihaab*, 1948, trans. Young Muslims Canada-wide. As of February 14, 2008:
http://www.youngmuslims.ca/online_library/books/peace_in_islam/index.htm

————, Jihad, undated(a), *Militant Islam Monitor*, "The Way of Jihad: Complete Text by Hassan Al-Banna founder of the Muslim Brotherhood," January 16, 2005. As of February 14, 2008:
http://www.militantislammonitor.org/article/id/379

————, "Two Faiths," *Our Message*, undated(b). As of February 14, 2008:
http://islamic-world.net/book/ourmessage.htm

————, *Our Message*, undated(c), trans. Majmuat Ar Rasail, "Compilation of Letters [of] Imam Shaheed Hassan Al Banna," Muslim American Society Minnesota Chapter (MASMN), undated. As of February 14, 2008:
http://www.masmn.org/documents/Books/Hasan_Al_Banna/Rasail/001.htm

Al-Barqawi, Isam Mohammad Taher (aka Abu Muhammad Asem al-Maqdisi), Interview, Al-Jazeera TV, July 2005, Associated Press (AP) "Al-Zarqawi mentor arrested for 'terrorist'

links," July 6, 2005. As of February 14, 2008:
http://www.usatoday.com/news/world/2005-07-06-jordan-arrest_x.htm

Al-Battar Training Camp, Issue 1, January 2004a, trans. MEMRI, "The Al-Battar Training Camp: The First Issue of Al-Qa'ida's Online Military Magazine," Special Dispatch Series, No. 637, January 6, 2004. As of February 14, 2008:
http://memri.org/bin/articles.cgi?Page=archives&Area=sd&ID=SP63704

————, Issue 10, March 2004b, trans. SITE, "Kidnapping the Focus of Al Battar Issue No. 10," May 24, 2004. As of October 23, 2006:
http://siteinstitute.org/bin/articles.cgi?ID=publications3804&Category=publications&Subcategory=0

Al-Dosari, Suleiman, Editorial, "Why Is Jihad Necessary in Saudi Arabia," *The Voice of Jihad*, Issue 1, October 2003a, trans. MEMRI, "New Al-Qa'ida Online Magazine Features Interview with a 'Most-Wanted' Saudi Islamist, Calls for Killing of Americans and Non-Muslims," Special Dispatch Series, No. 591, October 17, 2003. As of February 14, 2008:
http://memri.org/bin/articles.cgi?Page=archives&Area=sd&ID=SP59103

————, *The Voice of Jihad*, Issue 2, October 2003b, trans. MEMRI, "Al-Qa'ida Magazine Debates Attacks in Saudi Arabia – Proposes More Attacks in the U.S. Will Boost Support," Special Dispatch Series, No. 632, December 23, 2003. As of February 14, 2008:
http://memri.org/bin/articles.cgi?Page=archives&Area=sd&ID=SP63203

Al-Fahd, Nasir bin Hamd, "A Treatise on the Legal Status of Using Weapons of Mass Destruction Against Infidels," May 2003a, FBIS, "Use of weapons of mass destruction defended on basis of Islamic law," GMP20030602000454, May 1, 2003.

————, *The Voice of Jihad*, Issue 1, October 2003b, trans. MEMRI, "New Al-Qa'ida Online Magazine Features Interview with a 'Most-Wanted' Saudi Islamist, Calls for Killing of Americans and Non-Muslims," Special Dispatch Series, No. 591, October 17, 2003. As of February 14, 2008:
http://memri.org/bin/articles.cgi?Page=archives&Area=sd&ID=SP59103

Al-Falastini, Abu Qatada, "The Markers of the Victorious Sect. Tawheed.com," trans. CTC Translation Centre, October 2005.

Al-Faqih, Saad, Interview, December 12, 2005, Abedin, Mahan Spotlight on Terror, "New Security Realities and Al-Qaeda's Changing Tactics: An Interview with Saad al-Faqih," Vol. 3, Issue 12, December 15, 2005. As of February 14, 2008:
http://www.jamestown.org/terrorism/news/article.php?articleid=2369847

Algerian Salafist Group for Prayer and Combat (GSPC), The Counterterrorism Blog, "Known Al-Qaida Affiliate Applauds 7/7 in London, Urges More Terror Attacks," July 21, 2005. As of February 14, 2008:
http://counterterror.typepad.com/the_counterterrorism_blog/2005/07/alqaida_affilia.html

Al-Ghamdi, Sheikh Sa'd Bin Abdallah al-'Ajameh, Sermon at the Sa'id Al-Jandoul Mosque in Al-Taif, Saudi Arabia, undated, trans. MEMRI, "Contemporary Islamist Ideology Authorizing Genocidal Murder," Special Report, No. 25, January 27, 2005. As of February 14, 2008:
http://memri.org/bin/articles.cgi?Page=archives&Area=sr&ID=SR2504

Al-Ghamdi, Yahyah bin Ali, "The Years of Deception," *The Voice of Jihad*, Issue 9, January 22, 2004, trans. MEMRI, "Al-Qa'ida's 'Voice of Jihad' Magazine: Issue No. 9," Special Dispatch Series, No. 650, January 27, 2004. As of February 14, 2008:
http://memri.org/bin/articles.cgi?Page=archives&Area=sd&ID=SP65004

Al-Haramayn [Two Holy Places] Brigades, Communiqué, 2003, *The Voice of Jihad*, 2003, trans. MEMRI, "Al-Qa'ida Magazine Debates Attacks in Saudi Arabia – Proposes More Attacks in the U.S. Will Boost Support," Special Dispatch Series, No. 632, December 23, 2003. As of February 14, 2008:
http://memri.org/bin/articles.cgi?Page=archives&Area=sd&ID=SP63203

Al-Hilali, Abu Ayman, *The Real Story of the Raids on New York and Washington*, trans. FBIS, "Book Commemorates September 11 'Raid,'" Majallat al-Ansar Publications, September 1, 2002, GMP20031027000226. As of February 14, 2008:
http://www.why-war.com/files/qaeda_celebrate_911.html

Al-Hilali, Abu Muhammad, Internet post, September 25, 2005, trans. Reuben Paz, "Al-Qaeda's Search for New Fronts: Instructions for Jihadi Activity in Egypt and Sinai," The Project for the Research of Islamist Movements (PRISM), Vol. 3, No. 7, October 2005. As of February 14, 2008:
http://www.e-prism.org/images/PRISM_no_7_vol_3_-_The_new_front_in_Egypt_and_Sinai.pdf

Al-Hukaymah, Muhammad Khalil, "A New Strategic Method in the Resistance of the Occupier," trans. SITE Institute, October 2006.

———, "Jihad Studies . . . Facts and Realities," trans. SITE Institute, June 2007.

Al-Iraqi, Abu Abdelrahman, Letter, "To: Our Shaykh and Commander Abu Musab al-Zarqawi – may Allah protect him," Al-Qaida's Jihad Committee in Mesopotamia, trans. Global Terror Alert, "A letter from a soldier to his commander. All praise be to Allah . . . and prayers to his prophet . . . ," October 1, 2005. As of February 14, 2008:
http://www.globalterroralert.com/pdf/1005/zarqawi1005.pdf

Al-Jama'a (The Group), "Take Up the Weapon for Life," Issue 1, May 2004, trans. Stephen Ulph, "A New Journal for Algerian Jihad," *Terrorism Monitor*, Vol. II, Issue 15, July 29, 2004. As of February 14, 2008:
http://jamestown.org/terrorism/news/article.php?articleid=2368324

Al-Jaysh al-Islami fi Iraq [The Islamic Army in Iraq], "Our View of the Elections," January 13, 2005, trans. Global Terror Alert, "'Al-Jaysh al-Islami fi Iraq' ('The Islamic Army in Iraq') on the Upcoming Iraqi Democratic Elections." As of February 14, 2008:
http://www.globalterroralert.com/pdf/0105/islamicarmy0105-2.pdf

Al-Kalesi, Sheikh Jawad, *Le Monde*, in Al Jazzera.net, "Cleric says al-Zarqawi died long ago," September 17, 2005. As of February 14, 2008:
http://english.aljazeera.net/NR/exeres/73570F02-EA07-492F-9E04-C080950DF180.htm

Al-Khudayr, Shaykh Ali, Quote, undated, in Al-Salim, Muhammad Bin Ahmad, *39 Ways to Serve and Participate in Jihad*, August 2003, trans. FBIS, "Book Entitled: '39 Ways to Serve and Participate in Jihad,'" GMP20031113000204, November 29, 2003. As of October 10, 2006:
b13777.com/39%20Ways%20to%20Serve%20Jihad.doc

Allah, Louis Attiya, Interview, "An Interview with Mr. Luis Attiyatallah," *The Voice of Jihad*, Issue 6, November 2003, pp. 13–18, trans. RAND, March 2008. As of March 24, 2008:
http://ia340919.us.archive.org/0/items/ozoooS/s06.pdf

———, Commentary on bin-Laden's Speech ("Anticipate a Large-Scale Attack in U.S."), *The Voice of Jihad*, Issue 9, January 22, 2004, trans. MEMRI, "Al-Qa'ida's 'Voice of Jihad' Magazine: Issue No. 9," Special Dispatch Series, No. 650, January 27, 2004. As of February 14, 2008:
http://memri.org/bin/articles.cgi?Page=archives&Area=sd&ID=SP65004

Al-Maarek, Azmiray, Poem written after being selected for a suicide operation, in a letter to Osama bin-Laden, November 4, 2001, in Alan Cullison, "Letters from a Young Martyr," *The Atlantic*, September 1, 2004. As of February 14, 2008:
http://www.keepmedia.com/pubs/TheAtlantic/2004/09/01/586823?extID=10026

Al-Maqdisi, Abu Muhammad, *Millat Ibrahim (The Religion of Abraham)*, At-Tibyan Publications, 1985.

———, "Al-Zarqawi: Support and Advice, Hopes and Pains," *Amal wa Alam*, July 2004, trans. RAND, March 2008. As of March 24, 2008:
http://www.paldf.net/forum/showthread.php?t=20682

———, "Abu Muhammad al-Maqdisi . . . Salafi Jihadism," Al-Jazeera TV, July 10, 2005a, trans. RAND, March 2008. As of March 24, 2008:
http://www.aljazeera.net/channel/archive/archive?ArchiveId=129776

———, Interview, Al-Hayat, London, July 10, 2005b.

———, "Salafi-Jihadi Leader 'Differs' with Al-Zarqawi on Killing Civilians in Iraq," FBIS (OSC), GMP20050705550004 Daoha Al-Jazirah Satellite Channel TV, July 2005c (Interview with Abu-Muhammad al-Maqdisi of the Salafi-Jihadi current, by Yasir Abu-Hilalah, place and date not given).

———, *Democracy: A Religion*, undated(a), trans. MEMRI, "Contemporary Islamist Ideology Authorizing Genocidal Murder," Special Report, No. 25, January 27, 2005. As of February 6, 2008:
http://memri.org/bin/articles.cgi?Page=archives&Area=sr&ID=SR2504
As of January 19, 2007, entire trans. (different wording but same meaning) at: http://www.streetdawah.com/books/DEMOCRACY-%20%20A%20RELIGION.pdf

———, "The Caravan Is Moving and the Dogs Are Barking," undated(b), *Al-Battar Training Camp*, Issue 7, March 2004, trans. Northeast Intelligence Network. As of December 6, 2005:
http://www.homelandsecurityus.com/battar7.asp

Al-Marid, Ahmed, "The Situation Is Getting Worse by the Day," Jihad Unspun (JUS), "Live from Kashmir: 'The Situation Is Getting Worse by the Day,'" October 12, 2005. As of November 13, 2006:
http://www.jihadunspun.com/newsarchive/article_internal.php?article=104785&list=/newsarchive/index.php&

Al-Masri, Abu Hamza, Sermon, undated, in British documentary by reporter Deborah Davies, undated, cited in "A Web of Terror," *Journal of Counterterrorism and Security International*, Vol. 6, No. 3. As of February 14, 2008:
http://www.globalterroralert.com/webterror.pdf

Al-Moqrin, Abdulaziz (Muqrin), Video (purported), posted on Dirasat web site, trans. Maggie Michaels, Associated Press (AP), "Saudi Arabia's Al Qaeda Chief Vows to Eject U.S. from Arabian Peninsula," April 8, 2004. As of February 6, 2008:
http://www.foxnews.com/story/0,2933,116611,00.html

Al-Muhajiroun (Bakir School of Thought), June 21, 2004, IslamistWatch.org, "Some Quotes," undated. As of February 14, 2008:
http://www.islamistwatch.org/body_main.html

Al-Munajjid, Muhammad, Interview, Al-Majd TV, undated, trans. MEMRI, "Tsunami Reactions (2) – Saudi Cleric Muhammad Al-Munajjid: Allah Finished Off Richter Scale in Vengeance

Against Infidel Criminals," TV Monitor Project, Clip No. 452, January 1, 2005. As of October 9, 2006:
http://memritv.org/Transcript.asp?P1=452

Al-Muqren, Abd Al-'Aziz (Muqrin) (aka Abu Hajer), Interview, October 2003, *The Voice of Jihad*, Issues 1 and 2, October 2003, trans. MEMRI, "Al-Qa'ida Magazine Debates Attacks in Saudi Arabia – Proposes More Attacks in the U.S. Will Boost Support," Special Dispatch Series, No. 632, December 23, 2003. As of February 14, 2008:
http://memri.org/bin/articles.cgi?Page=archives&Area=sd&ID=SP63203

Al-Muqrin, Abdul Aziz, "Targets Inside the Cities," *Al-Battar Training Camp*, Issue 7, March, 2004a, trans. SITE, "Choosing Targets in Cities the Focus of Al Battar Issue No. 7," May 27, 2004. As of November 19, 2006:
http://siteinstitute.org/bin/articles.cgi?ID=publications3904&Category=publications&Subcategory=0

————, "The Story of the American POW: Apache Engineer Paul Marshall 'From POW to being killed,'" *The Voice of Jihad*, Issue 19, June 19, 2004b, trans. Ben Venzke, Intel Center, "Al-Qaeda Article on Johnson Kidnapping," July 10, 2004. As of February 14, 2008:
http://www.intelcenter.com/AQAP-SHK-PUB-v1-1.pdf

Al-Najdi, Sheikh Abdallah, "Soccer Is Forbidden, Unless with These Conditions," Al-Jazeera TV, May 1, 2005, trans. RAND, March 2008. As of March 24, 2008:
http://www.tarbya.net/SpSections/ArticleDetailes.aspx?ArtId=179&SecId=13

Al-Najdi, Sheikh Nasser, "Kill Americans Whose Blood Is 'Like the Blood of a Dog,'" *The Voice of Jihad*, Issue 1, October 2003a, trans. MEMRI, "New Al-Qa'ida Online Magazine Features Interview with a 'Most-Wanted' Saudi Islamist, Calls for Killing of Americans and Non-Muslims," Special Dispatch Series, No. 591, October 17, 2003. As of February 14, 2008:
http://memri.org/bin/articles.cgi?Page=archives&Area=sd&ID=SP59103

————, "Jihad Must Continue Until All Infidels Convert to Islam or Pay a Poll Tax," *The Voice of Jihad*, Issue 2, October 2003b, trans. MEMRI, "2nd Issue of 'Voice of Jihad' Al-Qa'ida Online Magazine: Strategy to Avoid Clashes with Saudi Security Forces, Convert the World's Countries to Islam," Special Dispatch Series, No. 601, October 31, 2003. As of February 14, 2008:
http://memri.org/bin/articles.cgi?Page=subjects&Area=jihad&ID=SP60103

Al-Nashmi, "A Special Interview with the Commander of the Jerusalem Brigade, Fawwaz bin Muhammad al-Nashmi," *The Voice of Jihad*, Issue 18, June 2004, pp. 20–26, trans. RAND, March 2008. As of March 24, 2008: http://ia340919.us.archive.org/0/items/ozoooS/s18.pdf

Al-Neda, eleventh article in a series about the war in Iraq, undated, trans. MEMRI, "Contemporary Islamist Ideology Authorizing Genocidal Murder," Special Report, No. 25, January 27, 2005. As of February 14, 2008:
http://memri.org/bin/articles.cgi?Page=archives&Area=sr&ID=SR2504

Al-Oshan, Issa bin Saad, "An Open Letter to the Youths in the Summer Camps," *The Voice of Jihad*, Issue 19, June 2004, pp. 22–25, trans. RAND, March 2008. As of March 24, 2008:
http://ia340919.us.archive.org/0/items/ozoooS/s19.pdf

Al-Qaeda, Video transcript, undated, ABC News, "Transcript: Alleged Al Qaeda Tape Warns of New Attacks," September 11, 2005. As of February 14, 2008:
http://abcnews.go.com/WNT/print?id=1116101

"Al-Qaeda Warns Sunni Muslims to Avoid Likely Targets of Terror Attacks in Iraq," purported statement of Al-Qaeda in Iraq, posted July 25, 2005, Associated Press (AP), July 25, 2005. As

of January 31, 2008:
http://www.signonsandiego.com/news/world/iraq/20050725-1445-iraq-al-qaidawarning.html

Al-Qaeda al-Jihad (Organization of), Political Bureau, "Statement from the al-Qaeda Organization Regarding the Explosion of the Christian Oil Tanker in Yemen," October 13, 2002, trans. Aimee Ibrahim, Intel Center, "al-Qaeda Threat to Oil Industry and US Allies," v1.0, October 16, 2002. As of February 14, 2008:
http://www.intelcenter.com/OilAllies-v1-0.pdf

Al-Qaeda in the Arabian Peninsula, "Notice in Regard to Warning the Muslim from the Crusaders and Heretics," June 6, 2004," trans. Ben Venzke, Intel Center, "Al-Qaeda in the Arabian Peninsula: Shooting, Hostage Taking, Kidnapping Wave – May/June 2004 (AQAP-SHK-WMJ04)," Vol. 2.2, July 10, 2004, p. 30. As of February 14, 2008:
http://www.intelcenter.com/AQAP-SHK-PUB-v1-1.pdf

———, Video, "The Incursion of Memory of Sheikh Omar Hadid," 2005, trans. SITE, "'The Incursion in Memory of Sheikh Omar Hadid'—A Massive Operation Executed in Baghdad and Detailed in a Film by al-Qaeda in Iraq," October 12, 2005.

Al-Qaeda in the Land of the Two Rivers, "Now, al-Zarqawi Upset with Aljazeera," Statement to Agence France-Presse (AFP), June 17, 2005a. As of October 20, 2006:
http://english.aljazeera.net/NR/exeres/6B665804-0AB0-4562-82C3-A19FDD4025C3.htm

———, Media Division, "Al-Qaida to Islam Memo: Stop Lying About Mujahideen," October 21, 2005b, trans. Ubaidah Al-Saif, Jihad Unspun (JUS), "Al-Qaida's Takes Issue with Islam Memo," November 26, 2005. As of October 31, 2006:
http://www.jihadunspun.com/newsarchive/article_internal.php?article=105004&list=/newsarchive/index.php&

———, Military Division, October 28, 2005c, trans. Ubaidah Al-Saif, Jihad Unspun (JUS), "Mujahideen Intensify Attacks," October 28, 2005. As of October 18, 2006:
http://www.jihadunspun.com/newsarchive/article_internal.php?article=105052&list=/newsarchive/index.php&

Al-Qaeda in Mesopotamia, "Our Doctrine and Our Creed," undated, Northeast Intelligence Network (NIN), "The Command of the Al Qaeda Network in Mesopotamia," undated. As of December 7, 2005:
http://www.homelandsecurityus.com/sta0323akida.pdf

Al-Qaida's Committee in Northern Europe, Communiqué, September 11, 2005, trans. Global Terror Alert, "Communique from 'Al-Qaida in Northern Europe,'" September 11, 2005. As of February 14, 2008:
http://www.globalterroralert.com/pdf/0905/qaidaeurope0905.pdf

Al-Qandahari, Abu Shihab, "The nuclear war is the solution for the destruction of the United States," December 26, 2002, trans. Reuven Paz, "The First Islamist Nuclear Threat Against the United States," Global Research in International Affairs (GLORIA) Center, January 10, 2003. As of February 7, 2006:
http://gloria.idc.ac.il/islam/nuclear_threat.html

Al-Qaradhawi, Sheikh Yousef, Al-Jazeera TV (Qatar), October 5, 1977, trans. Steven Stalinsky and Y. Yehoshua, MEMRI, "Muslim Clerics on the Religious Rulings Regarding Wife-Beating," MEMRI Special Report 27, March 22, 2004. As of February 14, 2008:
http://memri.org/bin/articles.cgi?Page=archives&Area=sr&ID=SR2704

————, Discussion hosted by Maher Abdallah, Al-Jazeera TV [Qatar], June 19, 2001a, trans. MEMRI, "The Prophet Muhammad as a Jihad Model," Special Dispatch Series, No. 246, July 24, 2001. As of February 14, 2008:
http://memri.org/bin/articles.cgi?Page=archives&Area=sd&ID=SP24601

————, Al-Jazeera TV (Qatar), September 16, 2001b, trans. MEMRI, "Terror in America (10): Prominent Leader of the Muslim Brotherhood Movement, Sheikh Yussef Al-Qaradhawi: 'Islamic religious law dictates that we join the Taliban's Jihad, not the US coalition; it is forbidden to attack American citizens, but permitted to attack the American military,'" Special Dispatch Series, No. 277, September 25, 2001. As of February 14, 2008:
http://memri.org/bin/articles.cgi?Page=archives&Area=sd&ID=SP27701

————, Sermon, June 13, 2003a, trans. MEMRI, "Sheikh Al-Qaradhawi: 'We Gave Up on Haifa and Jaffa'; 'I Am Opposed to Attacks in Islamic Countries,'" Special Dispatch Series, No. 531, June 27, 2003. As of February 14, 2008:
http://memri.org/bin/articles.cgi?Page=archives&Area=sd&ID=SP53103

————, Report to the European Council for Fatwa and Research, 11th session, "Jihad and Denying its Connection to Terror," July 2003b, trans. MEMRI, "Al-Qaradhawi Speaks in Favor of Suicide Operations at an Islamic Conference in Sweden," Special Dispatch Series, No. 542, July 24, 2003. As of February 14, 2008:
http://memri.org/bin/articles.cgi?Page=archives&Area=sd&ID=SP54203

————, Speech, December 2, 2005, trans. MEMRI, "Leading Islamist Sheikh Yousef Al-Qaradhawi: 'We Will Be Victorious, Allah Willing – Despite Traps Set by Judaism & Crusaders,'" Special Dispatch Series, No. 1045, December 9, 2005. As of February 14, 2008:
http://memri.org/bin/articles.cgi?Page=archives&Area=sd&ID=SP104505

Al-Qurashi, Abu 'Ubeid, "Al-Ansar: For the Struggle Against the Crusader War," Issue 4, February 27, 2002a, trans. MEMRI, "Al-Qa'ida Activist, Abu 'Ubeid Al Qurashi: Comparing Munich (Olympics) Attack 1972 to September 11," Special Dispatch Series, No. 353, March 12, 2002. As of February 14, 2008:
http://memri.org/bin/articles.cgi?Page=archives&Area=sd&ID=SP35302

————, "The 11 September Raid: The Impossible Becomes Possible," 2002b, trans. FBIS, "Book Commemorates September 11 'Raid,'" Majallat al-Ansar Publications, September 1, 2002, GMP20031027000226. As of February 14, 2008:
http://www.why-war.com/files/qaeda_celebrate_911.html

————, "Fourth-Generation Wars," undated, Al-Ansar: For the Struggle Against the Crusader War [now defunct], Issue 2, undated, trans. MEMRI, "Bin Laden Lieutenant Admits to September 11 and Explains Al-Qa'ida's Combat Doctrine," Special Dispatch Series, No. 344, February 10, 2002. As of February 14, 2008:
http://memri.org/bin/articles.cgi?Page=archives&Area=sd&ID=SP34402

Al-Qusaymi, Abu 'Asim al-Yamani, letter to "the Sheik" [Abu Musab al-Zarqawi], April 27, 2005, trans. SITE Institute, "Translation of a letter from Abu Asim al-Qusaymi al Yemeni to 'the Sheik,'" May 5, 2005. As of April 5, 2006:
http://siteinstitute.org/terrorismlibrary/government/government_1115299179.pdf

Al-Rantisi, Abd Al-Aziz, "Iraq Will Triumph, by Allah's Will," posted on Hamas web site, December 30, 2002, trans. MEMRI "Hamas Spokesman: Iraq Must Establish a Suicide Army," Special Dispatch Series, No. 457, January 9, 2003. As of February 14, 2008:
http://memri.org/bin/articles.cgi?Page=archives&Area=sd&ID=SP45703

————, "Which Is Worse – Zionism or Nazism?" *Al-Risala*, August 21, 2003, trans. MEMRI, Special Dispatch Series, No. 558, "The False Holocaust: The Greatest of Lies," August 27, 2003. As of February 14, 2008:
http://memri.org/bin/articles.cgi?Page=archives&Area=sd&ID=SP55803

————, Interview, Nida'ul Islam, undated, IslamicAwakening.com, "Interview with Shaheed Abdel Aziz Al Rantisi," undated. As of February 14, 2008:
http://www.islamicawakening.com/viewarticle.php?articleID=1129

Al-Rasheed, Madawi, *Contesting the Saudi State: Islamic Voices from a New Generation*, Cambridge, UK: Cambridge University Press, 2007.

Al-Sa'di, Abu Abdallah, "The Experience of Jihad and the Dead End," *The Voice of Jihad*, Issue 9, January 22, 2004a, trans. MEMRI, "Al-Qa'ida's 'Voice of Jihad' Magazine: Issue No. 9," Special Dispatch Series, No. 650, January 27, 2004. As of February 14, 2008:
http://memri.org/bin/articles.cgi?Page=archives&Area=sd&ID=SP65004

————, "Myths and Idle Prattle" ("Abatil wa-Asmar"), *The Voice of Jihad*, Edition 6, May 2004b, in Stephen Ulph, "A New Journal for Algerian Jihad," *Terrorism Monitor*, Vol. II, Issue 15, July 29, 2004. As of February 14, 2008:
http://jamestown.org/terrorism/news/article.php?articleid=2368324

Al-Salim, Muhammad Bin Ahmad, *39 Ways to Serve and Participate in Jihad*, August 2003, trans. FBIS, "Book Entitled: '39 Ways to Serve and Participate in Jihad,'" GMP20031113000204, November 29, 2003. As of January 30, 2008:
http://www.google.com/search?q=cache:4U8H35FUnOAJ:b13777.com/39%2520Ways%2520to%2520Serve%2520Jihad.doc+Book+Entitled+39+Ways+to+Serve&hl=en&ct=clnk&cd=1&gl=us&lr=lang_en

Al-Sayf, Sheikh Abu Omar, Letter, Al-Fath online magazine, December 2004, trans. MEMRI, "Zarqawi and Other Islamists to the Iraqi People: Elections and Democracy Are Heresy," Special Dispatch Series, No. 856, February 1, 2005. As of February 14, 2008:
http://memri.org/bin/articles.cgi?Page=archives&Area=sd&ID=SP85605#_edn1

Al-Shamari, Abd Al-Rahman Ibn Salem, "O Sheikh of the Slaughterers, Abu Al-Zarqawi, Mus'ab Go Forth in the Straight Path, Guided by Allah," *The Voice of Jihad*, Issue 23, August–September 2004, trans. MEMRI, "Al-Qa'ida Magazine: O Sheikh of the Slaughterers, Abu Mus'ab Al-Zarqawi, Go Forth in the Straight Path, Guided by Allah," Special Dispatch Series, No. 797, October 12, 2004. As of February 14, 2008:
http://memri.org/bin/articles.cgi?Page=archives&Area=sd&ID=SP79704#_edn1

Al-Sheik, Khaled, "Missile Squad," undated, trans. MEMRI, "Messages by Al-Qaeda Operatives in Afghanistan to the Peoples of the West (Full Version)," Special Dispatch Series, No. 992, downloaded in September 2005 from the web site of Al-Qaeda's Jihad Media Battalion. As of February 14, 2008:
http://memri.org/bin/articles.cgi?Page=archives&Area=sd&ID=SP99205

Al-Siba'i, Hani, Interview, Al-Jazeera TV, July 8, 2005, trans. MEMRI, "Director of London's Al-Maqreze Centre for Historical Studies Hani Sibai: There Are No 'Civilians' in Islamic Law; The Bombing Is a Great Victory for Al-Qa'ida, Which 'Rubbed the Noses of the World's 8 Most Powerful Countries in the Mud,'" Special Dispatch Series, No. 932, July 12, 2005. As of February 14, 2008:
http://memri.org/bin/articles.cgi?Page=archives&Area=sd&ID=SP93205

Al-Subh, Atallah Abd al-'Al Abu, "To Clinton," *Al-Risala*, December 3, 1998, trans. MEMRI, "Anti-American Statements in the Palestinian Media," Special Dispatch Series, No. 15,

December 3, 1998. As of February 14, 2008:
http://memri.org/bin/articles.cgi?Page=archives&Area=sd&ID=SP1598

———, "To America," *Al-Risala*, September 13, 2001, trans. MEMRI, "Terror in America
(2) Hamas weekly: 'Allah has answered our prayers; the sword of vengeance has reached
America and will strike again and again,'" Special Dispatch Series, No. 268, September 17,
2001. As of February 14, 2008:
http://memri.org/bin/articles.cgi?Page=archives&Area=sd&ID=SP26801

Al-Suri, Abu Mus'ab, "Da'wah lil-Muqawamah al-Islamiyyah al-'Alamiyyah" ("The Call
to Global Islamic Resistance"), trans. Reuven Paz, "Al-Qaeda's Search for New Fronts:
Instructions for Jihadi Activity in Egypt and Sinai," The Project for the Research of Islamist
Movements (PRISM), Vol. 3, No. 7, October 2005, Global Research in International Affairs
(GLORIA) Center. As of February 14, 2008:
http://www.e-prism.org/images/PRISM_no_7_vol_3_-_The_new_front_in_Egypt_and_Sinai.
pdf

Al-Takrouri, Bassem, and Mujahid Al-Jabari, Video prepared before suicide attack on May
17, 2003, trans. Itamar Marcus and Barbara Crook, "A Self-Portrait of Suicide Terrorists,"
Palestinian Media Watch, March 2, 2006. As of February 14, 2008:
http://www.pmw.org.il/Latest%20bulletins%20new.htm

Al-Tartousi, Sheikh Abu Baseer, undated, trans. MEMRI, "Sunni Sheikhs and Organizations
Criticize Al-Zarqawi's Declaration of War Against the Shi'ites," Special Dispatch Series, No.
1000, October 7, 2005. As of February 14, 2008:
http://memri.org/bin/articles.cgi?Page=archives&Area=sd&ID=SP100005

Al-Tartusi, Abu Basir, "Passion for Revenge or Sharia-based Judgment?" trans. CTC, July
2005. As of February 14, 2008:
http://ctc.usma.edu

Al-Timimi, Ali, message dated February 1, 2003a, in Daniel Pipes, "Convicting [Ali al-Timimi,]
the 'Paintball Sheikh,'" *FrontPage Magazine*, May 2, 2005. As of February 14, 2008:
http://www.danielpipes.org/article/2579

———, Interview with Lisa Myers and the NBC Investigative Unit, June 27, 2003b, "Muslim
scholar on trial for inciting jihad: Case against spiritual leader hinges on right to free
speech," MSNBC, April 15, 2005. As of February 14, 2008:
http://msnbc.msn.com/id/7421318

Alusi, Muhammad (Iraqi Shi'i cleric), "There Is No Jihad Without Islam," October 2004, trans.
Reuven Paz, The Project for the Research of Islamist Movements (PRISM), "Islamic Legitimacy
for the London Bombings," Occasional Papers, Vol. 3, No. 4, July 2005. As of February 14,
2008:
http://www.e-prism.org/images/PRISM_no_4_vol_3_-_Islamic_legitimacy.pdf

Al-Utaybi, Sa'ud Bin Hamoud, Editorial, *The Voice of Jihad*, Issue 27, 2004, trans. MEMRI,
"Al-Qa'ida Internet Magazine Sawt Al-Jihad Calls to Intensify Fighting During Ramadan—
'The Month of Jihad,'" Special Dispatch Series, No. 804, October 22, 2004. As of February 14,
2008:
http://memri.org/bin/articles.cgi?Page=archives&Area=sd&ID=SP80404

Al-'Utaybi, Sheikh Ubay Abd Al-Rahman Al-Athari bin Bajad, "Oh Demonic Rulers, There Will
Be No Surrender!" *The Voice of Jihad*, Issue 20, June–July 2004, trans. MEMRI, "Al-Qa'ida
Magazine: 'We Reject Saudi Arabia's Ultimatum,'" Special Dispatch Series, No. 744, July 14,
2004. As of February 14, 2008:
http://memri.org/bin/articles.cgi?Page=archives&Area=sd&ID=SP74404

Al-Wahhaab, Shaykh 'Abdullah ibn Muhammad ibn 'Abd, "The Purity of Tawheed," undated, Islamic Information and Support Centre of Australia (IISCA), 2004. As of February 14, 2008: http://www.iisca.org/articles/document.jsp?id=96

Al-Wahhab, Muhammed ibn Abd, "The Clarification of Unclarity Concerning the Creator of Heaven and Earth" ("kashf al-shubuhat 'an khaliq al-ardi wa al-samawat"), undated, 'Abd Allah ibn 'Abd al-Rahman Al Bassam (ed.), 1st ed., Cairo: Dar ihya al-kutub al-'arabiyah, 1377 (1957 or 1958), quoted in Jamil Effendi al-Zahawi, "al-Fajr al-sadiq fi al-radd 'ala munkiri al-tawassul wa al-khawarig" ("The True Dawn: A Refutation of Those Who Deny the Validity of Using Means to Allah and the Miracles of Saints"), trans. Anonymous, "The Doctrine of Ahl Al-Sunna Versus the 'Salafi' Movement," undated. As of February 14, 2008: http://www.sunnah.org/publication/fajr/fajr.htm

Al-Zahar, Mahmoud, Interview by Ali Elsaleh, Asharq Al Awsat, "Asharq Al-Awsat Interviews Hamas's Mahmoud al Zahar," August 18, 2005a. As of February 14, 2008: http://aawsat.com/english/news.asp?section=3&id=1294

———, Interview, posted on web site www.elaph.com [in Arabic], October 2005, trans. MEMRI, "Hamas Leader in Gaza Dr. Mahmoud Al-Zahar: We'll Join the Legislative Council—and Keep Our Guns," Special Dispatch Series, No. 1028, November 18, 2005b. As of February 14, 2008: http://memri.org/bin/articles.cgi?Page=archives&Area=sd&ID=SP102805

Al-Zahrani, Faris, quote, London Al-Hijaz, "Al-Zahrani Has Not Departed from Salafi Doctrine in His Political Views: A Reading in the Thought, Opinions, and Teachers of Faris al-Zahrani," FBIS, "Ideology of Recently Captured Saudi al-Qa'ida Theoretician al-Zahrani Analyzed," GMP20040820000143, August 14, 2004.

Al-Zarqawi, Abu Musab, Letter to al-Qaeda Operatives (purported), February 2004a, trans. Coalition Provisional Authority (CPA), National Review Online, "Zarkawi's Cry: A Terrorist's Words of Despair," February 12, 2004. As of February 14, 2008: http://www.nationalreview.com/document/zarkawi200402121818.asp

———, "Political Fortress," Audio, April 6, 2004b, Federation of American Scientists, "'Text' of Al-Zarqawi Message Threatening More Attacks," undated. As of February 14, 2008: http://www.cpa-iraq.org/transcripts/20040212_zarqawi_full.html

———, Speech on several Islamic web sites, September 11, 2004c, trans. MEMRI, "Al-Zarqawi's Message to the Fighters of Jihad in Iraq on September 11, 2004," Special Dispatch Series, No. 785, September 15, 2004e. As of February 14, 2008: http://memri.org/bin/articles.cgi?Page=archives&Area=sd&ID=SP78504#_ednref1

———, "Find Out the Ways of the Criminals," in The Comprehensive Book of the Speeches and Words of the Sheikh Who Is Proud of His Religion, January 23, 2005a, pp. 211–229, trans. RAND, March 2008. As of March 25, 2008: http://al-boraq.org/showthread.php?t=16103

———, Audio, May 18, 2005b, trans. SITE, "A Speech by Abu Musab al-Zarqawi from the Information Department of al-Qaeda Organization in the Land of Two Rivers—Wednesday, 05/18/05," May 18, 2005. As of October 31, 2006: http://siteinstitute.org/bin/articles.cgi?ID=publications47405&Category=publications&Subcategory=0

———, Audio (purported), Caroline Faraj, "Tape justifies killing innocent Muslims: Voice purportedly belongs to al-Zarqawi," CNNArabic.com, May 19, 2005c. As of February 14, 2008: http://www.cnn.com/2005/WORLD/meast/05/18/iraq.main/

————, "Could Religion Decline While I Am Alive?" in *The Comprehensive Book of the Speeches and Words of the Sheikh Who Is Proud of His Religion, Abu Mus'ab al-Zarqawi*, July 7, 2005d, pp. 288–325, trans. RAND, March 2008. As of March 25, 2008:
http://al-boraq.org/showthread.php?t=16103

————, "A Statement and Clarification on What Sheikh al-Maqdisi Has Sparked on al-Jazeera Channel," July 14, 2005e, trans. RAND. As of March 24, 2008:
https://alltalaba.com/board/lofiversion/index.php/t12470.html

————, Speech (purported), released on the Internet, September 11, 2005f, trans. SITE, "Speech of Abu Mussab A-Zarqawi About the Events in Tal Afar," September 11, 2005. As of October 9, 2006:
http://siteinstitute.org/bin/articles.cgi?ID=publications93005&Category=publications&Subcategory=0

————,"This Statement Is to the People and Let Them Be Warned," in *The Comprehensive Book of the Speeches and Words of the Sheikh Who Is Proud of His Religion, Abu Mus'ab al-Zarqawi*, September 14, 2005g, pp. 283–289, trans. RAND, March 2008. As of March 25, 2008:
http://al-boraq.org/showthread.php?t=16103

————, Audio, Al-Qaida in the Land of the Two Rivers, September 14, 2005h, trans. Omar al-Faris, Jihad Unspun (JUS), "Zarqawi Declares All Out War Against Shia," September 14, 2005. As of October 17, 2006:
http://www.jihadunspun.com/newsarchive/article_internal.php?article=104178&list=/newsarchive/index.php&

————, Audio (purported), November 18, 2005i, Halaby, Jamal, Associated Press (AP), "Al-Zarqawi Threatens to Kill Jordan's King: Purported al-Zarqawi Tape Threatens to Kill Jordan's King Abdullah II and Bomb More Hotel Sites, ABC News, November 18, 2005. As of November 2, 2006:
http://abcnews.go.com/International/wireStory?id=1326396

————, "Taste, You Are the Mighty and Noble," November 2005j, trans. RAND, March 2008. As of March 25, 2008:
http://www.alltalaba.com/board/lofiversion/index.php/t18630.html

————, Document found on computer disk (purported), undated(a), International Institute for Counter-Terrorism (ICT), "Full Text of 'Al-Zarqawi Letter,'" February 12, 2004. As of February 14, 2008:
http://www.ict.org.il/documents/documentdet.cfm?docid=62

————, Audio posted on several Islamic Jihadist Internet sites, undated(b), trans. World News Connection, "Transcript: Al-Zarqawi Denies Jordanian Intelligence Story on Chemical Bomb," April 29, 2004. As of February 14, 2008:
http://www.why-war.com/news/2004/04/29/alzarqaw.html

————, "The Return of Ibn Al-'Alqami's Grandchildren," Audio, undated(c), trans. RAND, March 2008. As of March 24, 2008:
http://www.hanein.net/images/iraq/vdo/abnalkami.rar

Al-Zawahiri, Ayman (Abu al-Muizz), Letter to Abu Yasir, April 19, 1999, trans. *Asharq Alawsat* (English edition), "Al-Qaeda's Secret Emails Part Three," June 19, 2005. As of February 14, 2008:
http://asharqalawsat.com/english/news.asp?section=3&id=428

————, *Knights Under the Prophet's Banner: Meditations on the Jihadist Movement*, FBIS, "Al-Sharq Al-Awsat Publishes Extracts from Al-Jihad Leader Al-Zawahiri's New Book," GMP20020108000197, December 2, 2001.

————, Video, Al-Jazeera TV, August 4, 2004a, BBC News, August 8, 2004. As of February 14, 2008:
http://news.bbc.co.uk/go/pr/fr/-/2/hi/middle_east/4746157.stm

————, Video, al-Jazeera TV, September 9, 2004b, trans. MEMRI, "Ayman Al-Zawahiri's Message for the Third Anniversary of 9/11," TV Monitor Project, Clip No. 250, September 9, 2004. As of October 18, 2006:
http://memritv.org/Transcript.asp?P1=250

————, Speech, February 10, 2005a, trans. Joseph Braude, "Daily Express: On Message," The New Republic Online, February 11, 2005. As of February 16, 2008:
http://www.aijac.org.au/updates/Feb-05/140205.html

————, Letter to al-Zarqawi, July 9, 2005b, trans. Office of the Director of National Intelligence, "Letter from al-Zawahiri to al-Zarqawi," News Release No. 2-05, October 11, 2005. As of February 16, 2008:
http://www.dni.gov/press_releases/letter_in_english.pdf

————, Video, Al-Jazeera TV, September 1, 2005c, trans. MEMRI, "Al-Qaeda Leader Ayman Al-Zawahiri Defends the London Bombings: Even Those Who Did Not Vote for Bush and Blair Accept Them as Legitimate Rulers," TV Monitor Project, Clip No. 834, September 1, 2005. As of October 18, 2006:
http://www.memritv.org/Transcript.asp?P1=834

————, Interview, al-Sahab TV, September 11, 2005d, trans. MEMRI, "Newly-Released Video of Al-Qaeda's Deputy Leader Ayman al-Zawahiri's Interview to Al-Sahab TV," Special Dispatch Series, No. 1044, December 8, 2005. As of February 16, 2008:
http://memri.org/bin/articles.cgi?Page=archives&Area=sd&ID=SP104405

————, Interview, al-Sahab, September 11, 2005e, trans. MEMRI, "Al-Qaeda Leader Ayman Al-Zawahiri's interview to Al-Sahab (Part IV): I Call Upon Americans to Join Islam. The Torah and the New Testament Are Distorted. We Will Continue to Attack the US Until Our Prisoners Are Released," TV Monitor Project, Clip No. 957, December 7, 2005. As of October 10, 2006:
http://memritv.org/Transcript.asp?P1=957

————, Interview, by Farraj Isma'il, undated(a), trans. James Olberg, "Bin Laden's Right-Hand Man, Al-Zawahiri, Interviewed on Fighting In Afghanistan," December 21, 2001, *Al-Majallah*, Issue December 16–22, 2001, pp. 12–13. As of February 16, 2008:
http://www.rense.com/general18/ex.htm

————, Interview, by Hamid Mir, undated(b) (prior to 9/11/01), "Report: Al Qaeda Has Nukes," Associated Press, March 21, 2004. As of February 16, 2008:
http://www.foxnews.com/story/0,2933,114760,00.html

Al-Zaydan, Khalid, "Al-Riyad Discusses the Secrets of the Cell and the Organization" (statements by unknown repentant jihadists), Al-Riyad, 2005, trans. FBIS, "Saudi Report on Causes of Emergence of Terrorism, Extremism (5)," GMP20052022514003, October 22, 2005.

Al-Zaydi, Mshari, "Terrorist Justifications for Kidnapping and Murder," *Asharq Alawsat* (English edition), June 23, 2005. As of February 16, 2008:
http://www.asharqalawsat.com/english/news.asp?section=3&id=546

Amira, Sheikh Issam, Speech on the Temple Mount, 2005, trans. Scott Shilo, FBIS, "Israel's Arutz 7: Islamic Radicals Plan World Revolution from Temple Mount," GMP20051114614010, November 14, 2005.

Announcer (unidentified), Video, "Sawt al-Khilafal" ("The Caliphate Voice Channel"), Global Islamic Media Front (GIMF), October 11, 2005, trans. FBIS, "Global Islamic Media Front Releases 'Third News Program,'" GMB20051012396001, October 12, 2005.

Anonymous, "Anti-ship Warfare," *Al-Battar Training Camp*, Issue 8, April 17, 2004a, trans. Jamestown Foundation, "Anti-Ship Warfare and Molotov Cocktails at the Siege of Acre, 1190," May 6, 2004. As of February 16, 2008:
http://www.jamestown.org/news_details.php?news_id=46

————, Message posted on a jihadist web site, December 2004b, trans. SITE, "Do not stop slaughters, may Allah keep you steadfast, for many have recovered because of it . . . Slaughter is a cure for the hearts; may Allah glorify you," December 23, 2004. As of October 5, 2006:
http://siteinstitute.org/bin/articles.cgi?ID=publications14004&Category=publications&Subcategory=0

————, Posting on a jihadist message board, February 12, 2005a, trans. SITE, "Map of Future Al-Qaeda Operations," February 14, 2005. As of October 19, 2006:
http://siteinstitute.org/bin/articles.cgi?ID=publications19805&Category=publications&Subcategory=0

————, Fatwa, "The Base of Legitimacy for the London Bombings, and Response to the Disgraceful Statement by Abu Basir al-Tartusi," trans. Reuven Paz, "Islamic Legitimacy for the London Bombings," Occasional Paper, Project for the Research of Islamist Movements (PRISM), Global Research in International Affairs (GLORIA) Center, Vol. 3, No. 4, July 20, 2005b. As of October 18, 2006:
http://gloria.idc.ac.il/columns/2005/paz/v3n4.htm

————, Volunteer interviews on Al-Arabiya TV, November 24, 2005c, trans. MEMRI, "The Battle of Falluja - Iraqi and Arab Mujahideen Speak to Al-Arabiya TV," TV Monitor Project, No. 946, September 24, 2005. As of October 17, 2006:
http://memritv.org/Transcript.asp?P1=946

————, Message posted on a jihadist web site, undated(a), trans. SITE, "How Can You Become a Member of al-Qaeda?" January 27, 2005. As of March 3, 2006:
http://siteinstitute.org/bin/articles.cgi?ID=publications17105&Category=publications&Subcategory=0

————, Message posted on a jihadist web site, undated(b), trans. SITE, "Two Messages Reflect on the Recent Shootout Between al-Qaeda in Saudi Arabia and Saudi Security Forces," April 7, 2005. As of October 24, 2006:
http://siteinstitute.org/bin/articles.cgi?ID=publications34205&Category=publications&Subcategory=0

Asad, Muhammad, *Islam at the Crossroads*, Islamic Book Trust, 1934, rev. ed., 1982.

Ash-Shu'aybi, Sheikh Hammoud bin 'Uqla, "Terrorism: Its Meaning and Its Reality," undated, trans. Jihad Unspun (JUS), undated. As of December 13, 2006:
http://www.jihadunspun.com/sheikhhammoud-two.htm

Association of Muslim Scholars in Iraq, undated, trans. MEMRI, "Sunni Sheikhs and Organizations Criticize Al-Zarqawi's Declaration of War Against the Shi'ites," Special Dispatch

Series, No. 1000, October 7, 2005. As of February 16, 2008:
http://memri.org/bin/articles.cgi?Page=archives&Area=sd&ID=SP100005

Atallah, Missile Squad, undated, trans. MEMRI, "Messages by Al-Qaeda Operatives in Afghanistan to the Peoples of the West (Full Version)," Special Dispatch Series, No. 992, downloaded in September 2005 from the web site of Al-Qaeda's Jihad Media Battalion. As of February 16, 2008:
http://memri.org/bin/articles.cgi?Page=archives&Area=sd&ID=SP99205

Atiyah, Letter to al-Zarqawi, trans. Combating Terrorism Center at West Point, September 25, 2006.

Atta, Mohamed, Document found in baggage, undated, trans. RAND. As of April 8,2008:
http://www.fbi.gov/pressrel/pressrel01/letter.htm

Azmi, Rim, "Muslims in Name, Apostates in Fact," *Al-Ahram Al-Arabi*, April 23, 2005, trans. MEMRI, "Egyptian Journalist on Muslim Liberals in the West: 'Muslims in Name, Apostates in Fact,'" Special Dispatch Series, No. 905, May 6, 2005. As of February 16, 2008:
http://memri.org/bin/articles.cgi?Page=archives&Area=sd&ID=SP90505

Azzam, Abdullah Yusuf, *Join the Caravan*, London: Azzam Publications, 1987, 2nd English ed., ISBN: 0-9540843-0-6, 2001. As of February 16, 2008:
http://islamistwatch.org/texts/azzam/caravan/intro.html

———, quoted in Muhammad Bin Ahmad Al-Salim, *39 Ways to Serve and Participate in Jihad*, August 2003, trans. FBIS, "Book Entitled: '39 Ways to Serve and Participate in Jihad'," GMP20031113000204, November 29, 2003. As of October 10, 2006:
b13777.com/39%20Ways%20to%20Serve%20Jihad.doc

———, "From the House of the Brave Commander Jalaaluddin Haqqani, Monday Afternoon, 12th Shaban 1406 H, 20th April 1986," IslamicAwakening.com, "The Will of Abdullaah Yusuf Azzam," undated(a). As of February 16, 2008:
http://www.as-sahwah.com/viewarticle.php?articleID=532

———, "Martyrs: The Building Blocks of Nations," Extracts from "Will of the Shaheed" and "A Message from the Shaheed Sheikh to the Scholars," lectures, undated(b), downloaded by Religioscope, December 2001. As of February 16, 2008:
http://www.religioscope.com/info/doc/jihad/azzam_martyrs.htm

———, "Virtues of Martyrdom in the Path of Allah," undated(c). As of February 16, 2008:
http://www.as-sahwah.com/viewarticle.php?articleID=1012

———, "Defense of Muslim Lands," undated(d). As of February 16, 2008:
http://www.islamistwatch.org/texts/azzam/defense/defense.html

Azzam Publications, "How to Prepare for Jihad," undated, posted on several web sites, February 26, 2002. As of February 16, 2008:
http://www.confuddled.com/board/messages/7/37.html

Ba'asyir, Abu Bakar, Interview by Scott Atran, "The Emir: An Interview with Abu Bakar Ba'asyir, Alleged Leader of the Southeast Asian Jemaah Islamiyah Organization," August 13 and 15, 2005, Spotlight on Terror, Vol. 3, Issue 9, September 15, 2005. As of February 16, 2008:
http://www.jamestown.org/terrorism/news/article.php?articleid=2369782

Billah, Ahmad al-Wathe, undated, trans. Habib Trabelsi, Middle East Online, "Al-Qaeda takes jihad to media four years after 9/11: Al-Qaeda fighters become producers, film directors,

video cameras have become their most potent weapon," September 9, 2005. As of February 16, 2008:
http://www.middle-east-online.com/english/?id=14500=14500&format=0

Billington, James, *Fire in the Minds of Men: Origins of the Revolutionary Faith*, Basic Books: New York, 1980.

Bin Laden, Osama, "Declaration of War Against the Americans Occupying the Land of the Two Holy Places," Al Quds Al Arabi, August, 1996, PBS News Hour with Jim Lehrer, undated. As of February 16, 2008:
http://www.pbs.org/newshour/terrorism/international/fatwa_1996.html

—————, "Osama bin Laden Fatwah of 1998," Al-Quds al-'Arabi TV, February 23, 1998a. As of February 16, 2008:
http://www.mideastweb.org/osamabinladen1.htm

—————, Interview, Al-Jazeera TV, December 1998b, *News Telegraph*, "'Ever Since I Can Recall, I Despised and Felt Hatred Toward Americans,' Text of al-Jazeera interview with Osama bin Laden," filed July 7, 2001. As of February 16, 2008:
http://www.telegraph.co.uk/news/main.jhtml;jsessionid=CTWRPVXFGYSMLQFIQMFSFF4AVC BQ0IV0?xml=/news/2001/10/07/wbin07.xml&page=2

—————, Interview, Al-Jazeera TV, 1998c, in Bruce Lawrence (ed.), trans. James Howarth, *Messages to the World: The Statements of Osama Bin Laden*, London: Verso, ISBN 1-84467-045-7, 2005.

—————, Interview with Taysser Alouni, Al Jazeera TV, October 2001a, trans. CNN, "Transcript of Bin Laden's October Interview," posted February 5, 2002. As of February 16, 2008:
http://www.cnn.com/2002/WORLD/asiapcf/south/02/05/binladen.transcript/index.html

—————, Interview with Hamid Mir, "Osama Claims He Has Nukes," *Dawn*, November 10, 2001b. As of February 16, 2008:
http://www.dawn.com/2001/11/10/top1.htm

—————, Video, November 2001c, trans. and annotated independently by George Michael, Diplomatic Language Services; and Dr. Kassem M. Wahba, School of Advanced International Studies, The Johns Hopkins University, "Transcript of Usama bin Ladin Video Tape," December 13, 2001. As of February 16, 2008:
http://www.defenselink.mil/news/Dec2001/d20011213ubl.pdf

—————, Interview, Al-Jazeera TV, February 11, 2003a, in Bruce Lawrence (ed.), trans. James Howarth, *Messages to the World: The Statements of Osama Bin Laden*, London: Verso, ISBN 1-84467-045-7, 2005.

—————, "The Party Declaration," in *The Comprehensive Archive of the Words and Lectures of the Imam of the Mujahideen, Usama bin Muhammad bin Laden*, February 16, 2003b, pp. 97–142, trans. RAND, March 2008. As of March 25, 2008:
http://al-boraq.org/showthread.php?t=15020

—————, Audio (attributed), "Exposing the New Crusader War," February 2003c, trans. FBIS/OSC, "Islamist Site Posts Translation of Purported Bin Ladin Audio Message," GMP20030214000152, February 14, 2003. As of February 16, 2008:
http://www.islamistwatch.org/texts/comms/newcrusaderwar.pdf

————, Sermon, 2003d, trans. MEMRI, "Contemporary Islamist Ideology Authorizing Genocidal Murder," Special Report, No. 25, January 27, 2005. As of February 16, 2008:
http://memri.org/bin/articles.cgi?Page=archives&Area=sr&ID=SR2504

————, Audio, Al-Jazeera Satellite Channel TV, ISRC, January 4, 2004a. As of February 16, 2008:
http://www.why-war.com/news/2004/03/04/fulltext.html

————, Speech, Al-Jazeera TV, *The Voice of Jihad*, Issue 9, January 22, 2004b, trans. SITE Institute, "Ninth Issue of Sawt Al-Jihad Released," January 23, 2004. As of October 17, 2006:
http://siteinstitute.org/bin/articles.cgi?ID=publications2504&Category=publications&Subcategory=0

————, Statement (purported), posted to jihadist web site Al-Qal'ah, May 6, 2004c, trans. World News Connection (WNC), "Transcript: Alleged Bin Ladin Statement—May 6, 2004," May 7, 2004. As of February 16, 2008:
http://www.why-war.com/news/2004/05/07/allegedb.html

————, Video, Al-Jazeera TV, October 29, 2004d, trans. MEMRI, "Osama bin Laden's Speech on the Eve of the 2004 US Elections," TV Monitor Project, Clip No. 312, October 29, 2004. As of November 3, 2006:
http://memritv.org/Transcript.asp?P1=312

————, "A Statement to the Saudi Rulers," December 16, 2004e, trans. Jihad Unspun, December 16, 2004. As of November 13, 2006:
http://www.jihadunspun.com/BinLadensNetwork/statements

————, Speech, Al-Jazeera TV, December 16, 2004f, trans. MEMRI, "Osama Bin Laden: 'Today There Is a Conflict Between World Heresy Under the Leadership of America on the One Hand and the Islamic Nation with the Mujahideen in Its Vanguard on the Other,'" Special Dispatch Series, No. 838, December 30, 2004. As of February 16, 2008:
http://memri.org/bin/articles.cgi?Page=archives&Area=sd&ID=SP83804

————, "To the Muslims in Iraq in Particular and the [Islamic] Nation in General," Al-Sahab Institute for Media Productions, December 27, 2004g, trans. MEMRI, "Osama Bin Laden to the Iraqi People: It Is Forbidden to Participate in Iraqi & PA Elections; Jihad in Palestine and Iraq Is Incumbent upon Residents of All Muslim Countries, Not Just Iraqis and Palestinians; Zarqawi Is the Commander of Al-Qa'ida in Iraq," Special Dispatch Series, No. 837, December 30, 2004. As of February 16, 2008:
http://memri.org/bin/articles.cgi?Page=archives&Area=sd&ID=SP83704

————, Audio (purported), Al-Arabiya and Al-Jazeera TV, undated(a), trans. BBC News, April 15, 2004. As of February 16, 2008:
http://news.bbc.co.uk/2/hi/middle_east/3628069.stm

————, "Letter to the American People," undated(b), *The Observer* (UK), November 24, 2002. As of February 16, 2008:
http://observer.guardian.co.uk/print/0,,4552895-102275,00.html

Bin Muhammad, Hafiz Abdul Salam, undated, ed. Kashif Jamal, "Jihad in the Present Time," Al-Huda International, General Discussion, Topic: some info about jihad to clear doubts, March 28, 2005. As of October 4, 2006:
http://www.alhudapk.com/forum/forum_posts.asp?TID=2260

Bir, Abu Omar Abdul, Interview, "Interview with Abu Omar Abdul Bir from the Media Wing of the Algerian Salafist Group for Prayer and Combat (GSPC)," Global Terror Alert, January

31, 2005. As of February 16, 2008:
http://www.globalterroralert.com/pdf/0105/gspc0105-5.pdf

Center for Islamic Studies and Research (CISR), *The Operation of 11 Rabi Al-Awwal: The East Riyadh Operation and Our War with the United States and Its Agents*, August 1, 2003, trans. FBIS, "Islamic Research Center Publishes Book on 12 May Riyadh Operation," GMP20031004000119, August 1, 2003. As of February 16, 2008:
http://www.why-war.com/files/qaeda_east_riyadh_operation.html

————, Lecture, undated, trans. SITE, "Al-Qaeda's 'Center for Islamic Studies and Research' Warns Muslims About Information Leakages and Call for the Use of Denial and Deception Technique," May 17, 2005. As of October 23, 2006:
http://siteinstitute.org/bin/articles.cgi?ID=publications47005&Category=publications&Subcategory=0

Coll, Steve, and Susan B. Glasser, "Terrorists Turn to the Web as Base of Operations," *The Washington Post*, August 7, 2005. As of February 16, 2008:
http://www.washingtonpost.com/wp-dyn/content/article/2005/08/05/AR2005080501138.html

Committee for the Defense of Legitimate Rights (CDLR), Press release given by Sheikh Abu Iyad the Amir of the Mujahideen of Baghdad, April 16, 2003. As of January 31, 2008:
http://www.apfn.net/messageboard/4-16-03/discussion.cgi.16.html

Cooley, John K., *Black September: The Story of the Palestinian Arabs*, London: Frank Cass, 2002.

Crawford, Angus, "Iraq's Mandaeans 'face extinction,'" BBC News, last updated March 4, 2007. As of January 31, 2008:
http://news.bbc.co.uk/2/hi/middle_east/6412453.stm

Cullison, Alan, "Inside Al-Qaeda's Hard Drive," *The Atlantic*, September 2004. As of January 31, 2008:
http://www.theatlantic.com/doc/200409/cullison

Faraj, Muhammad Abd al-Salam, *The Neglected Duty (Al-Faridayh al-Gha'ibah)*, 1979, trans. Johannes J.G. Jansen, *The Neglected Duty: The Creed of Sadat's Assassins and Islamic Resurgence in the Middle East*, MacMillan Publishing Company, November 1986.

"From Youth of the Summer Camps to Issa al-Oshan, a Response Letter," *Risala Jawabiya*, June 2004, trans. RAND, March 2008. As of March 26, 2008:
http://www.saaid.net/Anshatah/mr/23.htm

Frontline, "Battle for the Holy Land," PBS presentation of a Goldvicht Productions/October Films production for the BBC in association with the Kirk Documentary Group, WGBH Educational Foundation, Program 2015, Original airdate on PBS: April 4, 2002. As of February 16, 2008:
http://www.pbs.org/wgbh/pages/frontline/shows/holy/etc/script.html

Global Islamic Media Front (GIMF), The Voice of the Caliphate (Sout Al-Khilafa), Issue 1, 2005a, trans. MEMRI, "New Al-Qaeda Weekly Internet News Broadcast Celebrates U.S. Hurricanes and Gaza Pullout, Reports on Al-Zarqawi's Anti-Shiite Campaign and Chemical Mortar Shells in Iraq," Special Dispatch Series, No. 993, September 23, 2005a. As of February 16, 2008:
http://memri.org/bin/articles.cgi?Page=archives&Area=sd&ID=SP99305

————, Video, "Third News Program," The Caliphate Voice Channel, October 11, 2005b, trans. FBIS, "Global Islamic Media Front Releases 'Third News Program,'" GMB20051012396001, October 12, 2005.

————, Announcement of initiative to sign an oath of loyalty posted on Islamic internet forums, undated, trans. MEMRI, "Now Online: Swear Loyalty to Al-Qaeda Leaders," Special Dispatch Series, No. 1027, November 18, 2005c. As of February 16, 2008: http://memri.org/bin/articles.cgi?Page=archives&Area=sd&ID=SP102705

GlobalSecurity.org, "Al Qaeda Organization in the Arabian Peninsula," undated. As of January 30, 2008: http://www.globalsecurity.org/military/world/para/al-qaida-arabia.htm

Global Terror Alert, "The Association of Muslim Scholars in Iraq: Statement No. 157—in regard to the latest statements from Abu Musab al-Zarqawi," September 15, 2005. As of February 16, 2008: http://www.globalterroralert.com/pdf/0905/zarqawi-amsulema.pdf

Habeck, Mary, *Knowing the Enemy: Jihadist Ideology and the War on Terror*, New Haven, CT: Yale University Press, 2006.

Hadith quoted in *Al-Ansari*, Shaykh Abu al-Waleed, "The Termination of "Israel"—A Qur'anic Fact," trans. Abu al-Waleed al-Hamawi, undated. As of February 16, 2008: http://www.missionislam.com/nwo/termination.htm

Hadith quoted by Muhammad Abd al-Salam Faraj, *The Neglected Duty (Al-Faridayh al-Gha'ibah)*, 1979, trans. Johannes J.G. Jansen, *The Neglected Duty: The Creed of Sadat's Assassins and Islamic Resurgence in the Middle East*, Macmillan Publishing Company, November 1986.

Haim, S. G., "Sayyid Qutb," *Journal of Asian and African Studies*, Vol. 16, 1982, pp. 155–156.

Hakimi, Abdul Latif, Statements, on an URDU TV channel in Pakistan, undated (following Afghan elections on September 18, 2005), trans. Ahmad al-Marid, "Islamic Emirate Is Now in 11 Afghan Provinces!" Jihad Unspun (JUS), September 22, 2005. As of October 18, 2006: http://www.jihadunspun.com/newsarchive/article_internal.php?article=104368&list=/ newsarchive/index.php&

Hamad, Ghazi, Editorial, *Al-Risala*, September 13, 2001, trans. MEMRI, "Terror in America (2) Hamas weekly: 'Allah has answered our prayers; the sword of vengeance has reached America and will strike again and again,'" Special Dispatch Series, No. 268, September 17, 2001. As of February 16, 2008: http://memri.org/bin/articles.cgi?Page=archives&Area=sd&ID=SP26801

Hamas, "The Covenant of the Islamic Resistance Movement (Hamas), 18 August 1988." As of February 16, 2008: http://mideastweb.org/hamas.htm

————, Web site discussion, July 2, 2002, trans. Israeli Defense Forces, in *Israel National News*, "Hamas Chat: How to Murder Americans," July 2, 2002. As of October 23, 2006: http://israelnn.com/news.php3?id=26111

Hegghammer, Thomas, "Global Jihadism After the Iraq War," *Middle East Journal*, Vol. 60, No. 1, 2006, pp. 11–32. As of July 1, 2007: moyen-orient.sciences-po.fr/.../17042007%20Hegghammer%20Global%20Jihadism%20 after%20the%20Iraq%20War.pdf

The Highest Intuition, Issue 1, March 2, 2005, trans. SITE Institute, "Al-Qaeda in Iraq Releases New Publication, 'Thurwat al-Sanam' ('The Highest Intuition')," March 2, 2005.

History World, "History of the Ismailis," undated. As of February 18, 2008:
http://www.historyworld.net/wrldhis/PlainTextHistories.asp?historyid=ab17#1275

Hunt, Emily, "Zarqawi's 'Total War' on Iraqi Shiites Exposes a Divide Among Sunni Jihadists," The Washington Institute for Near East Policy, Policy Watch No. 1049, November 15, 2005. As of February 18, 2008:
http://www.washingtoninstitute.org/templateC05.php?CID=2400

Hussein, Foad, "Al-Zarqawi: The Second Generation of Al Qaeda," *Al-Quds Al-Arabi*, Vol. 17 (serialized), 2005, trans. SITE Institute, April 2006.

Ibn Hamed, Sheikh Nasser, "A Treatise on the Ruling Regarding the Use of Weapons of Mass Destruction Against the Infidels," undated, trans. MEMRI, "Contemporary Islamist Ideology Authorizing Genocidal Murder," Special Report, No. 25, January 27, 2005. As of February 18, 2008:
http://memri.org/bin/articles.cgi?Page=archives&Area=sr&ID=SR2504

Ibn Taimiya (Taymiyyah), "Enjoining Right and Forbidding Wrong," undated, trans. Salim Morgan, undated. As of September 25, 2006:
http://www.java-man.com/Pages/Books/alhisba.html

Ibn Taymeeyah (Taymiyyah), Letter (7) from Prison (to the King of Cyprus and the religious leaders, princes and priests replying to their enquiries), undated, in "Ibn Taymiyyah's Letters from Prison," undated. As of January 15, 2007:
http://thetruereligion.org/modules/wfsection/print.php?articleid=70

Ibn Taymiyyah, Sheikh Ahmad, "The Religious and Moral Doctrine of Jihad," undated. As of September 25, 2006:
http://www.sullivan-county.com/z/tay.htm

Ibrahim, Najih, Asim al-Majid, and Isam-al-Din Darbalah, *The Islamic Action Charter*, 1984, trans. FBIS, Mahmud Sadiq, "Egyptian Islamists' Ideologies Viewed," April 14, 2000, GMP20000417000177.

Ilyas, Ustad, Interview, Luqman, Hakim Arifin, Gatra, "Terrorizing the US Is an Obligation," *Gatra*, November 12, 2005, FBIS, "Indonesia: 'Convicted Terrorist' Discusses Azahari's Ideology, Tradecraft," SEP20051114071001, November 12, 2005.

Iyyad, Abu, with Eric Rouleau, *My Home and My Land: A Narrative of the Palestinian Struggle*, New York: Times Books, 1984.

Izz-al-Din al-Qassam Brigades, "The Crime of Assassinating Amjad al-Hinnawi, Commander of the Northern West Bank District, Will Not Go Unpunished," November 14, 2005, FBIS, "Al-Qassam Brigades Vows to Avenge Killing of Commander in Nablus," GMP20051114566003, November 14, 2005.

Jamestown Foundation, "Anti-Ship Warfare and Molotov Cocktails at the Siege of Acre, 1190, A Translation from al-Qaeda's Military Journal al-Battar," trans. Jamestown Staff, 2004. As of January 30, 2008:
http://www.jamestown.org/news_details.php?news_id=46

Jane's Terrorism and Insurgency Centre (JTIC) and The Middle East Media Research Institute (MEMRI), "JTIC/MEMRI Joint Investigation: Jihad on the Web—Part 1," posted March 18, 2004.

Jihad Fighter No. 1, "The Nuclear Bomb of Jihad and the Way to Enrich Uranium" [aka "The Encyclopedia for the Preparation of Nuclear Weapons"] posted on October 6, 2005 on the Islamist forum Al-Firdaws (in Arabic), trans. MEMRI, "On Islamic Web sites: A Guide for Preparing Nuclear Weapons," Special Dispatch Series, No. 1004, October 12, 2005. As of October 23, 2006:
http://memri.org/bin/articles.cgi?Page=archives&Area=sd&ID=SP100405

Kahn, Mohammad Siddique, Al-Qaida video, July 2005, Richard Norton-Taylor and Riazat Butt, "Queen is target for al-Qaida, Security sources confirm," *The Guardian*, November 14, 2005. As of January 9, 2005:
http://www.guardian.co.uk/alqaida/story/0,,1642055,00.html

Kelley, Jack, "Militants wire Web with links to Jihad," *USA Today*, July 10, 2002. As of February 6, 2008:
http://www.usatoday.com/news/world/2002/07/10/web-terror-cover.htm

Lia, Brynjar, and Thomas Hegghammer, Norwegian Defence Research Establishment (FFI), "FFI Explains al-Qaida Document," March 19, 2004. As of October 19, 2006:
http://www.mil.no/felles/ffi/start/article.jhtml?articleID=71589

Makki, Hafiz Abdur Rehman, in Sikand, Yoginder, "Quake Aid and Lashkar Politics," *The Sentinel*, November 7, 2005, FBIS, "Indian Writer: Islamic Group Uses Quake Relief Work to Promote Political Agenda," SAP20051115379020, November 15, 2005.

The Manchester Document, undated, trans. and released by the Department of Justice (DOJ) on December 7, 2001. As of November 14, 2006:
http://cryptome.org/alq-terr-man.htm#6

Mansour, Mu'aadh, "The Importance of Military Preparedness in Shari'a," *Al-Battar Training Camp*, Issue 1, January 2004, trans. MEMRI, "The Al-Battar Training Camp: The First Issue of Al-Qa'ida's Online Military Magazine," Special Dispatch Series, No. 637, January 6, 2004. As of October 5, 2006:
http://memri.org/bin/articles.cgi?Page=archives&Area=sd&ID=SP63704

McCants, William (ed.), *Militant Ideology Atlas: Research Compendium*, West Point, NY: Combating Terrorism Center, 2006. As of July 1, 2007:
http://www.ctc.usma.edu/atlas/Atlas -ResearchCompendium.pdf

McGeough, Paul, "Zarqawi: the New bin Laden," *The Sydney Morning Herald*, 2004. As of April 10, 2008:
http://www.smh.com.au/articles/2004/10/16/1097784103533.html?from=storylhs

MEMRI, "Al-Qa'ida Web Site, Back On-Line, Publishes Book About Its War on the U.S. and Bombing in Saudi Arabia," Special Dispatch Series, No. 560, September 9, 2003. As of December 8, 2005:
http://memri.org/bin/articles.cgi?Page=archives&Area=sd&ID=SP56903

———, "Lebanon's Largest Government University Hosts Hizbullah's Al-Manar TV Symposium Calling to Wipe Israel Off the Map: 'Just Like Hitler Fought the Jews . . . We Too Should Fight the Jews and Burn Them,'" Special Dispatch Series, No. 1049, December 15, 2005a. As of September 7, 2006:
http://memri.org/bin/articles.cgi?Page=archives&Area=sd&ID=SP104905

———, "Now Online: Swear Loyalty to al-Qaeda Leaders," Special Dispatch Series, No. 1027, November 18, 2005b. As of May 6, 2008:
http://memri.org/bin/latestnews.cgi?ID=SD102705

Mishal, Khaled, "Our Programme Is Ejection of the Occupier," Interview with London-based Quds Press, undated. As of October 12, 2005:
http://www.hamasonline.org/indexx.php?page=Hamas/interviews/Khaled_3

Mish'al, Khalid, "Text of Address by Khalid Mish'al, Head of the Political Bureau of the HAMAS Movement, at the Inauguration of the Global Anti-Aggression Campaign Conference," Al-Qassam Brigade web site, February 24, 2005, trans. FBIS, "Al-Qassam Brigades Posts Mish'al Speech at Qatar Conference," GMP20050307000062, March 6, 2005.

Mohammed, Omar Bakri, Interview, in Edward, Rhiannon, "Radical cleric attacks Muslim 'hypocrites,'" The Scotsman, July 22, 2005. As of June 29, 2006:
http://news.scotsman.com/international.cfm?id=1664052005

Mudeiras, Sheikh Ibrahim, Sermon, Palestinian TV, May 13, 2005, Intelligence and Terrorism Information Center (ITIC), Special Information Bulletin, May 2005. As of March 1, 2006:
http://www.terrorism-info.org.il/malam_multimedia//ENGLISH/HATE-ANTI%20SEMITISM/PDF/MAY21_05.PDF

Mujahideen of Jaish-i-Mohammad, "Reasons for joining a jihadi organization," October 2001, in Muhammad Amir Rana, A to Z of Jihadi Organizations in Pakistan, trans. Saba Ansari, Lahore: Mashal Books, 2004. As of October 31, 2006:
http://www.mshel.com/book00085.html

Musa, Dr. Muhammad Yussif, Humankind's Need for Islam Also Found in Necessity for Islam [Dari], Islamic Unity for Afghanistan, [s.i.], republished 1984 (1386 A.H.).

Mustafa, Abu Ibrahim, Fatwa, "Fighting the Foreigners," undated, trans. SITE, "Salafi Group for Call and Combat Issues Fatwa for Jihad Against Foreigners in Algeria," March 11, 2005. As of February 28, 2006:
http://siteinstitute.org/bin/articles.cgi?ID=publications25505&Category=publications&Subcategory=0

Mustafa of Tikrit, Sheikh Muzahem, undated, trans. MEMRI, "Sunni Sheikhs and Organizations Criticize Al-Zarqawi's Declaration of War Against the Shi'ites," Special Dispatch Series, No. 1000, October 7, 2005. As of October 31, 2006:
http://memri.org/bin/articles.cgi?Page=archives&Area=sd&ID=SP100005

Naji, Abu Bakr, The Management of Savagery: The Most Critical Stage Through Which the Umma Will Pass, 2004, trans. William McCants, John M. Olin Institute for Strategic Studies, Harvard University, May 2006. As of July 1, 2007:
http://www.ctc.usma.edu/Management_of_Savagery.pdf

Nasr, Seyyed Hossein, Islam: Religion, History, and Civilization, New York: HarperCollins Publishers, 2002.

Nasrallah, Hassan, Speech, Al-Manar TV, November 25, 2005, trans. MEMRI, "Hizbullah's Leader Hassan Nasrallah Discusses Martyrdom and Declares: It Is Our Right and Our Duty to Kidnap Israeli Soldiers," TV Monitor Project, Clip No. 944, November 25, 2005. As of December 15, 2005:
http://memritv.org/Transcript.asp?P1=944

Qari, Sheikh Abd Al-'Aziz, Sermon at the Ka'ba Mosque in Al-Madina, undated, trans. MEMRI, "Contemporary Islamist Ideology Authorizing Genocidal Murder," Special Report, No. 25, January 27, 2005. As of October 11, 2006:
http://memri.org/bin/articles.cgi?Page=archives&Area=sr&ID=SR2504

Qutb, Sayyid, *Social Justice in Islam (Adalah al-ijtima iyah fi al-Islam)*, 1949; rev. ed., trans. John B. Hardie, 1953; rev. ed., trans, Hamid Algar, 2000, New York: Islamic Publications International, 2000.

————, *Milestones*, 1964, Cedar Rapids, IA: The Mother Mosque Foundation, ISBN No. 0-911119-42-6, undated. As of December 5, 2006:
http://www.youngmuslims.ca/online%5Flibrary/books/milestones/Introduction.asp

————, Quotation, undated(a), trans. MEMRI, "Contemporary Islamist Ideology Authorizing Genocidal Murder," Special Report, No. 25, January 27, 2005. As of October 10, 2006:
http://memri.org/bin/articles.cgi?Page=archives&Area=sr&ID=SR2504

————, *In the Shade of the Qur'an (Fi Zilal Al-Qur'an)*, undated(b), trans. Adil Salahi, United Kingdom: The Islamic Foundation, ISBN: 0860373894, 2004, fn 1, MEMRI SR 25, January 27, 2004. As of December 13, 2006:
http://www.memri.org/bin/articles.cgi?ID=SR2504

Rami, Ahmad, Interview, Al-Manar TV, September 30, 2005, trans. MEMRI, "Hizbullah's Al-Manar TV Interviews Head of Swedish 'Radio Islam': The Muslims' War Is with the Jews; Judaism Is a Criminal Mafia, Not a Religion," Special Dispatch Series, No. 1002, October 11, 2005. As of July 25, 2006:
http://memri.org/bin/articles.cgi?Page=archives&Area=sd&ID=SP100205

Rennie, David, "I'd Do It All Again, Says Film-Maker's Killer, *The Telegraph*, July 13, 2005. As of April 10, 2008:
http://www.telegraph.co.uk/news/main

Rishawi, Sajida, "TV Confession," November 13, 2005, trans. Jackie Spinner, "The Amman Bomber Who Failed," *The Washington Post*, November 14, 2005. As of October 19, 2006:
http://www.epic-usa.org/Default.aspx?tabid=2065

Riyashi, Reem, Video prepared before suicide attack on January 14, 2004, trans. Itamar Maracus and Barbara Crook, "A Self-Portrait of Suicide Terrorists," Palestinian Media Watch, March 2, 2006. As of October 5, 2006:
http://www.pmw.org.il/Latest%20bulletins%20new.htm

Rodriguez, Paul M., "'Job Application' online for suicide bombers: Iranian group recruiting for attacks on U.S. citizens, forces, Israel," Insight/News World Communications Inc., posted June 10, 2004. As of June 29, 2006:
http://www.worldnetdaily.com/news/article.asp?ARTICLE_ID=38895

Saeed, Hafiz Mohammad, Friday prayers sermon, October 14, 2005, trans. FBIS, "Pakistani Jihadi Chief Says Rulers Believe in US as God," SAP20051016002002, October 14, 2005.

Safuri, Ali, Interview, "Battle for the Holy Land," *Frontline*, PBS presentation of a Goldvicht Productions/October Films production for the BBC in association with the Kirk Documentary Group, Program 2015, original airdate April 4, 2002. As of October 23, 2006:
http://www.pbs.org/wgbh/pages/frontline/shows/holy/etc/script.html

Sakr, Hala, *Al-Ahram Weekly*, Issue No. 734, March 17–23, 2005. As of January 19, 2007:
http://weekly.ahram.org.eg/2005/734/sc2.htm

Salaheddin (Saladin) II (*nom de guerre* of the Emir of the Global Islamic Media Front (GMIF), Internet exhortation, undated, trans. Habib Trabelsi, Middle East Online, "Al-Qaeda takes jihad to media four years after 9/11: Al-Qaeda fighters become producers, film directors, video cameras have become their most potent weapon," September 9, 2005. As of October 20, 2006:
http://www.middle-east-online.com/english/?id=14500=14500&format=0

Sayyaf, Abu Yasser, "An invitation to all the fighting brothers on the frontiers to keep the faith in their struggle," January 8, 2005, Global Terror Alert, "Communique from the Algerian Salafist Group for Prayer and Combat (GSPC)," January 8, 2005. As of March 1, 2006:
http://www.globalterroralert.com/pdf/0105/gspc0105-2.pdf

Shakir, Shaykh Ahmad, Kalimat al-Haqq, quoted in *The Operation of 11 Rabi Al-Awwal: The East Riyadh Operation and Our War with the United States and Its Agents*, The Center for Islamic Studies and Research (CISR), August 1, 2003, trans. FBIS, "Islamic Research Center Publishes Book on 12 May Riyadh Operation," GMP20031004000119, August 1, 2003. As of October 13, 2006:
http://www.why-war.com/files/qaeda_east_riyadh_operation.html

Sister Al, "Sister's Role in Jihâd," www.islaam.org.uk, January 18, 2001. As of January 17, 2007:
http://www.sunnahonline.com/ilm/jihaad/0005.htm

SITE, "Call to Kill Dutch MP Hersi Ali on Jihadist Message Board," January 27, 2005a. As of October 19, 2006:
http://siteinstitute.org/bin/articles.cgi?ID=publications17205&Category=publications&Subcategory=0

———, "How to Face the Interrogator (Security/Safety Advices)?" February 18, 2005b, trans. of first part of summary of *The Philosophy of Confrontation Behind Bars*, undated. As of August 8, 2006:
http://siteinstitute.org/bin/articles.cgi?ID=publications20505&Category=publications&Subcategory=0

Siyami, Sheikh Adnan Ahmad, Sermon at a Mecca Mosque, trans. MEMRI, "Contemporary Islamist Ideology Authorizing Genocidal Murder," Special Report, No. 25, January 27, 2004. As of October 11, 2006:
http://memri.org/bin/articles.cgi?Page=archives&Area=sr&ID=SR2504

Taheri, Amir, "Al-Qaeda's Agenda for Iraq," *New York Post*, September 4, 2003. As of October 9, 2006:
http://www.benadorassociates.com/article/544

Terrorist #3, Interviews with detained Iraqi terrorists, Al-Arabiya TV, January 10, 2005, trans. MEMRI, "Terrorists Caught in Iraq Confess: We Murdered People by Orders of Al-Zarqawi; We Committed Murders Under Death Threats," TV Monitor Project, Clip No. 481, January 10, 2005. As of October 20, 2006:
http://memritv.org/Transcript.asp?P1=481

Terrorist #4, Interviews with detained Iraqi terrorists, Al-Arabiya TV, January 10, 2005, trans. MEMRI, "Terrorists Caught in Iraq Confess: We Murdered People by Orders of Al-Zarqawi; We Committed Murders Under Death Threats," TV Monitor Project, Clip No. 481, January 10, 2005. As of October 20, 2006:
http://memritv.org/Transcript.asp?P1=481

"Tips for the Traveling Terrorist," sidebar in Alan Cullison, "Inside Al-Qaeda's Hard Drive," *The Atlantic*, September 2004. As of February 16, 2008:
http://www.theatlantic.com/doc/prem/200409/cullisonsidebar1

Um al-Shahid, "Message Addressed to the Spouse of the Infidel Paul Johnson from the Spouse of a Martyr in the Arab Peninsula," in *The Voice of Jihad*, Issue 21, July 28, 2004, trans. SITE Institute "Message from the spouse of a martyr to the widow of Paul Johnson." As of October 5, 2006:

http://siteinstitute.org/bin/articles.cgi?ID=publications5504&Category=publications&Subcategory=0

Umar, Warith Deen, former Islamic Chaplain of New York's prison system, Dinner communication with the author, undated, Paul M. Barrett, "Captive Audience: How a Chaplain Spread Extremism to an Inmate Flock—Radical New York Imam Chose Clerics for State Prisons; Praise for 9/11 'Martyrs'—Saudi Arabia's Helping Hand," *Wall Street Journal* (Eastern edition), February 5, 2003, p. A.1. As of October 20, 2006:
http://proquest.umi.com/pqdweb?index=28&did=283327141&SrchMode=3&sid=1&Fmt=3&VInst=PROD&VType=PQD&RQT=309&VName=PQD&TS=1138732223&clientId=61650&aid=5

Umm Badr, "Obstacles in the Path of the Jihad Warrior Woman," *al-Khansa*, Issue 1, August 2004, pp. 19–22, trans. RAND, March 2008. As of March 24, 2008:
http://ia300003.us.archive.org/2/items/ozoooK/129.pdf

Umm Saburah (wife of a Shaheed), Conversation recollected in diary of Sister Al, "Sister's Role in Jihâd," www.islaam.org.uk, January 18, 2001. As of January 17, 2007:
http://www.sunnahonline.com/ilm/jihaad/0005.htm

"USC–MSA Compendium of Muslim Texts," undated. As of February 2, 2008:
http://www.usc.edu/dept/MSA/

The Voice of Jihad (Sawt Al-Jihad), Issue 4, November 2003, trans. MEMRI, "Escalation of Incitement to Violence During the Month of Ramadan," Special Dispatch Series, No. 612, November 20, 2003. As of October 5, 2006:
http://memri.org/bin/articles.cgi?Page=archives&Area=sd&ID=SP61203

————, Issue 9, January 22, 2004, trans. MEMRI, "Al-Qa'ida's 'Voice of Jihad' Magazine: Issue No. 9," Special Dispatch Series, No. 650, January 27, 2004. As of January 16, 2007:
http://memri.org/bin/articles.cgi?Page=archives&Area=sd&ID=SP65004

Weimann, Gabriel, in "Terrorists Turn to the Web as Base of Operations," *The Washington Post*, August 7, 2005. As of July 13, 2006:
http://www.washingtonpost.com/wp-dyn/content/article/2005/08/05/AR2005080501138.html

Wright, Lawrence, "The Master Plan," *The New Yorker*, September 11, 2006.

Yassin, Sheikh Achmed, Interview, Al-Jazeera TV, undated(a). As of October 5, 2006:
http://www.radio786.co.za/special_reports/ahmed_yassin/articles/The_life_and_death_of_sh_Yasin.asp

————, Quotes, undated(b). As of December 6, 2005:
http://www.hamasonline.org/indexx.php?page=yassin

About the Author

Ambassador David Aaron is Director of the Center for Middle East Public Policy at the RAND Corporation. He has served in both the government and the private sector. After graduation from Occidental College and Princeton University, he entered the Foreign Service, where he held a variety of posts, which included serving on the U.S. delegation to NATO and to the Strategic Arms Limitation Talks with the Soviet Union. After leaving the Foreign Service, he remained in government, where his posts included the National Security Council staff, where he was responsible for arms control and strategic doctrine. Subsequently, he became a Task Force Director for the Senate Intelligence Committee and then Deputy National Security Advisor to President Jimmy Carter. In the latter capacity, he chaired sub-Cabinet committees dealing with arms control and intelligence. He also served as a confidential presidential emissary to Europe, where he negotiated the deployment of medium-range missiles; to the Middle East, where he helped prepare for the Camp David negotiations; and to Africa, Latin America, and China.

Upon leaving government, Ambassador Aaron became Vice President for Mergers and Acquisitions at Oppenheimer & Co. and Vice Chairman of the board of Oppenheimer International.

During the Clinton administration, he served as Ambassador to the Organisation for Economic Co-operation and Development (OECD) in Paris, where he negotiated the international anti-bribery convention. At the same time, he was appointed Special White House Envoy for Cryptography to develop international guidelines for encryption technology in trade and communications. Subsequently, he was appointed Undersecretary of Commerce for International Trade, where he negotiated the US/EU privacy accord.

After leaving government in 2000, he became Senior International Advisor to the law firm Dorsey LLP, where he remained until his appointment as a Senior Fellow at RAND. He is the author of three novels published in ten languages, as well as two PBS documentaries, including "Lessons of the 1991 Gulf War."